PRAISE FOR *TOMORROW'S CAPITALIST*

"Alan Murray illuminates the path for anyone who aspires to be on the right side of the history of capitalism. From his unique vantage point, Murray paints an inspiring portrait of how business can and *ought* to work—and of how leaders can and *ought* to lead—in our now-fused world where political, social, environmental, biological, ethical, and moral issues that were once considered tangential to an organization's agenda are increasingly viewed as inescapably at the center of it. Murray assembles the right playbook for what business does best—innovating at scale—but designed to meet the imperatives of a post-pandemic world: creating value by truly serving people and putting their concerns and hopes at the core of operations."

—Dov Seidman, author of *How* and founder and chairman, LRN and the HOW Institute for Society

"Is the shift to stakeholder capitalism for real? Could business indeed discover a moral compass? Drawing on hundreds of conversations with the world's leading CEOs, Murray makes the case that we are living through a moment of profound change in how business leaders understand their role, and argues that this shift is already changing the way that business operates."

—Rebecca Henderson, John and Natty McArthur University Professor, Harvard University, and author of *Reimagining Capitalism in a World on Fire*

"With decades of experience studying, investigating, and educating the public about business and capitalism, Alan Murray has tapped into a fundamental truth—one that is both pragmatic and moral: Companies can only grow and prosper if they invest in their employees, serve their customers, support their communities, and recognize their responsibility to help lift up all of society—rather than ignore or 'drive by' those who have been left behind. Murray gets it, and in *Tomorrow's Capitalist* he lays it out in a compelling, thought-provoking work that can benefit every budding capitalist and business leader."

—Jamie Dimon, chairman and CEO, JP Morgan Chase

"Practical, hopeful, and convincing. A must-read for all in leading positions who want to seize the biggest opportunity we have of our times and position themselves well for a prosperous future. As more companies commit themselves to a purpose larger then profits, there is increasing evidence that it might be to the shareholders best interest as well."

—Paul Polman, cofounder and chair, IMAGINE, and former CEO, Unilever

"Alan Murray's keen insight, gleaned from decades of in-depth conversations with corporate leaders and his own shrewd, front-row observations of the shifting priorities of American business, is on abundant display in *Tomorrow's Capitalist*. His surgical dissection of the motives and pressures driving decision-making at the heart of capitalism, combined with often warm (but always revealing) firsthand anecdotes finds there is reason to hope."

—Ginni Rometty, former chair, president, and CEO, IBM

"No American journalist has a keener understanding of the interrelationships between business, public policy, and society than Alan Murray. In this landmark work, he shares all he has learned in forty years as a premier economic journalist. Murray has the rare quality of balance in these polarized times as he assays all that is transpiring in the business world and what it means."

—Lawrence H. Summers, Charles W. Eliot University Professor and president emeritus, Harvard University, and former secretary of the treasury under President Clinton

"Alan Murray tracks the essential moments—and seminal leadership—that brought us to this new era of stakeholder capitalism with characteristic verve and unrivaled industry insights."

—Alex Gorsky, executive chairman, Johnson & Johnson

"In *Tomorrow's Capitalist*, Alan Murray shows us that profit needn't be separated from purpose. It's a false choice. The task now is to answer which principles will shape capitalism 2.0."

—Satya Nadella, executive chairman and CEO, Microsoft

"Alan Murray is at the vanguard of rethinking capitalism to meet the great challenges of our times. He has convened global leaders across sectors, asked the difficult questions, and led the rigorous and honest dialogue that is necessary for change. *Tomorrow's Capitalist* is the compelling story of Murray's journey at the center of this critical discussion, and it is required reading for all who believe that capitalism needs an upgrade. Through his belief in the possibilities of capitalism and the clarity of his call to action, Murray inspires and challenges all of us to do better."

—Dan Schulman, president and CEO, PayPal

"Many CEOs today are listening more deeply to all their stakeholders and asking themselves: What can I do to improve the state of our world? *Tomorrow's Capitalist* captures this critical move toward a new capitalism that is more equal, fair, and sustainable, where profit and purpose go hand-in-hand, and business can be the greatest platform for change."

—Marc Benioff, chair and co-CEO, Salesforce

"Business as usual is over. The journey forward—which Murray expertly captures in this book—starts with realizing we're all part of an interconnected system. And then it requires putting the tools of business to work constructing a stronger, safer, more inclusive, and more sustainable future. There's much work to be done and we're going to need a lot of shoulders at the wheel to do it."

—Ajay Banga, former CEO and executive chair, Mastercard

"Insightful. Alan Murray leverages his years of business journalism to describe how the relationship between business and society is being redefined in the current world. A must-read."

—Indra Nooyi, former CEO and chair, PepsiCo, and author of *My Life in Full*

"The role that business must play in our society has never been more important. Alan Murray saw this early and has been a compelling voice to inspire CEOs to lead in these areas. *Tomorrow's Capitalist* captures the challenges and lays out a clear path forward."

—John Donahoe, CEO, Nike

TOMORROW'S

CAPITALIST

My Search for the
Soul of Business

TOMORROW'S

CAPITALIST

Alan Murray

with Catherine Whitney

PUBLICAFFAIRS

New York

PublicAffairs
Hachette Book Group
1290 Avenue of the Americas, New York, NY 10104
www.publicaffairsbooks.com
@Public_Affairs

Printed in the United States of America

First Edition: May 2022

Published by PublicAffairs, an imprint of Perseus Books, LLC, a subsidiary of Hachette Book Group, Inc. The PublicAffairs name and logo is a trademark of the Hachette Book Group.

The Hachette Speakers Bureau provides a wide range of authors for speaking events. To find out more, go to www.hachettespeakersbureau.com or call (866) 376-6591.

The publisher is not responsible for websites (or their content) that are not owned by the publisher.

Print book interior design by Amy Quinn.

Library of Congress Cataloging-in-Publication Data
Names: Murray, Alan S., 1954– author.
Title: Tomorrow's capitalist : my search for the soul of business / Alan Murray with
    Catherine Whitney.
Description: First Edition. | New York, NY : PublicAffairs, 2022. |
    Includes bibliographical references and index.
Identifiers: LCCN 2021047539 | ISBN 9781541789081 (hardcover) |
    ISBN 9781541789104 (ebook)
Subjects: LCSH: Organizational change. | Industrial management. |
    Diversity in the workplace. | Business ethics. | Social responsibility of business.
Classification: LCC HD58.8 .M874 2022 | DDC 658.4/06—dc23/eng/20211116
LC record available at https://lccn.loc.gov/2021047539

ISBNs: 9781541789081 (hardcover); 9781541789104 (e-book)

LSC-C

Printing 1, 2022

To the women who gave me life and gave my life meaning:
My mother, Catherine; my daughters, Lucyann and Amanda;
and my life's partner, Lori.

CONTENTS

FOREWORD
THE REDESIGN IS UNDERWAY

By Ellen McGirt

As I think about the future of stakeholder capitalism, I feel a bit like the pig in the age-old business parable. In a bacon-and-egg breakfast, what's the difference between the chicken and the pig? The chicken is involved but the pig is committed.

I'll come back to this in a moment.

Now, let me be clear from the outset: If you read this book, you will have enough of an understanding of the history of modern economic drama to have a clear idea of why the business world is changing, and what that means for you. You'll also have smart things to say to any Keynesians, Friedmanites, Fukuyama fans, market fundamentalists, Brexiteers, or any barbarians at any gates you might encounter. This alone is worth the price of admission.

But that's not only what the world needs now, is it?

In this book, Alan Murray has accomplished the near impossible: to document, often in real time, the quest to redefine the guiding principles of business in the middle of numerous, deadly, and often intersecting crises.

It wasn't simply a roiling pandemic that overtook the globe. It was the disparate outcomes that followed, revealing systems of entrenched, racist inequality—from access to food to health care, credit, education, digital tools, and beyond—and that the people now known as stakeholders increasingly refused to ignore.

It wasn't just the murder of an unarmed Black man at the hands of the police. Instead, George Floyd's death became a long overdue tipping point that spurred an unquenchable demand for equity and accountability, and that brought the conversation about race and justice to every living room and boardroom across the United States and in many places around the world.

All of this pushed a real but relatively slow-moving inquiry into the purpose of business into sudden overdrive, and very specifically to the doorsteps of the CEOs who were interviewed for this book and on the *Leadership Next* podcast, which I co-host with Alan.

To a person, these conversations were an equal mix of personal reflection and tactical resolve and revealed the truth of Alan's central thesis that tomorrow's capitalists are prepared to ask better questions, listen more deeply, and amend the shareholder playbook for good. "We need to show society who we are and what we believe in," Cisco CEO Chuck Robbins told Alan and me on *Leadership Next* about how the company responded to George Floyd's murder. "I think the world's changed, and businesses are held accountable for these other issues now. Even our shareholders are asking us to get involved in a lot of these issues."

If business now has a role to play in addressing pressing social issues, particularly those that they helped create, then CEOs must exercise latent muscles of empathy, courage, resilience, and grace to rethink how power unfolds in their organizations and understand who is not represented in important rooms—on their boards and leadership teams; in their high-potential pools, supplier networks, and customer bases; even their own LinkedIn feeds and birthday parties—and ask why. In the "why" is the work.

And that's where things get tricky.

As I was writing this foreword, the *Washington Post* published a grim report card on the outcome of the $50 billion pledged by corporations for racial justice initiatives following Floyd's murder. Their analysis "reveal[ed] the limits of their power to remedy structural problems." In many cases, the pledges were a fraction of the capital they could have deployed. "Corporations are not set up to wield their power for the greater good as much as we give them credit for, a lot of times," said Phillip Atiba Goff, a professor at Yale University and cofounder of the Center for Policing Equity. "They are constrained by things they feel they need to do to manage their brand in a world where Black liberation does not have consensus."[1]

That's a very polite way of saying this is all much harder than it looks. That said, know hope.

I established the race and inclusive leadership beat at *Fortune* in 2016 with a now award-winning newsletter called *raceAhead*. Back then, I used to joke that I was prepared for it to be a dull duty, reporting on diversity reports that never changed, interviewing the outliers who made it to the top of some corporate ladder, and reminding people not to be racist at Halloween. I never expected white supremacists marching in the streets, a racist immigrant ban, or the now permanent psychic scar of viewing so many Black bodies lost to police violence. I was also not expecting serious investments in corporate diversity, albeit in its early stages, and the number of big company CEOs who have made serious and credible efforts to take bold stands on social issues.

From two completely different perspectives, Alan and I have arrived at the same hopeful place, with one caveat.

Which brings me back to my breakfast joke.

There are many unanswered questions about the future of capitalism, all of which involve trusting the already powerful, who have little real incentive to share their power, with the heady task of inventing it. For it to be real, I think the people who have been on the wrong side of inequitable systems need to lead the way. Right? Handing the breakfast reins to the pig in the proverb is the only way to be sure that the one creature least likely to survive the exercise gets a shot at the redesign.

The redesign is now underway. Congratulations, capitalists of tomorrow, Alan has given you an enormous head start with this book. Now, it's your job to pay it forward.

PROLOGUE
GOD AND MANNA

On December 3, 2016, the titans of business and commerce gathered in the house of God. One hundred corporate chieftains assembled early in the morning in the Sistine Chapel, before it opened to the public, for an hour of contemplation under Michelangelo's magnificent *Creation*. Then they moved to the ornate Clementine Hall, where they met with Pope Francis to answer his call for business to respond to the needs of people and the planet. The Vatican Global Forum in Rome was convened by *Fortune* and *Time* magazines at the invitation of the Holy Father. I have been fortunate to witness many important moments in my career, but this was one of the most dramatic and, ultimately, most meaningful. In retrospect, I now know it marked a fundamental inflection point in the world of business. That inflection point, and the changes resulting from it, are the subject of this book.

The attendees at the two-day conference represented iconic companies: Ford, Dow Chemical, IBM, Johnson & Johnson, Allstate, Lenovo, Barclay's, Royal Dutch Shell, TIAA, Baxter International, Walgreens Boots, Novartis, Siemens, Virgin Group, Deloitte, McKinsey, BCG, and others—the largest and most powerful companies in the world. Their mission was in its title: "The 21st Century Challenge: Forging a New Social Compact." There was a growing sense among these CEOs that capitalism was under threat, that it wasn't working as well as it could or should, and that they needed to do a better job demonstrating its value to society.

The impetus for this remarkable gathering was not just the clear needs in society that Pope Francis frequently cited. Going in, the CEOs recognized that public support for the capitalist system was waning. Brexit had just passed in the UK over the objections of nearly every business leader. Donald Trump had triumphed after a campaign attacking the globalization that these companies had driven. His opponent, Hillary Clinton, had nearly been defeated for the Democratic nomination by Bernie Sanders, who openly embraced democratic socialism. Polls showed that among young people, a majority did not favor capitalism. Clinton later told me she thought that declaring she *was* in favor of capitalism might have hurt her in the primary campaign.

Pope Francis himself was also a symbol of the rising discontent. His official pronouncements often had been distinctly skeptical of capitalism, informed in particular by the excesses in his native Latin America. Meanwhile, government effectiveness in addressing important social and environmental problems was clearly being hobbled in many Western countries, brought down by political polarization.

The CEOs felt they needed to change that trajectory. Self-preservation was part of what motivated them. They needed to step up and tackle important issues like climate change, inequality, and diversity and inclusion, or run the risk of losing their license to operate. Their presence that day also reflected fundamental changes in how businesses operate. This was a new generation of leaders charged with organizing a new generation of employees and exciting a new generation of customers and investors in a twenty-first-century economy whose underlying dynamics were profoundly different from those of the twentieth century.

I had spoken with these leaders on many occasions, and I knew how serious they were about making changes. They weren't in Rome for the photo op. They had greater ambitions for how the corporate world, which is often seen as the problem, actually might become a bigger part of the solution.

Welcoming the gathering the day before their Vatican meeting in a Rome hotel ballroom, I put the context in frank terms. "I don't think I have to convince anyone in this room that we are in a moment of crisis in global capitalism," I said.

Dov Seidman, the author of *How: Why How We Do Anything Means Everything* and chairman of LRN, a corporate ethics compliance company, joined me on stage for a conversation on the need for CEOs to provide "moral leadership"—a topic that had seldom, if ever, been discussed at CEO confabs in the past. The global transparency brought on by social media was one of the factors driving the change. He related a cautionary tale involving the Minneapolis dentist who woke up one day and posted on Facebook about a trip he was planning to Zimbabwe to hunt a lion. He had a permit for the hunt, but within minutes of slaying a lion, he was engulfed in global outrage. People went on Yelp to try and drive him out of business with ugly reviews. In the span of a few days some four hundred thousand people went online to spew vitriol. The outrage extended to Delta for flying back trophy killings, which led to a ban on the practice that spread to other airlines.

"David Hume, the moral philosopher, says the moral imagination declines with distance," Seidman told the assembled CEOs. "As a corollary, I think it would follow that as distance decreases, the moral imagination increases. . . . We are living in a no-distance world, where people are morally awakened and activated, are able to feel the plights and challenges and vanquishes and actions of people far away, viscerally and directly." The result, he said, is a dramatically reshaped world, placing new demands on business leadership. And it was the obligation of today's leaders—of those gathered in Rome—to be thoughtful and to formulate meaningful change for this morally awakened world.

The "crisis in capitalism," which I had framed at the beginning of the meeting, arose from a complex collection of causes. It was not just a rebellion, especially among young people, against capitalism's perceived evil byproducts. Nor was it simply the failure of government to do a better job regulating those evils. Rather it was the result of far-reaching changes in the world that were demanding a new social compact between business and society, and a new set of governing principles that went beyond pure profit and loss.

Over the years, speaking to many of these CEOs, I had often heard variations on the idea that profit need not be separated from purpose. Being socially responsible, prioritizing employee well-being, tending to community needs, encouraging diversity, and contributing positively to the environment were all actions that, in the long run, could also improve market share and lift long-term profits. But while these ideas weren't new, the gathering forces had propelled them to the front of business conversation, with a force and a conviction I had not seen in my four decades as a journalist.

In working groups on the first day of the Rome conference, we grappled with what the private sector could do to address fundamental social issues, such as job creation, fair wages, environmental responsibility, access to education and health care, and financial inclusivity. The groups emerged with specific proposals on how business could help reach the billions of people in the world who lacked basic financial services; support the effort to fight climate change; expand training programs for those whose jobs were threatened by technological advances; and provide basic community health services to the half-billion people who had no access to care. These proposals were written up by *Fortune* editor in chief Clifton Leaf, and translated into Italian to be presented to Pope Francis.

On day two we entered the Vatican with hushed reverence and spent an hour in the Sistine Chapel. It was a humbling experience for a not so humble crowd. One of the CEOs came up to me, in front of *The Last Judgment* fresco on the far wall, to complain of the long wait for coffee in the small café beyond. "Look at this," I said, pointing up.

Later, we were ushered into Clementine Hall, where the pope greets official guests. The location's symbolism was inescapable, calling to mind groundbreaking convocations held over the centuries in this very place. We were all fully aware of the gravitas of the Vatican and its stake in the globe's moral imperatives and public welfare. It was a solemn occasion.

As the president of *Fortune* and host, along with *Time* editor in chief Nancy Gibbs, I introduced the Holy Father, who rose to address a rapt audience. He spoke warmly to the gathering as we sat surrounded by stunning Renaissance frescoes.

He thanked us for the work we had done, while asking us to look beyond the concepts to the human dimensions. He could read the room as he cautioned, "Important as this is, what is required now is not a new social compact in the abstract, but concrete ideas and decisive action which will benefit all people and which will begin to respond to the pressing issues of our day."

The pope set forth a mandate for what he called the "noble vocation" of business, asking the leaders to rise to the challenge of caring for the planet and increasing the equitable opportunity for prosperity. He, too, called on the CEOs to assert moral leadership.

His message urged the CEOs to be more than just maximizers of profit. They must step outside their comfort zones.

"This fundamental renewal," he told us, "does not have to do simply with market economics, figures to be balanced, the development of raw materials, and improvements made to infrastructures. No, what we are speaking about is the common good of humanity, of the right of each person to share in the resources of this world and to have the same opportunities to realize his or her potential, a potential that is ultimately based on the dignity of the children of God, created in his image and likeness.

"I pray that you may involve in your efforts those whom you seek to help; give them a voice, listen to their stories, learn from their experiences, and understand their needs. See in them a brother and a sister, a son and a daughter, a mother and a father. Amid the challenges of our day, see the human face of those you earnestly seek to help."[1]

Afterward, I sat under the magnificent frescoes and watched as each of the business leaders was invited up to personally greet the pope. As they turned away from their encounters, I saw the looks on their faces. Many of the Catholics in the group were in tears. Denise Morrison, then CEO of Campbell's Food, gave the pope a new zucchetto (skullcap) to place upon his head and then returned to her seat. Even those who were not Catholic were visibly moved by their personal moment with the pope. By the time we left the Vatican, there was a sense of shared purpose. It was impossible not to be inspired by the vision, the collegiality, and the magnetic words of a man who believed it was all possible. But it was also impossible not to be impressed by the sincerity of those global CEOs, who were committing themselves to make business better.

In the subsequent weeks, as I talked about the event, I often got looks of disbelief and skepticism. I heard frequent criticism that it sounded more like moral posturing than real change. We live in a time suffused with narratives about the failures of capitalism, the greed of the one-percenters, and the blindness of corporations to public need. Exchanging blessings with the pope, some people told me, was just a way to try and hide the wounds.

But as someone who had spent more than four decades covering the relationship between business and society, I knew something different was afoot. The CEOs who went to Rome knew that as well. The status quo was changing, for a host of reasons. And the burden was on these CEOs to find a new and better path forward. They knew that things had to change—not just the kind of cosmetic fixes that typically generated so much cynicism, but real transformation.

I am not a particularly religious person, nor am I an ideological one. As a lifelong journalist (I started a one-page neighborhood newspaper when I was nine years old) I have always seen my role as explaining the world, not changing it. And I have always started my reporting journeys with a good dose of skepticism.

But throughout my career, like many journalists, I have enjoyed unusual, and often undeserved, access to people in power. In my first job, I started the business section for the *Chattanooga Times*, my hometown newspaper. Later, as Washington bureau chief for the *Wall Street Journal* in the 1990s, I covered the intersection of politics and business. For several years early in the new millennium, I co-hosted a television show on CNBC with Gloria Borger, where we frequently interviewed CEOs as well as government leaders. Afterward, *Wall Street Journal* managing editor Paul Steiger invited me to New York to start a new column for the paper, called simply "Business." While there, I created the *Wall Street Journal* CEO Council, which gathered top business leaders to discuss issues of policy. And since joining *Fortune* in 2014, first as editor, then as president, and now as CEO, I have had many opportunities to talk with the world's top business leaders in both public and private settings—for *Fortune* events, for our *Leadership Next* podcast, for the *CEO Daily* newsletter that I headline, and in other venues.

All of that has given me unique opportunities to talk with CEOs— hundreds of them—about how they were doing their jobs. And what was clear to me by the time we reached the Vatican in 2016 was that the way

CEOs talked about their jobs and thought about their responsibilities had changed profoundly. They were all on a journey, driven by forces that they faced every day in their positions of enormous responsibility and consequence. And I was fortunate to be a passenger on those journeys. My conversations gave me a prime opportunity to travel along with them.

Looking back, I would pinpoint the first sign of this rethinking of corporate capitalism that I heard to a 2008 speech Bill Gates gave at the World Economic Forum at Davos—his last year as Microsoft CEO. The financial crisis and the Great Recession that followed had sown new doubts about free market economics. And the ramifications of that recession were being felt far and wide. Countless books have been written about that colossal market failure, and there is no need for me to revisit it in detail here. But in response, capitalism's greatest victor, Bill Gates, was making the case for a new approach. He challenged businesses to be better and to have "a twin mission": making profits and also improving lives for those who don't fully benefit from market forces.

"The world is getting better," he said, "but it's not getting better fast enough, and it's not getting better for everyone. The great advances in the world have often aggravated the inequities in the world. The least needy see the most improvement, and the most needy see the least."[2] He emphasized, "The genius of capitalism lies in its ability to make self-interest serve the wider interest. . . . But to harness this power so it benefits everyone, we need to refine the system. The challenge is to design a system where market incentives, including profits and recognition, drive the change. I like to call this new system 'creative capitalism'—an approach where governments, businesses, and nonprofits work together to stretch the reach of market forces so that more people can make a profit, or gain recognition, doing work that eases the world's inequities."

That wasn't the Bill Gates I had gotten to know back in the 1990s, when I was running the Washington bureau of the *Wall Street Journal* and he was desperately fighting the government's antitrust case against his company. I had met him at a dinner on one of his very first visits to Washington, and even his body language made it clear that he had no interest in being there. In those days, he was all about protecting his company's profits. The bigger problems of the political world were not his concern.

But I was struck by Gates's words in Davos. Something new was going on. Something was changing.

In subsequent years, I heard others articulate variations on the same theme. Harvard Business School professor Michael Porter called it "shared value capitalism."[3] Whole Foods cofounder John Mackey described it as "conscious capitalism."[4] Salesforce CEO Marc Benioff spoke of "compassionate capitalism."[5] Hedge fund billionaire Paul Tudor Jones called it "JUST Capital." Lynn Rothschild, who had married into the legendary banking family, called it "inclusive capitalism." Increasingly, the leaders of business found it necessary to put adjectives before the economic system that had brought them their success. Capitalism needed a modifier.

Today, the results of that change have burst loudly onto the world business scene. Business leaders who not long ago hid under their desks rather than confront controversial social or political issues now routinely feel compelled to speak out on a broad array of tempestuous topics, from transgender access to public bathrooms to restricting food and water for people in voting lines. Companies that once led the charge against costly climate policies that could crimp their bottom lines now lead the way in adopting plans to reach "net zero" by 2050 or sooner. New corporate efforts to promote diversity, to encourage racial justice, to provide new opportunities to societies less fortunate, have become a daily deluge.

Conservative critics of this movement tend to view it as "virtue signaling." The editorial page writers of the *Wall Street Journal* attack "woke CEOs" for kowtowing to the liberal mob. In the more left-leaning opinion pages of the *New York Times*, on the other hand, those same CEOs are often portrayed as craven opportunists, trying to distract from the damage corporations are doing elsewhere. The controversy over CEO activism, in particular, has reached a fevered pitch in the US, with companies weighing in on voting laws that have become ground zero for partisan warfare. Some CEOs who are opposed to corporate activism have called on their peers to take a deep breath, pull back, and think carefully before diving into the most polarizing political issues of the day.

But behind all that partisan noise are some more fundamental forces that cannot be ignored and will not be reversed. Business is inexorably changing. The purpose of this book is to explore and explain those forces, look at why they are happening, where they are heading, and what they mean for the future of business. It is an account of my own journalistic journey, attempting to understand things that I heard so clearly in the conversations with CEOs at the Vatican and since.

Clearly, we're on a journey. I'm not trying to portray the business world as being suddenly converted to idealism. That would be ridiculous. Nor am I suggesting that we've entered a golden era of the end of greed or corporate misdeeds. This is not a fairy tale. But as a journalist I'm intrigued by the prospect of the first major change in corporate ideology since at least the 1970s. This book is a chance to explore one of the most profound questions of the day: What principles will shape the soul of tomorrow's capitalist?

PART ONE

RAISING THE STAKES

CHAPTER 1

THE BIG CHANGE

MILTON FRIEDMAN, THE NOBEL PRIZE–WINNING ECONOMIST, WAS NOT above introducing serious economic lessons into his children's lives. In the late 1950s, when Jan and David Friedman were teenagers, the family was planning a long train journey across the country. Friedman presented them with a proposition. They could either have rooms with sleeping berths or they could travel in coach and receive the price difference in cash. The choice epitomized a couple of Friedman's key libertarian principles—life was about freedom to choose, and you don't get something for nothing. Both children chose to ride coach and presumedly the lesson was learned.

I received my own taste of Friedman's economic pedagogy as a young reporter for the *Wall Street Journal*, when I would occasionally call him to get quotes for my economic stories. He always returned my phone calls, but he alone among my sources insisted on returning them "collect," so that the charges were reversed to me. I was the one who wanted to speak to him, he figured, so I should pay.

By all accounts, Friedman was an affectionate parent, and a caring man. But when it came to matters of the economy, he had very clear views about how the world was supposed to operate. Born in Brooklyn in 1912 to Jewish immigrant parents, he grew up poor but always strived for the happiness inscribed on the Statue of Liberty. As his biographer Lanny Ebenstein wrote, "Friedman lived his life for a purpose, the utilitarian goal of producing the greatest good for the greatest number while being happiest oneself."[1]

In his long career, Friedman advanced a variety of influential theories and was most known in the academic world for his analysis of monetary policy. But the one he became known for in the corporate world was his view on the importance of private companies pursuing their own profits without consideration for social goals. He popularized it in a 1970 *New York Times* essay whose headline summarized the main point: "A Friedman Doctrine—the Social Responsibility of Business Is to Increase Profits."[2] In it, he criticized those who spoke of business as having a "social conscience." In particular, he claimed that the decision-makers in corporations didn't have the right to "spend someone else's money"—referring to stockholders—to address social problems. He quoted his own book *Capitalism and Freedom*, where he wrote that in a free society "there is one and only one social responsibility of business—to use its resources and engage in activities designed to increase its profits so long as it stays within the rules of the game, which is to say, engages in open and free competition without deception or fraud."[3]

As a graduate student at the London School of Economics in the late 1970s, I had studied economic history and read the works of Adam Smith, who laid the foundation for Friedman's view of a market economy. Smith wrote of an "invisible hand" that ensured the self-interested strivings of individuals combined for the greater good. "By pursuing his own interests, he frequently promotes that of the society more effectually than when he really intends to promote it," Smith wrote. "I have never known much good done by those who affected to trade for the public good."[4]

Friedman's warnings—and Smith's—about the consequences of companies pursuing social good particularly resonated in the 1970s, when the economy was stalling, and both inflation and unemployment were rising. There was widespread concern that in the decades following World War II, American corporate leadership had grown complacent, and wasn't responding sufficiently to competition from abroad or doing enough to ensure profits for owners. Friedman railed against the shortsightedness of business leaders who gave speeches about social responsibility while failing to meet the competitive challenge. "This may gain them kudos in the short run," he wrote. "But it helps to strengthen the already too prevalent view that the pursuit of profits is wicked and immoral and must be curbed and controlled by external forces. Once this view is adopted, the external forces that curb the market will not be the social consciences, however highly developed, of the pontificating executives; it will be the iron fist of Government bureaucrats."[5]

Over the final years of the twentieth century, Friedman's dictate found its way into corporate thinking as well as the political class. It helped pave the way for the rise of free market politicians like Margaret Thatcher in the UK and Ronald Reagan in the US, and the rise of corporate raiders and buyout firms that attacked companies with complacent and underperforming leadership. For the last quarter of the twentieth century, Friedman's doctrine seemed to be the rule of the land. The business of business was business. Companies existed for the benefit of their shareholders. Society could take care of itself.

THE BEST SYSTEM IN THE WORLD

Like most Americans I grew up believing that capitalism was the best system in the world, and that socialism was a dangerous dead end. When I was in college, my father would clip articles out of *Fortune* magazine and send them to me, fearful I might be led astray by left-leaning professors (and never imagining I might one day run the company that produced his favorite magazine!). He once sent me a book called *The Incredible Bread Machine*, which put Smith's invisible hand into simplistic, almost cartoonish language, to make sure I didn't miss the point.

But the truth is, he need not have worried. Any remaining sympathy I, or others, might have had for alternative economic systems pretty much evaporated in the final decades of the twentieth century. Inflation and slow growth took their toll in the 1970s and early 1980s, and the need for a market-based revival became more than apparent. I had studied English literature as an undergraduate but decided that to understand what was happening in the world, I needed a grounding in economics, and enrolled in the master's degree program at the London School of Economics. While in London, I watched Thatcher implement her tough-minded free market policies that first produced a recession, then a flowering of the British economy. Shortly after I came back to the US, Reagan was elected and began a similar exercise here, embracing tight monetary policy while pushing through sweeping deregulation and tax cuts. Around the world, countries with controlled economies began turning to more Friedmanesque policies to awaken their sclerotic economies.

And then, after the long and bitter Cold War that pitted capitalism against communism, the Berlin Wall fell in 1989, and the Soviet Union collapsed, revealing the economic rot that communism had caused. It soon appeared that Friedman, Thatcher, Reagan, and their faith in markets had conquered the world. Capitalism was triumphant.

I had the opportunity to visit Moscow shortly after the collapse of the Soviet regime and saw the gleaming new McDonald's franchise constructed at Pushkin Square. The store had many cash registers, but at first the Russians kept lining up in the longest line of people because they had been conditioned to think that's where the good stuff was. There was a joke at the time about a Russian seeing Lucas Cranach's famous painting of the Garden of Eden and concluding Adam and Eve must be Russian, because they had no clothing, no shelter, only a single apple to eat between them, and yet someone had told them they were in paradise.

I traveled to Poland with a group of cabinet secretaries in the administration of George H. W. Bush (1989–1992) to meet with Leszek Balcerowicz, who was building the postcommunist policies for the Polish economy. One of the US cabinet secretaries asked him if he was considering a "third way" that blended capitalism and socialism. "There is no third way," he responded without hesitation. "Capitalism has won."

Political scientist Francis Fukuyama went even further, writing a popular book called *The End of History and the Last Man*, in which he argued, "What we may be witnessing is not just the end of the Cold War, or the passing of a particular period of postwar history, but the end of history as such: that is, the end point of mankind's ideological evolution and the universalization of Western liberal democracy as the final form of human government."[6]

To be sure, capitalism had earned its triumph. Countries that turned away from central planning and embraced market economics saw sizable economic gains as a result. The most remarkable example was China, which by embracing market reforms was beginning its long and successful ascent that would bring hundreds of millions of its citizens out of poverty. "The Washington Consensus," a set of free market economic principles developed jointly by the International Monetary Fund, the World Bank, and the US Treasury, all based in Washington, became the bible for addressing economic crises around the globe. In February 1999, *Time* magazine enshrined the state of global economic thinking with a dramatic cover that anointed Federal Reserve Chairman Alan Greenspan, Treasury Secretary Robert Rubin, and his deputy Lawrence Summers as the "Committee to Save the World."

Summers, who later that year succeeded Rubin as Treasury Secretary, was particularly a product of the times. Considered one of the brightest economic thinkers of his generation, he had grown up in a family of Keynesian economists. In an interview with author Daniel Yergin in 2001, he said that "in many ways, Milton Friedman was a devil figure in my youth."[7] But the experiences of the final years of the twentieth century had changed his view. "If you think about it, it cannot be an accident that it is the same 15-year period when communism fell, when command-and-control corporations like General Motors and IBM had to be drastically restructured, when planning industries through the developing world were closed down, and when the Japanese model of industrial policy proved to be a complete failure. There is something about this epoch in history that really puts a premium on incentives, on decentralization, on allowing small economic energy to bubble up rather than a more top-down, more directed approach."

As for his views of Friedman, Summers said at the time, "I . . . ultimately have come to have an enormous respect for Friedman's views on a wide range of questions."[8]

In the corporate world, those last fifteen years of the twentieth century were also a period of upheaval, led by corporate raiders and private equity firms who attacked companies they viewed as having underperforming leadership. Their view was that many CEOs weren't looking after the best interests of their owners—the shareholders—and needed to be displaced. One of the most famous early examples was the leveraged buyout of RJR Nabisco, led by Henry Kravis and his cousin George Roberts, and chronicled in Bryan Burrough and John Helyar's classic book, *Barbarians at the Gates*.

Frequently, the buyouts left the acquired companies with large loads of debt and forced widespread layoffs in the name of efficiency.

In response, corporate leaders began catering more to shareholders, striving to provide predictable increases in quarterly earnings so those shareholders wouldn't be tempted to side with the raiders. GE CEO Jack Welch, who was dubbed "manager of the century" by *Fortune*, epitomized the trend. It was during this period that "shareholder primacy" became the rule. In 1997, the Business Roundtable, big business's lobbying arm in Washington, even put it into writing. "The paramount duty of management and boards of directors is to the corporation's stockholders," it pronounced, adding that "the interests of other stakeholders are relevant as a derivative of their duty to stockholders."[9] As the century came to a close, Friedman's rule had become the reigning corporate dictum.

The twenty-first century got off to a rocky start. A wrenching stock market collapse in 2000 put an end to a decade of frenetic market activity, led by technology stocks. Some big companies like Enron and Worldcom succumbed to spectacular, and scandalous, collapse. And then the terror attacks of September 11 made it clear that, contrary to the Fukuyama thesis, history had not ended, and ideological combat continued in a particularly brutal manner. The faith in markets that characterized the last decade of the twentieth century suddenly seemed shaken.

It was the financial crisis of 2007–2008 that really rocked market fundamentalism to its core. It was a market failure on a grand scale, and countless players bought into the notion that fancy new securities based on shaky home mortgages could somehow be treated as risk-free as government securities. The resulting Wall Street bailouts fed the impression that capitalism was a rigged game that elites would win regardless of the outcome. Homeowners who had taken out loans they couldn't afford to repay found themselves underwater, with houses valued at less than their debt. The crisis led to a recession, with widespread unemployment that was painfully slow to recover. Wages for the least-well-paid stagnated, even as profits recovered. Wealth for the fortunate who kept their savings in the market soared.

Wealth for the unfortunate whose only asset was their house plummeted. Trust in business, and in all institutions, also plummeted.

And capitalism got a second look. People had experienced the painful effects of markets gone haywire. The invisible hand had developed serious arthritis. And as the economy recovered, everyone looked around and saw an enormous and widening gap between the very rich and the working poor, between the ample rewards going to the owners of capital and the stagnating wages being paid to labor, between the plight of the protected few and the vulnerable many.

The irony of the moment was that even as capitalism was being reconsidered in the US and Europe, it was scoring its greatest global triumph. China was soaring, largely from its embrace of market-based policies, and the result was the greatest reduction in poverty in the history of the world. World Bank statistics showed that during the years since the collapse of Communism, the rate of extreme poverty around the world had fallen at about one percentage point a year—from 36 percent in 1990 to 10 percent in 2015.

But within the prosperous countries of the US and Europe, those global gains seemed to come at the expense of low-wage workers, causing inequality to rise. In the US, for instance, Pew Research found that households classified as "middle income" saw only modest increases in income between 1970 and 2018, while upper-income households saw their income nearly double. The share of all income going to the middle-income group dropped from 62 percent to 43 percent, while their share of wealth dropped even faster.

The 2008 shakeup led to a cascade of events, including Brexit—a bold and potentially disastrous rejection of corporate and political common sense—and the advent of leaders like Donald Trump and Boris Johnson, who flouted centuries of conventional wisdom without replacing it with any stable alternative. And just as real was the backlash on the Left, personified in the United States by Bernie Sanders. Sanders launched two presidential campaigns that, while ultimately unsuccessful, harnessed the impressive energy and influence of the younger population and pulled the Democratic party in his direction. Corporations were viewed as bastions of privilege, with CEOs who were paid hundreds of times more than their average worker. A slow rage was building in the public.

THE CHANGING ARENA

The growing backlash against market fundamentalism, however, is only half the story. At the same time, technology was transforming the fundamental structure of business, in some profound ways. The corporation of the twenty-first century increasingly had little in common with that of the twentieth. And the economic rules that applied to it were dramatically changed.

When I was first approached about coming to *Fortune* in 2014, a friend whom I admired advised me not to do it. "Why?" I asked. "Because *Fortune* is the magazine of big companies, the Fortune 500. And all the excitement in the economy today is in smaller tech companies."

I sort of understood his point. The top ten on the Fortune 500 in 2013 included four energy companies—Exxon, Chevron, Phillips, and Valero; two car companies—General Motors and Ford; Berkshire Hathaway, which earned much of its money from railroads; and General Electric. These were twentieth-century goliaths, the champions of a previous era of business. The only tech company on the top ten list was Apple.

But what that missed was the dynamism driving change in business. By the end of the decade, Amazon and Alphabet had rocketed into the top ten, along with a quartet of health care firms, while the oil and auto companies had fallen out (save Exxon, still hanging on at number ten).

In his book *Prosperity*, the author Colin Mayer cites a single statistic that captures the sweeping nature of these business changes. He looks at the assets on the balance sheets of the five hundred largest corporations in 1970 and again in 2018, and what he finds is striking. "Forty years ago, 80 per cent of the market value of US corporations was attributable to tangible assets—plant, machinery, and buildings—as against intangibles—licenses, patents, and research and development. Today, intangibles account for 85 per cent of the market value of US corporations."[10]

That shift has changed the power dynamics of business. In the twentieth century, power rested with those who controlled physical capital—land, plants and equipment, railroads, inventory, oil in the ground—as well as the financial capital needed to maintain those physical assets. But in the twenty-first, that power had shifted to companies that were relatively light on physical capital, and built their businesses on intellectual capital and brands, or on talented people and trust. Human capital and social capital had become the fundamental sources of value.

Other profound changes in how businesses operate have accompanied that. Because they require relatively little physical capital, modern businesses scale rapidly, expand their customers almost infinitely, and disrupt legacy competitors quickly. As a result, the pace of business competition and disruption has accelerated. A quarter century ago, if you asked the head of an investment bank or a retail giant or a media company who its main competitor was, they would quickly point to another company in the same industry. But ask the question today, and the answer is far less clear. It could be Amazon, which is making inroads in multiple industries; or a startup that is challenging the industry's entire business model; or even a new technology, like artificial intelligence or the blockchain, which promises to reshape the entire industrial landscape. Disruption has become a constant in business.

Information flows also have changed. A half century ago, corporations were set up as information hierarchies. The people in the field all reported information up to the C-suite, where the leaders would take that information, analyze it, formulate a strategy, and then send orders back down the hierarchy.

Today, information flows in all directions at once. Information no longer moves vertically; it moves omnidirectionally. And if you wait for the folks at the top to take it and analyze it, you've probably waited too long. So, decision-making has to be pushed to the edges to allow big companies to move faster, adjust quicker, and stave off disruption.

All of those changes have led to a very different challenge for the people at the top. The CEO's job today is less about telling people what to do, and more about representing the corporate vision and values, setting a North Star, and providing motivation and necessary guardrails. The main challenge of the modern leader is less about husbanding physical and financial resources, and more about attracting the very best talent and giving that talent an environment that ensures they provide their best work efforts.

And they must do all of this in a fishbowl. With social media abundant, the world is watching with an intensity unheard of in the twentieth century. Social media has enhanced transparency and made leaders more accountable for their performance, including their impact on society.

The business changes also are fueled by a generational shift. When I served as president of the Pew Research Center in the early years of the new millennium, we did research showing that the younger generation is indeed different—perhaps not in their desire for meaning, but in how they fulfill it. Millennials are slower to marry, less likely to belong to organized religion, less inclined to join civic clubs, than previous generations. That leaves the employer as their main formal connection to society. They want meaning and purpose in their work, placing new pressure on the workplace to be more than a faceless bureaucracy tallying profit and loss.

When Ellen McGirt and I interviewed Colin Mayer for our podcast *Leadership Next*, he spoke about the many ways the old rules no longer apply. "We need to think about how do we move forward from the model of the company and our capitalist system, which emerged in particular from the middle of the twentieth century with a focus on profits and shareholder returns, to a recognition that our capitalist system is more than that," he said.[11] "It is something that could really contribute to addressing the problems that we face as individuals and societies, and business can play a critical role in that, in a form that is not only beneficial for our societies and us as individuals, but beneficial for companies."

DREAM BIG

The idea that businesses should have a social purpose beyond making a profit is hardly a new one. It's been a strain of business thinking from the beginning. But in the last decade, what became clear to me was that the frequency and the intensity with which business leaders talked about purpose were increasing. More of them were putting it front and center. A growing group of CEOs felt the need to focus more consciously on their contributions to society.

John Mackey was an early example of this trend. He founded Whole Foods in 1980 with what then would have been considered peculiar ideas at its core. It wasn't just his advocacy of organic foods. Though a libertarian and strong advocate for free markets, Mackey felt business had to do a better job serving society. Whole Foods set strong standards for animal treatment, capped executive salaries relative to worker pay, and started the movement for what Mackey called "conscious capitalism"—a new ethical framework for business.

I've interviewed him several times over the last two decades. In our most recent interview, I asked him to spell it out: "What *is* conscious capitalism, and why the heck did you start talking about it?"[12]

"Real simple. I'll give you the elevator pitch for conscious capitalism," he replied. "It's not socialism, it's capitalism, but it's done in a more conscious way, and we recognize four major pillars in conscious capitalism. The first pillar is that every business, every organization has the potential for a higher purpose besides just maximizing profits. Number two, all the stakeholders matter, not just the investors. Customers, employees, suppliers, communities, investors, and business needs to create value consciously for all of them. Third, we need a different kind of leadership in the world. We need more conscious leadership. Leadership that's less about enhancing its own power and wealth. In leadership, it's about serving the organization and serving all the stakeholders. And fourth, we need to create cultures where human beings flourish, where people really like coming to work and being at work helps them grow to their highest potential as human beings."

Mackey reflected on the seminal moment that changed his view of capitalism—a flood in 1981 that wiped out his company. "That's when I discovered stakeholders, because hope shouldn't die," he said. "We had a near death experience, and I didn't have the language back then, but our stakeholders saved us. Our customers and neighbors came up and cleaned up our store and everybody pitched in and gave us money." Mackey's bank initially turned him down for a loan, but the decision was reversed. He later found out that his banker had personally guaranteed the loan, knowing Mackey would pay it back. "I got that sense of stakeholders very early on," he said. "And then I wanted to get the Conscious Capitalism Movement going because I really feel like business is misunderstood in the world. It's seen as a bunch of selfish, greedy bastards that are just in it to make as much money as possible."

Mackey doesn't believe that's true of most businesspeople and companies. And he set out to show the world that there's more to business than "a bunch of selfish, greedy bastards."

Mackey was early in this journey, and his words sounded discordant to many CEOs weaned on Friedman. But as I listened to leaders in the wake of the Great Recession, I heard more and more of them sound similar views. Tech CEOs, at the center of the battle for talent, for instance, were early to recognize the importance of articulating purpose for their employees.

In November 2015, I had the rare opportunity to interview Google founder Larry Page on stage at the *Fortune* Global Forum in San Francisco, before an audience of a couple hundred CEOs. Throughout his career, Page had largely avoided public interviews. But at that time, he had just created his new umbrella company, Alphabet, and was ready to talk about it. He was in a buoyant mood, and unlike most of the CEOs I have interviewed, he came with few prepared talking points.

What was most striking about the interview was Page's clear disdain for his fellow business leaders. In coming up with the plan to form Alphabet, I asked, was "there any company out there that you look at and say, 'That's kind of what we want to be'?"

Page thought for a moment, saying, "Mmmm," and then answered, "No."

"Companies have pretty bad reputations in the world," he said. "It's not like most people get up and say, 'Hey, I wish I could go work for a company.' I mean, they do it because they have to."

Alphabet's goal was to be different, to take on big problems. "We have to be more ambitious, we have to do things that matter to people, we've got to do less things that are zero-sum games, and more things that cause a lot of benefit." In short, companies needed a higher purpose. Whether Google has achieved that goal is open to debate, but the mindset of its founders clearly reflected a generational change.

The Vatican meeting came just one year after the San Francisco event where Page spoke, and in the weeks that followed it, many of the CEOs who had attended urged *Fortune* to keep that important conversation going. We agreed to create the *Fortune* CEO Initiative, as a venue for sharing ideas and best practices among companies striving to improve their social impact.

Salesforce CEO Marc Benioff was one of the first to step up, offering to support the Initiative as founding sponsor. Speaking at our meeting in 2019, he explained how he came to be viewed as one of the first "activist CEOs."

"I didn't become all of a sudden this activist CEO. I got kind of pushed by my employees," he said. "I think they just realize they have a choice where they work. They want to be in a business that is about purpose. They want to make sure the company they are in is actually committed to improving the state of the world. What is going to happen is that you have these very young people getting involved with next-generation technologies, and they are going to use it to create this [new] industrial revolution, which is actually about saving the planet."

Apple CEO Tim Cook, speaking to my colleague Adam Lashinsky at a CEO event in San Francisco in 2018, put it this way: "For Apple, we have always been about changing the world. It became clear to me a number of years ago that you don't do that by staying quiet on things that matter. And so, for us, that's been the driving issue. . . . I don't think business should only deal in commercial things. I think that's a fallacy. Business to me is a collection of people. If people should have values . . . then companies should have values, because it's just a collection of people."

And it wasn't just technology leaders who were focusing on values and purpose. JPMorgan CEO Jamie Dimon came to the CEO Initiative's 2017 meeting and had this to say in an interview with *Fortune* editor in chief Clifton Leaf about his bank's effort to rescue the failing city of Detroit, which included a $100 million investment (later extended to $200 million): "I have never had this conflict between shareholders and corporate social responsibility. I look at business very personally. If I have a store in a town, you participate in the neighborhood, you help the homeless, you might help the local church or synagogue, a Little League team, might give some summer jobs, that's what you do. That is called humanity. I've never been conflicted on that."

FROM TYRANNY TO OPPORTUNITY

All these conversations reinforced my conviction that the world of business had changed, and in some important ways. A conversation I had with Bill McDermott, the CEO of software company ServiceNow, helped me focus on how dramatic that change really had been. I had first met McDermott a decade earlier, when he was the newly minted CEO of SAP, the German software company. The occasion was the World Business Forum, a massive event held at Radio City Music Hall for aspiring executives from multiple companies. McDermott was getting ready to speak. I was there to interview Jack Welch, the former CEO of General Electric, still considered a legend and a role model for the up-and-coming business leader.

So, when McDermott and I met again in mid-2020, we began to talk about Welch, who had died earlier that year at age eighty-four. "Jack Welch at the end of the twentieth century, he was *it* when it came to leadership," I said.[13] "His book [*Jack: Straight from the Gut*[14]] sold like crazy, he developed a whole generation of CEOs who went on to lead Boeing, Home Depot, 3M, et cetera. He was a phenomenally successful businessman who increased shareholder value at GE a hundredfold. But there is a sense that the rules of the game have changed pretty dramatically since he left the stage. I wonder if you could talk about that."

McDermott, who remembered with pleasure our conversation backstage with Welch and his wife Susie, said, "Jack was an incredible force of nature and figured you had to be number one and two in any business and held people highly accountable, and if you didn't perform, you didn't last long. I think that is absolutely a leadership style that proved to be highly successful for him. But I do think the rules of the game have changed so much. There's a bigger war for talent now than I believe there ever has been. I believe you have to create cultures that have an enormous focus on purpose, and you have to create environments where people feel inspired to come to work."

The good news, according to McDermott, is that "the pendulum has really swung more towards a leader being absolutely in service to the employees and absolutely finding new ways to inspire them, new ways to innovate, new ways to bring out the best in them, and the accountability is actually in unleashing the entrepreneurial spirit itself versus managing things hard line. So, there's a soft touch that you need today that's pretty unique."

None of this, of course, means that big businesses have become paragons of virtue, or that the rules of human nature have been repealed. Greed-driven misbehavior always has been and always will be part of the business landscape. Many, if not most, of the companies mentioned in this book have been involved in activities that cast shadows over their more altruistic efforts.

JPMorgan was home to the London Whale scandal, where a single trader accumulated outsized positions in credit default swaps that led to a $6 billion loss and called into question the bank's risk management systems. Google, despite its initial "Don't Be Evil" motto, has been dogged by accusations that its business has been built on its misappropriation of other people's work, and that its search engine favors its own services over outside competitors. Apple, like many of its tech brethren, manipulates global rules to pay an unconscionably low rate of tax on its activities. Facebook is currently embroiled in a debate about whether its business model deliberately encourages toxic speech and misinformation. Like the people who work at them, these companies are complex organizations, capable of doing bad as well as good.

But something clearly has changed. The demands that companies deliver for society as well as for shareholders—from employees, from customers, from investors, and from society at large—have intensified. The incentives to behave in ways that benefit the broader needs of people and the planet have become more woven into the very structure of business. And the consequences for taking a narrow, Friedmanesque view of corporate responsibility have been dramatically heightened. Business is evolving, not in a straight or unbroken line, and perhaps not as fast as many would like, but in a clearly discernible direction.

CHAPTER 2

THE BASTION SHAKES

JAMIE DIMON HAD BECOME A HOUSEHOLD NAME DURING THE 2008 FINAN-cial crisis. He was one of the rare banking giants who emerged from the rubble, applauded for being part of the solution. While other financial in-stitutions were struggling or crashing, Dimon's company, JPMorgan Chase, was gobbling up market share. By 2009 it had become the leading finan-cial institution in America—the one most graduating students said they wanted to work for. Dimon in turn became the titular spokesperson for the industry—the man many financial journalists turned to for insight.

One reason was his ability to look beyond the narrow interests of his own company. His biographer Duff McDonald characterized him during that period as "a creative thinker and a man with the ability to shape the culture not just of his company but also of his industry and even the country itself."[1] During the financial crisis Dimon's mantra was that banks (and by exten-sion other businesses) are important partners in problem-solving financial solutions to benefit the nation. Although Dimon said his bank did not need a loan from the Troubled Asset Relief Program (TARP), he accepted it at the request of the Treasury Secretary to assure the stability of the TARP program. JPMorgan repaid the loan with interest by June 2009.

In 2019, Dimon was about to make another bold move. As chairman of the influential Business Roundtable (BRT), an association of CEOs that had traditionally been devoted to lobbying for business interests, he acknowledged that the concerns expressed by many Americans about the state of capitalism were worthy of attention. He thought that the BRT was the right vehicle to address the issues. And he was in a unique position to change things. Each year *Fortune* polls the Fortune 500 CEOs asking which of their members they most admire. Jamie Dimon was mentioned most in 2019 and 2020.

The Business Roundtable might have seemed an unpromising place to start. Since 1997, it had formally embraced the Friedman-style definition of capitalism, declaring that "the principal objective of a business enterprise is to generate economic returns to its owners." However, deeper in the BRT's history there was a glimmer of another philosophy. In 1981, the BRT issued a measurably different kind of statement about corporate purpose: "Corporations have a responsibility, first of all, to make available to the public quality goods and services at fair prices, thereby earning a profit that attracts investment to continue and enhance the enterprise, provide jobs and build the economy." The BRT further stated that there was a "symbiotic relationship" between business and society. By the 1990s, when Reaganomics had taken hold, much of that thinking had moved to the back burner, at least in corporate boardrooms and C-suites. Faced with activist investors, the companies were paying extra attention to pleasing their shareholders.

But even the BRT couldn't ignore the changes that were happening in business. In June 2018, the business and economics columnist Steven Pearlstein wrote a *Washington Post* column decrying the short-term corporate mentality that he said was crushing many corners of the economy. Harking back to the BRT's 1997 statement, he wrote that the "decision to declare maximizing value for shareholder[s] as the sole purpose of a corporation" is "the source of much of what has gone wrong with American capitalism."

Piling on, the Drucker Institute's Rick Wartzman, who had once worked with me in the Washington bureau of the *Wall Street Journal*, wrote a scathing verdict in *Fast Company*, noting that for all its efforts to address pressing social issues, "the Roundtable is failing in an area that lies at the very core of the connection between business and society: It continues to elevate shareholders' interests above everybody else's."[2]

As chairman of the BRT, Dimon was taken aback by the criticism. In October 2018, he chose to face the critics head-on, inviting Pearlstein, Wartzman, Judy Samuelson from the Aspen Institute, and several others to an off-the-record dinner at JPMorgan headquarters. The dinner was friendly at first, but grew testy. Dimon attempted to explain his position, which was that most BRT companies were already giving serious attention to a range of stakeholders when they made decisions—effectively transgressing the statement of purpose. Others at the table pressed for more, arguing that informal gestures weren't enough. At the end of the dinner Dimon said he would take a new look at the 1997 statement. Those attending the dinner thought their discussion would end there, with no action.

But in the coming months, Dimon led other members of the BRT in an animated debate about the purpose of a corporation and its role in the greater society. Meanwhile, Dimon himself was poking the bear.

In his annual letter to shareholders in April 2019, Dimon noted that "the American Dream is alive—but fraying for many."[3] He wrote that the federal government had lost the trust of the American people and needed to step up: "Governments must be better and more effective—we cannot succeed without their help." Still, he noted, "the rest of us could do a better job, too. . . . One consistent theme is completely clear: Businesses, governments and communities need to work as partners, collaboratively and constructively, to analyze and solve problems and help strengthen the economy for everyone's benefit."

Meanwhile, the BRT discussions were coming to a surprising conclusion. BRT CEO Joshua Bolten told me that despite the controversial nature of the discussion and the lively debates, most of the members were on board with dropping the 1997 statement and adopting a new articulation of purpose. The board agreed "that it is really important for us collectively to highlight and proactively communicate the positive role of business in society." Bolten hastened to add that traditional economic policies that promote or hinder growth were still the "bread and butter" of the association. But a new "opportunity agenda" was unfolding.

On August 19, 2019, the BRT surprised the business and political worlds with the release of an official statement. Because I followed these issues closely, they had given me a heads-up, enabling me to write a cover story for *Fortune*.

Statement on the Purpose of a Corporation

Published by the Business Roundtable, Aug. 19, 2019

Americans deserve an economy that allows each person to succeed through hard work and creativity and to lead a life of meaning and dignity. We believe the free-market system is the best means of generating good jobs, a strong and sustainable economy, innovation, a healthy environment and economic opportunity for all.

Businesses play a vital role in the economy by creating jobs, fostering innovation and providing essential goods and services. Businesses make and sell consumer products; manufacture equipment and vehicles; support the national defense; grow and produce food; provide health care; generate and deliver energy; and offer financial, communications and other services that underpin economic growth.

While each of our individual companies serves its own corporate purpose, we share a fundamental commitment to all of our stakeholders. We commit to:

- Delivering value to our customers. We will further the tradition of American companies leading the way in meeting or exceeding customer expectations.
- Investing in our employees. This starts with compensating them fairly and providing important benefits. It also includes supporting them through training and education that help develop new skills for a rapidly changing world. We foster diversity and inclusion, dignity and respect.
- Dealing fairly and ethically with our suppliers. We are dedicated to serving as good partners to the other companies, large and small, that help us meet our missions.
- Supporting the communities in which we work. We respect the people in our communities and protect the environment by embracing sustainable practices across our businesses.

- Generating long-term value for shareholders. [They] provide the capital that allows companies to invest, grow and innovate. We are committed to transparency and effective engagement with shareholders.

Each of our stakeholders is essential. We commit to deliver value to all of them, for the future success of our companies, our communities and our country.

The statement may not seem revolutionary, but the headlines were immediate and dramatic. It was no less than a redefinition of the purpose of a corporation. Shareholders were still there, to be sure—but mentioned only after employees, customers, communities, and the natural environment. Overnight, decades of adherence to the dogma of shareholder supremacy were ended. That's not to say that corporations instantly reconfigured themselves. But in the long game, change begins with purpose.

For Dimon, it was a matter of pragmatism. "Major employers are investing in their workers and communities because they know it is the only way to be successful over the long term," he said. "These modernized principles reflect the business community's unwavering commitment to continue to push for an economy that serves all Americans."

The Business Roundtable was hardly in the vanguard of this movement. And even many of its members argued that nothing really had changed— that they had always operated this way. But those statements ignored the history of the last three decades of the twentieth century. The Roundtable's action showed how pervasive the movement had become. Business was changing, in response to the needs of society, and under pressure from a new generation of employees, customers, and investors. History had taken a turn.

THE CONTRARIANS

Not everybody, of course, was so enamored with this new declaration of stakeholder capitalism. The breakthrough came with a lot of baggage. Generations of Americans had learned to equate social responsibility with socialism and state control of the means of production, and held a stubborn mistrust of anything that strayed from the traditional purpose, fearing that corporations would be unable to protect shareholders if they invited additional stakeholders in. Others who distrusted any action by business cynically viewed the Roundtable's statement as a head fake—an effort on the part of corporations to look "woke," and perhaps derail the aggressive regulatory actions of a coming Democratic administration. Some critics discounted the idea out of hand, such as economist Michael R. Strain, who stated, "As a matter of practicality, asking CEOs to make society better— the environment cleaner, working conditions safer, compensation higher—is beyond their competence and ability."[4] Some critics argued that stakeholder capitalism actually makes companies *less* accountable by reducing the natural controls wielded by shareholders.

One of the most thoughtful contrarians was Harvard Law's Lucian Bebchuk. In "The Illusory Promise of Stakeholder Governance," he stated that stakeholder capitalism was not real—that when faced with actual decisions, CEOs don't have an incentive to give weight to other stakeholders and therefore won't do it.[5] In follow-on research published in 2021, he found that the companies that signed the Business Roundtable statement had made few if any changes to their corporate governance guidelines, corporate bylaws, proxy statements, director pay policies, or responses to shareholder proposals as a result. His conclusion? That the Business Roundtable statement was "mostly for show."

I decided to host a debate on the topic on *Fortune*'s podcast *Leadership Next*, with cohost Ellen McGirt, pitting Bebchuk against Harvard Business School's Rebecca Henderson, a proponent of stakeholder capitalism and author of *Reimagining Capitalism in a World on Fire*.[6]

I gave Bebchuk the first chance to speak and asked him directly, "Why do you believe this is all hot air?"[7]

"I believe it's largely cosmetic," Bebchuk replied. "And if we keep talking about it, and have more interviews and more calls, we should not expect very substantial benefits to stakeholders to follow. And two reasons for this. One is that corporate leaders do not have significant incentives to protect stakeholders beyond what would serve shareholder value. They simply don't. And, secondly, we have to look at the evidence. And the evidence that colleagues and I've put forward is that, in fact, when CEOs and other corporate leaders face choices, they do not give independent sway to the interest of stakeholders."

Bebchuk's point was not without merit. This is exactly the kind of thing even the ardent fans of stakeholder capitalism worry about—that when push comes to shove, corporations will revert to form, and that openness can't withstand economic crises. Bebchuk pointed out that most of the CEOs who signed the BRT letter didn't even get board approval for their actions, raising questions about the seriousness of the effort. For Bebchuk, this was a telltale sign that the letter was "largely for show." He added, "We reviewed all their board-approved corporate governance guidelines, that public companies all have on their website. And we found that companies that are Business Roundtable statement signatories, by and large, still have guidelines that are largely reflective of a commitment to shareholder primacy."

Then Henderson, who had been listening quietly, and who consults with many companies and sits on the board of Amgen, spoke up.

"I respectfully disagree with Lucian. I think that the BRT statement is indeed quite important. And here I think is the root of the fundamental disagreement between us. Lucian says quite correctly, 'Well, they said this, but they didn't change the rules. And they're not changing their behavior. So, it doesn't mean anything.' Well, not quite. Because I believe that what we might call rhetoric, or culture, or our understanding of what the goals of the corporation are, is super important.

"And for the last twenty, thirty years, we've said that 'the goal of the corporation is to maximize shareholder value.' Which is . . . one interpretation of fiduciary duty, but only one. And there are other goals that the corporation could have, and those goals are really important. And I believe that shifting the goals of the corporation would make an enormous difference. I don't think you need to do a wholesale shift in corporate governance in order to do that."

In other words, words matter. The statement didn't change the world, but it did change the way business leaders talked about the world. And that was an important start.

I then turned to the second part of Lucian's argument, which was in effect to say, even if you could make stakeholder capitalism real, and put incentives together that would motivate people to act on it, it was still a bad idea.

Bebchuk elaborated, "I don't have any legitimate issue about if we found some way to make corporate leaders act in the way that economics calls 'the

Benevolent Dictator.' People who would act to maximize the social good, I would say, 'Sure, let's do that. And we'll bring society to a better place.' My problem is that I find that this would be very, very difficult and challenging. And the proposals on the table are just not going to do it. And in my view, we don't have any good reason to expect them to use their discretion to benefit stakeholders."

I interjected, "But you *do* argue in your paper that if companies actually had the incentives to pay more attention to stakeholder needs, that it would be a bad idea. Because they'd take their eye off the ball. They'd be less accountable to shareholders, and therefore they'd perform less well."

Bebchuk agreed that he was worried about loss of accountability, which in turn would lead to underperformance, "without actually delivering countervailing and offsetting benefits."

At this point Henderson broke in to delve deeper into the question of incentives.

"Lucian makes a very important point. Which is, we cannot expect business leaders to do good without the incentive to do good. I completely agree. I have twenty-five years of corporate board experience. Is the CEO going to say, 'I'm just going to give up my pay'? Or give up a chunk of money, and give it to the workers for no reason, except it's good for the world? No. Well, I think the debate is more interesting than this. I believe there's an important class of actions, which benefit both the firm and stakeholders that many firms have not focused on. Because they've been so focused on shareholder value that they've not taken a longer-term perspective, have not thought more broadly.

"We could think of this as instrumental stakeholderism. That is, 'I'm being stakeholder oriented, but don't worry, shareholders, I'm going to make you a bunch of money.' And those firms that have started down this road have some metrics that they think really give them a sense of the well-being of the workforce, or the reductions in environmental damage in their supply chain, and they're tracking those metrics. And they think that those metrics are giving them a route to profitability that they didn't have before. And they also think that embracing purpose, saying, 'I want to have a broader purpose,' is a better way to run the railroad."

She was describing the type of win-win situation I had heard so often from CEOs committed to stakeholder capitalism. It seemed to me that this was a fight well worth having. Profit maximizing, in theory, was clear-cut behavior. But in fact, it was anything but. As chief content officer, I had the opportunity to sit in the C-suite of the legendary media company Time, Inc., parent of Fortune, during the final days of its existence, before it was sold to Meredith. I saw the decisions that were made when you're faced with a shareholder activist who's demanding quarterly results. I saw the pressure to make decisions that were clearly not in the long-term interest of the company—much less the interests of the employees, or society, or any definition of stakeholder that you may choose—solely to goose quarterly returns. Everyone in business knows this happens. There are clearly tradeoffs, where the interests of the shareholder and the interests of other stakeholders diverge.

But if you focus on the longer term, that view changes. You can't have a successful company in the long term if your employees can't make a decent living; you can't have a successful company if social turmoil is undermining the community, the society, or the political context you must operate in; you can't have a successful company if the climate is creating chaos. In the long term, shareholder concerns and stakeholder concerns begin to converge.

Bebchuk agreed that a focus on long-term thinking was required, noting that it was something CEOs were not necessarily adept at. Henderson was happy to agree. She related an experience of her own. "As the Eastman Kodak Professor of Management [when at MIT], I spent the first twenty years of my career working with firms, like Kodak, trying to persuade them that the world was changing. I spent six months with Nokia, in Finland, in saunas, in the middle of February, trying to persuade them that Apple was really a threat to their business. And what did they say? They said, 'We're selling a million phones a week. Simmer down, Rebecca, it's going to be fine.' We know that there are real cognitive and institutional barriers to doing things differently."

"What we should do is look at what people do, rather than what people say," Bebchuk said in closing. And Henderson agreed but reiterated her belief that rhetoric from purpose-driven CEOs matters. Pushing them to act on their messaging is a way forward out of the desperate times society finds itself in today.

I've had a number of opportunities to speak to people who are skeptical about the new social consciousness in business. Skepticism is not a bad thing. It's important that we hold businesses accountable for what they say is their new purpose. Anand Giridharadas, author of the book *Winners Take All: The Elite Charade of Changing the World*, has emerged as one of the most vociferous and most skeptical critics. In his book, Giridharadas charges that the elite societies are often very visibly philanthropic while at the same time drilling down on the systems that actually keep the old order in being. When I spoke to Giridharadas about stakeholder capitalism, he readily acknowledged that he'd seen the change. "It has become socially unacceptable as a company or a rich person not to be doing good," he said. "CEOs are asking the question, 'What can I do to make the world better?' But what many are failing to do is ask, 'What have I done that may be drowning out any of the do-gooding I'm doing?'" He cited the 2017 US tax bill, supported by the Business Roundtable, as an example. The lion's share of the benefits, he argued, ended up in the hands of the top 1 percent, increasing the income inequality underlying many social problems.

"What I see are well-meaning activities that are virtuous side hustles," he argued, "while key activities of their business are relatively undisturbed. . . . Many of the companies are focused on doing more good, but less attentive to doing less harm."

It's an understandable argument. And ultimately, the success of stakeholder capitalism will require a new and transparent system of corporate accountability, so that companies can be held to their commitments. Corporations know how to measure shareholder returns—they and their accountants have spent more than a century building an elaborate infrastructure to do so. But new metrics are needed to measure stakeholder returns. We will come back to that point later in the book.

BATTLING FOR INDEPENDENCE FROM OVERSIGHT

The political implications of the BRT letter also were clear, especially as the nation approached a presidential election season. Happy to join the fray was Senator Elizabeth Warren, the financial reform activist who had announced her candidacy for the presidency. Appearing on CNBC, Warren challenged Dimon directly: "If Jamie Dimon thinks it's a good idea for giant corporations like JPMorgan Chase to have multiple obligations, he and I agree," she said.[8] "Then let's make that the law." Warren had introduced the Accountable Capitalism Act in 2018, and she told *Fortune*, "I asked ten major CEOs who signed the Business Roundtable statement to take tangible action to provide real benefits to workers and other stakeholders, but all they've offered up are hollow commitments and publicity stunts. If these companies are truly committed to a stronger economy for workers, communities, and other stakeholders, they would make the necessary reforms I have laid out in my Accountable Capitalism Act."

Warren's reaction was not surprising, especially in a political season. But her message was crystal clear: in her view, only a government agency could ensure proper accountability. Her underlying presumption was that the CEOs weren't really serious and wouldn't follow through unless forced by the government.

BRT CEO Josh Bolten wrote to Warren reconfirming the commitment of its members to their stakeholders and specifying four areas where they've been especially active—minimum wage, infrastructure, training, and data privacy.

But he strongly disputed the idea that Warren's proposed Accountable Capitalism Act was the only way to hold CEOs' feet to the fire. "Given our diverse economy, business decisions about how best to serve employees and deliver high-quality goods and services to customers require flexibility within the private sector," he wrote.[9] "Creating a new government entity to oversee those decisions would undermine U.S. competitiveness and result in less innovation."

Watching the back and forth, I realized that this debate was just getting started. At stake was whether the American people could trust the private sector to address the most pressing needs of society—or whether companies needed to be forced to do so by government regulation. And if regulation was going to be the answer, there was a danger we would quickly return to an era of government overreach that would stifle business creativity and innovation and dampen its ability to create jobs. There was a risk we would return to the stagnation of the 1970s, and business dynamism would move to other countries less willing to interfere with the invisible hand.

But the political battle lines were drawn.

NO REAL DEBATE

Despite all of the heated discussion in the media and politics over the legitimacy of stakeholder capitalism, one thing was becoming increasingly clear to me: there was very little debate among CEOs themselves. A new consensus had formed. And while there might be holdouts from the new doctrine of stakeholder capitalism among big businesses, they were distinctly in the minority.

I was continually struck by the difference in CEOs from just a decade ago. It was most evident in their willingness to speak out on controversial social issues. A decade ago, if there was a big cultural controversy being publicized across the airwaves, you couldn't get a CEO to comment on it to save your life. The attitude was very clear across the board: "If it doesn't directly affect my bottom line, I want nothing to do with it."

But more recently CEOs are speaking out boldly, even on topics that would once have gotten them in hot water. This was already happening in the year or two before the BRT statement. As Tim Cook put it at the 2018 Fortune CEO Initiative conference, you can't change the world by staying quiet. Among other things, Cook was outspoken about President Trump's immigration policy, especially child separation, which he called inhumane and said it had to stop. Immigration is not just a "numbers" conversation, he said. "There's real people behind this that have real feelings."[10]

This approach, virtually unheard of a decade earlier, was becoming more common. In the year or so after the BRT statement, I had many conversations with CEOs, both on the record and off, who were genuinely struggling with their role in a time of change. We talked openly about social issues—combating climate change, providing employee opportunities and training, increasing diversity and inclusion. The CEOs repeatedly told me that they felt a sense of obligation to fill a huge need that government had left unmet. And they reaffirmed that doing so was good for their business and their shareholders.

A good example of the trend is Chip Bergh of Levi Strauss. Bergh was present at the Vatican conference of CEOs, remembering that "I may be the only person who has met the Pope wearing jeans."[11]

"I firmly believe that CEOs have a role to play in making the world a better place," Bergh told Ellen McGirt and me on our *Leadership Next* podcast.

"One of the reasons I joined Levi Strauss is that this company has had for its entire 167 years a practice where the CEO is expected to take stands on important issues of the day. It goes back to our founder."

Bergh emphasized that the public stance on issues is important for his customers. "We target Gen Z and understanding where their mindset is on what's important in this world. It's gun control. It's climate change." And it's also important to employees. "We sit in the heart of Silicon Valley, and the reason we are able to attract great talent and retain great talent is because of the values we have and our fearlessness in taking these stands."

This view received widespread validation at the World Economic Forum in Davos in January 2020. It was clear the Business Roundtable statement, released the previous August, had marked an inflection point. We had been talking about these issues at our annual Davos dinners since January 2017, when Salesforce CEO Marc Benioff first stood up and offered, as noted earlier, to be founding sponsor of Fortune's CEO Initiative. Three years later, the intensity of the conversation had changed. The focus on social impact was no longer the diversion of an enlightened minority of CEOs. The Business Roundtable had made it mainstream and altered the tenor of the conversation.

We gathered about fifty CEOs at circular tables in a room at the Steigenberger Grandhotel Belvédère. A back-of-the-envelope calculation showed the assembled leaders ran companies earning over a trillion dollars in revenue and directly employing more than two million people. As I told them in my welcome, "You folks *can* change the world."

Among those present was Microsoft's Satya Nadella, who in *Fortune's* CEO polls over the previous three years had consistently been chosen by his peers as the "most underrated" CEO. In an announcement just a few days before our dinner, Microsoft had made a major commitment to go "carbon negative" by 2030, and by 2050 to "remove from the environment all the carbon emitted either directly or indirectly or by electrical consumption since it was founded in 1975." It also established a $1 billion innovation fund to accelerate the "global development of carbon reduction, capture and removal technologies."

I asked Nadella why Microsoft had made such a big commitment to address the climate problem.

"Why are we doing it?" he responded. "I think we are doing it out of enlightened self-interest. How do we as a company succeed? The world has to do well. I love Colin Mayer's definition of a corporation. In fact, it's a social enterprise, and a social enterprise's value is that it solves the challenges of the planet and its people."[12]

"Profitably solves" the challenges of people and planet, I interjected, correcting Nadella's citation of the definition Mayer gives in his book *Prosperity*.

"Yes, profitably," he said. "Key word is profitably. Sorry, it's eight p.m. on a Thursday. That definition is what it is all about. . . . If the planet is in danger, what exactly happens to capitalism? The best system we've ever developed to be able to allocate our productive resources is capitalism. So, if you want to keep the party going, you have to think about all the unintended consequences."

There was the key point. This move toward stakeholder capitalism wasn't just a public relations exercise. It was an existential necessity. *If you want to keep the party going, you have to think about all the unintended consequences.* Climate change. Growing inequality within nations. Historic injustices due to race. Societal tension over issues like guns, or LGBTQ rights. These were all "social" issues, once thought to be the exclusive domain of government. But the business community was acknowledging that could no longer be the case. The issues had grown too large. They had become of fundamental importance to the company's employees and its customers and even its investors. They had been too long ignored or mishandled or even exacerbated by the actions of governments. And if business didn't step up to the plate to address them, the whole system of democratic capitalism was in danger of collapse.

I heard so many other CEOs echo Nadella's point—and consistently arguing that by adopting broader social goals, they were also serving the interests of their business. Unilever CEO Alan Jope described it at a breakfast meeting in Davos that year. "The predominant paradigm—either deliver financial performance or pay attention to social impact"—is flawed, Jope stated, assuring the audience that Unilever didn't buy into the false choice.[13]

Jope said his company's focus on sustainability "has made us an absolute magnet for talent. Unilever has gone from being an unknown company in the talent market to being ranked by LinkedIn as number three after

Google and Apple." No small accomplishment for a company best known for selling soap.

As 2020 began, the world seemed to be taking note of this new focus for business. Skeptics, of course, remained legion. And even many of those who acknowledged the change argued it wasn't big enough, or happening fast enough, to meet the magnitude of the challenges. Still, I couldn't help but think it was a change for the good.

Then the world shook.

CHAPTER 3

WHIPLASH

THE WORLD DOES NOT STAND STILL AWAITING OUR NEXT MOVE. JUST AS THE fault lines of global capitalism were beginning to shift, COVID-19 shook the world to its core. Talk of the virus that had begun in Wuhan, China, swirled around Davos that January, but with no effect yet on people's behavior. While there, I ran into Li Chuyuan, chairman of Guangzhou Pharmaceutical, and his advisers, and we warmly shook hands, without any thought of the social distancing to come. (Chuyuan later came under some criticism for suggesting his company's herbal medicine could stave off the disease.)

But unknown to the Davos crowd, the first case had already arrived within the United States—later confirmed in Washington state on January 21. The virus hit southern Europe in force in February, and by March, it was declared a global pandemic.

The "global society," long heralded as a supreme advance of the modern era, aided the spread of the disease. In the coming weeks travel bans were announced, and when the spread continued, lockdowns began. California was the first with a statewide stay-at-home order. On the East Coast, New

York state became the epicenter of the coronavirus, with Governor Andrew Cuomo ordering all nonessential businesses closed.

The blow to the economy was immense. Without customers, the airline industry was effectively shuttered. Restaurants closed. Theaters shut down and Broadway went dark. Businesses sent workers home. Schools closed. The streets of Manhattan, the global heartbeat of finance, were empty. One almost expected to see tumbleweeds.

From my office—now at home—I watched the virus's effects on the economy, and talked with many business leaders, in video calls, as they tried to get a handle on how to predict what we faced. The problem was that there were no benchmarks and no history that would allow for predictions. We lived at the dawn of a new technological age of predictive analytics. But such predictions required past data, and in this case, there were none. We just didn't know. On some days it felt like being in one of those movies where aliens arrived and hovered in spacecrafts over the planet. Everyone waited and feared, but no one knew what would happen next. We were shocked when deaths were reported in the tens of thousands. We could not have imagined that they would grow to the hundreds of thousands and then millions.

The sheer unknowability of the virus sent the markets into a frenzy. In the early months, what cratered the public confidence was the lack of certainty. No one knew how long it would last, when a vaccine would be available— the estimate based on past experience was a decade—or when life could return to normal.

When the pandemic hit, my first instinct was that it would cause a temporary reprieve in business interest in stakeholder capitalism. Finances had been sent into a shambles. Bottom lines had suddenly collapsed. And I thought the natural reaction of corporate leaders would be to say, "Let's put all these stakeholder concerns on a back burner until we get our finances back on track."

After all, we had lived through something similar in the previous recession. In the years leading up to the financial crisis, a growing number of businesses stepped up their advocacy for policies to address climate change. In 2006, companies like General Electric and Duke Power, both at the heart of the twentieth-century fossil-fuel-driven economy, created a coalition called US CAP (Climate Action Partnership) that called for new and aggressive action to address greenhouse gas emissions. And as we moved into the US elections of 2008, both leading candidates, Republican Senator John McCain and Democratic Senator Barack Obama, had come out in favor of legislation to create a cap on carbon emissions. But then the financial crisis hit, and the Great Recession followed, and business interest in climate action seemed to evaporate.

As I spoke to more and more leaders after the pandemic hit, however, it became clear to me that this time, it was different. The opposite was happening. It might be argued that you don't plan a revolution during a pandemic. But the stakeholder revolution was already happening, and the pandemic, by its very nature, propelled it forward. Unlike the previous recession, which had been fundamentally financial in nature, this one was rooted in public health. It was a stakeholder crisis from the start, and it highlighted a host of stakeholder issues.

The pandemic put workers at risk, as they were forced to address the threat of being exposed to the virus in the workplace. And it quickly became clear the pandemic would widen the rifts that had plagued Western society in recent years—between knowledge workers and manual workers, between well-educated and less well-educated, between top-tier cities and the rest.

Faced with that new reality, CEOs became even more convinced that it was time for business to step forward and play a greater role in healing society's divides. As Emmanuel Faber, CEO of Danone, told me, "Everything we have seen during the last several months suggests companies will have even more stakeholders than before, with government stepping in, health authorities stepping in, and so on. Whether you want to call them stakeholders or not, they are. . . . This idea of stakeholder capitalism is going to be significantly bigger than it was before the crisis, whether you like it or not."[1]

Roger Crandall, CEO of MassMutual, echoed this sentiment. "I think we have a unique opportunity, in part driven by the lack of leadership in our government, for companies to make a huge difference," he said. "It has become very common for people to say Covid is accelerating trends already in place. The trend of companies driving real societal change is absolutely huge. It's literally like a snowball going downhill, picking up momentum."[2]

When I first began speaking with business leaders to hear their thinking about the crisis and its effects, I lamented that it was coming just as the dramatic movement for change was gathering momentum across the business community. Since that auspicious gathering in Rome, much had happened to cement a commitment to increasing the positive social impact of corporations.

ENTERING THE FRAY

When I spoke with JUST Capital CEO Martin Whittaker in early April 2020, he had just been exposed to the coronavirus and was experiencing symptoms. He'd later call it the biggest test of his career.

Whittaker is a thoughtful guy, who once told an interviewer that he derived strength from the words of Theodore Roosevelt in his famous speech about courage, delivered in Paris in 1910. Roosevelt discounts the critics and praises the person who is "actually in the arena, whose face is marred by dust and sweat and blood; who strives valiantly; who errs, who comes short again and again, because there is no effort without error and shortcoming; but who does actually strive to do the deeds; who knows great enthusiasms, the great devotions; who spends himself in a worthy cause; who at the best knows in the end the triumph of high achievement, and who at the worst, if he fails, at least fails while daring greatly, so that his place shall never be with those cold and timid souls who neither know victory nor defeat."

It's a dramatic mantra, yet the soaring prose is fairly typical of the kind of comments I was receiving from CEOs in the early days of the pandemic. I asked Whittaker the question that was on everybody's mind: Would the new social initiatives adopted by corporations suffer? What was JUST Capital's tracking showing about how companies were responding?

"We are seeing companies, for the most part, react quickly, especially to the needs of their workers and customers," Whittaker said. "In some cases, like in retail and in hospitality, layoffs are inevitable. But it's a question of how they do it."[3]

Whittaker, who has been watching companies along these lines for twenty years, described seeing steady movement over that period, away from pure shareholder metrics, and toward nontraditional measures of performance. "It started with the environment," he said, "but now has moved on to other social issues. Companies are stepping up." He said this is the only option, warning that a return to the previous status quo would lead to real problems. "This is a moment when we really should reflect on what new normal we should create. You cannot grow the pie if people just don't think the system is working for them." Whittaker added that stakeholder capitalism was the key. "I expect it to be the defining criteria for business performance in 2020," he said.

GO BIG

"None of us has the luxury of choosing our challenges. Fate and history provide them for us. Our job is to meet the tests we are presented."[4] This was Fed chairman Jay Powell's sober note as the COVID-19 pandemic hit the nation. And he was ready to act, announcing a bold economic rescue program to buy risky corporate debt. He was widely praised for his leadership during a crisis.

As crises often do, this one provided some opportunities for innovation, forced some long overdue changes in the way companies operate, and shined a bright light on the inequities that existed within corporations.

The pandemic delivered an unprecedented shock to the economy, making financial performance an existential imperative for many companies. Moreover, a historically tight labor market—which gave talented young employees unprecedented power to demand better pay, benefits, and social responsibility—had overnight given way to unprecedented unemployment. What could companies do? It was the ultimate test.

Mark Cuban has always been a showman and is a popular media personality on the highly rated *Shark Tank*. He's also a billionaire, an effective entrepreneur, and owner of the Dallas Mavericks. He dabbles in politics and has been mentioned on occasion as a potential presidential candidate.

One thing I know about Cuban. He understands the big gesture. When I interviewed him early in the coronavirus pandemic, he had just announced that he was paying all hourly employees of the Dallas Mavericks their normal wages, even though the Mavericks' home arena was closed, and the NBA was shut down for the foreseeable future. He explained, "It's not going to cost me nearly as much as it would cost the hourly employees to go without."[5] He added that he was rich and could afford it.

When I interviewed him, Cuban explained that this wasn't generosity but obligation. "As a CEO or entrepreneur, if you can afford to keep paying your employees, you should, simply because it's the right thing to do. And if you can't afford it, prioritize clear communication to explain why you're taking the steps you are to get to the other side of the crisis."

Cuban's go-big-or-go-home action got lots of attention as the entire business world grappled with ways to keep going and support their employees. In the early months of the pandemic, my email box was flooded with press releases from companies touting their coronavirus good works. The serious contenders, in my view, were the companies who were actually trying to make a measurable difference, either for their employees or in the COVID-19 fight. Target announced an investment of more than $300 million in added wages, paid leave, and backup childcare. Allstate offered free coverage to those who were using their vehicles to deliver food and medicine. MassMutual offered free life insurance to frontline health care workers. Jack Dorsey dedicated $1 billion in Square stock for coronavirus relief. The list went on.

COVID-19 has presented an opportunity for CEOs to do more than pay lip service to change. Paul Polman, who became CEO of consumer goods giant Unilever back in 2009 (retiring in 2019 and handing the reins to Alan Jope) and steered it toward a new kind of capitalism, expressed the view of many: "Governments in this world right now have a little bit of a hard time, and global governance is broken," he said.[6] "Populism, xenophobia, nationalism . . . all these things are going in the wrong direction. Meanwhile these issues are piling up. Cybersecurity, financial markets, climate change, coronavirus. These are global issues that need global coordination." He added, "I believe it is the duty of the private sector to step up and fill that void and be responsible. We are not elected bodies, but we do have to fill that void. And it's in the interest of business. And increasingly, business understands that."

"This is truly the mother of all defining moments. . . . In previous defining moments, if as a business leader you came out with the top and bottom line intact, that was defined as good enough. Now that is no longer good enough. People want to see that you're making a positive contribution to some of these societal issues."

—Mark Schneider, CEO, Nestlé

Was this just a knee-jerk reaction to a crisis, or was it a harbinger of a shift in corporate purpose? In the beginning, I couldn't have answered that question. But as weeks turned into months, it became clear that COVID-19 had a more permanent effect on business attitudes than anyone had imagined. It had created an opportunity for business to reshape the future.

LEADING WITH EMPATHY

From the outset, the hospitality industry was among the hardest hit by the pandemic, and by the summer things had only grown worse. When I interviewed Hyatt Hotels CEO Mark Hoplamazian, his company had already suffered major blows. With bookings down 94 percent and the company forced to lay off 1,300 people and furlough others, it was a unique challenge for a leader who often spoke about leading with empathy. I asked Hoplamazian how it was possible in the midst of a crisis that required such brutal choices. He replied, "Empathy has never been more important because everyone's experience of COVID is so different."[7]

He acknowledged that the layoffs had taken a serious toll and called it "the most difficult and challenging time that I've ever experienced as a person."

Hoplamazian had given a lot of thought to my question. He explained that one key to delivering the tough decisions with empathy was to be bold and up-front, thus avoiding the strain of uncertainty on his employees. Other measures included a care fund to supplement the financial safety net the government provided to laid-off employees. Hyatt also set up a support network for those who had been laid off to help people keep in touch with the company. This gesture was meant not only to help those who had lost their employment, but also to recognize that many of them would become future employees when rehiring was set in motion.

He also cited an innovative program for furloughed workers. "We're partnering with over ten companies that are currently hiring—companies like Walmart and Pepsi and CVS and Walgreens. We're very grateful to them for allowing us to plug straight into their application process online to help our colleagues find work there if they want to work during their furlough."

CRISIS UPON CRISIS

The nation hobbled into June 2020, still not having a handle on COVID-19 as it spread across the US. And then, as if to underscore that the foundations of the system were unstable, a racial justice crisis stormed to the forefront of public attention, and Black Lives Matter, the nascent civil rights movement, achieved new prominence.

There had been other high-profile incidents of police violence against Blacks in recent years, but the tragic death of forty-six-year-old George Floyd, a Minneapolis Black man, became a tipping point. On May 25, Minneapolis police officers arrested Floyd after a convenience store clerk claimed he'd passed a counterfeit $20 bill. The arrest, which was recorded by bystanders and caught on security cameras, showed Floyd handcuffed facedown on the ground while a police officer knelt on his neck. The officer pressed down for nine minutes and twenty-nine seconds while Floyd complained that he couldn't breathe and bystanders shouted for him to stop. Floyd finally lost consciousness, and when officers checked on his condition, they found that he had no pulse.

Floyd's death outraged the nation. Ignoring the pandemic, massive rallies formed in cities and towns across the United States, and unlike previous protests, they won support from a majority of Americans. The rallies and protests lasted well into September.

Suddenly a new dynamic was present that hadn't been observed before—companies getting behind the BLM banner. They did this because they judged it to be the right thing to do, but also because they were compelled by the overwhelming response, mainly from their employees. A survey by JUST Capital found that a large majority of Americans wanted CEOs to weigh in on the protests—with a statement about ending police violence (84 percent), promoting peaceful protest (84 percent), elevating diversity and inclusion in the workplace (78 percent), condemning racial inequity (75 percent), and condemning police killings of unarmed Black people (73 percent).

Beyond such statements, companies used the moment to make new commitments to increase diversity within their own ranks. JUST Capital tracked the companies taking action. For example:

PepsiCo created a $400 million initiative to increase the number of Black managers by 30 percent in five years and more than double Black-owned suppliers. PepsiCo subsidiary the Quaker Oats Company announced that it was canceling the Aunt Jemima brand.

Bank of America announced a $1 billion, four-year commitment to strengthen economic opportunities in communities of color.

Google set a target to drastically support Black executives and achieve at least 30 percent minority representation on their executive team by 2025.

Adidas, also the owner of Reebok, committed to filling 30 percent of new positions with Black or Latinx workers.

NASCAR banned the Confederate flag from appearing at its races.

When I spoke to CEO Brian Moynihan about Bank of America's response, he described the scene at that time. The company was already ramping up its employee and community support efforts because of the pandemic. But the George Floyd murder and the demand for a response hit the company solidly. "You had the combination of the impact of the virus on communities of color and then you had the impact of the racial justice question, and we decided, look, we just can't let this die down," Moynihan told me.[8] "We have to put our money where our mouth is to double our efforts or more." That's where the four-year plan to donate $1 billion to increase economic opportunities in communities of color came from. In this way, the pandemic and social justice issues went hand in hand. Such corporate actions shifted to conversations about Black representation in companies, underscoring the importance of diversity—one of the signature platforms of stakeholder capitalism.

It's worth noting that only six years earlier, a police officer in Ferguson, Missouri, had shot and killed Michael Brown in the middle of the street, witnessed by many bystanders. The event sparked large protests and fed the growth of the Black Lives Matter movement. But big company CEOs were, for the most part, silent.

Their reaction following George Floyd's death was different, indicating how much business leadership had changed in the few intervening years. Many CEOs had conversations with their employees about race for the first time. The intersection of BLM with the pandemic created a striking new awareness. A *Fortune*-SurveyMonkey poll taken in May had revealed that Black adults were more than twice as likely to have been laid off or furloughed as a result of the pandemic. This stark reality was rolled into the other inequities the Black population faced. George Floyd seemed to underscore the systemic lack of equality and civil rights that Blacks and other people of color experience in their daily lives.

At the June virtual meeting of the *Fortune* CEO Initiative, we heard from Ryan Williams, a thirty-two-year-old Black entrepreneur who has built a technology-driven real estate investment platform called Cadre, which reportedly oversees some $800 million in assets. The meeting was off the record, but Williams agreed to talk with me afterward.

Speaking of George Floyd, Williams told me, "I could very well have been in that same position because of how I looked. My professional accomplishments don't matter that much at the end of the day." Williams grew up in Baton Rouge, Louisiana, and remembered older relatives telling horror stories from the Jim Crow era. "Will I be able to tell my children and their children that the world they grow up in is more just?" he asked. "It hit me that we haven't made that much progress."[9]

Williams applauded other CEOs for openly discussing the problem, but also called on them to take concrete actions. He listed several of them: "Put in place immediate steps that increase diversity and inclusion at the table, actually make metrics related to diversity public, make your interviewing and hiring process public, and incentivize people off that." He acknowledged that these efforts might not prevent the next George Floyd, but "there is no one-size-fits-all solution. There are going to be multiple paths that have to be invested in. As CEOs, one of the best things we can do is start with our own home."

Hyatt's Hoplamazian theorized that the vulnerability created by COVID-19 actually allowed the movement for equity and inclusion to prosper in a way that will have long-term effects on the business world and society at large. He shared with me a profound admission. "My own personal journey in this has been now—and I'm embarrassed to say this—to really understand, probably for the first time, how deep systemic racism is and also how much of an ecosystem it requires in order to rectify," he said. "I think we're seeing the whole forest now, not just the individual trees of representation or minority content in our supply chain, but seeing how this extends to our communities. And that to me is the major difference."[10]

AVOIDING MISSTEPS

In the days after George Floyd was killed, there was a range of responses from the business community. Public statements of support for Black Lives Matter were issued from major brands. Public promises were made about doing better to incorporate diversity and inclusion in their own ranks. But even early on, what everyone was looking for was how the words would be followed up with actions.

To help us get our minds around the tricky issue of corporate engagement in social issues, Ellen McGirt brought in Dr. Erin Thomas for *Leadership Next*. Dr. Thomas is a researcher, a social scientist, and the vice president, head of diversity, inclusion, and belonging, for the freelance platform Upwork. But lately she's been working overtime, sharing her best advice for leaders at every level, on how to understand what's happening now and respond, and what's at stake for both Black employees and society.

Ellen asked Dr. Thomas if we could trust this moment as the beginning of true change, and she bluntly replied, "I'm not sure we can."[11] An explanation: "I think for some companies, they have been taking strides to be very action oriented and forward focused, in terms of the commitments that they're making. Others have not. I'm happy to talk about some of the missteps that I've seen. Both with public messages, but also with the messages that my friends all over the country have been sending me privately from their leadership teams, that I think really missed the mark. And have been stirring up this lack of trust amongst employees."

The first big misstep she pointed out was what she called performative messages. "If a statement is without commitment, it's really just a blackout Tuesday, it's a hashtag, it has no meat to it. I think the general structure of those messages is, this isn't right, we stand with Black people. That says nothing about what the company is investing in or committing to, moving forward. That just doesn't land well with anybody, including employees who are not Black."

Externally focused performative messages have the same flaws. "Corporate giving and donations, and aligning with Black Lives Matter, certainly are important. But they're not sufficient in having companies look in the mirror to understand, articulate, and act on the systemic racism that likely exists within their own organizations. Those statements are usually toned as this isn't right and we're giving to Black causes."

The problem with that? "There is no internal focus," Dr. Thomas explained. "It's sort of putting the problem out there and outsourcing the responsibility."

HUMBLING AND INSPIRING

These back-to-back crises—COVID and George Floyd—felt like whiplash to the status quo. Commentators repeatedly said that each in its own way will change the country as we know it—and that means the economic engines too. Yet the changes were actually accelerating some fundamental trends already underway.

As 2020 came to an end, Ellen and I spoke with Joe Ucuzoglu, CEO of Deloitte US, the domestic arm of the international business consulting company. Joe had been a partner throughout the year, sponsoring our *Leadership Next* podcasts, and I had come to appreciate his dedication and insight.

He began with reminiscing. "Alan, I'm reflecting back on the very first time we got together in your studio, which was literally just about a week before the pandemic hit the US in full force," he recalled.[12] "And we couldn't have possibly known that the nine months over which the series has run would coincide with this unprecedented period in society. So it wasn't that many months ago that society was literally turned on its head." Joe's recollections were certainly bittersweet, but he put an interesting spin on them, which felt optimistic.

"Despite all the challenges and the very dire public health situation, the economy has actually held up better than anyone could have expected. And I do think that's a reflection of the way in which the business community has stepped up and helped lead society through this very difficult period of time . . . and demonstrate the very best of business and a real-life manifestation of stakeholder capitalism."

Joe believed that the difficulties had presented a big growth opportunity for leaders. "Usually these difficult and challenging circumstances are where you grow the most," he said. "And I do think that this period has debunked the myth of this invincible CEO that sits in a corner office, is all knowing, issues edicts." The new reality is CEOs who use words like *empathy* and *vulnerability,* and do more listening than speaking, he observed—different attributes required in the complex world we live in.

What occurred to me as Ucuzoglu spoke was this: At the end of the day, CEOs are paid to be problem solvers and pragmatists. They're not ideologues. They are less interested in staking out positions and more interested in getting things done. They see big problems out there that aren't being solved by government. And many of them have concluded that if they don't take on the problems, nobody else will.

BRIGHT SPOTS EMERGE

With any dramatic societal event, you can observe in the aftermath some lasting changes. During the course of the COVID-19 pandemic, it soon became apparent what some of those changes would be:

> The shift toward talent as the most important source of corporate value had continued. The trend could have been weakened by historic levels of unemployment, which made labor plentiful. But plentiful labor is not the same as plentiful talent, and the pandemic seemed to be leading an increasing number of talent-forward companies to take an "employees first" approach. Indeed, as the economy bounced back from COVID in 2021, it became clear that there was an unprecedented battle for talent, giving knowledge workers even more power in the economic debates to come.

> Demands for systemic change also intensified. The pandemic exposed flaws in business's approach to global markets, deepening the divisions within countries and between them, and threatening supply chains. Geopolitical tension between the US and China also challenged the globalist model. Yet at the same time, the clear global imperative, made more urgent by the pandemic, was for business leaders to get their act together and nurture global progress. Globalization isn't going away.

> The dearth of political leadership also became more evident. In the US in particular, the prevalent political ideologies proved poorly suited for the moment. Presidential power changed hands in the US, but the new president's calls for a bipartisan approach to problem solving

struggled. The need for practical-minded business leaders to step up to help fill the gap was greater than ever.

What became clear by year's end—and what the critics of stakeholder capitalism seemed to miss—was this: Stakeholder capitalism wasn't a choice. It was an imperative. It was being driven by trends in business and society that showed no sign of reversing. The outpouring of CEO sentiment after the George Floyd killing wasn't just because "woke" CEOs suddenly decided to speak up. It happened because talented employees demanded it, and talent is today's top driver of corporate value. The renewed focus on employee safety wasn't just because of a wave of CEO empathy. It was forced by employees, government officials, health experts, and others—"stakeholders," all.

It was interesting that concern over climate also grew—unlike what had happened in the previous recession. COVID's effects on travel and commerce reduced greenhouse gas emissions in the short term. But the sense of collective vulnerability caused by the pandemic fed concern over the earth's future. Pragmatic business leaders, reinforced by their customers, investors, and employees, recognized that society faces an existential threat. All of these fed the continuing rise of stakeholder capitalism. None of them are things a responsible CEO, with a focus on the long term, could safely ignore.

CHAPTER 4

THE COVID-19 REDEMPTION

In 2019, when Gallup polled Americans about which industries they liked least, the pharmaceutical industry won the prize.[1] The reason wasn't hard to fathom. Persistent publicity over pricing scandals—Martin Shkreli and Valeant took top honors there—as well as the pill-pushing behind the opioid scandal, had poisoned the industry in the public mind.

Capturing the public imagination (and not in a good way) a few years before the pandemic was the story of Shkreli, a hedge fund manager and CEO of two fledgling pharmaceutical companies, Retrophin and Turing Pharmaceuticals. Only in his thirties, Shkreli seemed to think of himself as a boy genius. But what briefly earned him the tagline of the most hated man in America in many press accounts was a scheme to earn high profits on individual drugs while creating untold human suffering.[2] His company Retrophin, started in 2011, began to purchase old drugs that were only used by relatively small populations, and substantially jacked up their prices. When the company fired him in 2014, Shkreli raised the capital to start another pharma company, Turing Pharmaceuticals. That's when he became a household name.

In the fall of 2015, Turing acquired the license for the manufacture of a drug called Daraprim, which was used to treat a severe parasitic infection, often suffered by people with HIV. The price of the drug was immediately raised from a more manageable cost of $13.50 per dose to $750.

There was an immediate outcry, which Shkreli shrugged off, citing two arguments: first, the drug wasn't used by many people, so not that many would be affected; and second, that he had a right to charge prices that would help him stay in business.

Daraprim would later be called the "poster drug" of price gouging, but Shkreli was completely nonplussed by the criticism. "My investors expect me to maximize profits," he declared, saying if there was any blame to be had, "blame me for capitalism."[3]

Before the public momentum against Shkreli had a chance to reach full steam, he was arrested in December 2015 on an entirely different matter— fraud. When he was running his first pharmaceutical company, Retrophin, he was taking money out of the company to pay off investors to his faltering hedge funds.

Shkreli was tried and convicted in 2019, and he was sentenced to seven years in prison. He briefly emerged during the COVID-19 pandemic to request early prison release so he could work on a treatment for the virus, which he said he'd already begun researching in prison. His request was denied.

Stories like Shkreli's drowned out any positive news about the pharmaceutical industry. Even when fraud didn't exist, most people thought drug pricing was capricious and unfair. Large movements formed to illegally cross the border into Canada to get cheaper drugs. The government gave pharmaceutical companies patent protection in order to encourage research and development, and shield them, for a period, from generic competition. But in the public mind, pharma companies came to represent the worst version of a capitalist system focused solely on profits to the detriment of the public good. The government imposes virtually no price controls or limits on drug marketing, giving companies mostly free rein to charge what they want. While generics are modestly priced, certain high-use "innovative" drugs such as biologics used for arthritis and cancer are exorbitantly expensive.

COVID-19 provided an opportunity for redemption, and the leading companies seemed eager to take it. Suddenly, a purpose had been thrust upon them: defeating the virus. And that purpose caused a near immediate transformation. When I interviewed Albert Bourla, CEO of Pfizer, I found him talking about how employees were filled with this new sense of purpose as they searched for a vaccine. Bourla, who signed the BRT statement in 2019, characterized the response this way: "The word is proud," he said. "It's as if this were a world war. They feel very proud of what we are doing."[4] And that pride drove productivity and innovation.

That's a big change for an industry that had come to represent lack of regard for the public well-being. Bourla acknowledged the shift. "It was clear for us that our business model was not sustainable if we don't create value for patients and value for society."

MAKING A MIRACLE

Everyone knows the drill for the development of drugs, including vaccines. They go through several trials and take a long time—normally years. So when the Trump administration and some drug companies began to talk about a much shorter development and review period, measured in months, many people worried that corners would be cut. In part because of aggressive rhetoric coming from the White House, there was a real concern that the vaccine would become politicized and rolled out far too soon.

In fact, behind the scenes the manufacturers of vaccines, including Pfizer, Moderna, and Johnson & Johnson, had accepted the challenge to accelerate the timeline in a safe way. During this period Bourla told me, "I was amazed by how quickly my organization moved, and I think it was only because of the purpose." He said that Moderna was the first company to put its vaccine into clinical trials, followed by Pfizer two months later. Yet they both began Phase III trials on the same day. He acknowledged that such speed "is not what you expect from a big, monolithic, goliath company like Pfizer. I was surprised we were able to do that, and the only reason is because we gave them [the employees] one purpose: go back and calculate how many people will die if you don't do it this fall." Bourla repeatedly told his employees, "The competition is the disease."

I also interviewed Noubar Afeyan of Flagship Pioneering. Afeyan, who had been a cofounder of Moderna, was equally bullish on getting a vaccine to market.

He characterized the industry response this way: "We're running in our lane. And other people have their lanes. And we're not competing against them. We're competing to finish the race. And if we can finish the race, then we will have had an impact."[5]

Afeyan is an Armenian entrepreneur who was born in Lebanon and left the country with his family during its civil war. He talked about the significance of his immigrant experience in his personal success, and the connection between innovation and immigration.

"I view innovation as just intellectual immigration," he said. "When you leave the comforts of what you know, expose yourself to criticism, go to something that people don't believe is possible, persist, persist, persist, until you make it habitable so that people come and tell you how obvious it was years later. That is what an immigrant does."

Although Afeyan's new company Flagship is not limited to pharmaceuticals, its task is to create and incubate such companies by producing "innovation at the extreme." Gesturing to the grand challenge of vaccine development, he added, "I would invite people to think of the immigrant mindset when they are doing these kinds of innovations, particularly cutting-edge innovation, and recognize that it is a strength that the kind of resilience, the adaptivity, all the things that we think are rarefied skills in an entrepreneur, that's what every immigrant has to go through."

Johnson & Johnson CEO Alex Gorsky, who had led the process behind the Business Roundtable statement in August 2019, made the point even more broadly when I talked to him in October 2020, praising the actions of the business community. "I'm incredibly proud to see the way CEOs are trying to step up in times like these. It's a noticeable change from what I think it would have been five years ago, ten years ago, and before."[6]

"The crisis brings out the best in a people-driven organization. We believe the social contract at work is a source of resilience. We don't give this up in a time of crisis. It actually makes us stronger."

—John Driscoll, CEO, CareCentrix

Meanwhile, the pharmaceutical companies were doing everything they could to reassure the public about their commitment to a safe and effective vaccine. When the White House began promising a vaccine by October 2020 (before the election), pharmaceutical companies were alarmed that the timing would appear to be politically driven. They took out full-page ads in the *New York Times* and *Wall Street Journal*, promising that the vaccine timing would be driven by science, not politics. As it would turn out, the vaccine delivery began in December.

Bourla admitted to me that they were partially to blame for public lack of trust. "For years the CEOs of Pfizer were speaking of how much money we made from Lipitor instead of pointing out how many hundreds of millions of lives were saved by Lipitor. We did it to ourselves. You have the Martin Shkreli's, but also the philosophy of just jacking up prices as much as you can and cutting the research. It's just the exact opposite of what we're talking about. And now, you really do see a scramble. They're all saying, 'Wow, this is our chance to redeem ourselves, to prove that we have real value to society.'"

Bourla confirmed what many of us were already observing—that the coronavirus was giving the industry a chance to redeem itself and restore its reputation through a commitment to purpose. This earnest desire to work together to help society get through the crisis was reflected in the actions of many industries, he said. "Look at what all the pharmaceutical companies are doing right now, scrambling to show that they contribute real value to society, look at how companies like Target and Walmart are trying to deal with this, or even the hotels, which have to do these massive furloughs, but are trying to do it in a much more thoughtful and humane way than they have in the past. Look, it's hard. It's hard to judge because at the end of the day, people are still getting laid off. But it feels like there's a different consciousness out there that's going to survive through this crisis."

BEYOND THE PANDEMIC

Even as COVID-19 was continuing to rage across the country, many leaders were looking ahead to a post-pandemic world, with a question: Would the burst of innovation lead to a revolution in health care science? That was the possibility we investigated at *Fortune* Brainstorm Health in July 2020. Our first virtual conference, it was led by *Fortune* editor in chief Clifton Leaf, who assembled a who's who of health care leaders to talk about the future.

"Well, hasn't it been beautiful to see the entire industry come together and redefine the competition as the virus, not each other?"

—Paul Hudson, CEO, Sanofi

Many of the participants emphasized the extraordinary cooperation the pandemic has prompted in health science. "We are all on various collaborations together," said Novartis CEO Vas Narasimhan. Bristol Meyer Squibb CEO Giovanni Caforio said that there was "an unprecedented level of cooperation" between institutions of business, government, academia, and institutions like the National Institutes of Health. "My hope is this will be a galvanizing moment," he said. "What we have learned is to work collaboratively like never before, to challenge our thinking, and to accelerate the drug development process. We have done things in six months that would have taken five to ten years." He emphasized that the industry could "take the learnings of the last six months and apply them to other challenges, like cancer."

COVID-19 exposed multiple problems in the US health care system—the lack of surge capacity, the fragility of the financial model, and the vagaries of the payment system, to name a few. But it also sparked remarkable innovation. You could begin to see the unveiling of new ways of operating that would make health care better and more accessible after the pandemic. One clear example is telemedicine. Millions of people discovered that they could see their doctors and other medical professionals more often and more easily with web appointments. "The pandemic sent a lot of challenges our way," Genentech CEO Alexander Hardy told me on *Leadership Next*, "but there were also these really inspiring moments, as you saw the industry coming together" to defeat the virus.[7] Hardy said the virus "required us to be very innovative, fast, and flexible." So, the question he and others in the industry were asking was how they could maintain that level of speed, flexibility, collaboration, and innovation to attack other great health care challenges. Could the same skills that were used to develop a vaccine in record time be turned to addressing cancer or Alzheimer's? Could the nationwide rollout of vaccines serve as a model for making health care treatments available in corners of the nation that have been cut off in the past, such as rural areas and the inner cities?

Genentech is one of the oldest biotech firms, founded in 1976 in San Francisco. In 2009 it was acquired by Roche. At the time, some people expressed concern that a big company takeover would compromise the entrepreneurial spirit of the company. When Hardy arrived as CEO in 2019, he focused on strengthening the innovative culture of the company.

Then COVID hit, changing the way Genentech worked with others. "We have about eight drugs in various stages of development as therapeutics for COVID," he told me, "but we decided to give over a large proportion of our manufacturing and our largest biologic site to manufacturing one of our biggest competitors, monoclonal antibodies. And this is a competitor whom we compete very, very fiercely against." He described it as a "deep partnership"—the kind of collaboration that can change the course of the global response to the pandemic.

Looking ahead, Hardy saw the potential for such private-private partnerships to continue, addressing other health issues. "Normally you go through tremendously long negotiation processes and the pandemic, obviously nobody can wait around for that. We basically had very, very broad deals with not every eventuality mapped out like they normally are. And we moved ahead and actually we started working together even before the deal was fully inked, because again, time was of the essence."

So, how could that apply to other issues? Genentech has been on the front lines in fighting the major health scourges of the era—cancer, neurological diseases, Alzheimer's, ALS. I asked Hardy how the lessons learned during the pandemic could help conquer those big ticket health issues.

"This [the pandemic] has required us to be really innovative, fast, and flexible," Hardy said. "Innovative was always a characteristic of Genentech and our industry. Fast and flexible, not so much. Again, that focus on perfection in many cases meant that sometimes we moved slower than we really needed. So during the pandemic, because we had to, we've already pushed decision-making down the organization. So, things don't have to work up to a very, very senior level. People are empowered to make decisions themselves, and we've challenged those teams, those empowered teams to challenge themselves to do things differently. And the speed of change has been really remarkable.

"For example, it would normally take us from FDA approval to initiating a study, in some cases, four to five months. During the pandemic, we did that in three weeks. We shifted production around. We've done in three weeks—moving one of these biologics lines from one site to another—what took eight to twelve months before the pandemic. So, there's so many opportunities here for us to do these things differently. Some of them come from the pandemic, some of them I think are the results of technological trends and scientific understanding, which is starting to break as we speak."

In the process, Genentech has been attentive to the systemic inequities in the health care system, which were exacerbated by the pandemic. In the wake of George Floyd's death, Hardy published a piece articulating Genentech's stand on racial justice and equity:

The consequences of discrimination are far-reaching and acutely evident in every aspect of our lives, including and especially in connection with the current coronavirus pandemic. Black people and other communities of color continue to be devastated by disproportionate health impacts of COVID-19, including higher rates of infection, hospitalization, and mortality, as well as significant economic hardship.

Our company's efforts to advance social equity have been centered on our people, patients, and communities. We've worked hard to foster belonging for our employees, tackle racial disparities in clinical research, and forge partnerships in order to help spur societal transformation in the community. But it is painfully clear that we must do better as an organization, as individuals, and as a nation. Together we must acknowledge what's happening, speak up in allyship, and take action against this destructive force in our society.[8]

"Before the pandemic, Genentech was already focused on the topic of equity and particularly health inequity," Hardy told me. "We realized that, clearly our own development efforts needed to make sure that we were recruiting into our studies, these underserved populations, because they were suffering at a really unimaginable level. As we all know, it's not just the virus that they're facing, but health equity issues that expand the whole continuum from diagnosis to treatment, as well as underlying conditions. We have a really significant responsibility as an industry, as a society to never let these sorts of issues impact these populations as they've done now."

On the anniversary of the pandemic I celebrated by getting my second shot of the Pfizer vaccine, waiting in a long line in the Lord & Taylor parking lot in Stamford, Connecticut. Coincidentally, I also had an interview scheduled later that day with Pfizer's Bourla. His tone was optimistic. "I think it is very impressive that a year from a major disaster for humanity, we are emerging with a sense of liberation." The impact of the vaccine, he said, "is the best demonstration of the power of science and the power of human ingenuity."[9]

When *Fortune*'s Brainstorm Health reconvened in the spring of 2021, transformation was a recurrent theme. "The tempo of drug development has changed as a result of the lessons of the pandemic," Amgen CEO Bob Bradway said.[10] "There is no reason we can't replicate (the vaccine experience) with some of these other large diseases that we talk about—like heart attack and stroke." Mayo Clinic CEO Gianrico Farrugia said the pandemic "has given health care organizations the confidence that they can tolerate change more than we thought they could." And change is now an imperative. "We have to transform health care. We can't be satisfied with simply making things better."[11]

THE LEADERSHIP CHALLENGE

Closing the *Fortune* office in March 2020 was an easy decision to make. However, we had no idea it would be for a year or more. We thought we'd be working from home for a week or two, then back to normal. None of us knew what was in store for us.

But Mike Roman, the CEO of 3M, had an inkling. I sat down with him in person in *Fortune*'s offices shortly before we closed them, as the pandemic was breaking news across the globe. He was feeling the pressures around personal protective equipment, the N95 masks in particular. 3M had started ramping up its manufacturing of PPE before it hit the American public that the need was desperate here at home.

Roman explained: "Coming out of SARS, we had developed a strategy to have idle capacity available for the next pandemic. We didn't anticipate a global pandemic like we're facing with COVID-19. We responded and have been ramping up capacity ever since."[12]

The priorities were clear to his leadership: "Protect our employees, so we could keep executing, fight the pandemic from every angle, and deliver for our customers and shareholders, as we went through the uncertainty that we were facing. We had to add capacity. We had to shift from serving traditionally industrial customers to health care workers and first responders. It was an incredible responsibility, but really an opportunity for our people to step up and make a difference."

Roman described a company effort of great magnitude, doubling output while opening up avenues for creating more capacity. By midyear they'd doubled output again. Roman noted it was a fourfold increase by the end of the year over what the company did in 2019. "It was adding capabilities and turning on capacity, and then it was investing in and doing things in weeks that would have taken months or even years to add additional capacity. Going from March and turning on capacity in September, we've never done anything like that."

The key to this ability to rise above was partnerships—public-private and private-private. It was also figuring out how to overcome the risk of operation for 3M's own employees. While factories were shutting down elsewhere, or severely limiting operations, 3M needed to do just the opposite. About half of its 95,000 employees work in factories, and the protocols had to be reengineered for safety. The rest of the employees worked remotely. And they got the job done.

However, it was not without some external challenges. In April 2020, President Trump went on the attack against 3M, threatening to take action if the company did not stop distributing N95 masks and respirators to its overseas partners and send material manufactured in its overseas factories back to the United States. Trump tweeted that 3M would have "a big price to pay" over their distribution of masks, adding that the administration was hitting the company hard.

"It was really an awakening for us as a company," Roman said.[13] "When you step up in the face of a pandemic, there are increased expectations for leadership. Part of our focus from the beginning was delivering product to where we needed frontline health care workers and first responders. We quickly realized that we had to do more. We were in the spotlight as a company. We had to help fight fraud and price gouging that was going on in the N95 marketplace. It took us time to recognize what else we could do. Through that March/April time frame in particular, it took a while for us to get to where we had a clear, very effective working partnership, but we've had very strong partnerships throughout the year as a result of that."

I could see the difficulty. "It seems like this is a really fundamental challenge for a company's system," I said. "You can't run your company to prepare for a once in a century pandemic or a once in a century weather event or a never before cyberattack or all the things that the world can throw at you."

Roman acknowledged that, but the leadership lesson is clearly that companies need to be a few steps ahead as a constant posture. "A common theme throughout the pandemic is that many trends, that were there even before the pandemic, accelerated and really have driven a clear view that business is changing, the world is changing. I would expect that to impact supply chain significantly as we move ahead."

It was also to some extent business as usual for 3M. "I would say, for us as a company, this reaffirmed our model," he said. "Our model has been to manufacture close to customers, to do that regionally around the world. When other countries moved offshore from the United States, we never left. We manufactured nearly everything we sell in the United States in factories in twenty-nine states in the United States. We've always had a domestic supply chain and that's true for our companies around the world. Our model is to innovate for our customers. Our vision and our purpose, in its simple form, is to apply science to improve lives. We do that close to customers around the world. That takes innovation. That takes research and development. It takes market innovation. It takes manufacturing innovation. You have to keep that close to those markets and it's helped us serve those markets well and effectively."

Thankfully, it was a strategy that had the benefit of being well-positioned when the pandemic hit. They had a large manufacturing footprint in the

United States, which they were able to use as a base to expand. "Coming out of it, as our customers start to think about shifting their supply chains, we are positioned around the world to be able to move with them," he said confidently. "It is something that goes hand in hand with how we innovate. I think it certainly looks like it's going to serve us well as we take those learnings through the pandemic."

NO LOSS OF MOMENTUM

Competition is the core of the free market economy. It is competition that drives companies to improve quality and reduce prices, to become more efficient, to innovate. Competition is the magic that makes capitalist economies successful.

But solving society's biggest problems—like a global pandemic—requires cooperation as well as competition. The scientists at pharmaceutical companies were competing with each other to be the first to develop vaccines and treatments for COVID. But they also were sharing data, knowledge, and even their facilities in ways that never would have been imaginable before the pandemic.

"There's so much collaboration, cooperation going on," Daniel O'Day, chairman and CEO of Gilead Sciences, agreed. "The only competition in COVID is the virus itself. Companies have come together and collaborated in ways that we've never seen before. I'm optimistic that we're going to continue to do that."

The question for the future of stakeholder capitalism is how to continue that level of creative collaboration in normal times. The climate change challenge, for instance, will require massive collaboration among companies, throughout their supply chains, and with governments. It does little good for one company to develop the technology for producing a carbon-free alternative to cement, for instance, if a higher price prevents other companies from purchasing it.

Likewise, no one company, no matter how large, can address a problem as daunting as the training and reskilling challenge that the economy faces as technology advances. We are already seeing examples of companies like IBM working to train, not only just their own workers but a broader group of workers. And no one company can address the gender and racial inequities in business. That's why groups like the OneTen initiative are working across companies to create new opportunities. More about that later.

Classic economic thinking—the Milton Friedman view—argues that it's the government's job to deal with the coordination required to fight a pandemic, or the "externalities" caused by climate change, or the societal challenges of retraining workers and creating broad-based opportunity. Business's responsibility is simply to obey the laws and compete for profit.

But government action to address social issues has always worked better in theory than in practice and today is particularly challenged by polarized politics. Moreover, the size and complexity of the issues facing society require the innovation and skill and dynamism that only business can bring to bear. The question for the future is whether the kind of extraordinary efforts focused on a common goal that were evident in the fight against the pandemic can be aimed at society's other big challenges.

RADICAL COLLABORATION

As the pandemic, extreme weather, and other crises ripped through the nation, some forward-thinking folks were looking at a silver lining—the opportunity for "radical collaboration" among government, business, and philanthropy. "We live in a world that is more complex than ever," Ford Foundation President Darren Walker told the fellows at the Fortune Connect Summit in the summer of 2021. Ben & Jerry's CEO Matthew McCarthy weighed in as well, with, "If you want to do things that matter, you've got to do them together."

This profound notion wasn't new. But the pandemic had opened a pathway that wasn't there before, connecting even the most unlikely partners. It was something to appreciate going forward. Imagine the impact of harnessing such powerful collaborations. As we headed into 2022, many CEOs I spoke with chose to be optimistic, even given the paralyzing partisanship on Capitol Hill, the turmoil in many state legislatures, and the ongoing struggle to get a handle on COVID—not just in the US but around the globe, especially in places like Africa where vaccine accessibility is very low.

One of the brightest signs regarded the climate. Business—once the resistance in the climate policy debate—has moved to the vanguard and is calling for action. A survey of more than a thousand CEOs conducted by the UN Global Compact and Accenture ahead of the UN Climate Change Conference (COP26) beginning October 31, 2021, found that 79 percent said the pandemic has highlighted the need to transition to more sustainable business models. "I would have predicted that a crisis like COVID would have slammed the brakes on anything other than conventional bottom-line thinking," said George Oliver, CEO of Johnson Controls.[14] "The fact that it did the exact opposite is extraordinary. It has accelerated the trajectory of sustainability."

I've heard many echoes of this sentiment, which we'll explore in this book. Companies no longer want to be trapped in the past or frozen in place. There is an energy for looking to the future that has been missing in recent years, and I'm eager to explore where it might take us.

PART TWO

WHAT DO STAKEHOLDERS WANT?

CHAPTER 5

AN EMPOWERED WORKFORCE

ALONG WITH MY COLLEAGUES AT *FORTUNE* I HAVE HAD MANY OPPORTUNI-ties to talk with CEOs about prioritizing projects with social impact. We created the Fortune CEO Initiative as a forum for global corporate leaders to address major social problems as part of their core business strategy. During conversations at the CEO Initiative conference since its founding in 2017, it had become apparent that the members were focused on climate, on diversity, on the ramifications of the pandemic. But consistently at the top of their list was the issue of worker reskilling and training. They realized it was an urgent need in an era of technological transformation. And as leaders driving that transformation, they felt personal responsibility.

Capitalism had thrived in the last half of the twentieth century because it was seen as an escalator to opportunity. But by the beginning of the twenty-first, it was clear that the escalator had stalled. And there was every reason to think that technology would make the problem worse. Most of the CEOs I talked to believed that, as in the past, technology would create new jobs even as it eliminated old ones. But they weren't at all convinced that we had the systems in place to prepare the workforce for these new jobs at a fast enough pace.

Then the pandemic hit, dealing its hardest blow to those who weren't knowledge workers—those who worked in factories, or restaurants and retail stores, or in health care or public service, the very people who were most at risk of being left behind by technology. They didn't have the option of simply taking their work home. Many were furloughed or lost their jobs altogether. Others dropped out of the workforce to take care of children who were not in school, or elderly parents who were most at risk of contracting the disease. Statistics showed the pandemic's greatest hardships disproportionately fell on women, minorities, and those with less education. As the economy began to bounce back, half of the workforce was in boats that rose quickly; the other half seemed stuck to the bottom. John F. Kennedy's aphorism that "a rising tide lifts all boats" seemed to have lost its potency.

It was this issue, more than any other, that the CEOs felt they had to step up and take responsibility for. The pandemic had accelerated technological change. "Our clients have done things in the last five or six months that they thought would take five or six years," Genpact CEO Tiger Tyagarajan, who works with companies on their technology transformations, told a *Fortune* CEO Leadership Roundtable in November 2020.[1] With change accelerating, how would companies get the escalator of opportunity moving again? How would they create jobs for the people who had been left behind by the economy of the twenty-first century, who had been pummeled by the unequal effects of the pandemic, and whose ranks were likely to swell as a result of the technology revolution underway?

When I was working in Washington in the 1980s, the issue of worker training had been seen as a government responsibility. The public education system, and particularly the wide network of community colleges, had the charge of preparing workers for the jobs of the day, and the federal government provided funds for workers displaced by growing international trade.

But the CEOs in our Initiative had come to realize that *they* were the ones creating the jobs, and that they therefore had to play an active role in making sure people had the opportunity and the skills needed to fill them. Big companies came to recognize that their mandate was not just to provide training to the people they currently employed. For long-term success, they had to build new systems, new platforms to provide training to those who had been left behind by the technology-driven economy. Unless they solved that problem, they not only risked being without the skilled workforce they needed in the future, they also risked allowing social acceptance for the existing system to fray to the breaking point. Their operating license was at stake.

Workers, both current and future, became the critical stakeholders of far-thinking companies. The workforce challenge became the most immediate and most urgent economic challenge of our times. And that challenge involved two critical steps: First, creating a new world of work. And second, preparing for the technology-driven job disruption to come.

RETURN TO WORK

In the history of modern business, there has never been anything like it. Millions of Americans stayed home for more than a year (some are still home as of this writing), and with the aid of technology, worked remotely from living room couches, dining room tables, and bedrooms. In the first instance, it was a stressful time, requiring huge adaptations, but the ultimate impact was something more transformative. Thrive CEO Arianna Huffington called it a new opportunity, the "first since the Industrial Revolution" to truly redesign work.[2]

Beginning in mid-March 2020, I was among those working from home. Zoom, Teams, WebEx, Google Meet—they became my conference hub, seminar hall, and interview room. As we headed toward spring in the second year of the pandemic, we began to talk about what it would look like when we began to "go back" to work. In March 2021 *Fortune* held a Reimagine Work Summit in partnership with the Future Forum created by Slack, the collaboration software company, to envision what was next.

The Future Forum had done some interesting surveys about what workers want and had found that only 17 percent of knowledge workers wanted to return to the office full time. However, only 20 percent wanted to work from home full time. Most workers wanted some kind of flexibility about where and when they worked. This should have surprised no one. Calls for workplace flexibility—which used to be called flextime—have been out there for decades, usually framed around family needs and work-life balance. However, in recent years, with the competitive demands of a fast-paced global economy, there has been less talk of flextime. In many industries, like tech and finance, workers have been afraid of requesting flextime for fear of looking lax. Many work cultures prided themselves on burning the midnight oil.

However, because of the pandemic a widespread interest in flextime has emerged, based on the actual experience people have had working from home. The old stigma that being at home meant slacking off has all but disappeared, especially among knowledge workers. Indeed, many companies were able to report that the movement to work from home actually led to increased productivity. At our summit, people were excited about developing a hybrid approach, which would involve using the office for collaboration, serendipitous interaction, social bonding, and culture building, but allowing for individual work to be done elsewhere.

> "Workers have earned the right to do work differently."
>
> —Kristin Peck, CEO, Zoetis

When those general ideas came down to actual execution, however, there was a lot of uncertainty about how to make it work. What would such a system mean for office organization, accountability, and effectiveness? There were concerns, for example, that the office-home divide would lead to a hierarchy of influence, with those on the scene always having more resources and better opportunities for advancement. And what would it mean for inclusion? Would women and minorities be less likely to be "in the room" and therefore less likely to be taken seriously? There was good reason to believe that the playing field would tilt toward the existing elite, further stalling the escalator of economic opportunity.

As companies began to contemplate heading back to the office, I interviewed Diane Hoskins and Andy Cohen, co-CEOs of the design and architecture firm Gensler. They are dealing with hundreds of clients these days trying to figure out the post-pandemic office.

"We are seeing that collaboration has dropped off 40 percent" during the pandemic, Cohen told me. "People just aren't collaborating as much. They are missing the interaction."[3] But employees also want flexibility to decide when they go to the office, and executing on the vision of a hybrid workplace is no simple task. Particularly challenging is having some people in the room and others on Zoom. "People really need to feel they are in the room when they are Zooming in."

In an analysis for the *Harvard Business Review*, Harvard professor Prithwiraj (Raj) Choudhury asked whether work from anywhere (WFA) was here to stay. He studied companies that utilize remote or majority-remote models. Among the benefits of WFA to workers he cited the freedom to live anywhere, the flexibility to enjoy more quality time outside an office, and a more affordable cost of living. For society there was the potential to reverse the "brain drain" that had afflicted areas that are not considered business hubs.[4]

Obviously, not every organization can institute a WFA culture. Some industries, such as manufacturing, are tied to a place. But increasingly it seems that flexible options are going to be on the table in the coming years— responding to needs that existed long before the pandemic.

For some, that flexibility was seen as providing an improvement in workforce opportunity. Now, you could work from anywhere. You didn't have to be in Silicon Valley to join a big tech company, or in Manhattan to go into high finance.

But CEOs also worried that increased remote work would cause a dangerous fraying of corporate culture. Workday CEO and cofounder Aneel Bhusri told me he was eager to get his employees back to the physical office. Workday makes cloud-based software used by other companies' human resources and accounting departments. Bhusri is a member of the Business Roundtable and his company is ranked fifth on Fortune's 2020 list of the 100 Best Companies to Work For.

Bhusri explained, "I'm not a believer that having a significant population work from home forever is a great idea. You can't really develop a great culture. . . . You can execute well during this time, but you really can't collaborate and innovate in the same way. It's really important that we come up with a model that works for our culture, but also gives some flexibility if people want to work a couple of days a week from home."[5]

I asked Bhusri about the impact of the ongoing COVID-19 pandemic on Workday's business and on stakeholder capitalism. "Companies need to have a soul and need to step up in tough times," he said, echoing a refrain I'd been hearing from other CEOs—that the pandemic opened a mandate to do *more*, not less.

That takes leadership. And the fundamental rules of how to lead were changing with everything else. In their classic management book *In Search of Excellence*, Tom Peters and Robert Waterman wrote about the importance of "management by walking around." That doesn't work when the office is empty. There's also agreement that leaders need to focus more on worker well-being—continuing to lead with empathy after the pandemic. As AI tech company Pymetrics CEO Frida Polli put it, "The human elements of empathy and connection (are) critical to making this distributed workforce function properly."[6] Beyond the pandemic, companies are still grappling with the fundamentals of stakeholder capitalism, including finding new ways to empower the key internal stakeholders, the workers. The post-pandemic battle for talent has strengthened the demands of workers who want more flexibility to work remotely. As McKinsey's Bill Schaninger told CEOs meeting virtually at *Fortune*'s Leadership Roundtable, "Now that you have let the genie out of the bottle, all sorts of things are going to come into question. . . . This has been a real opportunity for people to question their own purpose, and whether what they are doing is what they want to do."[7]

In March 2021, Dov Seidman, who had been with us at the Vatican in 2016, released a survey of one thousand professionals in the United States who moved to remote work during the pandemic. His primary interest was in the matter of connectedness, which he had previously explored in his book, *How: Why How We Do Anything Means Everything*.[8] "Humans are social animals," Seidman said. "For human organizations to thrive, connections between and among individuals need to be meaningful and rooted in common purpose."[9]

One survey response was surprising and actually encouraging—that a feeling of connection to direct supervisors and organizations actually went up during the pandemic. However, 44 percent reported that their feelings of connection to coworkers declined.

Seidman believes that the difference between employees being connected gets back to the issue we had discussed together at the Vatican in 2016: "moral leadership."

"Moral leadership is about how leaders touch hearts, not just minds," Seidman said. "Given our physical distance from one another due to the pandemic, it is even more imperative that moral leaders work harder—and differently—to bridge that physical space to create a sense of connection and community."

What does moral leadership actually look like? Seidman mentioned a few actions that were part of a moral leader's toolbox, such as cultivating a sense of hope for the future, working to inspire others, showing patience and flexibility, encouraging workers to share their concerns and fears, explaining decisions in the context of purpose, and demonstrating a commitment to do the right thing. According to his research, employees at organizations whose leaders demonstrated those values were three times more likely to feel connected to their manager and their organization.

The takeaway is that companies have a responsibility, even in times of crisis—or *especially* in times of crisis—to help workers strengthen their bonds. A big part of the process is acknowledging the extent of the change employees are experiencing and being intentional about helping them feel a sense of purpose in their company and their work.

> "This is a new world. We won't go back to the old world, that's just gone. So what do we do? Do we just wait? Or do we accelerate transformation?"
>
> —Alexandre Dayon, chief strategy officer, Salesforce

All of this only further accelerated the changes in corporate leadership that had led to the stakeholder movement. More than ever, CEOs couldn't rule by fiat. They couldn't simply pass orders down the ranks. Instead, they had to embrace new strategies that accepted their employees' increased freedom and increased power, that recognized that engaged workers were their greatest asset, and that gave those workers a moral framework, a North Star, a purpose. According to McKinsey research, employees "living their purpose" had four times higher engagement and five times higher well-being than those who do not connect their work to their purpose. Yet only one-third believed their own employers strongly connected their actions to purpose.

THE UPSKILL REVOLUTION

For centuries, people have worried that workers will be replaced by machines. The fears were prevalent as employment moved from agriculture to manufacturing, and again as automation took hold in the manufacturing sector. The new wave of technology, and particularly the specter of artificial intelligence, caused those fears to be raised anew. Mankind had successfully moved from farmer to factory worker, and from factory worker to knowledge worker. But if machines took over knowledge work, what then?

In their important 2013 study, "The Future of Employment: How Susceptible Are Jobs to Computerisation?," Oxford professors Carl Benedikt Frey and Michael A. Osborne began by noting that "concern over technological unemployment is hardly a recent phenomenon. Throughout history, the process of creative destruction, following technological inventions, has created enormous wealth, but also undesired disruptions."[10]

They tell an amusing anecdote about William Lee, who invented the stocking frame knitting machine in 1589 as a replacement for hand knitting. Lee traveled to London to present his invention to Queen Elizabeth I, hoping to receive patent protection. Fearing for the workers, the queen refused to grant him a patent. "Thou aimest high, Master Lee," she said. "Consider thou what the invention could do to my poor subjects. It would assuredly bring to them ruin by depriving them of employment, thus making them beggars."

Reviewing the current trends, Frey and Osborne analyzed the probability of computerization for over seven hundred occupations and estimated that 47 percent of them were at high risk for being automated over the next decade or two. These included occupations in transportation and logistics, most office and administrative support workers, production occupations, and even a large percentage of service workers.

By forcing workers to work from home and increase their daily reliance on technology, COVID has contributed to a speeding up of tech trends that were already transforming society at a mind-spinning pace. When I interviewed Jeff Lawson, the cofounder and CEO of Twilio, the communication platform that has seen its stock soar since the pandemic, he perfectly captured the technology ethic that has been unleashed by the pandemic. "I would consider 2020 to be the great digital acceleration," he told me, citing Twilio's own study. Twilio asked various corporate leaders how much the pandemic had accelerated their digital strategy, and "the average response was six years. Telemedicine got accelerated by a decade."[11]

Lawson had just published his book, *Ask Your Developer: How to Harness the Power of Software Developers and Win in the 21st Century.* While most of it was written before the pandemic, Lawson had an opportunity to share some current insights in the epilogue. He wrote that the big lesson of the pandemic "is that great things can happen when people stop worrying about making mistakes or not getting everything perfect the first time around. During the COVID-19 crisis, change was free. There were no alternatives, no office politics and no fear of mistakes—because the alternatives were far worse. It's what happens when management doesn't have time to hold a bunch of meetings, to send requests and approvals up and down the chain of command, or to insist on huge master plans that never end up being what you build."[12]

This rapid innovation is proving a boon to business. And if history is any guide, there will be legions of new businesses and, ultimately, new jobs that result.

But the rapid pace of change is daunting, as is the need to gird workers for the new realities of the fast-moving twenty-first-century workplace. Some have called it our Sputnik moment. It is the leap we have to take to be competitive in a new era. In the US, it involves addressing the education divide and the digital divide, which is a part of it—the stark contrast in preparedness and resources among different populations in this country.

We have a long way to go. According to the Digital US Coalition's May 2020 report, "Building a Digitally Resilient Workforce: Creating On-Ramps to Opportunity":[13]

> 18 million households lack internet access;
> 32 million adults can't use a computer effectively;
> One-half of Americans aren't comfortable using technology to learn.

Whether the mandate is upskilling (training in new skills) or reskilling (training in skills to do a new job), it's a key interest of stakeholder capitalism. According to the World Economic Forum's 2018 Future of Jobs Report, by 2022 (the year this book is being published) seventy-five million jobs in twenty major economies will be displaced by emerging technologies.[14] At the same time there will be new jobs created, to the tune of 133 million, to meet the technological demand. Training is an urgent matter for a large percentage of the workforce.

Even before the pandemic, I had written of the need to reskill workers displaced by technology as "the challenge of our times." The urgency has been building in recent years. And it's not just a US workforce issue but a global issue. In 2019, the ILO Global Commission on the Future of Work stated, "Today's skills will not match the jobs of tomorrow, and newly acquired skills may quickly become obsolete."[15] *Obsolete* is a chilling word. We know from history that industries once the cornerstone of economies can die and leave large numbers of workers out in the cold. In the last half century this has happened repeatedly, partially because of the introduction of new technologies. The ILO has adopted what it calls the Centenary Declaration for the Future of Work, stating that it is the joint obligation of governments and the organizations supporting businesses and workers to establish lifelong learning systems to prepare for the next era of work.

"We see many companies today, on the one hand, laying off, restructuring, and at the same time hiring new people. It's quite strange. What we say is it is much cheaper and much more socially responsible to look at your own workforce and look at the people you can upskill and reskill and make that investment."

—Alain Dehaze, CEO, Adecco

A report from the McKinsey Global Institute concluded that 17.1 million Americans may need to switch occupations by the end of the decade—up from 13.4 million before the pandemic.[16] Similar increases in displacement were found in the other advanced economies. Basically, the pandemic speeded everything up—digitization, e-commerce, and automation. And as a result, even more people are now exposed to job displacement than before.

This is a wakeup call for those who are still hanging on and hoping the old technologies and industries will make a comeback, especially since many of these trends have been evident for a long time, including the shift to e-commerce, which has been shaking the retail world for at least two decades. Turning a blind eye to the endurance of these trends doesn't make them go away. They have to be faced head-on.

According to Susan Lund at McKinsey, the trends don't just mean people will need to find new jobs, but the "jump they will need to make from the old job to the new job [to be effective] is even bigger." This will be especially hard on women and minorities.

The upshot: the next decade demands a massive effort by business and government to upskill the workforce and create new training programs for those who are displaced. "Companies need to step up their investment in redeploying workers and creating alternative career pathways," Lund says. "And it is also going to take investment from educational institutions and government."

The investment doesn't come cheap. A paper by the World Economic Forum and Boston Consulting Group estimated that the cost of reskilling was around $24,800 per person in the United States. And leading human resources expert Josh Bersin believes it could cost as much as six times more to hire from the outside than to build from within.

CEOs are engaging on this issue in a number of different ways, such as increasing workplace learning opportunities and lobbying government for worker-friendly policies like paid family and medical leave.

A *Fortune* article in early 2021 by S. Mitra Kalita isolated several fascinating shifts in workplace organization and opportunity.[17] Kalita cited Ambika Nigam, the founder of Zeit, a platform for career path discovery. Nigam found several unexpected influences on the job market:

> Geography has disappeared as a major factor in hiring. It used to be that employees in certain industries were stuck in particular cities or regions, but now the opportunity is more spread out and hybrid remote office cultures offer more spatial flexibility.

> Employees, who were once judged by their IQ or by their EQ (emotional quotient), are now being evaluated by their AQ (adaptability quotient).

> The challenges of shifting industries, layoffs, and emergency measures have led companies to be more flexible about whom they hire. It used to be that open jobs would be filled with those who had done the same thing before. Now more job-switchers are getting a chance.

CLOSING THE SKILLS GAP

All of the CEOs I talk with are well aware of the dangerous fissures that this technology change has exacerbated between the highly educated and the less so. While the pandemic, racial injustice, and climate change may get more attention from society at large, it's that training and reskilling challenge for which the CEOs feel most directly responsible.

Deanna Mulligan, who stepped down as CEO of Guardian Life Insurance at the end of 2020, was committed to reskilling and expressed her views in *Hire Purpose: How Smart Companies Can Close the Skills Gap*, which was published during the last months of her tenure. She writes that the new age is upon us, and "we have the tools to prepare ourselves for the future of work. Indeed, we have an unprecedented opportunity to adapt to a new reality." But to do that, she warns, "we must not only act; we must act with intelligence. . . . The worst mistake we can make at this point is to get so caught up in imagining what could happen that we forget our own agency in determining what *will* happen."[18]

When I spoke with Mulligan, she told me about her evolution on the issue. Mulligan joined Guardian in 2008, in the midst of the Great Recession. Guardian "wasn't wildly impacted by the recession, but I was looking around and seeing so many of my friends losing jobs." When she became CEO in 2011, she realized a combination of pervasive low interest rates and technological change was going to drive huge disruption for her company and her employees. "I said to myself, I don't want to be one of those companies that has to turn all these people out on the streets."[19]

Mulligan made several practical moves. She started a program to teach people in the company's call centers to write code, joined a program to teach actuaries to be data analysts, and developed a program of "train in, train out," which provided two years' tuition at a local community college for workers whose jobs were eliminated.

"Companies have an obligation to society to try and do this," she said. "And it's less expensive than firing people." Like a number of her CEO colleagues, she is committed to finding ways to extend such programs beyond her own employees. "It's very important that we do this at scale."

There are creative ideas out there, but they require letting go of some beloved sacred cows. In 2019, while she was still CEO of IBM, Ginni Rometty took aim at the four-year college degree, a typical way that workers have been divided into haves and have nots for generations. With rising technologies, Rometty proposed that companies create "new collar" jobs that wouldn't require four-year degrees. This was a matter of some urgency, she said, and required most companies to rethink the requirements they use when posting jobs.

"If we don't do something, this is not going to be an inclusive era," she said. "This is true in every country. In the United States, all the riches cannot go to the West and the East Coasts. If people look at the future and say, 'This technology is great, but I don't have a better job,' then that isn't going to be good for anyone."[20]

She reiterated this idea at the Fortune Most Powerful Women Summit in October 2020, raising this question: "Can you embrace people that do not have a four-year degree and give them a path into your company to start?" She said that process was already underway at IBM, where 43 percent of open jobs no longer required a four-year degree. "It didn't dumb down our workforce," she added. "What we found is their ability to perform, their curiosity, matched everyone's."

I was interested in talking with Rometty for *Leadership Next* because I knew how passionate she had always been about the jobs and training challenge, and spoke with her just after the announcement that she was stepping down as CEO of IBM.

"I think there's a rate and pace of technology change that is moving so fast that the discontinuities are coming faster," she said. "I believe that it's our job. If I'm going to build these technologies, I've got to bring them into the world safely, and bringing them into the world safely means you look at the communities, you look at the people, you look at their skills, you look at the impact."[21]

I asked, "So the speed of change and the impact of change has raised the bar?"

"Yes," she said. "And it's put it on everybody's radar screen. And I think those who don't do it, by the way, are what cause some trouble out there. And therefore, we want everyone to aspire to a higher position on this because you don't want bad behavior by a few to derail a digital economy."

> "We've hired 9,000 people in the last year, none of whom have been to the office."
>
> —Michael Neidorff, CEO, Centene

THE NEXT AI WAVE

When *Fortune*'s Jonathan Vanian looked at investment in AI during the pandemic, he found it had gone on pause. "Some people were stepping back," Rachel Roumeliotis, vice president of O'Reilly Media, told him. She explained that those who thought AI was merely "nice to have" had been slowed down.

Some would dispute characterizing AI as merely "nice to have," but it is expensive technology, and there was plenty of belt-tightening during the pandemic, as companies focused on improving the existing digital pipelines that connected them with their employees, their customers, and their suppliers. A May 2021 report from IBM added some texture to the trend. The company surveyed several thousand IT decision-makers in seven countries and found only 31 percent said their company "has actively deployed A.I. as part of its business operations." That was down slightly from 34 percent in a similar October 2019 survey. A larger 41 percent said they were "exploring, but have not deployed, A.I. in business operations," up slightly from 39 percent in 2019.

Limited AI expertise and knowledge remain the top obstacles to AI adoption, followed by data complexity and data silos. I asked IBM CEO Arvind Krishna, Rometty's successor, what accounted for the slowdown. "When people went through the pandemic, the first thing they invested in was resiliency and making sure people could work remotely," he told me.[22] Shortage of good AI talent was also a restrictive factor.

But the slowdown may just be a pause before the breakthrough. "Almost all companies recognize AI is going to improve the customer experience, automation inside the enterprise, and everything around natural language processing. Those are the three areas where we see huge amounts of interest. People were pausing because they were squeezing ten years of digital transformation into two years." But now that that's done, AI looks to be the second wave. "Significant investments are planned," Krishna says. The world is watching to see how this story develops.

AN INFLECTION POINT

In January 2020, in what might now be termed "the before times," I had a long conversation with Julie Sweet, who had recently taken the top job at consulting firm Accenture. She was just in the process of unveiling Accenture's growth plan for the new decade, and she told me with great confidence, "2020 is a new inflection point. We are now beginning the decade of delivery on the promise of digital and technology."[23]

Her prediction was true, but not necessarily in the way she expected. It came to fruition as we grappled with the pandemic. When I spoke to her later in the year, she described the rapid acceleration of those trends she had tagged earlier. "Today we are 20 percent in the cloud," she said. "We are moving to 80 percent." But, "instead of happening in a decade, it is going to happen in five years."[24]

It was now clear that digital skills would become central to virtually every business. "Digital is technology," Sweet said, "but digital is also transformation of how you work, how you make decisions, how you interact with customers." As a result, you need "digital everywhere."

And that, in turn, meant that industries would become more interdependent. "Digital disruption has blurred industry lines," Sweet said. "You have industry convergence. You have cross-industry platforms. And you have CEOs who are benchmarking the best, regardless of industry." That requires a different approach.

These trends led Sweet to a new guiding principle of "shared success"— her company's version of stakeholder capitalism. As she pointed out, the demands of innovation meant companies, communities, and governments must rely on each other. "The impact of digital and technology without a shared success mindset can be very detrimental to communities around the world," in terms of its impact on job opportunity, climate, and other pressing issues.

And she added, "Young people today want to have both value and values. . . . To get the best people, you have to have this mindset of shared success."

Sweet is in a position to know. Accenture isn't a cloud technology company, but it is the leading partner for most of the cloud companies in implementing wide-ranging enterprise applications, and it is also an enormous employer of young talent, bringing in tens of thousands of young people each year. She calls the coming transition "a complete re-platforming of global business. This is the Henry Ford moment of the digital era."

THE TRAINING CHALLENGE

Technology is driving the need for training and upskilling, but Anousheh Ansari, CEO of XPRIZE, believes technology can also help solve the problem. XPRIZE is a nonprofit that creates public competitions to encourage tech development that is beneficial to humanity. "The future of work is one of the most critical puzzles that we need to solve in our societies," she told me.[25] "In the midst of the pandemic, as we saw millions lose their jobs, disproportionately in lower paying employment, we saw a window of opportunity to tackle the immediate problem and give people new options."

In June 2020, Ansari launched a $5 million "Rapid Reskilling" competition, with ten finalists announced in March 2021. Their challenge is to leverage novel solutions that will rapidly train 350 individuals in ninety days at no up-front cost and place them in good jobs within sixty days. The winner needs to demonstrate their solution is scalable, deployed for at least 5,000 individuals in three industries.

Finalists have some interesting approaches, such as offering training through conversations with virtual humans, online mentoring for experiential learning, and coding skills for disadvantaged students.

Another company plowing this same field is Guild Education, which is pioneering a new financing model for continuing education. Traditional tuition reimbursement programs force workers to front the cost for their training. Guild connects workers with the right university training programs, and then works with the company to cover the cost. "If you are a frontline worker, you don't have $5,000 to pay up front," CEO Rachel Carson told me. "Guild at its core is a deep payments company. The employee no longer has to front the money."[26] Guild also employs coaches to ensure that participants find the appropriate education program. Partners include Walmart, Disney, Lowe's, and Chipotle.

> "I think the number one constituency that I serve is my employees, because I think the only sustainable advantage that a company has is the talent and the passion of their employees. If you put employees first—and employees come to companies that have an inspiring mission and values, then you will serve customers better, and, ultimately, shareholders."
>
> —Dan Schulman, CEO, PayPal

Starbucks turned fifty during the pandemic, and it had some special challenges. With thousands of stores in China, it was hit before America had truly woken up to the fallout. Yet when I asked CEO Kevin Johnson whether the crisis had made the company stronger, he replied, "Absolutely. We are more resilient and stronger today than we were pre-pandemic."[27]

In the US, it managed to thrive through multiple lockdowns by convincing millions to preorder drinks on its app and drop by stores to pick them up. By the middle of 2021, its same-store sales had fully recovered in its key markets of the US and China.

Going forward, Johnson believes, people will return to in-store service. "We are on the cusp of the great human reconnection," he said. "As human beings we were meant to connect, to socialize . . . and Starbucks was built for this moment."

A LIVING WAGE

Income inequality became a rallying cry in the last decade that in part inspired corporations to move toward stakeholder capitalism. It's a huge challenge, but many people believe that one way to begin tackling it is to raise the minimum wage.

While I was writing this, the debate about raising the minimum wage was once again heating up in Congress, as it regularly does. The issue has a long and often contentious history in this country.

In 1938, in the waning period of the Great Depression, President Franklin Roosevelt signed a significant piece of legislation into law. For the first time in US history, the Fair Labor Standards Act established a federal minimum wage of 25 cents per hour. Although it fell 15 cents short of what Roosevelt had hoped for, it was an impressive first, which established that the government had a right to intervene in setting wages. Already, individual states were taking the matter into their own hands, as they continue to do today, but the federal standard was a critical sign of progress.

Clearly, Roosevelt intended this rate to be "more than a bare subsistence level." He spoke of it being a way that all workers could "earn a decent living." That, in turn, would increase their purchasing power and boost the economy. In a fireside chat after signing the bill Roosevelt expressed enthusiasm for the effects of the bill. "Without question it starts us toward a better standard of living and increases purchasing power to buy the products of farm and factory," he said.

In the subsequent decades, the US federal minimum wage was raised twenty-two times. The last increase, to $7.25, occurred in 2009, on the heels of the financial crisis. Although a few individual states have raised the minimum wage for their residents, there has been no federal increase in over a decade. At about $15,000 per year, pretty much everyone agrees that this is not a living wage.

Complicating the equation is the matter of purchasing power. Although wages for most workers are higher than they were in the 1970s, according to Pew Research the actual purchasing power has not moved for almost fifty years. A report in *Fortune* detailed how the United States is falling behind other nations on the living wage front. Adjusting for US dollars, the minimum wage in Australia is $12.60 per hour, in France it's $12.10, and in Germany it's $11.80.

Dr. Amy K. Glasmeier, professor of economic geography and regional planning at MIT, created an analytic tool in 2004 that brings that fact home.

Glasmeier's Living Wage Calculator, which is updated regularly, charts the living wage in counties across America for eleven categories of people, from single adults with no children to two working adults with two children, and a number of categories in between. For example, the living wage for a single person in relatively expensive Fairfax County, Virginia, is $19.92. The living wage for two adults with one child and one of them working is $33.58. In Miami-Dade County, those numbers are $16.08 and $31.41, respectively; and in Los Angeles County they're $19.35 and $39.06.[28]

Whichever part of the country you live in, these numbers are far from the legal minimums. What is the obligation of companies to make sure their workers earn a living wage?

Critics of the minimum wage hike argue that it would lead to increased unemployment, particularly among young people. But the evidence on that point is not conclusive. JUST Capital released a study in July 2020, in collaboration with MIT, challenging the idea that raising the minimum wage is a burden on companies and ultimately leads to unemployment. Even with the pandemic well underway, they found that companies at the top level of paying a living wage reaped a return of 12.3 percent, compared to companies at the bottom whose return was 1.1 percent. JUST Capital concluded, "The reality is that divesting in workers was bad business during good times, and is equally short-sighted during an economic downturn. Leading research shows that investing in workers—raising wages and providing strong benefits—improves business outcomes. As companies are developing strategies to weather the current recession, they should start by considering how to improve the financial security of their workforce."

In spite of this, when Walmart announced in February 2021 that it was raising the company's minimum wage to between $13 and $15 for 425,000 of its lowest-paid workers, the stock market rebelled, sinking share prices by 6 percent. This was reminiscent of 2015, the last time Walmart raised wages. At that time, shares fell by 10 percent.

That may be a commentary on the gap between Wall Street's priorities and those of real-world companies. Walmart founder Sam Walton was known for paying the lowest price the market would bear for *everything*—labor included. But current CEO Douglas McMillon has taken a different approach. As chairman of the Business Roundtable, McMillon has made it clear that he believes in investing in workers, even if he has to take a temporary hit to the bottom line. It's a real-life demonstration of the stakeholder capitalism that he advocates. And it's an investment he believes will pay off for the company in the long run—even if investors reject it in the short run.

ON THE FRONT LINES

It was one of the last New York City galas before the coronavirus took hold. The glittering February 2020 event by the Museum of Finance attracted luminaries from both the private and public sectors. The year's honoree for the Schwab Award for Financial Innovation, which would be presented that evening, was Dan Schulman, the charismatic and sometimes offbeat CEO of PayPal. A standout amid the tony, well-dressed crowd, Schulman was wearing jeans.

But it was his words not his wardrobe that got the most attention. Schulman, who had been early to recognize that capitalism needed a reboot and the CEOs had to do more than just make money for their shareholders, had been speaking out for years. And on this evening, he laid it out for his peers. "If you look at the state of our country today, it's clear that capitalism needs an upgrade," he said. "People don't believe that the system is working for them." He went on to call on business leaders to stand for more than just making money for shareholders, and to serve "multiple stakeholders, whether they be our employees, our customers, the environment, [or] the communities that we serve." It was time, he told those gathered, to use their power for good—for a moral purpose.

Schulman's words about capitalism needing an upgrade stuck with me, and a few months later when I had a chance to interview him for *Leadership Next*, it was the first question I asked. What did he mean by that?

Schulman believes that counting on the market to make the changes necessary to include those who have been left out isn't working. He describes the change in emphasis advocated by corporations through the Business Roundtable a form of "reverse Friedmanism."

I'd heard Schulman talk about the importance of businesses asserting moral leadership in their communities for a long time—well before the BRT statement. "The people who argue that profit and purpose are two separate things, I think don't really understand that they don't work against each other," he told me. It was a simple and clear declaration of what stakeholder capitalism was all about.[29]

Schulman elaborated, when accepting the award, that what he meant about capitalism needing an upgrade is that "this idea of just counting on market forces to create a just and equitable society isn't working." He described how he saw that firsthand with his own workers. He prides PayPal on paying at or above market rates across the globe. Yet when they did a study of the net disposable income of their employees—what they had left after essential living expenses and taxes—he found that their entry level call center workers had disposable incomes below 10 percent. "And we feel that 20 percent is the bare minimum you need for somebody to have savings, to be able to not struggle to make ends meet at the end of the month. We were paying at or above market rates. So clearly, the market isn't working for a segment of our population. I really felt companies, like those companies at that event, had an obligation to measure how we're doing in serving our employees and then to step up and to make sure that they had a sense of financial health. Because you cannot have passionate employees if every month they're worrying about how they're going to make ends meet."

Schulman was raised with an activist mentality—his mother took him to civil rights marches—so it's no surprise that he has found himself among the frontline CEOs for critical issues, including the reaction to the Charlottesville racial violence. After the rally, the Southern Poverty Law Center, which calls out radical extremist groups, announced that some of the organizations and people who organized the rally used PayPal to raise money. The company responded by removing those accounts. Schulman understands that vigilance is needed. After an August 2017 terrorist incident, when a van ploughed into a crowd in Barcelona killing thirteen, he sent this message to PayPal's global employees:

Like many of you, I have been extremely affected by the events of the last week. First in Charlottesville and then in Barcelona, brutal expressions of intolerance and hatred have left innocent people injured and many have tragically died. Our thoughts go out to those who have been traumatized or harmed by these terrible events.

Our values are the heart and soul of our company. They guided us when we fought against efforts to diminish the rights of transgender citizens in North Carolina. They guided us when we opposed efforts to restrict people from entering the United States based on their religion. And they guide us now, as we work to heal the wounds that were created by the hateful acts in Charlottesville and Barcelona.

Schulman studied economics so he is versed in the standard belief that it is the job of business to build profits and the job of government to address social issues. He rejects it. "I think that the foundation of our democracy rests upon some degree of financial health to all of our citizens," he told me. "Why do I say that?" He cited the famous but unattributed quote, "Democracy is two wolves and one sheep voting on what to have for lunch," and said it has to be more than that. "So, what that really means is that democracy can depend on people rising above their own self interests. Thinking about the whole greater than the individual, how does that happen when every single day you're worried about whether you're going to actually be able to pay your bills, when you're worried about whether your kids will have a better life than you do? This is the first generation ever to believe that they won't have a better life than their parents"—a decline in the American Dream.

"You have a populace that is frustrated with the system because they don't think it's working for them. I think you have people both on the left and on the right who are very, very unhappy. I think that undermines the very foundations of our democracy. In fact, I would argue if you don't have purpose, if you don't have values that support the purpose of your company, you can never attract the very best talent into your organization. The very best talent is what assures that a company over the medium and long term can move from being a good company to a great company, an enduring company. It's just a matter of what your framework looks like: Are you maximizing profits next quarter or are you building, hopefully, a great company over the medium and long term? That is what I think our shareholders expect from me and expect for PayPal."

WORKFORCE HUMANITY

"Most people in the twenty-first century want to work for more than just a paycheck," Whole Foods cofounder John Mackey wrote in *Conscious Capitalism*.[30] "They crave work that is stimulating and enjoyable. They're looking for meaning; they want their work to make a difference, to make the world a better place. They're looking for a community of friends. They're looking for opportunities to learn and to grow and to have fun."

This might seem like an idealized description of work at a time when people are feeling such tremendous stress about the rapidly changing workplace environment. But it captures the aspirations of millions of workers, especially the younger demographic, who don't see themselves toiling for lifetimes in workplaces that offer no human rewards.

Now, as always, it's the millennials and younger people who are driving change, although workers of all generations reap the benefits. For example, the idea of "work-life balance" used to be described solely in the context of traditional families, particularly moms and dads having time to spend with their children. Today, flextime and workplace wellness are standard benefits in many well-run companies, and they are presented as quality of life benefits that can be used personally or intergenerationally. Increasingly, working yourself sick is not seen as the route to career advancement.

Great Place to Work, which partners with Fortune for its "100 Best Companies to Work For" and other rankings, conducted a study of Best Places to Work for Millennials and found that they are "just searching for a position with great leaders, fair base pay, and support for their real life needs. And when organizations deliver on those requests, millennials deliver big time for their organizations." One of its examples is Panda Restaurant Group. Millennials find the culture to be in sync with their priorities. That culture is described as the "Panda Way," which has four components—healthy lifestyle, continuous learning, developing others, and acknowledging others. These trends seem to have accelerated post-pandemic.

In this environment we can visualize workforce empowerment as three points of a triangle. The first is training workers to take advantage of opportunities supplied by new technologies. The second is delivering a living wage to all workers. And the third is creating a workplace with human values. As I argue throughout this book, the rising tide of technology has not devalued workers; it has enhanced their value—at least those who have the skills demanded by the new economy. Human capital now makes up the most important capital of most companies, and employees have become the most important "stakeholder." Companies fight for talent. They are forced to recognize their most important assets are not factories or finances or oil in the ground or inventory on the shelves. They are people, who walk out the door every night and are under no obligation to return the next morning. Companies need to serve their needs, or pay the price.

Colin Mayer makes the case that those talented workers have also become the most scarce resource. Whereas in the twentieth century a company's top challenge might have been securing access to oil, or access to financing, or perhaps access to manufacturing plants and equipment, today it is access to talent. That changes the way business leaders lead in the new world, and it also puts a high priority on developing new pipelines of talent.

In other words, in the long run, the needs of most companies and the needs of society converge. A massive training and reskilling effort over the coming decades is essential to both.

CHAPTER 6

INNOVATION FROM DIVERSITY

THERE WAS A LOT OF ENERGY AT THE FORTUNE MOST POWERFUL WOMEN Summit, held virtually between September 29 and October 1, 2020. The event, which has been held annually for the last two decades, brings the most prominent women in the Fortune 500 together with leaders in government, philanthropy, education, and the arts for both an uplifting and hard-hitting conference. And it lost only a little of its spark in 2020 by being virtual. Among the speakers were powerful CEOs such as GM's Mary Barra, AT&T Business's Anne Chow, Chase Consumer Banking's (and now CEO of TIAA) Thasunda Duckett, Boeing Defense, Space & Security's Leanne Caret, and others. The summit even attracted Meghan Markle, the Duchess of Sussex, who sat down with *Fortune* senior editor Ellen McGirt. Markle spoke about the Stop Hate for Profit Campaign, which she and Harry had joined during the summer, and called on the business community to reject the toxic elements within the internet.

The conference is based on Fortune's annual list of the Most Powerful Women in Business, which got its start back in 1998. Since then, it has provided a venue for the top women in business to meet and share business ideas. And in 2020, in the wake of the George Floyd killing, it became an opportunity to promote diversity and inclusion more broadly within companies. Ginni Rometty challenged the underrepresentation of Black and brown executives in the ranks of company leaders. "We can't wait a generation to fix this," she declared.[1]

GM CEO Mary Barra is also committed to promoting racial diversity, although she acknowledged that progress had been slow. "We're trying to be very transparent with the workforce in that, yes, we're going to continue to make progress. But this is a journey that we're beginning," Barra said at the summit.[2] "We want to have realistic expectations. And we want to keep everyone engaged. Part of this is being vulnerable, and sharing that we don't have all the answers. The other day, somebody said, 'We're all learning [about racial diversity] real-time.' And I was so encouraged by it. We have a long way to go. But I'm encouraged by the engagement."

At GM, Barra has asked her 230 senior leaders to consider diverse candidates any time an internal position opens up, but also to be proactive about developing employees of color for such future promotions. "If you don't have a diverse slate, then tell me what you're going to do so that three years from now, the slate will be diverse," she said. "And that's causing a lot of discussion."

As always, this is driven in large part by business interest. When talented people are the scarcest and most valuable form of capital, no company can afford to rule out people because of their gender or race or sexual orientation. In a true talent economy, the "old boy" network has to give way to a new approach. Supporting this today is some research suggesting that more diverse workplaces with policies of inclusion do better on key financial measures than other companies.

But old ways aren't easy to disrupt. Progress is halting. And increasing numbers of corporate leaders are convinced they need new tools and new tactics to change deeply ingrained practices.

WOMEN LEFT BEHIND

Ginni Rometty and Mary Barra made it to the very top of the business hierarchy, where women and minorities are still relatively scarce. The pandemic also exposed some deep inequities that exist for women further down the ladder. About 55 percent of job losses from COVID in 2020 were suffered by women, and more than two million women disappeared from the paid workforce during that time. Women also accounted for a majority of frontline workers in deeply affected industries like retail, food service, hospitality, and health care, and also picked up a disproportionate share of the additional loads of schoolwork, housework, and elderly care. Projections based on economic scenarios modeled by McKinsey and Oxford Economics estimate that employment for women may not recover to pre-pandemic levels until 2024—two full years after a recovery for men.

Meanwhile, women also are failing to move up the hierarchy. An IBM study on women and leadership found that women have stalled in gaining seats on corporate boards or rising to C-suites. This is a global trend. Despite increased advocacy for diversity, and even mandates in some countries, there was no real movement in numbers of women on boards of directors (8 percent) or in C-suites (10 percent) between 2019 and 2021. More alarming, the pipeline that feeds these positions from the ranks of company executives has narrowed. Fewer women are coming up through the ranks.

Bridget van Kralingen, former IBM senior vice president and the lead sponsor of the study, told me, "We are backsliding. If you are a CEO, you've got to get serious about this."[3] Among the solutions, she says, are better on-ramps for women returning to work, more flexible working arrangements, gender-blind hiring, and more childcare support. She added that mentoring is crucial to female opportunity, and currently only 30 percent of junior female managers had sponsors or mentors. Why? In part because there are so few senior women to play the role.

Van Kralingen wrote a compelling commentary, sharing her views on the subject for Fortune.com. "Despite a growing body of evidence showing that businesses are more likely to see higher rates of revenue growth when they place greater value on gender equity, 70% of organizations do not make it a top priority, according to IBM's research. And while many companies have started well-intentioned programs to address the gender gap, today's reality shows they are not delivering. This dilemma exacerbates undercurrents of fatigue and waning optimism about the seriousness of corporate efforts.

"Businesses have the ability to reverse this trajectory today and begin carving a path out of this global crisis," she wrote.[4] "At the top of the list is implementing ways for women to return to work now. This means supporting them with access to training, tools, and technology, as well as giving them work assignments on technical projects that match their expertise. That last point is especially noteworthy. In my own experience, it is when women are empowered with the tough roles—the big and thorny turn-around jobs—that our next generation of leaders emerges."

It's an uncomfortable reality check. Who can imagine a scenario where women actually backslide in business, disappearing from the workplace and becoming less prevalent in executive positions? Is that even possible? The pandemic shows that it is.

According to the 2020 Women in the Workplace study coauthored by McKinsey and LeanIn.org, one in four women are now considering leaving the workplace or downshifting their careers.[5] While the stressors they experience aren't limited to those affecting parents, a massive increase in caregiving responsibilities at home and at work jeopardizes women's ability to stay in the workforce and progress. Forty percent of mothers (compared to 27 percent of fathers) have added three or more additional hours of caregiving a day to their schedules—the equivalent of a part-time job. This extra burden affects women at all levels, but those in senior roles feel an additional pressure to be "always on."

> "What COVID has done is expose underlying issues in the economy in an even more stark way. Small and medium-sized enterprises and service-oriented businesses which tend to employ more women and minorities have been more heavily impacted."
>
> —Ajay Banga, CEO, Mastercard

Once again companies are facing the hard truths about how society at large has let down women by asking them to shoulder the bulk of the caretaking responsibilities, not only for children but for elderly parents as well. There's a disconnect between what we say we value as a society, including having children and maintaining strong family relationships, and what we actually do to enable that. Too often, when it comes down to the actual responsibility, women fill the roles with very little support from their companies. Many companies are now acknowledging that they have a key role in helping to work this out.

In October 2021, the Most Powerful Women Summit returned to an in-person format, with more than three hundred prominent women executives in attendance (all vaccinated, tested, and wearing masks except while on stage). Everyone was eager to talk about the new realities imposed on workplaces. A session at the beginning of the summit called "The Great Hybrid Experiment" turned into a lively discussion of how to respect the true needs of workers.

"I think the word hybrid is super loaded," said Colleen McCreary, chief people, places, and publicity officer for Credit Karma. "It locks you into certain ways of working. Flexible work is what we are talking about. We are freeing up the conversation to think about things we never thought about before."

"We don't call it hybrid. We don't call it flexible. We call it being intentionally flexible," said Nickle LaMoreaux, chief human resources officer at IBM. "It's about people coming together as a team and intentionally deciding what flexibility works for them and their team."

This flexibility, we are reminded, is something women and families have been seeking for decades, but it has to happen within an environment of inclusion and collaboration.

"We don't want to come to the office and sit in front of our laptops or a video screen to talk to people who aren't there," said Francine Katsoudas, chief people, policy, and purpose officer at Cisco. "We will be reconfiguring our space to be someplace where collaboration and team building happens. It's really about the experiences we want to happen."

A BETTER WORLD

When Ursula Burns stepped down from her job as CEO of Xerox in 2016, she had the distinction of being the first and only Black woman to run a Fortune 500 company. (Burns served as CEO from 2009 to 2016 and Xerox chairwoman from 2010 to 2017.) She is known to be outspoken and sometimes fiery, and she earned her position by fighting the odds. Raised in a struggling neighborhood on the Lower East Side of Manhattan by a single mother, she developed an individual style and learned to persevere even when her aspirations seemed far away. "I can assure you that no one at my commencement was pointing at me and predicting that I would be the CEO of anything," she told the 2009 graduating class of the Rochester Institute of Technology.[6] "Women presidents or CEOs of large global companies were non-existent at that time. Black women presidents of large global companies were unimaginable." She succeeded in part because of her willingness to speak her mind under any circumstances, to speak truth to power in a way, but from inside the company. And she has never held back.

Burns didn't step down from Xerox to go quietly into retirement. She had new missions in mind. Her latest project is the Board Diversity Action Alliance, a no-nonsense plan to diversify corporate boards to address what in her view is the glacial pace of progress in corporate diversity. She cofounded the project with another prominent Black woman, private equity's Gabrielle Sulzberger. Sulzberger is on the boards of many prominent companies and organizations, including Eli Lilly, Whole Foods, Mastercard, and the Ford Foundation.

When Burns spoke with Ellen McGirt and me for our *Leadership Next* podcast, she brought her usual force and honesty to subjects many people have difficulty speaking about. I asked her about quotas. She and I had spoken many times on the subject, and she had always been firm in opposing them. I asked if that had changed.

"Oh, I'm still not high on the notion of quotas," she said, "but I think that we may have earned our comeuppance when it comes to quotas. I actually was under the impression, still am, that when you have a challenge, that you have a gap, that you do some study, you put your best minds to it, and you work on it, and most of the time businesses solve problems. That's why we've got an R&D department. We can invent new drugs. We can get ourselves to the moon. My belief was that it would be enough to actually have very smart multibillion-dollar companies do what is reasonable. What has happened though, Alan, is that we have failed across the board. And every year we say, oh my God, it's a problem. We still haven't met it. And we're going to keep working on it. I thought about this. I was trying to reflect on, so now what else do you do?"[7]

Burns concluded that when they tell you over and over and over again that they're going to do something, and they don't do it, you have to bring other forces to bear. She used the example of a parent who is not paying child support. After a couple of attempts to receive voluntary payment, the court ultimately garnishes the salary. "They take away the right from the individual to fail again. And the one thing that I think about quotas and the reason why I'm even opening my mind towards it, is because with quotas, you're removing the right for people to fail again."

"So, Ursula, why have we failed so badly?" I asked.

Burns said that one reason was a sense of entitlement: "The structure believes that it owns these roles, it owns these seats. The structure is a white male structure. We have to change everything about how we approach this." She added that it's always been this way. People get used to where they are, even if it's unjust. And they may say they want change, but they also want it to be painless. "And if we can't make it painless to make a transition from an unfair, unbalanced system, to a more fair and more balanced system, we don't want to do it. We don't want to upset people because they don't want to give something up. We are at the point now where voices in the world that were silent before are starting to speak up a little bit more. I don't know if it will last forever, but it's happening for sure. So, we have the young people, we have women—the people in general, who were not part of the system, they're starting to articulate more and more. At least they'd like to understand what the heck the system is." The bottom line for Burns is simple: "We have a responsibility to leave behind a world that's better than when we inhabited it."

NOOYI'S DUALITY

Indra Nooyi was a leading voice for change in the corporate world for many years, as CEO and board chairman of PepsiCo. After stepping down as CEO in 2018 and from the board in 2019, she has continued to engage in discussions about the future of business—especially the human necessities. Ellen McGirt and I interviewed her in 2021 after the publication of her powerful book, *My Life in Full: Work, Family, and Our Future.*[8]

She described the subject that had been her passionate concern for many years. "I talk [in the book] about this duality that I grew up in two cultures," said Nooyi, who was raised in India. "But my duality went beyond growing up in two cultures; it was also about being a mom and an executive trying to balance short term and long term in my business dealings, performance, and purpose. It was duality all through my life—balancing and juggling. And the thing that surprised me while I was in my final years at PepsiCo, and most certainly now, post-PepsiCo, is all the talk about the future of work, the future of offices. Everyone talks about hybrid work, automation, remote work, technology, disruption. But the word *family* and helping young families and women balance family and work seems to be absent."

This pains Nooyi because we need women in the workforce. "Women are getting all the top degrees—they are wicked smart. They are graduating in larger numbers. They want economic freedom, and the country needs their talents. At the same time, women are also primary family builders. We want them to build families too, if they want to. Somehow the fact that we need young women to do both doesn't enter the equation at all. And we don't talk about what we need to do to make their lives easier."

I observed that women who achieved the top positions had traditionally been reluctant to tackle family-oriented issues. "In my experience, there was kind of a reluctance among those pioneers to talk about what it was like being a woman, because you wanted to be seen as a CEO," I suggested. "You didn't want to be seen as a female CEO. You didn't want to be put into a pigeonhole. And so, we haven't talked about these issues, and I think it's very bold what you've done, and I hope it will spark a renewed conversation."

"I approached this whole issue more as an economist than a feminist," Nooyi explained. "I said, 'Look, if you want to think of the resources of the country—all the talented women out there—how do you deploy them to further the country, to grow the country, to grow the GDP of the country?' And if you think that way, you want to make sure you grease the skids for women to come into the workforce and perform at their best. You will not just make it a feminist and a female issue. . . . It's about the future of the country, the economic promise of the country, the future of work. I think we need to soften the discussion from the future of work to include all this because right now it's too hard—technology, destruction, hybrid workplaces. But hybrid workplaces to enable what? Flexible working to enable what? I think we need to get more expansive and have a holistic conversation. And I think the time for that has come."

This is an example of the way in which Nooyi has taken the lead on important issues, which we saw during her tenure at PepsiCo. Relatively early in her days as CEO, she decided that the company had to do more than provide high-sugar drinks and snacks. But there wasn't a lot of support at the time for introducing healthy choices. I asked her how she made the decision and dealt with the blowback.

"Well, PepsiCo has a fantastic portfolio of great-tasting products, and I love every one of those products," she told us, smiling. "But as I looked to the population, I saw a trend toward consuming healthier products. Not necessarily purely nutritious products, but healthier for us versus what people were consuming in the past. So, I looked at this as a great opportunity to future-proof the company. And what did I want to do? Something very simple. I said, 'Look, our products, many of them are fun for you, great treat-like products. What if we were to offer zero-calorie versions of these products? It will be better for you.' So, dial up all the zero-calorie options in beverages. But in snacks, you can't really do zero calories because by themselves they are caloric, so reduce the salt and fat levels in those products.

"And then dial up the products with nutritional content like Sabra hummus or Naked Juice. It was a very nuanced strategy of fun for you, better for you, and good for you. The strategy was keep sending fun for you, but reduce the salt, fat, and sugar in the fun for you. Dial up the better for you and really dial up the good for you. There was only one problem: when you take a product that tastes so great and optimized over the years, when you try to take down the sugar or salt or fat, you want to make sure consumers don't say, 'God, it tastes so different, I don't want it.' So, it required the R&D capability, and a very careful formulation. I embarked on making the investors really think over this whole product line, and we were successful. We reduced the salt and fat in our products substantially—they still tasted great. And in core blue can Pepsi we reduced the sugar levels and dialed up the zero calories."

"But, Indra, I know in those early days, you got pushback from investors who said, 'Don't make me healthy, make me money,'" I prodded. "And I think you mentioned you got some pushback inside the company as well."

"Yeah, that's normal for transformations in retrospect in those days. I was miffed that people didn't see the strategy because many of those very investors who questioned my strategy had changed their eating and drinking habits. If you've changed your eating and drinking habits, why do you think we shouldn't? Because at the end of the day, you are a consumer, we're all consumers, and we should reflect how the marketplace has changed."

In these ways Nooyi has shown leadership in the areas that matter and that people care about. When she talks about a "softer" approach, she is referring to a human approach, which is a way of future-proofing a company.

LEVELING THE INVESTMENT FIELD

Tristan Walker is a rarity—a Black entrepreneur who successfully raised $40 million from Silicon Valley to start his own company, Walker & Company Brands, which makes health and beauty products for people of color. Studies show that less than 3 percent of venture dollars go to Black or Latinx entrepreneurs. But Walker beat the odds with a company that he sold to P&G. Today it operates as a wholly owned subsidiary of P&G, with Walker as CEO. When Ellen McGirt and I interviewed him for *Leadership Next*, he talked about the new challenges and opportunities brought by COVID and by the social justice uprising of 2020—and what it means to be a human being in a company today. "The thing I like to say to our team, particularly over the events of the past year, is, before I'm a CEO, before you're a colleague or an employee, we're people first. I am a Black husband, I'm a Black son. I have a Black brother, father, et cetera. And I think our leaning in with empathy to our *personness*, not only as colleagues together, but as consumers who are people too, made us not only well positioned to articulate with authenticity the side that we're standing on, but certainly it was an added plus for our business, quite naturally. Because folks are trying to gravitate towards businesses and companies that live their values truly and authentically in the real world."[9]

Ellen asked Walker, "What, in your estimation, is it going to take to make sure that talented people such as yourself don't become outliers?" It was not an easy question to answer, but one to which Walker had given a lot of thought. For him the key word was inevitability, driven by three factors—the demographic shift happening in the country, the cultural influence of people of color, particularly Blacks, and the influence of tech. "And everything that I tried to do over the past decade and, God willing, the next fifty years, really sit at the center of those three concentric circles," he emphasized. "There are a lot of folks like me that are developing a nuanced view around the importance and criticality of this demographic shift. Every company in twenty years, when folks of color are the majority of this country, if they do not have a plan to serve this audience with empathy, I believe that they will not exist. I think it is that critical, it is that existential, and that's where the inevitability comes in."

He told us that as a person who had been fortunate in life, winning a scholarship for a private boarding school education, he felt an obligation to bring others into the room. "I take that job very seriously, not only being at Procter & Gamble, but I'm also on the boards of Foot Locker and Shake Shack. I sit on the nominating and governance committees of these boards too. So when push comes to shove and we need to bring on another potential board member, I can support folks who look like me to have those roles and positions. But when you think about CEO, CFO, C-level succession, we can have a point of view that points folks to diversity." Walker has also founded CODE 2040—a nonprofit dedicated to promoting Black and Latinx participation in the tech business. Its name is derived from estimates that Black and Latinx people will become the majority in the US around 2040.

I brought up stakeholder capitalism, noting that "something is definitely changing in the way that business leaders are talking about their business, are talking about their values, are talking about purpose, and are talking about diversity and inclusion. But sometimes people come back to us and say, 'It's just all talk. It's all talk.' You're inside. You're in a big company like P&G. You're on the board of Foot Locker. On the board of Shake Shack. You've seen how the entrepreneurial system works. Do you think we're going to look back and look at the last year as a turning point for these issues?"

Walker's response was a thought-provoking analysis—one I hadn't heard before. "I think the pandemic is going to create a crop of really successful culture-less companies," he said. "What I mean by that—before the pandemic the culture for folks working in the office together was built on this very big assumption that the people in the office *like* working with each other, *like* doing the same things that each other likes to do, and be-tween, let's say eight and six o'clock, everybody's together doing the exact same things. So, you don't have the space to reflect, to do the things that would help you and your mental health. . . . I think the pandemic has forced that for people, 'Hey, go take care of your kids.' So, I think the only way to get empathy at scale is to provide or create these culture-less companies."

Walker acknowledged that his idea is counterintuitive in many ways, and runs against the thinking of other CEOs, who are eager to have their employees in the office to build culture. But only by providing space for workers to think about what they really need, Walker said, do companies arrive at something more authentic for *all* of their employees.

FROM THE OUTSIDE IN

Stakeholder capitalism's principles of diversity and inclusion are not just about what goes on inside corporations. They also involve who gets a chance to build a company in the first place. One important metric is which companies win the support of venture capitalists. Walker is a standout for having secured venture funding, but his experience is also quite rare.

Women of all races are also at a disadvantage, with only 3 percent of venture capital directed to women-owned businesses. This imbalance is not only wrong for society, it is also bad for business. According to a *Harvard Business Review* study, underfunding women-run businesses equates to some $3 trillion being left out of the economy. In a *Fortune* column on the topic, Jo Ann Corkran, Loretta McCarthy, and Peggy Wallace, co-CEOs of the venture fund Golden Seeds, which invests in women-run businesses, cited some harsh realities. "Women are at the forefront of many market trends, but struggle for the capital," they write. "Since 90% of VC decision-makers are men, who in turn invest 86% of their capital in all-male teams, our burning question is this: What must happen for this to change? And—perhaps more importantly—what's standing in the way? First, we must look at access to capital. Only 20 women have ever led an IPO. Ever. Women have been excluded from the headwaters of capital, specifically venture capital, leaving angel capital (and a few workarounds that do very little) as essentially the only path to funding. As angel investors focused on women-led businesses, Golden Seeds has skin in the game, of course, but that doesn't change the facts."[10] Even when it comes to angel investing Corkran, McCarthy, and Wallace point out that women-led companies get the short end of the stick, garnering only 19 percent of about $24 billion a year.

Mellody Hobson is a high-profile financier who is aiming to change the imbalance. As the Black president and co-CEO of Ariel Investments, the largest minority-owned investment company in the world, Hobson is committed to lifting up those who haven't had a chance before. Ariel doesn't spend investment dollars on companies that don't have diverse leadership and boardrooms. A few years ago, Hobson used the occasion of Fortune's Most Powerful Women Summit to talk about how the difficulties she faced growing up influenced her perspectives on business. Raised by a single mom and the youngest of six, Hobson's life was all about insecurity. Nothing was stable. Evictions were common, getting the phone disconnected was common, having the car repossessed was common. Her life was defined by instability, to the point that even when she first started working in the investment business at Ariel, she used to *overpay* her phone bill to provide a cushion against disaster. "I couldn't get out of the mentality that it could all go away," she said.[11]

Now successful in her own right and married to George Lucas (she notes that she was the least-famous person at their wedding), Hobson is committed to helping advance women and minorities in business. In December 2020, she was named chair of Starbucks's board of directors, after serving as vice chair since Howard Schultz stepped down in 2018. It was a hopeful sign at a time when the higher echelons of US companies are still largely composed of white men. A small step in the right direction.

Hobson makes a point of promoting investment firms that are targeted toward supporting women entrepreneurs and founders. These firms, such as All Raise, Beyond the Billion, Astia, Halogen Ventures, and the BELLE Impact Fund, offer women founders guidance and connection to funders, provide and catalyze early-stage investments for firms with women founders, and invest in women's technology startups.

THE ONETEN INITIATIVE

In late 2020, following the George Floyd killing, a group of prominent CEOs and organizations decided to back a bold initiative to upskill, hire, and promote one million Black Americans over the next ten years through their program called OneTen. The founders were business powerhouses: Ken Chenault, Chairman and Managing Director of General Catalyst and former CEO of American Express; Ken Frazier, CEO of Merck; Charles Phillips, Managing Partner of Recognize, Chairman of the Black Economic Alliance, and former CEO of Infor; Ginni Rometty, Executive Chairman and former CEO of IBM; and Kevin Sharer, CEO of Amgen and former faculty member at Harvard Business School. All five founders serve on the board of OneTen with Ken Frazier and Ginni Rometty serving as cochairs.

Frazier explained, "This is a moment in time for Americans to move past our divisions to come together and reach our full potential as a nation. Our country's workforce of the future will be an increasingly diverse one. Through the creation of one million jobs for Black Americans over the next 10 years, OneTen has the potential to address persistent inter-generational gaps in opportunity and wealth."[12] The founders are quick to explain that OneTen is not a philanthropy in the traditional sense, but a coalition that is out to create an ecosystem of businesses, community leaders, government, and education.

Ellen McGirt and I spoke with one of the cofounders, Charles Phillips, on *Leadership Next*. Phillips has an impressive history under his belt, including as the former CEO and chair of Infor, a global software company that was sold to Koch Industries. He's also the former president of Oracle. And before that he had a busy career on Wall Street, and he was a captain in the US Marine Corps. Today he is managing partner of the technology investment company Recognize, and cochair of the Black Economic Alliance. Phillips described how OneTen stands out from other efforts.

"There's a much greater number of [Black and brown] people who just have no pathway to building wealth. That's the reason why household wealth in the Black community is 10 percent [of the wealth of the white community]. What's been holding the Black community back is the inability to create intergenerational wealth."[13]

Phillips pointed out that whether the issue is crime or education or health care—any big issue people care about—it gets better if the jobs picture is stable. So, in a holistic sense, this job program is good for the country. He said his organization sold CEOs on joining the program by telling them that the country's demographics are changing, and "whether you like it or not, that's just a fact. And so that means your future customers are going to be made up of a different demographic and it's in your interest to have them creating wealth and growing and be ready for the next generation of workers you have to hire."

OneTen is building a network between talent providers and employers and asking employers to step up and commit to training and hiring efforts. At its launch, OneTen had the support of thirty-seven founding CEOs and companies across industries. Members include Accenture, ADP, Allstate, American Express, Amgen, Aon, AT&T, Bain & Company, Bank of America, Cargill, Caterpillar, Cisco, Cleveland Clinic, Comcast, Deloitte, Delta Air Lines, Eli Lilly, General Motors, HP, Humana, IBM, Illinois Tool Works, Intermountain Healthcare, Johnson & Johnson, Lowe's, Medtronic, Merck, Nike, Nordstrom, PepsiCo, Roper Technologies, Stryker, Target, Trane Technologies, Verizon, Walmart, and Whirlpool Corporation.

MEASURING UP

"What gets measured gets managed." That's a well-known management aphorism that was behind an innovative partnership between Fortune and data company Refinitiv to pair metrics with ideals when it comes to diversity and inclusion. Without strong accountability metrics, companies often have difficulty holding to their commitments. Fortune's Measure Up Initiative, powered by Refinitiv's environmental, social, and corporate governance (ESG) data capabilities, is designed to help businesses improve their diversity and inclusion numbers by making them public. Companies are invited to self-report their data, and Fortune and Refinitiv support this call to action by providing executives with data-driven insights and in-depth conversations on key topics such as inclusive leadership, corporate anti-racism, and the racial wealth gap. Measure Up helps corporate senior leaders set transparent goals around inclusion, share tactics and strategies, and work collectively to deliver measurable returns to a broader set of stakeholders.

Refinitiv CEO David Craig said of the partnership, "I believe the corporate world overwhelmingly wants to see change and understands how vital diversity is in building successful and sustainable companies. However, efforts to tackle minority under-representation in the workplace will fall flat unless companies first have an accurate picture of their racial composition. As one of the world's biggest providers of ESG data, we are encouraging companies to share minority-related measures of their workforce with the world—just as they already do with gender. By teaming up with Fortune to create Measure Up, harnessing their unique link with the CEO community, I'm more hopeful than ever that the corporate world can fulfill its promises and respond to the cries for change that have only grown louder in the wake of the murder of George Floyd."[14]

Simultaneous with our effort, Tim Ryan, chairman of PwC US, the audit and assurance, consulting, and tax service firm, published a blog post describing his company's decision to release its diversity data. As he told our group, "We wanted the self-imposed pressure to do better."[15] Ryan's blog is an example of a deep reflection at the corporate level, which doesn't try to minimize the difficulties or present a rosy scenario. It's the kind of bold truth-telling that's a beacon for other companies who are intent on improving their diversity profiles.

On 26 August [2020], we publicly released our diversity data, including racial and gender representation, at all career stages, for all of our offices in the United States. While we were proud of progress in some areas, such as the progress we've made in diverse recruiting of late, we were admittedly disappointed by some of the things that data said: our representation of women and racially and ethnically diverse people at senior levels is not what we would like, and we also wonder how many people in communities that self-identify (such as those who are LGBTQ+, who are veterans or who experience disabilities) felt comfortable doing so.

. . . We're more outcome oriented. As we move with fresh energy, we're innately aware of the difference between activity and outcomes. Both are important, so when people ask me how we're doing, I say we're encouraged, but our results show us that we are not where we want to be yet. What will the results of our next promotion cycle, six months from now, show? How about the following one, which is 18 months away? The fact that we've started down the road of transparency makes these checkpoints very real—and for me, very exciting.

In a sense, we're simply providing the same kind of scorecard for our diversity efforts that we've long provided for our day-to-day operations. Said differently, diversity, equity, and inclusion should be treated like any other business issue, and we are treating it as such. Most organizations that stay in business for meaningful periods of time do so because they are living, learning, evolving entities. We want that same spirit of adaptation to pervade our diversity efforts, at all levels, because everyone can see exactly how we are doing.

People, myself included, often describe diversity as a journey. I suppose that's true, in the sense that it's not the work of a moment; at PwC, we've been at it for more than two decades. But it's also a business issue that demands focused attention, testing, learning, scaling what works and stopping what doesn't. A journey can sound like a grand adventure with no known destination. That's not diversity, and business leaders aren't just along for the ride. They're navigators, who set direction, check progress continuously and turn around when they hit dead ends. They also need their people up and down the line to do the same, because course-correcting involves a multitude of actors. There's no substitute for clear, widely shared information in that endeavor. Uncomfortable though transparency may be at first, I'm convinced that vulnerability is a necessity if we want to lead effectively on diversity—and as the business community has the greatest share of trust we've had in recent memory, now is the time.[16]

How effective all these programs will be in increasing diversity in the top ranks of business remains to be seen. But what is clear to me, given my four decades as a journalist watching business culture, is that there is a seriousness today among business leaders that is unmatched by anything I've seen in the past. The time, attention, and energy that people like Frazier, Chenault, Rometty, Phillips, Craig, Ryan, and many others are putting behind this effort make me think that it will bear fruit. It's just one more piece of evidence that the world of business is changing.

CHAPTER 7

CLIMATE COMMITMENT

In January 2020, BlackRock CEO Larry Fink dropped a bombshell in his annual letter to CEOs. It's a letter they pay close attention to, because BlackRock is the world's top asset manager with more than $9 trillion under management, making it one of the largest shareholders of most Fortune 500 companies, and *the* largest shareholder of many.

In the letter, Fink declared that BlackRock would henceforth place environmental sustainability at the core of all investment decisions. He stated, "As a fiduciary, our responsibility is to help clients navigate this transition. Our investment conviction is that sustainability and climate-integrated portfolios can provide better risk-adjusted returns to investors. And with the impact of sustainability on investment returns increasing, we believe that sustainable investing is the strongest foundation for client portfolios going forward."[1]

The financial industry paid attention. BlackRock is the largest asset manager in the world, overseeing more than $9 trillion. What Fink says cannot be easily ignored. Few companies represent traditional capitalism the way

BlackRock does, and its commitment to sustainability marked a major reconfiguration of priorities.

In conversations with CEOs over the last decade about their increasing emphasis on stakeholder issues, I almost always asked them why they were doing this. And invariably, their first answer had to do with their employees. In recent years, some brands—think Starbucks, or Patagonia, or Nike—also had been rewarded by consumers for their stands on social issues. But Fink's letter added a critical third leg to the triad of support for stakeholder capitalism—the investor. Indeed, if shareholders started demanding companies pay more attention to social and environmental issues, and propose an end to conflict between shareholders and other stakeholders, then CEOs would clearly have no choice.

In January 2021, a year after that first letter, Fink took a step further, asking companies to disclose plans for how they will achieve "net zero" global emissions by 2050—meaning they emit no more carbon dioxide than they remove from the environment. That marked a true turning point. When the world's largest investor was asking every major company to commit to specific targets for eliminating greenhouse gas emissions, it was clear the world had changed.

Later in January, *Fortune* hosted a virtual gathering of CEOs in place of the dinner we normally held each year in Davos. It was a who's who of the corporate elite—the CEOs of Best Buy, Levi Strauss, L'Oreal, Workday, Pfizer, IKEA, Western Union, Nasdaq, Kohl's, and others. But it was Mary Barra, CEO of GM, who captured the group's attention. Earlier that day, she had announced that her company plans to eliminate all tailpipe emissions from new GM cars by 2035. "I think we will look back and see '21–'22 as an inflection point that allowed us to start driving mass adoption of electric vehicles," she told the group.[2]

In her calm, deliberate way, Barra told the CEOs she had made climate change a key mission of the automotive giant, announcing a commitment of $27 billion between 2020 and 2025 as an investment in electric vehicles. "We understand to get broad adoption, we need to make sure we cross multiple price points and multiple segments, so that's exactly what we're doing. Because four years ago, we also started working intently on the technology to enable us to do that efficiently, to make sure we can reach as many people as possible."

Barra announced plans to be carbon neutral by 2040, as well as eliminate tailpipe emissions from light duty vehicles by 2035, and to align with the goals of the Paris Accord, which the United States rejoined when President Biden took office. In her announcement earlier that day, she said, "There's a tremendous amount of work, and we have to work together with corporations, governments, and provide the charging infrastructure, but we're very enthused about the path we're on and the opportunity that we can have working with not only the US government, but other governments, to accelerate electric vehicle adoption and really address climate change from a mobility perspective, whether we're moving [people] or goods."

CEOs in other industries who attended the event confirmed the message Barra was sending. IKEA CEO Jesper Brodin, for instance, said, "2021 looks like an historic year in many respects. On the climate issue . . . we have definitely shifted the dialogue from the why and are now focused fully on the how."[3]

Prince Charles, who has been advocating for climate action for a half century, also joined the group and told the CEOs that business attitudes had changed. "After all these years of trying to encourage corporate social and environmental responsibility, and having a certain amount of difficulty trying to raise awareness despite endless different initiatives, suddenly it seems the dams are beginning to burst and people are now taking a real interest in this, particularly, if I may say so, a lot more of the investors, a lot more of the shareholders. And of course, as many of you know all too well, you have a lot of younger employees who take these issues very seriously indeed."[4]

Months later, in September, I had an opportunity to catch up with Barra again. Noting that electric vehicles currently accounted for only about 3 percent of the company's sales, I asked if she was getting ahead of her customers. "You know, that can always be a possibility," she replied. "But we would rather be ahead than be behind. And actually, when we talk to customers, and we understand and do research, every time we do the research there's more of a willingness to consider an electric vehicle, and that's what gives us a lot of confidence. What I've learned is when you put something like that out there, quickly everybody gets aligned, and then they just amaze you with what they're able to do to achieve those objectives."[5]

The bold 2035 target is an example of Barra's leadership style. She likes to challenge her team with broad, hyper-ambitious goals: "Zero crashes, zero emissions, zero congestion"; "We want to become the most inclusive company in the world." It's an approach she says paid off well during the pandemic.

Later in the year, Fortune surveyed the CEOs of the Fortune 500 companies and asked about their plans to reach net-zero carbon emissions by 2050 or sooner. A majority of companies had not published plans at that time, but a subsequent CEO survey in January 2021 showed only 40 percent of companies had not adopted a net-zero plan. By the time we surveyed in October 2021 that percentage had dropped to 29 percent. It was clear that corporate leaders—who a couple of decades ago were leading the resistance to climate change—had now moved to the vanguard.

Resistance to making big commitments on the climate, while still a part of the broader US political debate, is rapidly fading from corporate America. As Bill Gates, a leading champion of climate commitment, related in a *Fortune* interview, it's been a rocky path. In the past, whenever there was any kind of economic crisis, climate change went on the back burner. It was seen as a drain on the economy, not an enhancement. "During the financial crisis [of 2007–2008] people were like, 'Hey, things are tough now and that climate stuff, that's way out there,'" he said. "Even by 2010, if you polled the public, you'd find that interest in the climate had gone way down. It began to build up gradually over the next decade, but as we hit the pandemic, I thought, 'Okay, what's gonna happen?'"

But this time was different. "It's actually gone up somewhat during the pandemic, which is kind of weird," Gates said.[6] Indeed, in our CEO poll in October 2021, 90 percent of those polled agreed "climate change needs to be addressed urgently," and 86 percent agreed that "my company can play a positive role in addressing climate change." Only 17 percent said executing on their climate change agenda would negatively affect long-term growth, and only 4 percent said it would "negatively affect long-term shareholder value."[7]

In his 2021 book, *How to Avoid a Climate Disaster: The Solutions We Have and the Breakthroughs We Need*, Gates presents an agenda for meeting net-zero carbon emissions. Clifton Leaf, *Fortune*'s former editor in chief, described reading the book like being on an expedition, with "the promised land—Gates's Ithaca—being a place called 'zero.'"[8] As Gates puts it so bluntly, "There's no scenario in which we keep adding carbon to the atmosphere and the world stops getting hotter, and the hotter it gets, the harder it will be for humans to survive, much less thrive."[9]

Gates does not have any illusions about current sources of renewable energy—mostly wind and solar—being enough. "The wind doesn't always blow and the sun doesn't always shine," he writes, "and we don't have affordable batteries that can store city-sized amounts of energy for long enough. Besides, making electricity accounts for only 27 percent of all greenhouse gas emissions."

The way out, Gates proposes, is through massive innovation.

When it comes to climate change, there's a constant effort to find rosy scenarios. Facing the facts head-on is hard to do. But as the prospects become more urgent, there is less effort to pretend that things are better than they seem. For example, Gates tackled one of these, the pandemic effect. Some have considered it a silver lining that the slowing down of the global economy has been good for the climate. Gates agrees that greenhouse gas emissions were reduced by about 5 percent in the first year of the pandemic. But that rate isn't sustainable post pandemic, and it's not really good news. "Consider what it took to achieve this 5 percent reduction," he writes. "A million people died, and tens of millions were put out of work. To put it mildly, this was not a situation that anyone would want to continue or repeat. And yet the greenhouse gas emissions probably dropped just 5 percent, and possibly less than that. What's remarkable to me is not how much emissions went down because of the pandemic, but how little."

> "Profit of the company can be earned in one of two ways. It can be earned through creating benefits for us as customers and societies in the natural world, or it can be done through wealth transfer, at the expense of others. Environmental degradation, for instance, is profiting at the expense of others and not accounting for the true costs of cleaning up the mess."
>
> —Colin Mayer, speaking to the Fortune Connect Fellows

BUSINESS STEPS UP

A year after its commitment to stakeholder capitalism, the Business Roundtable released a set of specific principles and policies to address climate
change, including market incentives for the development and execution of
technologies designed to reduce greenhouse gas emissions.

Walmart CEO and BRT chairman Doug McMillon spoke for his colleagues when he said, "Climate change is one of the greatest challenges facing the planet today, and we believe businesses are an essential part of the
solution. Representing more than 200 CEOs from America's leading companies, the new Business Roundtable position on climate change reflects
our belief that a national market-based emissions reduction policy is critical
to reducing greenhouse gas emissions to levels designed to avoid the worst
effects and mitigate the impacts of climate change."

BRT doesn't recommend specific actions, but its climate principles are
meant as a guide. They propose to:

- Align policy goals and greenhouse gas emissions reduction targets with
  scientific evidence;
- Leverage market-based solutions wherever possible;
- Increase global engagement, cooperation, and accountability;
- Provide for adequate transition time and long-term regulatory
  certainty;
- Preserve the competitiveness of US businesses, including avoiding eco-
  nomic and emissions leakage;
- Minimize social and economic costs for those least able to bear them;
- Support both public and private investment in low-carbon and GHG
  emissions reduction technologies along the full innovation pipeline;
- Minimize administrative burdens and duplicative policies while maxi-
  mizing compliance flexibility;
- Ensure US policies account for international emissions reduction
  programs;
- Advance climate resilience and adaptation;
- Eliminate barriers to the deployment of emissions reduction technolo-
  gies and low-carbon energy sources.

"We are committed to leading by example," said Ryan Lance, chief executive officer of ConocoPhillips. "The U.S. can do the same by adopting a credible, durable and comprehensive climate change strategy with market-based solutions to reduce emissions across the economy while increasing adaptation, resilience and regulatory simplification." BRT urges its members to invest in federal funding for energy innovation and climate research, while continuing to create energy efficient policies that incentivize continued improvement in buildings, equipment, appliances, transportation, and manufacturing as well as in the electricity sector—in effect, to do whatever they can to speed the transition to a low-carbon economy.

TURNING COMMITMENTS INTO ACTION

The statement by the Business Roundtable and the steady rise in companies that are committing to reach net zero by 2050 are a clear sign that something has changed in the business environment. But commitments to hit a target in 2050, made by CEOs who will not be running their companies then, do little to convince skeptics that real progress toward addressing climate change is underway. The statements themselves are a relatively cost-free way for companies to please environmentally aware employees, customers, and investors.

What's impressed me more over the past year is not just the commitments, but the actions that companies are taking to make progress now. You can follow the money: it is moving to solve climate problems.

At the virtual Fortune Global Forum in June 2021, for instance, Søren Skou, CEO of the giant shipping company Moller-Maersk, told of a partnership he had formed with Danish power firm Ørsted to build new wind-powered facilities to produce carbon-free hydrogen fuel for the company's ships. When asked why he was doing it, Skou responded that his customers were demanding it. Many of the large companies that transport their goods on his ships have made sweeping net-zero commitments of their own that require them to get carbon shipping out of their supply chain. So they need Moller-Maersk to come up with a carbon-free solution.

"We have moved away from thinking about decarbonization in terms of cost and capital expenditure investment to thinking about it equally as a market opportunity," he said. Big business "is way ahead of the politicians on this issue. . . . We are not driven by regulations. Actually, we are trying to drive regulation forward so that we can maintain a level playing field as much as we possibly can."[10]

Looking at the climate transition, not as a government-imposed cost but rather as a market-driven opportunity, is also leading financial firms to make sizable commitments to climate change. In April 2021, for instance, Bank of America announced it would deploy $1 trillion by 2030 to "accelerate the transition to a low carbon economy." That's not charity. It's money going to finance a huge business opportunity. Other banks and private equity firms have made similar moves.

> "It has to become a way of doing business. . . . We are integrating sustainability into the core commercial operations of our business, so that any initiative we're working on not only has that traditional financial P&L lens, but also has the sustainability lens as well."
>
> —Michele Buck, CEO, Hershey's

THE CORPORATE PUSH-PULL

We've seen how former PepsiCo CEO Indra Nooyi was on the front lines in dealing with important issues. One of them was climate. Nooyi recalled that in 2006, she decided that PepsiCo had to change its entire business model to be more sustainable, which meant finding ways to minimize impact on the environment while being profitable. The result was her initiative Performance with Purpose, which put sustainability at the center of operations and values. "It wasn't easy, and I faced significant resistance," she wrote in an October 2020 column for *Fortune* titled, "Why I'm Optimistic About Business's Role in Solving Climate Change." But that resistance gradually fell away as the public demanded more of businesses in protecting the planet.

At first, she wrote, the pandemic might have seemed like a climate benefit—that "the human cost of the coronavirus is nature's gain" as people traveled and consumed less. In India, where Nooyi grew up, "we saw a large improvement in air quality, especially in urban areas, as industries, transportation, and tourism stalled. Remarkably, the Himalayas were visible from Punjab for the first time in 30 years."[11]

Nooyi pointed out, as others have, that the decline in carbon emissions during the pandemic had little impact on the health of the planet. But Nooyi did find hope from the engagement of the private sector:

> Businesses have a crucial role to play in changing consumer behavior: the push factor. If companies like PepsiCo change their model to use less water and more recyclable packaging, then by purchasing these products, consumers are helping to protect the environment.
>
> But businesses also need the pull factor to help incentivize that change. They need consumers to purposefully not buy things that damage the environment. Our goals at PepsiCo would have been far easier to achieve if our consumers had voted with their wallets and forced us to change. Consumers are exercising this pull factor more vocally than before, but they also have some way to go.
>
> Innovation must be at the heart of this change. It is not just about putting climate responsibility at the heart of business models; it's also about companies being braver, fostering new innovations, and championing new ideas.
>
> But the private sector cannot do this unilaterally. Businesses need to work with individuals and organizations across the board, harnessing the talents of a new generation of thinkers, leaders, and dreamers to help repair the Earth.
>
> The reason I'm an optimist is that never before has the world been so aware of a problem and businesses so aware that they are part of the solution. Consumers have found their voice, and businesses—from JPMorgan Chase to Microsoft to BlackRock—are acting. Board members have to embrace change if they are to keep their customers loyal. We're at a tipping point, and I'm hopeful that massive, global change is possible—as long as we keep pushing and pulling!

THE SUPPLY CHAIN CHALLENGE

In January 2020, the World Economic Forum sent a letter to CEOs around the world in the Net-Zero Challenge—to achieve net-zero gas emissions by 2050 or earlier. The appeal was formulated by the Alliance of CEO Climate

Leaders, a group of eighty-three CEOs who had organized in 2014 to support the Paris Agreement with bold corporate climate action. The Net-Zero Challenge sparked many initiatives, such as the Race to Zero campaign, which has engaged hundreds of companies and includes efforts to encourage governments to create incentives for companies to commit to net zero in reasonable time frames, institute carbon pricing mechanisms that make low-carbon options more cost effective, and make investments in green technology.

A year later, in January 2021, the World Economic Forum urged CEOs to do even more, beyond their own footprints into an expanded supply chain. Rich Lesser, then CEO of Boston Consulting Group and a cochair of the Alliance of CEO Climate Leaders, unveiled a study by BCG showing that eight supply chains account for more than 50 percent of global emissions, including construction, fashion, fast-moving consumer goods, electronics, automotive, professional services, and freight. BCG recommended nine initiatives every company can take to reduce those supply chain emissions:[12]

1. Build a comprehensive emissions baseline, gradually filled with actual supplier data;
2. Set ambitious and holistic reduction targets, reducing emissions;
3. Revisit product design choices;
4. Reconsider geographic sourcing strategies;
5. Set ambitious procurement standards;
6. Work jointly with suppliers to co-fund abatement levers;
7. Work together with peers to align sector targets that maximize impact and level the playing field;
8. Use scale by driving up demand to lower the cost of green solutions;
9. Develop internal governance mechanisms that introduce emissions as a steering mechanism and align the incentives of decision-makers with emission targets.

In its report, BCG addresses the issue of cost, which is usually cited as the stumbling block—especially the passed-along cost to consumers—and revealed the surprising data that decarbonization can be less expensive at the end of any supply chain.

As an example, consider the steel that goes into a midsize family car with a $35,000 sticker price. Producing steel is one of the most emissions-intensive activities in the supply chain. Producing zero-carbon steel can increase the steel makers' costs significantly—by as much as 50% in some cases. But since steel accounts for only roughly $1,000 of total car costs, the markup on this final product will be much, much lower. In fact, the same car made with exclusively zero-carbon materials would cost only about $600 more—or roughly a difference of 2%. Considering that getting there will take even the most ambitious companies many years, the immediate economics look much less scary.

"We're in business to save our home planet."

—Ryan Gellert, CEO, Patagonia

CLIMATE GAME CHANGERS

Salesforce CEO Marc Benioff wrote in *Trailblazer*, his book about core values as the bedrock of a resilient company, that he had always been connected to environmental issues. But he was struck anew by the obligation of businesses when he hosted a panel during the World Economic Forum in 2019. His panel included such luminaries as anthropologist Jane Goodall, musicians and philanthropists Bono and will.i.am, Secretary of the UN Framework Convention on Climate Change Christiana Figueres, and CEO of Sompo Holdings Kengo Sakurada.

In the audience was a sixteen-year-old Swedish activist named Greta Thunberg. "When I asked her to say a few words," Benioff wrote, "little did I know she would outshine everyone in this room full of star power the moment she shyly took the microphone from me."[13]

Thunberg proceeded to direct a scathing verdict on who was to blame for the climate crisis. "Some people, some companies, some decision-makers in particular have known exactly what priceless values they have been sacrificing to continue making unimaginable amounts of money, and I think many of you here today belong to that group of people," she charged.

Benioff recalled that a stunned silence fell over the room as Thunberg finished: "The future of humankind rests firmly in your hands."

It was a striking moment of clarity for Benioff. "This teenage climate activist had thrown down the gauntlet to some of the world's most powerful business leaders, and they weren't entirely sure how to react—not least because they knew deep down that she was right."

Benioff has backed up his commitment with action, and Salesforce has already achieved net-zero greenhouse gas emissions. Its headquarters, Salesforce Tower, which is the tallest building in San Francisco, has the largest onsite water recycling system in a US commercial high-rise. This is especially significant in drought-prone California, where water conservation is an environmental priority.

Other CEOs have taken steps for action on climate that go beyond mere gestures. In September 2020, in the midst of the pandemic, Walmart CEO Doug McMillon announced that Walmart was going to up its game beyond the sustainability measures it had been employing for more than fifteen years. Those measures had been triggered by Walmart's engagement in helping the recovery from Hurricane Katrina. The goal now, he said, was to become a *regenerative* company. "Regenerating means restoring, renewing and replenishing in addition to conserving," McMillon explained. "It means decarbonizing operations and eliminating waste along the product chain. It means encouraging the adoption of regenerative practices in agriculture, forest management and fisheries—while advancing prosperity and equity for customers, associates and people across our product supply chains. And, working with our suppliers, customers, NGOs and others, we hope to play a part in transforming the world's supply chains to be regenerative."[14] As part of that plan, Walmart targeted zero emissions in the company's global operations by 2040 and committed to helping to protect or restore fifty million acres of land and one million miles of ocean by 2030.

In January 2020, Starbucks CEO Kevin Johnson published "A Letter to Our Starbucks Partners, Customers and All Stakeholders," explaining the company's commitment to the environment. He began by detailing the substantial commitment to sustainability that has been at Starbucks's core since the outset.

"We know that leadership in sustainability takes commitment, invest-ment, innovation, partnership and, yes, time," Johnson wrote. "It took nearly two decades of dedicated effort in partnership with Conservation International to achieve the milestone of sourcing 99% of our coffee ethi-cally through C.A.F.E. (Coffee and Farmer Equity) practices. Our environ-mental footprint research shows that by implementing these standards, we have more than halved what our coffee's carbon footprint would have been otherwise."[15]

Johnson emphasized that transparency has been a big part of Starbucks's corporate culture, citing the annual Global Social Impact Report that the company has published since 2001. The report details both the positive achievements and the places the company has fallen short—not something you see very often. "For example, we established reusability and recycling goals in 2008 that were unprecedented for our industry but also largely dependent on radical changes in customer behavior. What we learned was that, absent the same rigorous analysis, partnerships and investments that made us leaders in sustainable coffee and green building, our results under-performed our high expectations and underscored the need for a different approach."

The current times, Johnson wrote, called for bigger commitments and greater action—moving the goal post to a resource-positive future and out-lining five strategies to take them there:

1. Expanding plant-based options and migrating toward a more environ-mentally friendly menu;
2. Shifting from single use to reusable packaging;
3. Investing in innovative and regenerative agricultural practices, refor-estation, forest conservation, and water replenishment in our supply chain;
4. Investing in better ways to manage our waste, both in our stores and in our communities, to ensure more reuse, recycling, and elimination of food waste;
5. Innovating to develop more eco-friendly stores, operations, manufac-turing, and delivery.

In a conversation for *Leadership Next*, Johnson talked about how it is the absolute obligation of the private sector to make this commitment. "In a lot of ways our political infrastructure is not serving society as well as it needs to, and that creates an opportunity for the private sector to step up," he told me. "I think, actually, businesses going forward are going to have to have a mission that goes far beyond the pursuit of profit, a mission that somehow contributes back to society in a way that creates a positive dynamic."[16]

SAVING THE PLANET . . . AND SHAREHOLDER VALUE

Nestlé CEO Mark Schneider considers corporate decisions about climate change one of the most difficult challenges a CEO faces. How does one balance the competing interests and invest in the future? He compares it to the way automobile executives must have felt in the 1970s and '80s when they decided to invest billions of dollars in smaller, more fuel-efficient cars, or how IBM executives must have felt in the early 1980s when it made a huge investment in smaller, less profitable computers, instead of doubling down on their profitable mainframe computer business. In a December 2020 column for *Fortune*, Schneider described the journey he and his company took to get serious about the issue.

Among other measures, Nestlé has committed to net-zero carbon emissions by 2050, reformulating products to have a smaller carbon footprint, including introducing more plant-based foods, and moving toward 100 percent renewable electricity. Its Project ReLeaf will plant three million trees in Malaysia by 2023.

"Personally, I was not exactly an early adopter when it comes to addressing climate change," he confessed. "In the early 2000s, when I had just become CEO of a global health care company, I was agnostic and wanted to see more proof that the massive investments required to address global warming were really needed. However, as more and more evidence has arrived, the need for action has become quite clear to me. Not all the facts are in today, but we know enough to act with a sense of urgency to address what is contributing to droughts and causing oceans to rise. Business leaders can no longer afford to be skeptical and interminably patient, waiting for every theory to be vetted or every climate model to be proven. . . . This is a moment of truth for industry leaders."[17]

Schneider dismissed the often-repeated criticism of corporate climate initiatives that they negatively impact shareholder value. "Every person on earth is a shareholder in what must be a collective and international effort, and we are all served when measures to address climate change advance," he wrote.

As a chief executive officer, I am held to account for our top- and bottom-line numbers, and I value real data and business returns over rosy projections. For Nestlé's work combating climate change, I will expect and demand the same. We submitted our company's targets to the Science-Based Targets Initiative, a collaboration of nonprofit organizations that is considered the international gold standard on assessing net-zero commitments. They confirmed that our plan meets the toughest criteria of the Paris Agreement. Our many stakeholders also deserve a full accounting, and we will provide annual updates. In the coming years, we will build upon our reporting so the world can judge our progress.

As a company that will continue to provide the nutrition needs of a growing population, we understand that we will need to reduce our environmental footprint, even as our business grows. That's why we support stable and consistent government policies that will guide all sectors toward the targets of the Paris Agreement. We would welcome clarity on carbon pricing and the requisite regulations so that our business can plan, with some degree of certainty, our path to progress.

A company like Nestlé has been able to thrive for more than 150 years by always looking around the corner and anticipating the world's needs. This foresight is a key ingredient of our success. To my fellow CEOs and leaders across other industries, I would respectfully suggest that contemplation is not a viable strategy to address climate change or a sensible way to run a business. Let's come together and commit to a shared future so that we will be able to look back at this moment in history not with regrets of how we failed, but with admiration for what we achieved.

THE YEAR OF CLIMATE CHANGE ACTION

As we got deeper into 2021, I began to see it clearly as the year that business got serious about climate change. And the reason was because climate change is becoming ever more important to business. A survey from IBM, which covered 14,000 people in nine countries, underscored this point. Among its findings:

> More than 70 percent of people said they were more likely to work for, or stay with, a company with a good record or reputation on the environment.
> 55 percent said they were "willing to pay more for brands that are sustainable and environmentally responsible."
> 48 percent of investors said their portfolio "already takes environmental sustainability into account," and another 21 percent said they would likely add sustainability as a factor for investment decisions in the future.

Those numbers are a big reason that 84 percent of CEOs said in a separate IBM survey that sustainability would be important to their strategy in 2022—up from just 32 percent who said the same in 2018. "COVID has substantively raised people's awareness of general global connectedness," Mark Foster, senior vice president of IBM Global Business Services, told me. "The line has been crossed. It has gone from an intellectual conversation about sustainability to more of a gut sense." And "people are looking at it as a business opportunity."[18]

I also spoke with Heineken CEO Dolf van den Brink. He recently announced ambitious plans to make the company's beer production carbon neutral by 2030, and to make its entire supply chain, distribution, and packaging carbon neutral by 2040. Achieving those goals "is going to be painful." But he says the commitment is not only good marketing, it also motivates employees. "You do all this external messaging, but the real energy is inside the company." Van den Brink believes the pandemic has led to "a kind of expanded consciousness of vulnerability. People realize how dependent they are on the environment."

By the way, the IBM study showed that the US continued to be an outlier when it came to public attitudes on climate, with only 51 percent saying climate change is very or extremely important to them, compared to 73 percent in the other eight countries surveyed.

EXXON'S MOMENT OF TRUTH

No event more clearly signals how business has changed in recent years than the activist attack on ExxonMobil in the spring of 2021. Exxon was the biggest, and most unrepentant, of the oil giants. It had size—vying with Walmart for the top listing on the Fortune 500 list for the first dozen years of the new millennium. Its influence around the world was so large that author Steve Coll titled his book on the company *Private Empire*. And it had Texas swagger. Under legendary CEO Lee Raymond, Exxon steadfastly refused to recognize growing scientific evidence that human activity was leading to a change in the climate, and funded research to prove the opposite.

Rex Tillerson replaced Raymond in 2006 and took a more nuanced position. "We recognize that climate change is a serious issue," he told the *New York Times* shortly after taking the job. But he was quick to add that there is "still significant uncertainty around all the factors that affect climate change."[19] One analyst summed it up: "It's the same old wine in a new bottle."[20]

I had my own run-in with Tillerson in June 2012, when the Council on Foreign Relations asked me to interview him as part of its CEO Speaker series. Shortly before the day of the interview, I learned Tillerson was insisting on giving a fifteen-minute speech before submitting to my questions—a break with the council's usual format. I sat quietly in one of two chairs on the stage while he stood at the podium and gave his "fifteen-minute speech" that consumed a half hour. He used the time, among other things, to launch a broadside against the press and its coverage of new drilling techniques that were unlocking huge stores of oil and gas, and transforming the US into the world's leading energy producer.

Understanding the new technologies "requires a lot of education, requires taking an illiterate public—illiterate in the sciences, engineering and mathematics—and trying to help them understand why we can manage these risks," Tillerson said. "And we are not particularly aided in our efforts by the broad-based media, because it's a lot sexier to write fear stories than to write here's-how-you-manage-it stories."[21]

When he finally sat down for the interview, I noted, only half-jokingly, that his criticism of the press had been pretty broad brush. Did he want to distinguish between reporters or news outlets? "There's probably a couple of camel hairs in the brush that this doesn't apply to," he responded. "But for whatever reason, a large number of people in the journalism profession are simply unwilling to do their work. They don't do their homework. . . . They are just lazy. It's as simple as that."

On the transition away from fossil fuels, Tillerson also gave little ground. Asked about electric vehicles, he responded, "The technology has simply not advanced sufficiently to make those vehicles attractive for most individuals. So large-scale deployment to passenger use, we think, is going to continue to be pretty slow." As for broader concerns about climate change, Tillerson said, "There are more pressing problems that we as a race and society need to deal with."

Tillerson stepped down from the top job at the end of 2016 to become President Donald Trump's secretary of state. In doing so, he also left his position as one of the top CEOs on the Business Roundtable. Later, in an interview with Insigniam's Nathan Rosenberg, Tillerson indicated he would have opposed the BRT's statement on stakeholder capitalism. "I don't think it's healthy for a group of CEOs to get together and just say we are all going to agree to behave this way—because everybody's business is different. Their organizations are different. When you start trying to covey up like a bunch of quail to protect yourself, I'm not sure you've got your eye on your shareholders' interests."[22]

As it turned out, Tillerson would be the last Exxon CEO who could freely thumb his nose at journalists, at climate science, or at the broader concerns of stakeholders and society at large. His successor, Darren Woods, was soon facing a very different set of forces. The pandemic caused oil usage to plummet, and Exxon's finances to follow. Revenues dropped $83 billion in 2020 from the year before, and Exxon's perch on the Fortune 500 list fell from number three to number ten. After two straight decades without a negative quarter, the company lost $22.4 billion for the year.

And while profits returned in the first quarter of 2021, Exxon's swagger did not. Its long-held view that oil and gas would remain central to the global economy for decades to come looked more tenuous in a world where Tesla had become the darling of investors, and most companies were rushing to adopt plans to ban all greenhouse gas emissions by 2050. A newly created investment firm called Engine No. 1 launched a proxy battle to force the oil giant to invest more in alternative energy, and to replace four of its board directors. In response, Woods announced a series of initiatives, including one to commercialize Exxon technology to reduce carbon emissions during the drilling process.

But the moves were too little too late. At the company's board meeting in May, Engine No. 1 successfully mustered the votes to replace three of Exxon's directors—a rare defeat, and a clear signal that Exxon's era of imperial arrogance was over.

The same week as Exxon's board loss, a Dutch court told another oil giant, Royal Dutch Shell, that it needed to cut its greenhouse gas emissions by a whopping 45 percent by 2030 in response to a lawsuit filed by several environmental groups. And at Chevron's annual meeting, 60 percent of shareholders voted for a resolution recommending that the company reduce its emissions not only from its own production processes, but also from the products it sells to consumers.

Together, the moves marked a tipping point. The world is still a long way from weaning itself from fossil fuels. But shareholders and stakeholders are uniting to send a message to Big Oil that it can no longer ignore the looming climate crisis.

When my colleague Katherine Dunn asked Darren Woods shortly before the board vote what his employees were asking about the future of the company, Woods responded as follows:

"The questions internally are very consistent with the external questions, which is, you know, given the demand and desire for less carbon intensive energy sources, how does that demand realize itself with time? And what's the impact on the company? And how do we think about managing through the transition? . . . Our job here is to meet the evolving demands of society. And that's just what we have historically done."[23]

In November of 2021, business showed up in surprising force for the COP26 climate conference in Glasgow. The event was a disappointment to many observers who were looking for significantly stepped-up commitments from governments to address climate change. But the sizable business presence—a dramatic change from the Paris climate conference in 2015—was notable. Financial institutions in particular pledged trillions of dollars to the effort to reach net zero. The business showing was one more sign, as Fortune's Dunn wrote, that CEOs no longer see sustainability goals as "nice to have," but rather as "must have"—acknowledging they will fundamentally change the way business is done in the future.

Business cannot solve the climate problem alone, any more than it can solve the training and reskilling challenge alone. And the explosion of business commitments to net zero over the last few years still leaves the world far short of solving the climate problem.

But big business's transition over the last two decades from a laggard in the climate debate, worried about policies that might stunt corporate growth, into a leader, moving far ahead of government policies, is yet another clear sign of the times. The world of business is changing.

CHAPTER 8

WHAT'S GOOD FOR THE COMMUNITY

STEVE CASE IS A WELL-KNOWN PIONEER FROM THE EARLY DAYS OF THE INternet. A cofounder of America Online, he played a major role in bringing the internet to much of the country. After leaving AOL, Case started the venture capital company Revolution, focused on entrepreneurs, which he believes are the engines of future prosperity and the key to the revival of communities across the nation.

In his 2016 book, *The Third Wave: An Entrepreneur's Vision of the Future*, named as an homage to the futurist Alvin Toffler's groundbreaking 1980 book with a similar name, Case wrote that the first wave was getting people online, the second wave was adding connection through search and social media functions, and "the Third Wave of the Internet is coming, the moment where the Internet transforms from something we interact with to something that interacts with everything around us. It will mean the rise of the Internet of Everything, where everything we do will be enabled by the Internet connection, much in the way it's already enabled by electricity."[1] In his view, that should mean an opportunity for everyone to have a seat at the table.

Case's most visible operation is Revolution's Rise of the Rest Seed Fund, which promotes investment in entrepreneurial endeavors outside the coasts. With California, New York, and Massachusetts reaping 75 percent of all venture capital dollars, the rest of the country is struggling to get a slice of the remaining 25 percent. Since 2014, Case's signature Rise of the Rest Bus Tours have traveled to cities from Detroit to Omaha to Salt Lake City to Dallas to Nashville, and all points in between, to drive investments in the rising startup cultures of those cities. As Case points out, talent in America is equally distributed, but opportunity is not. He aims to distribute opportunity across the nation. Case envisions a country map where growing tech ecosystems rise up in all regions, with investments being made to homegrown entrepreneurs.

Rise of the Rest has helped inspire and promote the creation of some vibrant startup cultures in places like Detroit, which is experiencing an entrepreneur-fueled revival, and Miami, a rising tech center. Rural areas and smaller cities are also included in Case's campaign, and Rise of the Rest has engineered excitement in places like Salt Lake City; Montgomery, Alabama; and Albuquerque, New Mexico, as well as in my hometown of Chattanooga, Tennessee. Often these communities are the casualties of manufacturing downturns or are struggling to find new opportunities to replace dying industries. New technologies are also revitalizing agricultural regions.

Case's focus on rejuvenating communities by investing in emerging businesses has been supported by a host of business leaders, including Jeff Bezos, Eric Schmidt, Howard Schultz, Meg Whitman, and the Walton family.

A big part of the discussion about revitalizing cities is the distinction between homegrown entrepreneurial ventures and existing megacompanies that open up headquarters in locations across the country. The model for the latter is America's car industry, which boosted the fortunes of regions outside Michigan with plant openings and extended supply chains. A modern example is Amazon.

When Amazon announced in 2017 that it was launching a competition for a second headquarters—dubbed Amazon HQ2—cities across America jumped into a competition that Case described as comparable to an Olympics bidding season.

After the selection of twenty finalists, Case wrote a piece for *Fortune*, titled "A Memo to the Cities Amazon Passed Over." He pointed out that even those who lost the bid gained a tremendous advantage through the process. That advantage was connection.

"One of the things that makes coastal tech hubs so attractive is network density. In Silicon Valley, you can't turn the corner without running into someone who can connect you with a customer, a coder, or a potential funder," he wrote. "That's not the case for most entrepreneurs in the heartland. One solution is to broaden the aperture. Many of the cities that bid for Amazon's attention joined forces with other municipalities to pitch a connected region."[2] Case also pointed to the unprecedented coalitions of government officials, startup community leaders, and corporate executives that came together and could now be harnessed for other initiatives.

Ultimately, Amazon punted on a choice in the middle of the country, picking Arlington, Virginia (a suburb of Washington, DC) and Long Island City in Queens, New York. After a bitter fight by local activists, the New York location was scrapped. This demonstrated vividly the tension between a community stakeholder and a corporation. Many New Yorkers thought Amazon's headquarters would jeopardize the community in certain ways, especially by raising housing costs and undermining community identity through gentrification. They also balked at the hefty price tag of nearly $3 billion in incentives New York was planning to give Amazon to come to the area.

But in Case's view, the advantage for all the cities involved in Amazon HQ2 was lasting. As cities begin to create their own tech commerce hubs around startups, there is the promise that the connections they make will give them a stronger position. After all, Silicon Valley was once a handful of tech companies. It achieved dominance through its interconnected culture. The advantages of homegrown tech hubs can be seen in the commitment to preserving and enhancing the natural attributes of communities, and in the involvement of stakeholders from city governments to universities, local businesses, and investors.

DEFINING THE COMMUNITY

Commitment to community has long been a core value of many great companies, as the Drucker Institute's Rick Wartzman details in his excellent book, *The End of Loyalty*.[3] Wartzman looks at how Kodak served Rochester and Coca-Cola supported Atlanta. But there are many other examples—DuPont in Wilmington, Delaware, or Cummins in Columbus, Indiana, for example. When companies were headquartered in the communities where most of their workers lived, the common bond between company and community was inescapably clear.

That began to change as globalization took hold in the last quarter of the twentieth century. Companies soon had factories and facilities all over the world—and far from where management was based. There was no single community that defined the company—there were hundreds, and many of them far away and out of sight.

So, when the Business Roundtable says companies commit to "supporting the communities in which we work," that raises more questions than it answers. What does the statement mean by "community"? The world's largest companies today have facilities in thousands of "communities" around the world. What responsibility do they have to each? Is "community" in today's globalized world no longer geography based?

Beth Ford, CEO of the $15 billion farmer-owned cooperative Land O'Lakes, has a clear view of the community she serves. Indeed, she often sounds more like an activist than the chief executive of a big agricultural business. She exemplifies the interconnected relationship between corporation and community. Ford is an outspoken champion of rural America, the heartbeat of her business, and she recognizes her company's obligation to those stakeholders. When we spoke, she conveyed a combination of indignation and determination about the plight of rural America. "The reality is, 95 to 96 percent of farms are still family owned," she explained. "They may incorporate as a business structure, but these are still family owned. So, they have to worry about [their children's] education. They lack technology; a third of the schools in rural America lack broadband. Most of these families take their kids to a parking lot an hour away that has the best WiFi so they can finish work on their phone. This is simply unacceptable. It leaves us so uncompetitive. It's unbelievable. They have no health care, because hundreds of hospitals in rural America have shut down."[4]

For Ford, frustration has turned to a hardened commitment to make things better. The way she sees it, the company is owned by farmers, and owned by local retailers. She's in their communities all the time. She knows their families. "I always say to my board, this isn't about tech. This is about being the conveners. It is awareness, advocacy, action." She pointed out that most food insecurity in America is in rural communities. Why is that Ford's issue? Because although she's there to run a business, she believes that being a voice for change is part of her job.

"We should all be concerned about this and this isn't somebody else's problem," she said. "This is all of our problem. It's not just a rural issue. We need to understand that. It's an American competitiveness issue."

LAST TO CLOSE, FIRST TO OPEN

Vivek Sankaran had been CEO of Albertsons Companies for only ten months when the pandemic hit. Overnight, he had to take the grocery behemoth, with stores located in thirty-four states and the District of Columbia, and prepare to serve the public while other companies were sending their workers home.

"You ran a grocery store," I said when Ellen and I sat down with him for *Leadership Next*. "Nobody went home."[5] I wouldn't have thought running a grocery store would put a company on the front lines, but that was the reality during COVID.

The company had to reinvent the way it did things, Sankaran told us. "We found a sense of purpose. We had to be there to feed at least the communities where we operate." To do that, "we focused first on the safety of our people. I obsessed about it even before the CDC came out with the recommendations." He noted that it took almost six weeks before the government issued any safety guidelines. "What we found is when people felt safe operating and working in our stores, they made our customers feel safe," he said.

By the time we spoke in the summer of 2021, a semblance of normalcy had been restored, but Sankaran found himself thinking about the spirit of the company. "I wish we could continue to bottle that [spirit] and keep it," he said. "We moved with some speed, some degree of abandon to do things quickly at that time. . . . There was this odd combination of incredible compassion and empathy on one end and competitive fire on the other end, because that's what we do."

Most of all, Sankaran felt the company had expressed its commitment to the community, especially in times of crisis or when a weather disaster like a hurricane strikes—being the last to close and the first to open in those circumstances.

"We operate in communities," Sankaran emphasized. "We occupy space in the community. We employ from within the community. And we serve the community. In the toughest of times, we want to be stewards of those communities."

MAKING IT

Few things say community like the nuts and bolts of building and maintaining homes. When I spoke with Lowe's CEO Marvin Ellison in the midst of the pandemic, his company was all in on building and rebuilding the community. Ellison is one of just five Black CEOs to lead a Fortune 500 company, and he reported that the company was thriving in tough times. He believes that small businesses are the cornerstone of the American economy, and he's there to help.

During the pandemic, Ellison decided to do everything possible to help small businesses, launching a $55 million small business grant program, specifically for minority-owned and rural businesses.

Ellison credits his roots as "someone who grew up in a small town in the South with a large family that had a lot of love and not a lot of financial support, because the thing that my parents taught me was the power of an opportunity, and the power of taking advantage of an opportunity. And so, of course, we're not looking at this from a big financial return on investment, we're looking at it as a chance to take a small business that's minority owned and give these individuals an opportunity to take products that they probably nurtured and developed over the years, and have a chance to put them literally on the shelf, or virtually on the shelf of a major Fortune 50 company. And so, this is all about reaching back, doing our part to try to play a role in helping the small business community."[6]

The program is called Making It with Lowe's, and the company uses a process patterned after the popular television competition show *Shark Tank*, where people pitch their products to a panel of judges. Inevitably, Ellison's version caught the eye of the real Shark Tank, with Daymond John, one of the show's stars, joining Ellison as a judge. Ellison is excited about the tie-in, and thinks it will present a unique opportunity for small business owners to be coached by a *Shark Tank* star and successful entrepreneur who has been such a champion for emerging businesses.

Ellison plans to narrow the pool of applications down to roughly 375 businesses, and then work that list down to a smaller group of business owners that Daymond will help coach. Ellison acknowledged that it might sound disingenuous, but it was true that the program wasn't so much about generating revenues for Lowe's as trying to find a way to give some of these businesses a chance to get their products into Lowe's stores.

One of the main things Ellison has seen coming out of the pandemic is a redefinition of home. "We've all understood the value of home ownership," he said, "but in today's environment your home is now being redesigned as a home office. It's being redesigned as a homeschooling location. It's being redesigned as a place where you spend most of your time for entertainment and for recreation. And so, those do-it-yourself customers are coming to Lowe's, allowing us to help them define and redefine those three unique categories of the home. Twelve months ago, very few people were thinking about their home as a home office, homeschool, and place for recreation and relaxation." The business of home is being redefined by the cultural shift that happened with the pandemic, and for Ellison that presents an opportunity to help communities rebuild.

INNOVATING BEYOND BRICK AND MORTAR

One of the largest retail trends to flow from the pandemic has been a growing comfort level with online shopping. What had been a convenience became a necessity as brick-and-mortar stores closed or limited their on-site merchandise. But the online marketplace needed curating that enhanced the opportunity of small producers, and that was the genius of Etsy, which created a global marketplace that connects millions of local sellers with a universe of buyers.

Started in 2005, the fledgling company had its share of ups and downs in the early years and struggled after it went public in 2015. Then came the pandemic. In 2020, Etsy more than doubled its business to $10 billion in gross merchandise. As CEO Josh Silverman described it, "This was a time when opportunity met preparedness. This was sort of our Dunkirk moment."[7]

Silverman explained the dynamic and the opportunity to Ellen McGirt—who is a committed Etsy customer—and to me on *Leadership Next*. "We had a time when Americans desperately needed all kinds of things and the supply chains of the big mass retailers couldn't keep up. And so, cottage industry came to the rescue through Etsy, and as a result, 4.4 million sellers actually had a pretty decent year on Etsy last year. Two-thirds of our sellers said they made as much or more in 2020 in sales as they've made in prior years. And for a lot of our sellers whose offline income was really hard hit, Etsy provided a meaningful lifeline."

On the other side of the equation, millions of buyers responded to the convenience as well as the originality of the product line. Silverman suggested that Etsy taps into a weariness with commoditized goods and cookie-cutter purchases. "I think they discovered that you can keep commerce human, you can support another seller," he said. "You can have something that's made just for you that comes with a handwritten note and it's just a better way to shop. So, it was definitely a transformational year for Etsy, and we feel really great about that."

The first sign that Etsy was becoming a go-to shopping destination came during the early quest for masks. "Masks was basically not a thing until April 2 of 2020," Silverman recalled. "If someone was searching for a mask, they were looking for a Halloween mask or face cream. All of a sudden on April 2 this new thing was invented called a fabric face mask. Within two or three days we had over ten thousand sellers making and selling masks on Etsy. And between April 2 and the end of the year, there was about $740 million of masks sold on Etsy. And that provided a lot of income for our sellers. It allowed buyers to get a mask that expressed their sense of taste and style, and it kept PPE, proper medical equipment, reserved for the people who need it most—first responders and hospital staff and others. And again, that's the kind of thing that wouldn't have been possible before."

That was a compelling pitch, but I was curious about what was under the hood. "We all know that e-commerce boomed during the pandemic, but this is well beyond what most e-commerce outlets did," I said. "And I just want to dig a little deeper in what was driving that. What was it in the pandemic that made people want to go to Etsy? I mean, was it the desire for authenticity? 'I don't want to do Amazon. I want to do Etsy.' What's the emotional impulse that drives people?"

Silverman responded that on top of the list was Etsy's agility in the marketplace—"as fast as someone needs something, or someone can imagine something to be made, it appears on Etsy." He gave an example: "In May [2020], the world woke up and decided it wanted to make bread. I don't know why, everyone decided they wanted to be bread makers. And within hours you had thousands of sellers selling yeast-making mixes and bread-making mixes on Etsy." He described a baker in Florida who had a wonderful bakery that he'd been running successfully for many years, but it had shut down because of the pandemic. The baker Googled where he could sell things online, and he found Etsy. "He had a successful bakery in Florida serving people within two blocks of his bakery, who happened to walk in. All of a sudden, he starts a thriving business on Etsy that becomes very successful, but he's selling to people who have real passion for bread making. And they're trading recipes and they want to know about the yeast culture he's worked on for years and years. And it's about a community. And suddenly, he's finding a community of people that share his passion, and not only as a successful business but it's a successful relationship for buyers and for sellers."

One unique aspect of Etsy is the profit arrangement of the platform. As Silverman put it, "There's no commoditization of work or labor. Someone wakes up in the morning and has a passion to make something. They're a crafts person, or an artist. And they have many places to choose where they can sell. Etsy is one of them. And they decide what they want to make, they decide how they want to make it. They decide how they want to price it. They decide how they want to promote it and photograph it and brand it and they build the relationships with their customers. We're a marketplace, we're a platform for them to do that. And we're really proud of the fact that they hire us. We don't hire them. They hire us to help market their products.

And we do the best we can to create a community that lifts all of them up and helps them to compete on a more level playing field against the Amazons of the world." To do that, Etsy keeps fees low and provides plenty of optional services for sellers to market their products.

For a long time, "community" has been the poor stepchild of business interests—not exactly a stakeholder but an intermittent consideration. Think of the way companies signed on to United Way, for example. In the new stakeholder model, communities take a seat at the table of stakeholders, with the understanding that when communities thrive, all the other stakeholders do better too.

PART THREE

THE SOUL OF A CORPORATION

CHAPTER 9

THE ACTIVIST CEO

When Georgia Governor Brian Kemp signed new legislation on voting regulations in March 2021, there was an immediate public outcry, mostly from Democrats accusing the Republican majority of voter suppression. Within weeks, the outcry had become mainstream.

After a record turnout in 2020, followed by President Trump's naked attempt to overthrow the election despite no evidence of widespread voter fraud, this aggressive anti-fraud legislation was seen by many as an attempt at voter suppression, especially in Black communities. The new restrictions reduced early voting hours in those communities, restricted access to absentee balloting relative to the relaxed pandemic rules of 2020, and, in a highly publicized regulation, made it illegal to give water and food to people standing in line to vote. President Biden and others referred to it, and similar legislation being considered in several states, as a new era of Jim Crow—hyperbole, to be sure, but indicative of the strong emotions created by the law.

While recent trends had been to make voting easier, these new provisions did the opposite, creating impediments for voters in dense urban counties—home to many minority voters who generally voted Democratic—to vote.

And it put increased control over elections in the hands of party leaders, raising the possibility that a future president who tried to overturn election results, as Trump did, might have more success. The effort was immediately suspect as it occurred mere months after Georgia was the centerpiece of ultimately unsuccessful efforts by the Trump presidential campaign to overturn Joe Biden's win in the state. Recounts and audits unearthed no voter fraud, and court challenges failed to do the same. With that backdrop, the rush to pass new voting restrictions seemed political and was particularly unsavory given Georgia's history of Black voter suppression.

Two prominent Black executives, former American Express CEO Kenneth Chenault and Merck CEO Ken Frazier, acted quickly when the law was signed, leading a group of seventy-two Black executives in challenging the legislation. Virtually every Black executive of note signed a letter that was published as a full-page ad in the *New York Times*. In part it read, "As Black business leaders, we cannot sit silently in the face of this gathering threat to our nation's democratic values and allow the fundamental right of Americans, to cast their votes for whomever they choose, to be trampled upon yet again. We call upon our colleagues in Corporate America to join us in taking a non-partisan stand for equality and democracy. Each of us stands ready to work with you on what can and must be done."[1]

Soon, activists turned their sights on Georgia-based companies, demanding that they take a stand. At first Delta CEO Ed Bastian declined to publicly criticize the legislation, trying to get along in the Republican-dominated state. But within days he made a complete turnaround after he'd had time to study the law and listen to the blowback, which included boycott threats against the airline. In a letter to employees titled "Your Right to Vote" he pulled no punches. "I need to make it crystal clear that the final bill is unacceptable and does not match Delta's values," he wrote. "The entire rationale for this bill was based on a lie: that there was widespread voter fraud in Georgia in the 2020 elections." "I know it is not comfortable to be caught in a highly emotional debate. We are at our best when we bring our customers and our world closer together."[2]

The Georgia state house immediately responded to Bastian's statement by trying to pass a law removing the airline's state tax breaks, an effort that failed in the senate. It was political hardball. But it wasn't the first time

Georgia sought payback against the activist CEO. In 2018, when Delta ended a discount program for Georgia-based National Rifle Association (NRA) members, the legislature made the same effort to punish the airline.

Meanwhile, another Atlanta-based corporation, Coca-Cola, also entered the fray. CEO James Quincey told CNBC that the legislation was "a step backward" and said, "It makes it harder to vote, not easier." He issued a strong public statement:

> We want to be crystal clear and state unambiguously that we are disappointed in the outcome of the Georgia voting legislation. Throughout Georgia's legislative session we provided feedback to members of both legislative chambers and political parties, opposing measures in the bills that would diminish or deter access to voting. Our approach has always been to work with stakeholders to advocate for positive change, and we will continue to engage with legislators, advocacy groups, business leaders and others to work towards ensuring broad access to voting is available to every eligible voter in our home state. . . . Our focus is now on supporting federal legislation that protects voting access and addresses voter suppression across the country. We all have a duty to protect everyone's right to vote, and we will continue to stand up for what is right in Georgia and across the U.S.[3]

Leaders of companies outside of Georgia were speaking out as well. *Fortune* reported on a large wave of tech companies openly criticizing Georgia's voter legislation. Salesforce, Apple, Google, Microsoft, Facebook, Cisco, and IBM all issued statements condemning the laws. Their messages emphasized tech's role in making voting more understandable and accessible, a mission that ran counter to the new law.

Perhaps the most dramatic response came from Major League Baseball, with an announcement that the 2021 All-Star Game would be moved from the designated host city of Atlanta to Denver. The move won wide support but also sparked outrage among those who felt that the city and its major league team, the Atlanta Braves, were being unfairly penalized for decisions beyond their control. Of course, that's the nature of boycotts; there are unintended victims.

The Business Roundtable also weighed in with a statement:

The right to vote is the essence of a democratic society, and the voice of every voter should be heard in fair elections that are conducted with integrity. Unnecessary restrictions on the right to vote strike at the heart of representative government. Business Roundtable members believe state laws must safeguard and guarantee the right to vote.

Over the course of our nation's history, the right to vote was hard fought for so many Americans, particularly women and people of color. We call on elected officials across the country to commit to bipartisan efforts to provide greater access to voting and encourage broad voter participation.[4]

Georgia was not the only state with legislation to restrict voting. As Texas introduced a controversial package of voter restrictions, pressure increased on state-based companies such as American Airlines and Dell Technologies to take a stand. Again, there was aggressive pushback from Republican leaders. Governor Greg Abbott, who supported the legislation, refused to throw out the first pitch on the Texas Rangers' opening day, as a protest against Major League Baseball moving the All-Star Game out of Atlanta.

The most prevalent argument against CEOs speaking out was that they were stepping outside their lanes. Senate minority leader Mitch McConnell said they were behaving like a "woke parallel government" and said, "My warning to corporate America is to stay out of politics." He added, "I'm not talking about political contributions."[5]

Through political donations and lobbying, corporations have been deeply involved in politics for a long time, and it is disingenuous to suggest otherwise. Critics of the CEOs seemed to be saying that although money is the equivalent of free speech and should be welcomed, actual speech should be curtailed. Or, to put it another way, *we'll take your money, but keep your opinions to yourself.*

OUT IN THE OPEN

As a journalist, over the years I was often in the position of trying to convince CEOs to speak out on controversial social or political issues. And their answer, invariably, was no. If it wasn't something that directly affected their finances, they were inclined to keep their heads down and stay out of the line of fire. That began to change in 2014, when the state of Indiana passed a "religious liberties" law that was viewed as restricting the rights of gay people.

Salesforce CEO Marc Benioff was one of the very first to speak out. After then governor Mike Pence signed the bill into law, Benioff threatened to dramatically reduce his company's investment in the state and cancel all Salesforce programs that would involve travel to Indiana. Benioff inspired others to take a stand as well, forcing Pence to revise the law to forbid businesses from denying service because of sexual orientation. Benioff was applauded as an activist CEO, and a new term came into the business lexicon.

As he recalled in *Trailblazer*, at first Benioff wasn't happy with the label of activist CEO. "But over the next year, the term grew on me. Or more accurately, I grew into it. . . . Over time I've become convinced that there are two types of CEOs: those who believe that improving the state of the world is part of their mission, and those who don't feel they have any responsibility other than delivering results for their shareholders." This new point of view, he acknowledged, was part of the thought process that led to his support of stakeholder capitalism—reaching well beyond a narrow definition of fiduciary duty to consider the community at large. "With all due respect," Benioff wrote, "Milton Friedman was wrong. He was wrong then and he's doubly wrong in the context of today. The business of business isn't just about creating profits for shareholders."[6]

Then in 2016, the state of North Carolina passed a law prohibiting people from using public bathrooms of a gender that is different than the one on their birth certificate. The law was aimed at transgender people. The outrage was swift. PayPal CEO Dan Schulman, for instance, announced the cancellation of a new global operations center in Charlotte because of the bill.

But the criticism didn't just come from West Coast tech companies. Bank of America, the largest company based in North Carolina, and its CEO Brian Moynihan, took a strong stand, even though they faced the possibility of retaliation from the state legislature. Others got involved as well. The Associated Press estimated that the bathroom bill would cost North Carolina more than $3.76 billion in lost business in a twelve-year period.

When Moynihan later joined Ellen McGirt and me on our *Leadership Next* podcast, I remarked that speaking out on such a controversial political and social issue was something CEOs never did a decade earlier. Why had he done it? His response:

"It comes down to, we believe in diversity and inclusion in our company. We believe it's the way to get the best people who can be themselves at work. At the time that bill came out, we got emails from our teammates saying, 'I won't come to Charlotte for a meeting.' And we happened to have our global diversity and inclusion group's award ceremony in Charlotte that year, and they wouldn't come because they said, 'Wait a second, this environment is not the environment to be coming to.' . . . So we had to take a stand, not only because it was the right thing to do, but because it affected our teammates."[7]

On April 12, 2017, a "Unite the Right" rally in Charlottesville, Virginia, brought out a huge crowd of neo-Nazis and right-wing agitators, whose chants shocked onlookers. A crowd of counter-protesters gathered peacefully, but the event became deadly when a man plowed his car into their midst, killing a young woman. President Donald Trump, who had been in office less than three months, refused to condemn the violence or the messaging of the right-wing rally goers, blaming both sides for the violence, and also saying that there were "very fine people on both sides."

I listened to the president's speech that day and was shocked by what I heard. Any of Trump's predecessors would have made clear there was no place for such violent, racist hate groups in American society. (Indeed, his living predecessors *did* make such statements.) The president's ambivalent response became a huge red flag for many people, signaling that overt racism and anti-Semitism were acceptable behaviors.

BRT chairman Jamie Dimon and president Josh Bolten immediately issued a strong statement on behalf of their members: "America's business leaders are shocked at the violence that took place in Charlottesville, and we mourn the unnecessary loss of life. Racism has no place in our businesses, our communities, or our country. The CEOs of Business Roundtable will never accept such intolerance and hate," they added. "We will continue to build our companies around the principles of respect, trust and equal opportunity to all our employees. The business community will build on our strong record of leadership to stand against racism to promote equality and acceptance."[8]

But the most electrifying response came from Merck's Ken Frazier, who resigned from the president's Manufacturing Council and Strategy and

Policy Forum, tweeting, "America's leaders must honor our fundamental values by clearly rejecting expressions of hatred, bigotry and group supremacy." Frazier set in motion a mass exodus from the president's councils, including 3M CEO Inge Thulin, Intel CEO Brian Krzanich, Under Armour CEO Kevin Plank, Alliance for American Manufacturing president Scott Paul, Campbell Soup CEO Denise Morrison, and AFL-CIO president Richard Trumka. The White House was forced to disband the councils.

Among the statements by the resigning CEOs, two stood out for me. I had noticed that sometimes these statements can end up sounding generic, drummed up by public relations executives and skirting the true offense, which, granted, is hard to talk about. These two CEOs hit the issue square-on.

Campbell Soup's Denise Morrison's statement was, as she put it, unambiguous: "Racism and murder are unequivocally reprehensible and are not morally equivalent to anything else that happened in Charlottesville. I believe the President should have been—and still needs to be—unambiguous on that point. Following yesterday's remarks from the President, I cannot remain on the Manufacturing Jobs Initiative. I will continue to support all efforts to spur economic growth and advocate for the values that have always made America great."[9]

Intel CEO Brian Krzanich was equally strong: "Earlier today, I tendered my resignation from the American Manufacturing Council. I resigned to call attention to the serious harm our divided political climate is causing to critical issues, including the serious need to address the decline of American manufacturing. . . . I have already made clear my abhorrence at the recent hate-spawned violence in Charlottesville, and earlier today I called on all leaders to condemn the white supremacists and their ilk who marched and committed violence. I resigned because I want to make progress, while many in Washington seem more concerned with attacking anyone who disagrees with them. We should honor—not attack—those who have stood up for equality and other cherished American values. I hope this will change, and I remain willing to serve when it does."[10]

I had spent most of my journalistic career in Washington, DC, and I had never seen anything quite like this. Merck, keep in mind, is in a regulated industry—pharmaceuticals. The federal government can have an enormous impact on its business. For that reason, CEOs of Merck and other Fortune 500 companies had generally worked hard and spent millions of dollars to establish close ties with government leaders. And they were quick to accept advisory roles as an opportunity to influence policy. To withdraw from those advisory positions was a big deal. Their critics pointed out that the council had no involvement in the events in Charlottesville. But the leaders saw their withdrawal as a highly public statement of values. They would not be associated with an administration that wouldn't condemn racist violence when it clearly presented itself.

Then, on February 14, 2018, a gunman opened fire with a semiautomatic rifle at Marjory Stoneman Douglas High School in Parkland, Florida, killing seventeen and injuring fourteen. It was yet another devastating school shooting, the kind of incident that initially seemed to create a wakeup call for Americans on the gun control issue. The message was carried most dramatically by a group of kids from the high school whose social media activism went viral.

Another viral public voice belonged to Ed Stack, CEO of Dick's Sporting Goods. After learning that the shooter had purchased his gun at a Dick's store, Stack, who is the son of the founder, became the public face of gun control, announcing that Dick's would no longer sell assault weapons, and promising other measures to limit gun sales. His announcement struck directly at the heart of the gun debate:

> We at Dick's Sporting Goods are deeply disturbed and saddened by the tragic events in Parkland. Our thoughts and prayers are with all of the victims and their loved ones.
>
> But thoughts and prayers are not enough. . . . We believe it's time to do something about it. Beginning today, Dick's Sporting Goods is committed to the following:
>
> We will no longer sell assault-style rifles, also referred to as modern sporting rifles. We had already removed them from all Dick's stores after the Sandy Hook massacre, but we will now remove them from sale at all 35 Field & Stream stores.
>
> We will no longer sell firearms to anyone under 21 years of age.
>
> We will no longer sell high capacity magazines.

We never have and never will sell bump stocks that allow semi-automatic weapons to fire more rapidly.

At the same time, we implore our elected officials to enact common sense gun reform and pass the following regulations:

Ban assault-style firearms.

Raise the minimum age to purchase firearms to 21.

Ban high capacity magazines and bump stocks.

Require universal background checks that include relevant mental health information and previous interactions with the law.

Ensure a complete universal database of those banned from buying firearms.

Close the private sale and gun show loophole that waives the necessity of background checks.[11]

In spite of extremely heavy backfire from the NRA, customers, and pro-gun legislators, Stack held his ground, losing an estimated $250 million in sales. In the coming years he became a vocal activist in Washington, promoting gun control measures. (Stack stepped down as CEO in 2021, after thirty-seven years building the company his father started with two stores. His replacement, Lauren Hobart, is a woman who served as president for three years and was responsible for carrying out the gun policies and keeping Dick's profitable.)

After the mass shooting in Parkland, a number of companies, including Delta and United Airlines, canceled discounts that were in place for NRA members. Ed Bastian took a lot of heat locally for that decision as well, but he refused to back down.

THE DELTA AIR LINES CODE

As noted earlier, I grew up in Chattanooga, Tennessee, and when I turned thirteen, I got my first shotgun. It was a rite of passage; in Tennessee, gun ownership was considered part of a moral upbringing. The same culture existed in Georgia to the South. After Delta Air Lines canceled the NRA discount, I asked Ed Bastian, during a meeting of the CEO Initiative, about that cultural connection. "You're in a city and in a state where the people see the NRA as having protected that right for years and years and years. And yet you made the decision to end your relationship with the organization. Why did you do that?"

"Well, it ran counter to our values," he replied. "At Delta, our values are everything. It's the culture of the company, it allows us to be who we are. We've got 85,000 employees around the world that want to know what we stand for."

He decided to act in the wake of the divisive rhetoric he saw from the NRA after the shootings. Until then, he'd given little thought to the relatively modest discount program the airlines had with the NRA, "but any implied endorsement that anyone can ever attach Delta to the NRA, we couldn't be part of it at that point. We had to stand and take notice. We were not the only ones. A number of other companies did the same thing."[12]

To my surprise, Bastian said he didn't discuss the decision with his board of directors before he made it. But he said there wasn't much blowback from the board. For those who questioned the decision, he made it clear that "the decision to make it, to me, was crystal clear."

I observed that he was holding the organization to a higher standard than it had been held in the past, and there were repercussions. The state legislature at the time was considering legislation that would have reduced Delta's tax burden, to the tune of $40 million a year. Bastian said that as soon as Delta made the decision to end the NRA discount, "the NRA members of the state legislature were up in arms, which is most of the state legislature. And they said that publicly, if we did not drop our opposition to the NRA and reinstate that modest discount program, that they were going to eliminate the tax benefit we were ready to receive. And we said, 'Well, that's the decision you take. You take that decision, but we were not going to be moved by it.'"

That meant Delta lost $40 million a year. I wondered how Bastian justified that to his investors.

Bastian was very clear about his response. "From an investor's standpoint, the most important asset we've got on our balance sheet is our culture and our values. And I think that's a modest investment in the culture of the business."

Even so, Bastian couldn't escape the complexity of choosing where to stake a position. There are so many issues, and with social media it can seem like a new one goes viral every week. I asked Bastian, "How do you make the decision about which ones you speak out on and which ones you keep your head down and stay away from?"

Bastian hastened to qualify his role. "I think that's really important because the last thing that I want to be seen as a CEO, is a social activist; that's not my job. My job is to run the best airline in the business and to continue to keep all of our constituencies united in that mission. So you have to be very careful as to where you are going to pick to engage, and where we've picked to engage are those aspects where it runs directly counter to what we call our Rules of the Road," Delta's founding values.

He went on to tell me a fascinating story of the company's founder, C. E. Woolman. A few years earlier Woolman's original desk had been brought out of storage, and it's the desk Bastian uses. While rummaging through the desk, they found some of Woolman's writings in one of the drawers. "We updated it for today's times, but we have this whole document we call our Rules of the Road that we distributed to all of our employees worldwide," Bastian said. "And we require them to read it and understand how we approach each other and how we approach our business. And when you understand what you stand for and who you are in the context of the world at large, I think it helps make that decision clear. So, they're not viewed as one-off issues, they're viewed as, 'Is this something that's going to be offensive to the culture, to the people, to what we stand our business purpose?'"

"So clearly, as you just said, some of the sense of values dates back to the very founding of the company, but some of it is different and new," I said. "What do you think is driving the new piece? Why is this happening now?"

"Well, that's an interesting question and one I've asked myself a lot because you feel it. I feel the pace of change is moving faster than ever before. I think change promotes a lot of angst and anxiety." He sees this around the world, noting that "the populist movement is strong and robust. Whether it's here in our country, or the election of a populist in Mexico, or what's going on with Brexit, Spain, Italy, and many other parts of the globe. There's a lot of fear and angst, all of which causes people to move away."

Which brings him to Delta's core purpose. "Our purpose in the world is to connect. We feel we've got a mission. It's an honorable mission to connect the world, to make the world a smaller place. And we'd like to think that we do it better than anyone. Well, different businesses connect people in different sorts of ways. We do it physically and we do it emotionally, we do it personally. We're a lifestyle brand that we carry each year to two hundred million people around the world. And so, when you have that responsibility, and an issue that runs counter to where you stand arises, that's what activates that decision."

THE CHAUVIN MOMENT

I wrote about how the killing of George Floyd in an encounter with Minneapolis police electrified the nation at the height of the COVID pandemic and solidified the BLM movement as a significant cultural advancement. Nearly a year later, the trial of police officer Derek Chauvin, who had knelt on Floyd's neck until he stopped breathing, again held the nation spellbound, especially in viewing the devastating video record of Floyd's last minutes. On April 20, 2021, after a three-week trial, Chauvin was found guilty on all three counts—second-degree murder, third-degree murder, and second-degree manslaughter.

Once again there was an expectation that American businesses would speak publicly about the verdict, especially since so many had spoken and acted when George Floyd was killed. But the demand had intensified. As *Fortune* reporter Geoff Colvin wrote, "Companies now face a dilemma that they didn't face then. Over the past few years, employees and the public have come to expect companies to take positions on large issues of public interest. The latest research from the Edelman communication firm finds that 86% of respondents across 27 countries expect CEOs to speak out on at least some societal issues."[13]

On the other hand, Colvin noted, there were significant complications for businesses speaking out, such as the traditional reluctance of CEOs to weigh in on jury verdicts, and the probability that there would be an appeal. But the CEOs who did speak out placed the focus not on Chauvin but on the future of racial justice.

Facebook CEO Mark Zuckerberg tweeted, "Right now I'm thinking of George Floyd, his family and those who knew him. I hope this verdict brings some measure of comfort to them, and to everyone who can't help but see themselves in his story. We stand in solidarity with you, knowing that this is part of a bigger struggle against racism and injustice."[14]

General Motors' Mary Barra weighed in: "While the guilty verdicts in the trial seeking justice for George Floyd are a step in the fight against bias and injustice, we must remain determined to drive meaningful, deliberate change on a broad scale."[15]

From Microsoft president Brad Smith: "Today's verdict is a step forward in acknowledging painful truths and for the continued cause of defeating racism and fighting discrimination. Our company remains committed to the continued path ahead."[16]

Salesforce tweeted, "Today's verdict was a defining & important moment. We recognize this does not make up for so much loss and injustice experienced by the Black community. George Floyd should be alive today. The work continues. We will keep taking action for racial equality and a more just world."[17]

And from Starbucks: "George Floyd should be alive today. We still have work to do to address systemic racism and ensure everyone has an equal chance to succeed and thrive. Black lives matter, and we stand with our Black customers and partners."[18]

Industry groups also talked about the verdict in the context of what remained to be done. Rick Wade, senior vice president at the US Chamber of Commerce, said, "There has been much attention paid to the trial and today marks a step towards healing. As a nation, we need to remain steadfast in our pursuit of equality of opportunity for Black Americans and other people of color."[19]

The Business Roundtable delivered an equally strong statement: "Though today's verdict is a step toward justice in this case, unarmed Black men and women continue to die in encounters with the police. To ensure true justice and healing, our country needs to take steps to address its long history of racial inequity in law enforcement."[20]

The outpouring of CEO commentary marked a dramatic change from when Marc Benioff first made his unusual public statement back in 2014. The practice of CEOs speaking out on controversial social and political issues had gone from a rarity to a requirement in just seven years. Leaders now felt that their employees expected it of them and interpreted silence as a lack of concern. The genie was indeed out of the bottle, and wary employees were standing guard to make sure it didn't go back in.

> "Visionary CEOs, individually, are the engines of massive change. This is unprecedented in the history of information technology—possibly unprecedented in the history of commerce. Today CEO-mandated digital transformation drives the company's roadmap and goals."
>
> Thomas Siebel, *Digital Transformation: Survive and Thrive in an Era of Mass Extinction*

ARE CEOS ACCOUNTABLE?

Critics of CEO involvement in "social" issues often argue that CEOs should stay out of such matters because they aren't "accountable." Unlike politicians, they weren't elected to office and can't be removed if citizens disagree with their actions.

However, CEOs *are* accountable—to their boards. And as CEOs redefine their role in society, boards need to be intimately involved. In his critique of the Business Roundtable's 2019 statement on stakeholder capitalism, Harvard Law professor Lucian Bebchuk said he asked the public relations offices of BRT companies whether their CEOs had consulted with their boards before signing the statement. Forty-seven of the forty-eight that responded said no. Bebchuk took that as a sign of the lack of seriousness of the BRT change. But it also raises a question about whether boards are doing their jobs.

Dambisa Moyo, a former Goldman Sachs economist, explored the issue in her 2021 book, *How Boards Work: And How They Can Work Better in a Chaotic World*. She has a decade of experience in the space, currently serving on the boards of Chevron and 3M, and previously doing stints with SABMiller and Barclays. "We have a lot of anti-capitalism, anti-corporation sentiment out there," she told me. "The reason I wrote the book is because I wanted to reassert the importance of the corporation."[21]

In effect the book is a call for reform. "In all times, but especially in times of turmoil, corporate boards have a responsibility as custodians not just of a single organization, but of our economic well-being as a whole."

None of this is easy. "As the concept of shareholder primacy fades," she writes, "it is replaced by the competing and sometimes conflicting priorities of employees, consumers, governments and shareholders. . . . If a company adjusts too little, it leaves itself at risk of losing its license to trade. . . . But adjust too much, and the company risks becoming uncompetitive."

All of this puts more pressure on boards than ever before. Their role is evolving too.

DOES CORPORATE ACTIVISM WORK?

Aaron K. Chatterji and Michael W. Toffel, authors of a 2018 *Harvard Business Review* study on activist CEOs, admitted, "When we first started studying CEO activism three years ago, we never imagined how significant this phenomenon would become."[22] Although there is a long tradition of corporations being involved in politics and supporting various candidates and issues, "Until recently, it was rare for corporate leaders to plunge aggressively into thorny social and political discussions about race, sexual orientation, gender, immigration, and the environment."

This trend is certainly in sync with a commitment to stakeholder capitalism, but it takes it a step beyond, placing the CEOs themselves in a personal spotlight on behalf of their companies.

In their *HBR* article, Chatterji and Toffel investigated a big question: How effective is CEO activism? Does it help or hurt a company, and is the cost of silence becoming even greater?

They decided to conduct an experiment to determine if CEO activism had an effect on consumer behavior. They asked a nationally representative group of people about their intent to buy Apple products in the near future. Some of the respondents were first randomly shown a statement that the Apple CEO Tim Cook had made criticizing Indiana's religious freedom bill as discriminatory to LGBTQ individuals. Other respondents randomly received a generic statement about Cook's management philosophy. And some respondents were provided with no additional statement.

Those who heard about Cook's activism expressed a significantly higher intent to buy Apple products in the near future than those in the other two groups.

The authors concluded, "Learning about Cook's activism increased intent to purchase among supporters of same-sex marriage but did not erode intent among its opponents. These results indicate that CEO activism can generate goodwill for the company but need not alienate those who disagree with the CEO. But this most likely does not apply to all companies. Apple products are especially sticky, so while Cook's remarks might not provoke a backlash against iPhones, other business leaders should consider whether the political makeup of their consumers and the nature of their products might lead to a different result. It's critical for every CEO to proceed thoughtfully."

The authors noted that not every topic of activism is polarizing. For example, companies who get involved in issues such as parental leave or the minimum wage reap the benefits with support from members of both political parties. These issues are also deemed more appropriate for corporate commentary, whereas issues such as gun control or same-sex marriage can seem outside a company's brief. Obviously, many of our activist CEOs would disagree with this analysis.

One caution the authors suggest: get your internal stakeholders on board before you act. For example, Ken Frazier consulted his board members at Merck before he resigned from Trump's economic council, and they gave him their support. When the critics came out, they defended him and praised his courage and integrity.

REBUILDING TRUST

The Edelman Trust Barometer is an annual global survey of the level of trust in businesses, government, and institutions. Surveying 33,000 people in twenty-nine countries in January 2021, Edelman reported that "while the world seems to be clouded by mistrust and misinformation, there is a glimmer of hope in business. This year's study shows that business is not only the most trusted institution among the four studied, but it is also the only trusted institution with a 61 percent trust level globally, and the only institution seen as both ethical and competent.

"When the government is absent, people clearly expect business to step in and fill the void, and the high expectations of business to address and solve today's challenges has never been more apparent. The heightened expectations of business bring CEOs new demands to focus on societal engagement with the same rigor, thoughtfulness, and energy used to deliver on profits."[23]

Eighty-six percent of respondents agreed with the statement, "I expect CEOs to publicly speak out on one or more of these societal challenges, pandemic impact, job automation, societal issues, local community issues." And 68 percent agreed that "CEOs should step in when government does not for societal impact."

Having said that, in a year when disinformation was rampant, people are feeling shell-shocked and questioning all institutions. I recall a few years ago when Edelman's global chair of corporate practices, Kathryn Beiser, stated, "Business is the last retaining wall for trust." That seems to still be true. But the retaining wall needs shoring up. Among Edelman's recommendations:

- **Business must embrace its expanded mandate and expectations**, with CEOs leading on a range of familiar and unfamiliar issues. It's important to take meaningful action first and then communicate about it.
- **Societal leaders must lead with facts and act with empathy.** They must have the courage to provide straight talk, but also empathize with and address people's fears.
- **Provide trustworthy content** that is truthful, unbiased and reliable.
- **Institutions must partner with one another to solve issues.** Business, government, media, and NGOs must find a common purpose and take collective action to solve societal problems.

An updated survey taken in May 2021 found that trust had risen even higher, boosted by the pandemic experience. It remained higher than trust in NGOs, government, or the media. "My employer" ranked even higher than business in general. Majorities in every country agreed that "our country will not be able to overcome our challenges without business involvement." Upwards of 30 percent in each country said the pandemic "has led me to believe this is true."

"Business must lead on areas of comparative advantage—retraining, skills development, innovation—and it must continue to take meaningful action on societal issues from sustainability to racial justice, starting with getting its own house in order," wrote CEO Richard Edelman. "But it must resist the temptation to be the A student doing all the work on the group project because government is slacking. As in *The Odyssey*, business must steer a course between the Scylla of complacency and the Charybdis of over-reach. Navigating these roiling waters will surely require adjustments and course corrections, but there is no time to waste to help a shaken world regain its bearings."

MODELING SOCIAL PURPOSE

"We need to show society who we are and what we believe in," Cisco CEO Chuck Robbins told me when we talked after George Floyd's death. Robbins had spoken out about Floyd's killing, calling it "horrific," "maddening," and "truly abhorrent." He said, "I think the world's changed and businesses are held accountable for these other issues now. Even our shareholders are asking us to get involved in a lot of these issues. I mean, this is the whole notion of ESG [environmental, social, governance] investing that has occurred. Our shareholders aren't sitting around saying, 'What are you guys thinking?' They're actually saying, 'We're ready for this.'"[24]

Robbins saw his response in the context of the core mission of the company. "We have been working over the last six months to redefine and rebuild what we believe the purpose of our corporation is," he explained. That purpose—"to power and create an inclusive future for all"—Robbins explained, means that "we think about that through both our technology lens and the connectivity that we can bring to remote parts of the world. Just connect everybody so they can have education, health care, and opportunity." But he emphasized that when there is a social wrong, such as the murder of George Floyd, the company's employees, customers, partners, and community stakeholders all want to know, "Where do you stand?"

Robbins acknowledged something I noted earlier, that corporate activism at this level was unheard of even a few years earlier. If you turn the clock back to Ferguson in 2014, there was no outpouring of CEO sentiment. What happened? "Times have changed," Robbins said simply. "There's an expectation that CEOs are actually being asked to be more vocal on these issues in our society." He described the numerous occasions when he'd stood in front of the company and engaged in complicated discussions about social issues. These aren't easy things to do. But CEOs like Robbins view it as an obligation.

"When you think about running a company, one of the most important assets you have are your people," he said. "In order to create an environment where you want the best talent to be, there's an expectation that you're going to have an open dialogue about these issues. What I've talked to our employees about is, there are certain issues where as a company we're going to have a very binary take on what's happening. Like this issue that happened with George Floyd. It's just wrong. There are other issues where we're going to have a spectrum of our employees who are going to believe one way and a spectrum that are going to believe another way. And it's based on their upbringing, their political beliefs. In those situations, we just try to encourage conversation. We try to encourage them to seek a different opinion that doesn't align with theirs. Just try to learn and understand why people feel the way they do. But we've taken on every issue that has arisen in the last five years with our employee base. Because they've asked us to."

When Robbins chooses to take a public stand, he doesn't do it in a vacuum. He's very serious about educating himself about the issues so he can speak from a perspective of understanding. Being a CEO activist isn't about mouthing off because you have a spotlight. It's about adding a meaningful voice to the discussion.

In the case of George Floyd's death, "It's just not like I'm sitting around and trying to figure out what to say," Robbins said. "I mean, it's through really spending time with [the Black community] and understanding. One of the things that the white community struggles with significantly is, being very concerned that you're going to say the wrong thing. About nine months ago, I read *White Fragility*. It's an incredible book that educated me about talking to the people who are living the experience every day. You have to understand the situation from their perspective. Then you almost have to just up front say, 'Listen, we want to engage in this discussion. Anything that we say that's wrong, tell us it's wrong, but know that it comes from a spirit of a good place and it comes from within. We're trying to engage in this discussion. So, let's have an open dialogue.' I think that's all you can do. If you're sincere, it's going to work."

Activism isn't just about speaking out. The deeper question is, what are companies like Cisco doing to drive change? Robbins rightly gauges that the first step is being attentive to the experience of Black employees, because if a company doesn't get that right it doesn't really matter what they say in the public square. That action can be taken in partnership with the Business Roundtable and other organizations that are working on issues of equity and inclusion. Another way to help is to put financial resources behind the issues. And, Robbins added, "we can also improve the representation of the Black community at our executive level or our board, much like everybody else has. During this time, for those of us who have spoken out, we've all had microscopes put on our leadership teams and our boards for all the right reasons."

When Robbins first became CEO, he announced to the employees in a sweeping statement that they should throw away everything that had been tried in the past on diversity and inclusion because it hadn't worked. "Today, my leadership team is virtually 50/50, male/female. Then it begins to flow through the organization. I think we've now applied what we've learned to Cisco's Black community. It's incumbent upon us to really be much more aggressive on that front and just acknowledge that we haven't done the job we need to do."

LEADERSHIP TODAY

Business leadership used to be about setting strategy in the C-suite and then giving orders to everybody down the line about what they need to do to implement the strategy. Things are moving too fast today for that kind of a top-down approach. I asked Joe Ucuzoglu, the CEO of Deloitte US, who told me that "being a great leader in this environment requires a lot of listening, empowering one's people, setting the tone for a culture of innovation and strategic risk taking. Because, at the end of the day, you can't be involved in every interaction with your customers, with your employees, with your regulators. You have to instill in your professionals a sense of values to drive the way in which they'll make those on-the-spot decisions on behalf of the organization."[25]

He didn't say it in so many words, but the obvious conclusion is that activist CEOs also infuse their companies—top-down and bottom-up—with a sense of corporate values.

When we surveyed Fortune 500 CEOs in May 2021, we asked them which of the following statements came closest to their own view, even if neither was exactly right:

- *CEOs have a responsibility to speak out on important social and political issues and should continue to do so.*
- *CEOs have recently gotten too involved in commenting on social and political issues and need to pull back.*

Their answers were split right down the middle: 50 percent said keep it up; 50 percent said pull back. The mixed response demonstrates the awkward dilemma that the US debate over voting practices has created for corporate chieftains. More than 80 percent agreed that "everything possible should be done to make it easy for every citizen to vote." But countering that belief is a strong desire to stay out of the partisan crossfire (and perhaps not be called "woke" by the editors of the *Wall Street Journal*). Corporate activism is clearly on the rise. But it has its limits.

CHAPTER 10

THE PURPOSE OF BUSINESS

When Hubert Joly took over Best Buy in 2012, the company had been given up for dead by many analysts. After all, who needed a giant electronics store in the age of e-commerce? Joly, who had been born in France, came from the travel and hospitality business and had no real background in either retail or electronics. He recalled that he gathered his five hundred directors and officers together shortly after starting the job and told them, "The purpose of a company is not to make money, but to make a positive contribution in people's lives." He imagined that they were rolling their eyes as he said it. But no one would roll their eyes at him today. A month after Joly took over, Best Buy's stock bottomed out at $11. On May 3, 2021, it closed at $117. "Ten times is not bad," he told me with a smile. And while putting Best Buy's purpose—"to enrich lives through technology"—at the center of its business wasn't the only reason for the successful turnaround, he believes it was essential.[1]

Today, Joly teaches at the Harvard Business School and says we are in the midst of what he calls a "revolution"—an "urgent refoundation of business and capitalism around purpose." "The tide is turning," he said. "Employees

demand this. Customers demand this. Shareholders demand it. Society demands it." And the pandemic, which hit after he stepped down as CEO, has
"vastly accelerated it. You have a health crisis, an economic crisis, a societal
crisis, a racial crisis, an environmental crisis. The status quo is not an option."

I was interviewing Joly on the occasion of the publication of his book, *The
Heart of Business: Leadership Principles for the Next Era of Capitalism*. In it, Joly
described how in the course of his time at the helm of several companies he
had started to see shareholder primacy as the root cause of some overwhelming problems society was facing, from climate change to income inequality.
"Although making money is of course vital and a natural outcome of good
management, considering profit as the sole purpose of business is wrong for
four fundamental reasons: (1) profit is not a good measure of economic performance; (2) an exclusive focus on it is dangerous; (3) this singular focus antago-
nizes customers and employees; and (4) it is not good for the soul."[2]

Joly's perspective on shareholder primacy is unapologetic, and he speaks
truth in ways you seldom hear out loud. I'm sure many would argue with his
characterization that exclusively focusing on profit is "dangerous," but here's
the way he explains it:

> Profit—like the temperature of a patient—is a symptom of other underlying
> conditions, not the condition itself. And focusing on the symptom alone can
> be dangerous. . . .
>
> It is an easy game to rig, and not just through accounting. I can maximize
> profit by underinvesting in people and other assets that directly benefit cus-
> tomers. It works, but for a short time. Expenses go down, and the numbers
> look good for a time while the long-term health of the business suffers. This
> is precisely what happened at Best Buy between 2009 and 2012, when the
> company slowed spending on its stores and invested too little in e-commerce.
> At the same time, it increased prices. For a while, that helped sustain the bot-
> tom line—until customers grew tired of battling with the company's website,
> and of the dusty stores and poor customer service I encountered when I went
> to buy my flip phone. The path to bankruptcy is littered with retailers like
> Sears and others that focused more on short-term profits than on investing in
> talent and better serving customers.

My central message in this book is that a new age of business requires the new approach to leadership exemplified by Joly. Joly puts Milton Friedman, who articulated the doctrine of shareholder primacy, and Robert McNamara, who instituted scientific management at Ford, at the top of his "FBI most wanted" list. "This is what got us in trouble. So much of what I learned in business school is either wrong, dated, or at best incomplete." The new model, he said, requires leaders who can create "an environment that unleashes human magic, rather than pretend they can come up with all the answers."

Focusing on *purpose* over *profit* in business is, as noted earlier, nothing new. Many, if not most, companies start with sincere efforts to solve a problem, rather than just a scheme to make money. And many great companies—take pharmaceutical giant Johnson & Johnson, for example—work to keep that purpose at the center of their business. J&J's famous credo, crafted in 1943, is well known to every one of the company's employees, and many of its customers.

Indeed, business guru Jim Collins, whose book *Good to Great*, published in 2001, is considered one of the best business books written, insists "the greatest company builders have always" put purpose at the center of their business.[3] In his earlier 1992 book, *Beyond Entrepreneurship*, Collins warned against the Friedman doctrine of "maximize shareholder wealth" as not being supported by the reality of great companies. "For them, profit is simply a strategic necessity rather than the supreme end point."[4]

But even Collins acknowledged, when I pressed him about this, that something had changed in recent years. Purpose beyond profit had become a much bigger part of the business discussion. Often, Collins feared, the words weren't backed up with any real action—they were mere "purpose washing." But at the very least, the *pretense* of purpose had become much more common.

As I have tried to argue in this book, there is more than mere pretense to this change. Fundamental forces in business, driven by technology and society, have raised the importance of purpose on the business priority list, and made it a critical tool of success in the new leader's playbook. It is no longer enough for a leader to tell his people *what* to do. He or she must give people a compelling sense of *why* they are doing it and lay down the ethical foundations for *how* they do it.

Some of this, I am convinced, is generational. It's common these days to say that people don't work to make money—a belief rooted in research that dates back to Douglas McGregor's classic 1960 text, *The Human Side of Enterprise.*[5] But I'm fairly certain that my father, born in 1923, *did* go to work to make money. That's not to say he didn't have other goals in life, but he was a child of the Depression. His job was about making money. When it came to other goals, he turned elsewhere—his family, his friends, his clubs, his avid participation in community theater. (He was especially known in my hometown for his portrayal of *Scrooge* at Christmas.)

My children, on the other hand, are quite another matter. When I was president of the Pew Research Center from 2012 to 2014, we did a major research effort on the millennial generation, and what we found was, they were in many ways different from previous generations—slower to get married, less likely to belong to an organized church, less likely to join social clubs. These differences meant that for many of them, their employer was their most important formal connection to society. As a result, what they expect from work is far more than a paycheck. My daughters fit the type. They look to their jobs to give their life meaning, to give them a purpose—an aspiration that I suspect never occurred to my father.

Some of this is inherent in the changing nature of business itself. It was Frederick Winslow Taylor who laid the groundwork for the twentieth-century view of "scientific management." Work could be broken into individual components, he argued, and workers could be given a task to complete. Strategy was conceived at the top of the organization, and orders cascaded down the hierarchy. As my *Fortune* colleague Geoffrey Colvin put it, scientific management was all about making humans act more like machines. Each was a cog in the great wheel.

But the source of value has shifted from machines to people. The flow of information has moved from hierarchical to omnidirectional. The pace of change has forced decision-making to move from the center to the edges. And now business leaders increasingly recognize that their jobs have become less about telling people what to do, and more about giving them a good reason to do it. Hubert Joly was early in recognizing this, but today, it has become an inescapable reality of running a good business.

During the course of the pandemic, *Fortune* teamed up with McKinsey & Company to explore this reality through a series of virtual conversations with forty-five of the world's top CEOs, asking how they thought about purpose. McKinsey's Bruce Simpson and I attempted to synthesize what we learned from these conversations, focusing on seven clear takeaways:[6]

1. IN THE LONG RUN, THERE IS NO TRADEOFF BETWEEN PURPOSE AND PROFITS.

To a person, the CEOs we convened were passionate about having a positive societal impact and serving all stakeholders, while recognizing that in the long run this would also be good for shareholders. As IBM CEO Arvind Krishna put it, "Purpose and profit go together, reinforcing each other." PayPal CEO Dan Schulman took it one step further: "I'd actually argue if you don't have a purpose as a company, you will be less successful from a results perspective." PayPal did a lot during the pandemic to provide extra support for its workers, including lowering the cost of benefits, increasing salaries, offering stock, and increasing financial education. This contributed to drops in attrition and absenteeism.

In the short term, of course, tradeoffs clearly occur. McKinsey research shows that 61 percent of executives and directors said they would cut discretionary spending on positive value projects, including investments in employees and other stakeholders, to avoid an earnings "miss." But purposeful leaders, who deliver against a broader set of stakeholder interests, will tend to keep their eye on the longer term and create more value through time. In the long term, shareholder interests and stakeholder interests tend to converge.

"If you stay true to your purpose and it is very clear to every person that is working in this company, then there is a very clear direction, there is a compass, there is a star that is telling you this is where we all go," said Pfizer CEO Albert Bourla. "That unites the organization, creates cohesiveness, and brings results." Levi Strauss CEO Chip Bergh put it this way: "By doing right and doing the right thing, you are going to reward your shareholders over the long term."

2. PURPOSE BEGINS WITH YOUR EMPLOYEES.

In an economy where human capital drives business value, an employee-first approach has become essential. Research from the multinational professional services firm Aon and the research and education firm the Ponemon Institute shows that four decades ago, hard assets accounted for 80 percent of a company's value, while today it's intangibles—"soft assets" that include reputation, brand equity, patents, and R&D—that account for 85 percent. The focus on employees as the source of value was further reinforced by the pandemic.

"Purpose starts with supporting your own teams and front lines. They in turn support our customers, which takes care of business," said Best Buy CEO Corie Barry, Hubert Joly's successor, commenting on her company's transformation, underpinned by increased employee discounts, training, and broad engagement of frontline staff. Recent McKinsey research found that frontline employees who "feel purpose" at work are up to four times as engaged as those at organizations where purpose is not activated and aligned to that of individual employees, and twice as likely to stay in the job.

XPO Logistics CEO Brad Jacobs told us how the pandemic "actually brought a purpose to our drivers, warehouse workers, people on a cross dock. . . . They suddenly had a big purpose in getting people's toilet paper delivered, getting people's Purell delivered, getting medicines delivered. That was the prime thing that led to our employee satisfaction figures going up five percent."

3. PURPOSE DRIVES INNOVATION.

All the CEOs who took part in the McKinsey-Fortune conversations gave strong testament to the power of purpose in unleashing creativity and innovation. A recent Gallup survey shows that 70 percent of the workforce in North America and Europe is "not actively engaged," which means that while they may be bringing discipline, rigor, and obedience to work, they're leaving creativity, collaboration, and initiative at home.

"As leaders we always need to find a way to fundamentally attach what we are doing to that greater purpose," said Johnson & Johnson CEO Alex Gorsky. "I think it frees up a sense of energy, of ambition, of desire, and, frankly, a pride and accomplishment in our employees. . . . The impact that can have, and the power that has more broadly on our organization, can't be understated."

Honeywell CEO Darius Adamczyk said he had "never seen such a level of excitement, of pride on the part of employees" as when his company turned to making masks for the pandemic. "I think it's been transformative."

4. A COMPANY'S PURPOSE MUST BE AUTHENTIC, AND EMBEDDED IN ITS DNA, TO BE EFFECTIVE.

In an age of social media transparency, employees and others will be quick to call a company out if its words don't match its actions. We now have numerous examples of companies whose credibility has been undermined by their own employees who became "whistleblowers" on social media.

"It's important to talk about the values you want to speak out on internally [and explain] why it is core to your business," said John Donahoe, CEO of Nike. "Nike has a strong history of fighting for racial and social justice. [That's] core to our mission and purpose as a company. When the George Floyd events occurred, we ran the 'Don't Do It' campaign and made a $140 million commitment on racial and social justice."

Stan Bergman, CEO of Henry Schein, a health care solutions company, put it this way: "Social media is testing us to make sure we are authentic. . . . I think that's great."

5. "PROOF POINTS" ALONG THE WAY BUILD CREDIBILITY AND TRUST.

In an age of skepticism, it's not enough to merely state your purpose. You need to demonstrate it on a consistent and regular basis. "[You need to] take the purpose and demonstrate it with real proof points," said Lynn Good, CEO of Duke Energy. "When I say employee safety is important, I need to demonstrate it with unequivocal safety protocols. When I say climate is important, I back up my climate plan with investments to show we are making progress."

Other proof points can include tying executive compensation to delivering on the purpose of the business. This is the case for Danone CEO Emmanuel Faber, whose company links compensation to metrics on its contributions to health, the planet, its people, and inclusive growth—as well as financial returns to shareholders.

Decisions to stop doing something you were previously doing—like the CVS decision to stop selling cigarettes, or the Dick's Sporting Goods decision to limit gun sales, or IBM's decision to stop selling facial recognition software—also can be powerful in building necessary credibility.

6. A STRONG COMMITMENT TO PURPOSE CAN HELP YOU THROUGH TOUGH TIMES.

Many of the CEOs talked about purpose being especially valuable when times are rocky. "When the shit hits the fan—whether it is COVID or social injustice—we look to our purpose to figure out what to do," said Intel CEO Bob Swan. Ulta Beauty's Mary Dillon said that "you can't take for granted the notion of purpose, of putting that trust in the bank, so that at a time when you really need your employees, they feel good about stepping up and doing more."

7. MILLENNIALS AND GEN Z ARE DRIVING CHANGE.

While purpose helps drive performance across all generations, it is younger workers who seem most motivated by it. "In my career, I've never seen a generation who are more influential in driving this change," said John Seifert, CEO of Ogilvy. "Millennials are motivated by their 'why,' and they're demanding that we build purpose within our organizations today," said Penny Pennington, managing partner of financial services firm Edward Jones.

The younger generation is expressing itself not only in the workplace but also as consumers. In one sign of that generation's growing influence, some 70 percent of consumers overall now claim they buy or boycott products or services based on the social stances of the companies that make or sell them. And it's not just about being supportive of social causes but also proactively working to solve underlying problems.

If you have made it this far in the book, it should be clear that the job of leading a large business has become immensely more difficult than it was in the past. As another business guru, Gary Hamel, likes to remind us, it has also become immensely more *human*. The beauty of the shareholder primacy model, with its goal of profit maximization, was its simplicity. Here was a well-developed set of tools you could use to drive results.

But running a business today involves a much more complicated set of calculations. At the *Fortune* Global Forum in Paris in November 2019, James Manyika, chairman of the McKinsey Global Institute, posed a thought-provoking list of ten questions that today's best business leaders feel they must answer:

- What is our mission and purpose as a company?
- How far do we go beyond shareholder capitalism? How are we accountable to different stakeholders?
- Who benefits in our economic success? How?
- What is the time horizon for managing our economic success and impact?
- What is our responsibility to our workforce, especially given future-of-work implications?
- How do we leverage data and technology responsibly and ethically?
- What are our aspirations for inclusion and diversity?
- What is our responsibility for societal and sustainability issues involving our business, and beyond our business?
- What are our responsibilities regarding participants in our platforms, ecosystems, supply and value chains and their impact on society?
- How should we address the global and local (including national) imperatives and implications of how we compete, contribute, and operate?

These are the questions I have been asking CEOs in my journey into stakeholder capitalism, and this book has been my attempt to convey their answers. But always, the most important question to answer is the first: What is your company's purpose?

"Making profits is not a purpose of business. It's a derivative. A purpose is what problems it is solving for us as customers and communities."

—Colin Mayer, speaking at Fortune Connect

BUILT FOR THIS MOMENT

Microsoft CEO Satya Nadella has been thoughtful about the question of corporate purpose, and he put his interest front and center in his October 2021 letter to shareholders, colleagues, customers, and partners. Claiming that "Microsoft was built for this moment," he went on to detail an impressive array of technological transformations of business and society fed by the company's products. But what made me sit up and take note was the bold statement of purpose at the end of his letter. I thought it was a particularly good articulation of purpose.

> We aspire to create a culture where employees are encouraged to be curious, to experiment, and to share things they learn. This is why we put so much emphasis over the past few years on building a culture that centers on our commitment to a growth mindset. This growth mindset served us well during the past year of crisis, disruption, and transformation. It drives our passion to obsess about our customers, and to learn about and from them. It has helped us become more empathetic toward our colleagues and enabled us to work together as a team—as One Microsoft. And it underlies our approach to diversity and inclusion.
>
> We know that as we become more representative of the communities where we live and work, and the people around the world who we aspire to serve, we become better at helping everyone on the planet achieve more. Diversity and inclusion continues to be a core priority for every employee at Microsoft and is incorporated into our performance and career development approach. . . .
>
> Care is the new currency for every leader, and we've built a new framework to help our managers strengthen their teams and deliver success through empowerment and accountability. Our managers strive to model our culture and values in their actions, to coach their teams to define objectives and adapt and learn, and to care deeply for their employees, seeking to understand their capabilities, ambitions, and invest in their growth.

Nadella ended his letter with the declaration, "I couldn't be more optimistic," and that was important too. He made that statement in spite of the "immeasurable hardship and deep uncertainty" that we face right now.

A TIME TO REFLECT

A few years back, I received a visit from John Donahoe. At the time he'd been CEO of Bain and then of eBay, and he'd yet to become CEO of ServiceNow and then Nike. I vividly remember our conversation that day because he'd just finished a year-long sabbatical. It was quite amazing to me to see this high-powered executive take a year off to explore his personal purpose and what he wanted to see in business going forward. It was one of the first times I recognized that something different was happening in business today.

When I interviewed Donahoe again in 2020, I was eager to explore this matter further and talk about what he learned from this quest. So, I asked him about his journey and what other businesspeople could learn from it.

"I actually had given the advice so many times in my career when someone faced a transition, to take time off, and I had never really done it myself," he told me.[7] "I was fifty-five years old at the time. To be honest, in hindsight, I was more burned out than I realized after twenty years of Bain, and ten intense years at eBay, and so I took that year off to reflect on what it was I wanted to do with the next stage of my life. It was one of the most rejuvenating years of my life. I did a ten-day silent Buddhist retreat early on, and that was a very foundational portion of the experience."

As Donahoe contemplated his future, he began to ask himself what would be important to him in a decade. He knew plenty of people who became more negative as they got older—and there's actually some brain science to back that up. But he also knew people who at sixty-five or older had vitality, were young at heart, and were happy. He started reaching out to them and said, "Tell me a little bit about how you understand your life at this stage and how you have handled the transition since you turned fifty." Donahoe shared the four main lessons he had gained from those conversations, and they turned out to be not only important personal lessons but valuable insights for all corporate leaders.

"Number one," Donahoe said, "attitude's everything. As we get older, we get gray hair or our hair falls out, our knees hurt, our backs hurt. You feel the signs of visible aging. Well, our brains don't necessarily get older. [Business management guru] Jim Collins said to me, 'John, your fifties and your sixties and God willing, your seventies should be the most creative and productive years of your life, because you have the wisdom of your experience and you have the freedom to apply that wisdom where you want to do it, and you can do it out of service and not out of ego.'

"Second, someone said to me, 'You want to know about vitality. I hang out with people that have vitality.' He said, 'Every time I hang out at the golf club with guys my own age, all we do is bitch about how bad our golf swings are and brag about what red wine we drank the night before. That makes me old. I like being around young people.'" Donahoe observed that every one of those happy, productive older people found ways to be around young people. They coached young people. They mentored young people. They taught young people. They worked with young people. They volunteered with young people.

"Third thing, being conscious about time." He told this story about Tom Tierney, the chairman and cofounder of the Bridgespan Group, who was one of his mentors. "He put a glass out in front of me and he said, 'You know, Donahoe, this glass is your capacity,' and he said, 'You have spent the last thirty years trying to take a rock that's twice as big as the volume of that glass, jam it in to think you were going to get more done. All you did was spill a bunch of water on the table and the glass didn't really get bigger. You are who you are. Now your glass is empty. Don't just fill it with pebbles. Find things in your life for which you have accountability and there's consequence. It doesn't have to be one big thing, but find meaningful things in your life. You can add more time for kids, time with your grandkids, or travel with your spouse, but find things that have consequence and meaning for you.'

"Fourth thing. This was the thing that had the biggest impact on me," Donahoe said. "It was a guy that requested he be nameless because I've gone back to him. Sixty-nine years old. Two different people said I had to go see him. He lives in the South. I went and I saw him. I bought him a cup of coffee and he actually bought me lunch, and he's like, 'John, you want my advice about how you can have vitality when you're my age? It's this. Do not lose sight of your gifts. Now, when I was your age, I never would have used the word gifts because that sounded a bit egotistical. I use that word with not one shred of ego. God gave me certain gifts and my job has been to figure out which of those gifts, when I utilize them and utilize them in service to others, animates me inside and makes me happy, because I've learned that all the success and wealth and fame in the world cannot make me happy. Happiness cannot come from the outside. It can only come from the inside. I have determined that the best way I can contribute to this world at my age is to be happy. So, John, do not let anyone else tell you what your gifts are. You are the only one that has to go inside of yourself and figure out what are the things when you utilize them, animate you inside and makes you happy, but you need to go do some thinking young man.'

"I'm like holy cow. Just tell me what my gifts are. And then the last one, the role of serendipity. I'll use another example. Clay Christensen, who has passed in the last year, said, 'John, I'm very conscious about who I am as a husband, as a father, and as an educator. I'm very left-brained about who I am.'

But he said, 'I've learned to allow the role of serendipity to play a huge impact on how I spend my time. I think I have a big left brain,' apparent to anyone who knew Clay, 'but now, when I look to my future, I don't worry about it because I realize as much as my left brain wants to predict and control it, it's a waste of energy.' So now I try to be present for what life deals me. Almost everyone I talk with tells me how one thing led to another, that led to another. So, a long-winded way, it was an incredible learning journey, but those things informed what I wanted to do in the next stage of my life."

What Donahoe ultimately concluded was that his role was service-based leadership, sometimes referred to as servant leadership. When he was approached about being CEO of Nike, the first thing that came to his mind was how polarized and divided the world is—more than any other time in his adult life, with many institutions finding it hard to overcome the problem. "But, sports is one of the few things that still brings people together, both within and across countries on the ultimate level playing field. The color of your skin, your height, your weight, your personality don't matter. If you can play, you can play. Sport brings people together under a civil set of rules. You can be against your archrival that you play with a common set of rules and you shake hands at the end of the game. As I reflected upon it, I feel like the world needs sport more today, and that Nike is at the center of sport."

I asked Donahoe about Nike's decision to put controversial player Colin Kaepernick on the company's advertising. While the decision was made a year before Donahoe became CEO he had served on the board of directors since 2014.

Kaepernick, a former quarterback for the San Francisco 49ers, is well-known for kneeling during the playing of the national anthem as a protest against racial injustice. The gesture took hold as a form of protest by many players but effectively halted Kaepernick's once promising career. His critics saw it as an act of disloyalty to the country. But in 2018, Nike showed its support for Kaepernick and his message by featuring him again in its thirtieth anniversary "Just Do It" ad campaign.

I put the question to Donahoe in a straightforward manner. "When Nike made the decision to put Colin Kaepernick on its advertising, a lot of people saw that as a divisive move, not a uniting move. Why did you do it?"

"Well, Alan," he replied, "this gets to a conversation you and I have had many times, where in today's environment, it's important that companies not just look after the commercial interests and ignore what's going on in society. It's important that companies have a point of view on some societal issues, and every company needs to figure out what are the societal issues that are connected to your purpose as a company." He reminded me of Nike's long history of featuring elite athletes in its advertising, greats such as Michael Jordan, Bo Jackson, Tiger Woods, Kobe Bryant, Serena Williams, and LeBron James. "They are the heroes for our company. We also have a strong connection with Black culture. The Jordan brand, the Nike brand, both Black and Latinx, and many diverse cultures. Nike is a global brand that has strong connections with many diverse cultures. We view it as part of our core purpose to take a point of view and stand up for racial and social justice."

Donahoe was able to convincingly argue the point that Nike's culture was synonymous with this quest. "It's something we believe in," he emphasized, "because it's connected to our history, our heritage, and our purpose. Our athletes care about it. Our consumers care about it. We have a very diverse consumer base. We understand that not everyone's going to agree with our perspective, but we view racial and social and ultimately economic justice to be an extension of our core purpose as a company."

I believed him, but I also pointed out, "It's also damn good for your business." Which has been the case.

"That's one and the same," he said. "I'm still blessed to be part of the PayPal board and Dan Schulman always says so well, 'Good purpose and good business are not inconsistent with one another. When they're authentic and you do them well, they can be mutually reinforcing.' But we didn't do it because we think, oh, we're going to sell more Jordans or we're going to sell more Nikes. In fact, when you make those decisions . . . I remember the night before we ran the Don't Do It [anti-racism] brand campaign. You don't know how it's going to be received, but our internal discussion was it's the right thing to do for who we are, who our stakeholders are, our athletes, our consumers, and our employees. So, you do it, and we try to do the right thing with authenticity. We don't always get it right. When we get it wrong, we apologize. We acknowledge it, apologize, and try to do better next time."

> "I actually believe that humility and humor are great assets to have as a leader. . . . If you come into the prospect of leadership as a privilege you were granted, not as a birthright, it is easier to embrace the idea of humility and humor as your companions."
>
> —Ajay Banga, former CEO, Mastercard

THE CHINA SYNDROME

The 2017 Fortune Global Forum in Guangzhou, China, was a spectacular affair. The city of fifteen million people had planted fresh flowers throughout its gleaming center to welcome the CEOs from around the world. Traffic was restricted, to keep the streets clear and the skies blue. An epic cultural extravaganza was planned for the city's riverbank, followed by a dazzling display of more than a thousand drones in synchronous flight, operated by the Guangzhou-based drone firm eHang, with colored lights recreating the city scape and spelling out words like "innovation," "open," and "fortune," in both English and Chinese, in the nighttime sky.

I had first come to Guangzhou two years earlier, at the invitation of Ren Xuefeng, party secretary of the city, whom I had met earlier in Davos. After a welcoming dinner, and despite my jet lag, Ren insisted I join him on a boat ride down the Pearl River to the iconic Canton Tower, a sparkling, thin-waisted column that reached six hundred meters into the sky and defined the city's modern center. As we approached the tower in the night, Ren pointed to its top, and I looked up to see the words "Hello Alan" rolling in bright lights across the top, followed by "Welcome Fortune." The message was unmistakable: Guangzhou wanted to host the Fortune Global Forum, following in the path of Shanghai, Beijing, Chengdu, and Hong Kong, which had hosted it in earlier years.

The main sessions of the forum were held at the Shangri-La Hotel and opened with a speech from Wang Yang, China's vice premier and a member of the Communist Party standing committee in Beijing. Also on hand was Canadian Prime Minister Justin Trudeau, who was there to announce that the 2018 Fortune Global Forum would be held in Toronto.

Then I took the stage with Jack Ma, who was China's most recognizable entrepreneur, the irrepressible founder and executive chairman of Alibaba. The event was one year after the forum at the Vatican, but Ma spoke as if we were still there.

Alibaba was prepared to invest $15 billion in research and development, he said, and "it is not about investing in technology to empower ourselves. We want to build this thing like a Bell Labs, for human beings. Traditional technology companies try to empower themselves. I want to use this technology to empower others, making sure this technology is inclusive. A company like us, we are big, we have the resources, we have money, we are so profitable. The money we invest, of course, will benefit us, but it will also benefit all the small businesses."

Much of the planned investment, he said, would be in machine learning, but "we want to make sure this is improving human lives. We want to make sure human beings benefit from the technology." He added, "Innovation is about solving problems for today, tomorrow, and the future."

Ma made a big pitch for global trade, which had become a popular theme in China since US President Donald Trump had started his anti-globalization campaign two years earlier. "Globalization is a great step," he said. "It's just a baby. Let's improve it. Trade is so good because when trade stops, war starts. If trade stops, peace stops. We have to make sure every company benefits from free trade."

He urged the assembled business leaders from around the globe to step up and take a leadership position on issues important to society. "We should never wait for the politicians," he said. "Businesspeople, we have to do our best to build up the environment, to connect, to talk. We should never wait for policies. We should go before the policy and try to do it."

"Opportunity is everywhere," he told the CEOs. "Opportunity means responsibility. What problem are you solving for the world?"

And then his final salvo: "In the future . . . we have to focus on IQ, EQ, and LQ." What was LQ? "The love quotient."

Ma's cornball approach had clearly paid big dividends at Alibaba. Founded in 1999, the e-commerce company had conducted the largest IPO in world history in 2014, and just a few months after the Guangzhou event broke US records with $500 billion in market capitalization.

But for all the similarities between Ma's comments and those of the CEOs at the Vatican a year earlier, the forces that were driving Chinese business as the nation powered its way to becoming the largest economy on earth were very different than the forces driving change in the US and Europe. China's strong centralized government, controlled by the Communist Party, and the government's ownership stake in many of the nation's largest companies, had built a very different form of capitalism. Private shareholders had never achieved anything close to the "primacy" that they had in the US in the 1990s. And the leading "stakeholder" was never in question. It was the Chinese government.

In my visits to Guangzhou leading up to the forum, I had gotten to know the CEOs of Guangzhou Automotive, which ranked 206 on the Fortune Global 500 list, as well as the CEO of Guangzhou Pharmaceutical and others. But in meetings with them and Party Secretary Ren, there was never any doubt about where power lay. At one meeting, we were discussing a technology contest for Chinese startups that we were holding in connection with the forum, and Ren suddenly suggested, why don't we give the winners a car? He looked over to the CEO of Guangzhou Automotive, who, as I recall, simply nodded his head. Winners of each category in the contest were awarded a Trumpchi, Guangzhou Automotive's most popular model. (The name has no relationship, despite its similarity, to the former US president.)

China's state-controlled capitalism may have looked after the needs of society, but largely as those needs were interpreted by the Communist Party. And if Jack Ma didn't fully realize that in December 2017, he certainly learned it two years later. In 2020, Ant Group, an affiliate of Alibaba that ran China's largest digital pay platform, was preparing to do its own IPO, projected to top Alibaba's earlier listing and again set a global IPO record. But on the eve of the stock sale, the Chinese government stepped in and blocked it. Reporting at the time suggested Communist Party leader Xi Jinping was concerned about the wealth and power being created by the Alibaba group and its shareholders.

Clearly feeling the pressure, Jack Ma stepped down in 2020 from the chairman's position and adopted a distinctly lower profile. In April 2021, the *Wall Street Journal* reported that the Ant Group would be transformed into a financial holding company, overseen by the Chinese central bank.

This book has mostly dealt with CEOs and companies in the US and Europe. But the rise of China poses a distinct challenge to the economic world order in the years ahead. Today, there are more China-based companies on the Fortune Global 500 list than there are US-based companies. Many of them, like Guangzhou Automotive, are partially state-owned, and owe their huge size to their government-protected monopolies rather than to their business dynamism.

But the increasing bifurcation between US and European economic systems and the Chinese alternative raises some profound questions for the future of stakeholder capitalism:

> If US and European companies accept or impose restraints on the development of new machine learning technologies—limiting access to personal data because of concerns about privacy, for instance, or restricting the use of facial recognition technology because of concerns about bias—will they be forced to take a back seat to Chinese AI companies, where the government has no such qualms?

> If newly empowered US and European workers insist that the tech companies they work for stop doing work with government

defense agencies, do they run the risk of ceding geopolitical power to the Chinese, where the government has access to all "private" technology?

> If stakeholders demand companies pay more attention to human rights issues—focusing, for instance, on the treatment of Uighurs in the Xinjiang region, or on the crackdown on political protesters in Hong Kong—will they make it increasingly difficult for those companies to operate in China?

> Can US and Western companies successfully attack climate issues by reducing their reliance on fossil fuels if Chinese companies feel no such constraints?

This great clash between two very different systems of economic management will likely be as defining in the twenty-first century as the Cold War was in the twentieth. And ultimately, the outcome will be determined in the same way. Which of these systems can prove, over the long term, that it produces better prosperity and well-being for the broadest swath of its citizenry? That's the greatest challenge facing stakeholder capitalism in the decades ahead. The future of the world is in the balance.

A chilling postscript to this section: Ren Xuefeng, who brought the Fortune Global Forum to Guangzhou, was subsequently moved to the central Chinese city of Chongqing, where I visited him in September 2019. A month later, press reports said the fifty-four-year-old leader had died in Beijing, where he was attending party meetings, after falling off a building. I was never able to find further details of the unusual circumstances surrounding his death.

WALK THE WALK

When I've written about CEOs talking about stakeholder capitalism, people have often asked me, "Do they really mean it?" I believe they do, for a mix of positive reasons—a new generation of CEOs includes many who are committed to the idea, a growing army of employees are demanding it, and even some customers and investors are beginning to value it—as well as a negative reason: the political environment continues to look very threatening to business these days.

Still, what is real and what is merely public relations remains a big topic of conversation. At Fortune's 2020 Most Powerful Women Summit I was allowed to listen in on a fascinating off-the-record discussion among chief marketing officers of some of the world's largest companies. One of the topics they covered was "values washing," also called virtue signaling—a reference to companies that promote their values and purpose purely as a PR exercise, rather than backing them with action. If there is widespread support for companies that authentically support the environment, diversity, and other social issues, consumers will also respond quickly and fiercely to companies they perceive as being insincere . . . attacking them on social media, where powerful influencers can create embarrassment and even havoc for companies. In our divisive and cynical public environment, companies are often accused by opponents of virtue signaling whenever they support a social cause. How can you sort out the fake from the real?

At one of our meetings of the Fortune CEO Initiative, I asked Mark Weinberger, who was then global CEO of Ernst & Young, how he would measure sincerity around purpose. At the time, Weinberger was deeply involved in an effort to put metrics and accountability around stakeholder capitalism—an effort we will discuss in the next chapter.

But in the absence of such measures, he told me, the best thing to do is to go to the employees—talk with them, listen to them, survey them. They know, better than anyone, whether a company is living its purpose. They see every day how decisions are made and how culture gets formed. And they can tell you if it is purpose washing or true lived purpose. One more way in which employees have been empowered by the new trends in business.

CHAPTER 11

THE ACCOUNTABLE ERA

WE ALL KNOW HOW TO MEASURE SHAREHOLDER RETURNS. THERE IS A MAS-sive accounting infrastructure, built over centuries, that supports the effort. And its metrics are used to measure and manage businesses, and ultimately hold companies accountable.

But how do you measure stakeholder returns? To hold companies accountable for their promises, and to separate hollow commitments from meaningful change, metrics are essential. Fashioning such metrics is no easy matter.

Go back to the Business Roundtable statement, which said companies have responsibilities, not just to their shareholders but to their employees, their customers, the communities they live in, and the natural environment they inhabit. That's a pretty broad remit.

As Colin Mayer pointed out in his book *Prosperity*, since financial and physical capital were the primary source of value in the twentieth century it was critical that they were measured well, so they could be managed well.[1]

But in the twenty-first century, it's human capital, social capital, and natural capital that are in short supply. Intangible assets such as intellectual property, brand trust, and great people matter more than tangible assets such as plant, equipment, oil in the ground, or product in warehouses. And a company's effect on the environment is just beginning to be factored into values. Creating the tools to measure returns to human capital, to society, and to the natural environment, and to hold companies accountable for their performance against these measures, will be critical to making stakeholder capitalism a reality.

One group that has been attempting to solve that problem for several years is Paul Tudor Jones's JUST Capital. The folks at JUST have developed a methodology for scoring all the companies in the Russell 1000 on issues that their polling shows are important to Americans.[2] That includes treatment of workers and customers, as well as commitment to communities and the environment.

> "I think we wasted a lot on this philosophical debate over shareholder versus stakeholder, and I think now we need to get down to the nitty gritty, and actually work on some of the metrics and priorities and trade-offs involved."
>
> —Mark Schneider, CEO, Nestlé

So, how did the companies that signed the Business Roundtable statement do in comparison to their peers on these measures? Pretty well, it turns out. JUST Capital found that 34 of the 134 Business Roundtable signatories it measured ranked in the top 100—including Apple, P&G, GM, IBM, JPMorgan, Salesforce, and Accenture, among others. Roughly half—68—ranked in the top 200. The BRT members overall scored 22 percent better than the Russell 1000 average in their treatment of employees, 22 percent better on community issues, and 13 percent better on environmental issues. So, it appears there is more than rhetoric going on here.

Speaking to a group of executives who are part of Fortune Connect—our community of next-generation corporate leaders—Colin Mayer made a point: "Increasingly we're getting standard setters recognizing that we have to include metrics against which companies can measure their contribution to environmental and social standards. It is beginning to happen. But we've got a long way to go."

Everyone agreed that any stakeholder effort needed strong metrics, something Bank of America CEO Brian Moynihan has been involved in developing. Moynihan is chairman of the International Business Council (IBC), which is a community of over 120 global CEOs. The IBC has been working to establish a set of common metrics that the business community can use. At the January 2020 Davos meeting of the World Economic Forum, the IBC issued a preliminary report setting the terms for the discussion, and then followed it up in January 2021 with a final report.

The report identifies a set of Stakeholder Capitalism Metrics across four pillars considered the most critical for business, society, and the planet: governance, planet, people, and prosperity.[3] To summarize:

PILLAR 1: PRINCIPLES OF GOVERNANCE. "Governance is foundational to achieving long-term value by aligning and driving both financial and societal performance, as well as by ensuring accountability and building legitimacy with stakeholders," the report elaborated. In other words, governance is the basic organizing principle and operation of a corporation. We often hear the expression "good governance" to describe the ideal corporate environment.

PILLAR 2: PLANET. As the visibility of business impacts on the planet grows and expectations of corporate responsibility extend along the value chain, the business risk associated with failing to demonstrate a good understanding of and response to environmental impacts is amplified. The report noted, "In the absence of companies reporting effectively on their environmental impacts and framing the associated narrative, it is increasingly easy and common for third parties to fill the void of information with potentially spurious estimates and a damaging narrative of their own. This provides a clear business case for firms to report on material environmental impacts at a value chain level, alongside targets that are guided by science and clear plans to reduce negative impacts and increase positive contributions."

PILLAR 3: PEOPLE. "People are crucial for every organization: they represent employees, workers, customers, suppliers, distributors, retailers and contractors. People are also the investors and ultimate beneficiaries of providers of capital (e.g. pensioners). Their growth—in knowledge, prosperity and well-being—is central to the success of all organizations and societies. The business case for firms to measure, manage and disclose information on how they ensure an engaged, skilled and healthy workforce across their value chains is compelling. Such a workforce creates both financial and non-financial value that is critical for a company's business performance and competitive advantage, while enabling it to mitigate risks, maintain a license to operate and strengthen stakeholder relationships."

PILLAR 4: PROSPERITY. The UN's 2030 Agenda for Sustainable Development identifies prosperity as an area of critical importance: "We are determined to ensure that all human beings can enjoy prosperous and fulfilling lives and that economic, social and technological progress occurs in harmony with nature." The UN Secretary-General's *Synthesis Report* acknowledges that prosperity is an essential element in delivering on the Sustainable Development Goals and defines it as growing "a strong, inclusive and transformative economy." The report links prosperity with dignity and the fight to end poverty and inequality.

The report is a starting point—and an ambitious one. It certainly ticks most of the boxes within the pillars, providing something of a road map for company action. What it doesn't really do—yet—is provide actual accountability points to keep company policies aligned with their principles. We're expecting agencies like the SEC to put more teeth into accountability measures, but so far this is a work in progress.

In the summer of 2020, just weeks before the IBC report was released, I interviewed Moynihan for *Leadership Next*. "The key here," he told me, "is to get alignment between investors and operators and asset owners. If people can be measured along these metrics on a consistent basis, then people can make judgments about whether we are making progress."[4]

Currently, Moynihan said, "there are too many metrics out there," allowing companies to pick and choose the ones that show them in the best light. "What we have done is to consolidate into twenty or so metrics. The idea was to pick the best of the best metrics out there that measure the activities of the seventeen SDGs [Sustainable Development Goals, developed by the UN] that are closely aligned with progress on them, and asking companies to disclose the ones they are working on in an annual report.

"The key thing is you have to start with a few principles. One is, you can't solve the world's problems without getting private industry involved. There's not enough money in governments. Private money has to drive it.

"Second, how do you agree that private companies are driving it in the right direction? The metrics give you a scorecard, and when you have a scorecard, the entire company gets aligned.

"We aren't saying company A is good and all the others are bad. We are saying company A is good, and companies B, C, and D are above the line, too." He suggests one might invest in them all. But if company E is not trying—and therefore not reaping the known benefits—one might skip investing in that company.

LINKING MONEY TO DOING GOOD

Throughout this book, we have talked about the shift from shareholder primacy to stakeholder capitalism. But one of the most interesting developments of the last few years has been the steady increase in the number of investors—shareholders—who, like Larry Fink, are demanding that companies pay attention to social issues like climate change, inequality, and diversity. Between 2018 and 2020, the impact investing sector has doubled in size and by some measures now comprises as much as one in four investment dollars ($12 trillion).

The reason seems obvious. The rise of impact investing has a direct correlation to the other drivers of change we've been describing—a massive dissatisfaction with an economic system that has left many struggling while enriching the top 1 percent, and the evolving conviction in the corporate world that a broader range of stakeholders need to be attended to.

According to the Global Impact Investing Network (GIIN), there are four core characteristics of impact investing: intentionality—the desire to make a positive social or environmental impact; the expectation of a return on investment; a range of return expectations and asset classes; and ways of measuring the impact. This last one is an important characteristic that has relevance to accountability discussions around stakeholder capitalism. If you're asking investors to buy a stake in a company that's doing good, you have to show them that, first, it can be a healthy investment, and, second, you are responsible to your stakeholders. Without setting strong impact goals, metrics for measuring success, and regular accountability to investors, the system could not work.

More and more investors are talking about ESG investments—that is, investments related to environmental, social, and corporate governance, which are termed *sustainable investments*. A report from Morgan Stanley said up to one-third of all managed funds are now being invested in ESG. People want to own things that they think are doing good in the world, and it shows: the Morgan Stanley report noted that sustainable investments are outperforming other investments.

I spoke with Doug Peterson, CEO of S&P Global, which was formerly McGraw Hill Financial, and he confirmed the trend. "Whether you're somebody who is younger, or you're heading towards your retirement age, you're following carefully what's happening with themes around the environment, or social activities like what we saw last year with George Floyd, or how people feel about their own companies, and how they reacted after COVID. There's a whole new level of consciousness of the purpose of capitalism and the purpose of corporations, and people manifest that into how my funds are being invested."[5]

Peterson said that the greatest demand is coming from individual investors who go to their asset managers and say, "'I want you to tell me more about where my funds are invested, and I want to make sure that they're doing something that is going to improve the planet, is going to make us have a better future.' And because of that, you're seeing asset managers, endowments, and others starting to ask those questions and invest in new ways."

Within that framework, what do investors want? That varies, Peterson explained. "You have some that want to see all three of them [E, S, and G—environment, social, and governance], you have some people that just want to see the climate aspect of the funds. . . . It's very important that an investor who is looking to get into sustainability read the fine print to know that, if you're investing in a sustainability fund or an ESG fund, that that's exactly what they're going to invest in."

To help investors make decisions, S&P launched the S&P ESG Index. It began by reviewing all companies in the S&P 500 and found that only about 340 of them complied with the ESG screen they'd devised. The screen eliminated companies that produce certain types of weapons, or had a certain level of carbon production, or certain social scores. But here's the headline: Ultimately, those 340 companies outperformed the S&P 500.

Green investing, in particular, became a thriving investment category during the pandemic. A Morgan Stanley report on 2020 green investing showed that the median return on sustainable equity funds was 19.04 percent—compared to 14.77 percent for nonsustainable—4.3 percent improvement on return.[6] That may have been skewed by the astounding market performance of electric car company Tesla during the pandemic. But it is a sign of the times nonetheless.

The old suspicions about good works and financial security being at odds are fading away with this new construct. According to Morgan Stanley CEO James Gorman, sustainable investing has hit a tipping point. "When we started our Global Sustainable Finance Group in 2009," he told me, "we viewed sustainable investing as the future of finance. Today, we are seeing that it has reached the mainstream. As technology and data continue to advance and empower the field, more and more investors are making decisions with an ESG mindset."[7]

The problem, of course, is there are as yet no clear standards for what constitutes a "sustainable" investment—opening the door to "greenwashing" efforts by funds who want to capitalize on the trend, without doing the hard work needed to make it meaningful. The field of ESG investing, like all of stakeholder capitalism, is still in its infancy. For it to mature, we will need a clear set of agreed upon metrics that investors and managers can use to assure accountability.

At Fortune's CFO Collaborative in the summer of 2021, there was clear support for SEC action to require disclosure on sustainability and diversity metrics. Moynihan, who is immersed in the topic with the IBC, told the CFOs that the demand for standardized ESG metrics is coming from investors. "They want more accountability from the corporate world on what they are doing to drive progress on stakeholder capitalism, and if they weren't going to get it, they were going to start voting with their feet," he said. But CFOs were still struggling with how to measure stakeholder returns. As an example, Moynihan said, "in 2020, but for the pandemic, there would have been six-hundred [different] conventions in North America for environmental metrics." He said it was time for a higher level of accountability. "What will really change this dramatically is when someone from the official sector says, 'This is what you will do,'" he said.

Former SEC Commissioner Robert Jackson, now at NYU School of Law, told the CFOs to expect the SEC to jump into the act. "You should expect in the next six months out of this SEC a proposal to require disclosure on climate impact . . . and secondly, a human capital rule, which will require disclosure about workforce diversity and workforce pay."

THE B CORP EMERGES

Another effort to put metrics and accountability around stakeholder engagement is the B Corporation. It was the brainchild of three friends who met at Stanford and became successful businessmen: Jay Coen Gilbert, cofounder of the apparel/basketball footwear company AND1; Bart Houlihan, an investment banker who joined as president; and Andrew Kassoy, an investment manager at several firms who became involved in sustainable business models. Their idea was simple—that business could do well by doing good, and that the approach could be formalized into a legal structure.

In 2006 they created B Lab, a nonprofit with a framework for businesses that sought to be not only the "best in the world, but best *for* the world."[8] B Labs certifies companies for B Corp status, making them publicly accountable to stakeholders beyond shareholders. There are currently more than 3,500 certified B Corps in operation, including well-known companies like Patagonia, Eileen Fisher, Bombas, Uncommon Goods, and Danone.

The B Corp Declaration of Interdependence

We envision a global economy that uses business as a force for good. This economy is comprised of a new type of corporation—the B Corporation—which is purpose-driven and creates benefit for all stakeholders, not just shareholders. As B Corporations and leaders of this emerging economy, we believe:

- That we must be the change we seek in the world.
- That all business ought to be conducted as if people and place mattered.
- That, through their products, practices, and profits, businesses should aspire to do no harm and benefit all.
- To do so requires that we act with the understanding that we are each dependent upon another and thus responsible for each other and future generations.

THE FISHER WAY

Eileen Fisher was running a sustainable company long before others were even talking about the value of doing it. An interior and graphics designer who didn't even know how to sew, she started her Eileen Fisher clothing brand in 1984, and has grown it into an iconic privately owned brand. It was a pleasure to interview her because in her quiet way, she expresses the fundamental ideals that this movement is all about—ideals that were *organic* to her business. Remarkably, she has maintained 100 percent ownership, although she's surely had many opportunities to sell the company or take on investors.

"I'm really glad I did," she said of her decision to maintain ownership.

"I don't think I understood it at the time. I just felt that other people didn't understand my concept, and it was like my child. I didn't want to give my concept to someone who didn't really get it."[9] In this respect Fisher has stayed outside the norm. I think most businesses would agree that a top priority is growth, but that has never been part of Fisher's business plan.

"I don't get that growth is what it's all about. For me, it's about doing what I love and staying true to the concept and the soul of the company. I'm much more interested in growing in what we call a circular way: How do we grow this company so that it's taking full responsibility for its impacts on the environment, on the people working? That's where I'm passionate."

At first, there were few models in the business world of that kind of thinking. She gravitated toward other companies, such as Ben & Jerry's, but these were informal relationships. Then she heard about a new organizing principle found in the B Corporation. "We thought, 'Oh, that's a business model that actually represents us. That's what we're already working on and working with B Corp, we can work to do better.' It forced us to begin to really measure and track all the things we were doing. It wasn't enough just to say it or even just to do it. We had to actually measure it and account for it. That's what B Corp is all about, actually holding the companies accountable."

THE EXPERIMENTAL ORGANIZATION

Throughout the forty-eight-year history of Patagonia, the outdoor clothing company, the culture has been experimental. (The title of founder Yvon

Chouinard's memoir, *Let My People Go Surfing*, provides a hint.) It fell naturally into addressing a broad array of social, environmental, even political issues and is one of the leading B Corporations. As CEO Ryan Gellert explained it to me, "The company was founded to make equipment. First, hard goods, climbing equipment, and then apparel for outdoor exploration. And I think when you're passionate about the outdoors and you see the damage that's being inflicted by development, by changing climate and other forces, and you run a business, you feel a responsibility to use that business to try to be part of the solution to the degradation that we've seen."[10]

To express those commitments, Patagonia evolved along with the culture. "First, [our commitment] was around minimizing our footprint and then scaling solutions and then supporting activists, very much with a focus on grassroots activists on the front lines of the environmental crisis," Gellert said. "And then I think in the last handful of years, we have felt like we really needed to wade much more directly into activism ourselves, but our whole reason for being, and our mission statement is, we're in business to save our home planet."

I asked him to talk about the broader activism—the extraordinary battle going on in the United States over voting laws and hours of access, mail-in ballots, and other election issues. It has boiled down to a fiercely partisan matter between Republicans (for tighter restrictions) and Democrats (for more access). His reply was thoughtful.

"I think the narrative right now is that there's all these woke corporations who have somehow found a religion on these topics," he said. "And the reality for us on the voting topic, which is probably not well known by many, we've been encouraging both our customers and our employees to vote and vote with the environment in mind for two decades now. So, us taking a position on voting is not new. The existential threat, the climate and ecological crisis is man-made. It is real. And the only way we're going to solve it is if we bring to bear everything that we have via government, via business, and via individual actions. And part of those individual actions comes from people exercising their voice through civil society.

"I think on the specific issue of voting rights in Georgia, our democracy doesn't work if everybody is not treated equally. And being treated equally means having access to the polls. So, I think that's a critically important piece. And we're living in a period now that is going to define our future of intersecting and overlapping crises. The days of us being able to focus on one thing at a time, unfortunately, are probably behind us."

In 2018, Gellert joined with Dan Schulman of PayPal and Chip Bergh of Levi's to cofound Time to Vote, to encourage voter turnout—so this was not a new issue for him. And he strongly believes it is not a partisan issue, as much as it might seem that way on the surface. "I believe our democracy runs better if people participate," he said. "And I think it is fundamentally critical that people have equal access to participate. And I think that when it gets described as Republican versus Democrat, it overlooks the fact that we're an independent organization, we're not an extension of the Democratic Party."

One big question is, once a company decides to be an activist organization, how does it decide which issues to be activist on? Gellert went through a list of questions that get informally asked prior to making a decision: How does the issue affect the company? Does Patagonia have credibility on the issue? Is it something that the company has spoken out about before? Does Patagonia have its own house in order on the issue? How are the employees going to respond? Is Patagonia's statement additive—in other words, does it bring something new to the discussion? And finally, are the words combined with productive actions?

For example, when Patagonia spoke out on the voting rights issue, the company took three steps. First, it donated a million dollars to organizations working to fight voter suppression. Second, it advocated very publicly in support of two pieces of federal legislation—the For the People Act and the John Lewis Voting Rights Advancement Act. Third, it made a commitment to continue working against other restrictive voting laws.

As a private company, Patagonia is able to sidestep some of the prohibitions public companies face. As a B Corp, it already espouses a culture of public purpose. "We've got very dedicated owners," Gellert said. "Usually [when an issue arises] we bring some people together in the organization. We have conversations, we figure out what we think would be additive. And then we go to the ownership and say, 'Here's how we're thinking about things.' And I would say consistently and overwhelmingly the response has been, 'That sounds good, you've got our full support.'"

So, is responding to social issues good for business? Gellert hastens to clarify, "This is not part of a communication strategy. This is not part of a business or commercial strategy. This is out of a real belief that these issues matter and that they are critical to us delivering on our mission. We're in business to save our home planet. But with all that in mind, our businesses continue to grow as we've been more outspoken on these issues. Whether that's in giving away money or making some pretty big bets in technology or investments. Say it's decarbonizing our business or saving areas that we think are under imminent threat or whatever it may be." He cited an example that I found extremely relevant to the debate over corporate taxes. When the tax code change came through under the Trump administration, Patagonia benefited to the tune of about $10 million. "We committed immediately to giving that $10 million away to grassroots organizations working on environmental topics," Gellert told me. "Because we felt like the change in the tax code for corporations was irresponsible, particularly in the middle of this climate and ecological crisis. And so that would be where I think on the other end of it, we just continue to sort of tax ourselves."

To date, the B Corporation route remains a lightly traveled one. Even the most well-intentioned companies find it a difficult path to follow. But it does provide an important model for the future. If stakeholder capitalism continues its advance, governance structures that support and encourage it, like the B Corp model, are likely to follow.

DISCIPLINE AND TRANSPARENCY

In an August 18, 2021, op-ed for *Fortune*, JUST Capital's Martin Whittaker and Peter Georgescu, chairman emeritus of Young & Rubicon, addressed critics of stakeholder capitalism in a clear and compelling way. "Done properly, stakeholder capitalism is not defined by political activism, opportunistic virtue-signaling, or brand sloganeering," they wrote.

> It doesn't necessarily need policy interventions, corporate governance reform, or amendments to company documentation to be pursued. And it certainly doesn't work to the detriment of investors. It's about the disciplined generation of long-term value for each of the key stakeholder groups. It represents a more evolved form of capitalism that creates good jobs and

empowers workers; that provides for upward economic mobility and equality of opportunity for all; that builds healthy, prosperous communities and safeguards our planet; and that supports profitable businesses, integrity of leadership, and long-term investor returns.

Moreover, we know from seven years of surveying the public on the role of corporations in society that stakeholder capitalism is what Americans across the political, racial/ethnic, geographic, and economic spectrums want.

Rather than another "exposé" of so-called corporate stakeholder hypocrisy, what's needed now is the hard foundational work to strengthen the market infrastructure and build the operating norms that underpin this new approach. In this sense, the view of some Business Roundtable (BRT) companies, that they are already practicing stakeholder capitalism and that nothing needs to change, falls short. We need, for example, wider understanding and agreement on what stakeholder value creation actually means, how it can best be measured, and how it can be used as an engine for better financial performance. Greater transparency on reporting company progress and active engagement with stakeholders are critical, as is the provision of consistent, objective, and meaningful data on actual performance and impact.

CHAPTER 12

CONFRONTING THE SKEPTICS AND THE CRITICS

AS I SAID AT THE OUTSET, FOR MOST OF MY CAREER I HAVE SEEN MY JOB AS explaining the world, not changing it. My journey into the world of stakeholder capitalism was driven more by a journalist's curiosity than a crusader's zeal. Over time, however, I have become a believer. And the reason why I ultimately decided to write this book is to let readers see and hear what I have had the privilege to see and hear by virtue of my job. It seems absolutely clear to me that something important is happening in the world of business, and its effects on the world are, for the most part, good.

But clearly, not everyone agrees with my thesis. One of the pleasures of my job is the three hundred words I get to write each day for our newsletter, the *CEO Daily*. And one of the ancillary pleasures of newsletter writing is that recipients feel free to respond. I read each of those responses, and over the course of the last couple of years, I suspect I have gotten encouragement, but also heard every argument that anyone with a keyboard can muster. I've tried to sort them into general categories, with my responses to each below.

You are so naive, my friend. All this talk about purpose and stakeholders is a head fake, meant to deflect criticism. Greed is still the name of the game.

As a lifelong journalist, I appreciate skeptics. They are my native tribe. But at some point, I have to accept what my ears hear and my eyes see.

Yes, I am certainly aware of CEOs who have gone to their chief marketing officers and demanded, "Find me a purpose!" Indeed, I once worked for one who did exactly that. And I know many stories of companies that pursue good works mainly to deflect attention from their bad works—think of the Sacklers contributing to art galleries while pushing opioid pills on the public.

But I have spent too many hours in too many conversations hearing testimonials from too many leaders who have bowed to the forces of the stakeholder movement, sometimes even against their will. Under Armour CEO Patrik Frisk, for instance, said at one of *Fortune's* CEO Roundtables that if you had asked him when he first took the job to talk about the CEO's role in broader social issues, he would have said, "What are you talking about? I'm here to run a business." But demands from employees, consumers, and investors have changed his view. "It's become the expectation for us, both internally as well as externally."[1]

Okay then, maybe they mean it, but is there any evidence they are actually doing anything about it? At the end of the day, they still have to make a profit, and that drives all.

There is something to that argument. As discussed in the previous chapter, for stakeholder capitalism to become a powerful force, it will need to be supported by common and transparent metrics, and CEOs will have to be held accountable for meeting those metrics, by their boards, their investors, their employees, and their customers. We're not there yet.

In the meantime, though, what I've learned in four decades covering business, and a much shorter time practicing it, is that there is seldom only one answer to any problem, and only one path to a profitable outcome. If CEOs start to pay more attention to the social impact of their business decisions, it will matter at the margins. And in businesses of this size, those margins are large.

Don't you see, Murray, that this is all a big game of politics, and the CEOs are playing it poorly. They think they are appeasing liberal Democrats with their squishy talk of social goals. But in fact, they are only empowering them with appeasement. The result will be that government will turn those goals into regulated requirements.

Ahh, my friends on the *Wall Street Journal* editorial page have joined the dialogue. And again, there is something to their argument. As a political tactic, talking about how CEOs need to take more responsibility for social outcomes may provoke the Elizabeth Warrens of the world to take stronger action.

But what is clear to me is that most of these CEOs aren't being driven by political strategy. As Marc Benioff put it, they are being led by their employees, who in turn are their most important asset. This is nurturing the goose that lays their golden eggs. Political strategy is a secondary concern.

But then, why are you talking about stakeholder capitalism at all? If they are doing this for the sake of their business, isn't that good old-fashioned shareholder capitalism?

In some sense, yes. As we've said throughout this book, there isn't necessarily a conflict between social purpose and profits—at least in the long term.

But again, there is always more than one path to a profitable outcome. And if an increased focus on social benefits leads to the path that is better for people and the planet, isn't that a good thing?

You said, "at least in the long term." Is what we are really talking about here the difference between short-term and long-term profit seeking?

As I said earlier in this book, it takes very little imagination to think of ways you can goose short-term profits at the expense of society. Despoil the environment, slash research, take shortcuts in your product development that may cause problems years in the future, ignore long-term health effects. But over time, the interests of shareholders and stakeholders tend to converge. If you don't take care of your employees, your customers, the communities they live in, or the environment, eventually it will come back to haunt you.

So, yes, "stakeholder capitalism" and capitalism for the long term are closely related.

So, if all you are saying is that companies that pay attention to stakeholders will, in the long run, do better for their shareholders, then are you really saying anything new? Hasn't that always been true?

To some extent, perhaps it has. It is certainly possible to find companies that have always operated this way. I guess what has changed is the cost of *not* operating this way. If you don't look after your employees, if you don't listen to your customers, if you don't show concern for the future of the planet, the consequences are likely to come faster and harder.

What worries me is focus. Businesspeople aren't that smart. If you give them multiple goals, aren't you increasing the odds that they won't meet any of them? Setting total shareholder return as a goal keeps them focused.

Let's be honest, folks. Is there really any area of your life where you focus on a single goal, to the exclusion of all others? Do you obsess over your children's grades, and ignore their happiness or their health? Do you choose a home based solely on a calculation of return on investment, without any regard for what it looks like, where it's located, or whether it is arranged in a way that works for your family? Nothing in your life can be measured by a single metric; why do we think business should be different?

But aren't you worried that we will return to the economy of the 1970s, when businesses became complacent?

Not really. The rapid pace of technological change and the onslaught of disruptive innovation have left most big companies anything but complacent. Regularly, I speak to companies that are more concerned with startups than with their legacy competitors. That's a common refrain in today's business world. We are in a period of Schumpeterian creative destruction that is driving the best big companies to transform themselves faster than ever before in their histories, or be subjected to disruption. Frankly, I've never seen CEOs *less* complacent. The elephants feel like they have to dance . . . or else.

"We're seeing [legacy] companies being replaced with companies with new DNA," serial tech entrepreneur Tom Siebel, now CEO of C3.ai, said at the virtual Fortune Global Forum in December 2020. "Amazon replaced ten thousand retailers in the US last year, applying technology to completely disrupt retailers. Companies like Tesla are using AI and big data to disrupt the automobile business. Airbnb is disrupting the hospitality industry." No cause for complacency.

Okay, even if you could convince me that CEOs can successfully address social goals, why should we let them? Who elected those CEOs? Shouldn't that be the job of democratic governments?

Fair enough. But unfortunately, our governments have been proving themselves sadly incapable of addressing even some of our most obvious needs. Government too often seems to be set up to exploit problems for political gain, rather than solve them. Companies, on the other hand, are set up to solve problems, and CEOs are trained to do the same. Why not let them do what they can?

In fact, what I'm seeing today is that the desire to solve social problems is itself driving dynamism. Increasingly, companies are applying their profit-making superpowers to some of the world's most stubborn problems, and they are driving real change. It's been said that companies today are taking on unsolvable problems and solving them, while government is staring at solvable problems and doing nothing. That's why Marc Benioff calls business "the greatest platform for change."[2]

UNFINISHED BUSINESS

In a book called *The Six New Rules of Business*, Judy Samuelson, founder of the Aspen Institute's Business and Society Program, describes the fundamental changes that have occurred as hard assets and financial capital have become less important, and reputation, intellectual property, and human capital have become more so.[3]

Like me, Samuelson believes those changes have led business to focus more directly on its impact on society—a change reflected in the Business Roundtable's statement on stakeholder capitalism in 2019. "The BRT statement was an important marker," she writes. "It clarified intentions."

But when we spoke in January 2021, Samuelson also told me about the "blind spots"—three significant pieces of unfinished business, which she said are holding companies back from fulfilling their vision for stakeholder capitalism:[4]

> **Executive pay.** Over the last decade, senior executive pay has gone up 7 percent a year, she says, while middle managers on down have seen only 3 percent increases. Why the discrepancy? Because top managers are paid in equity-related rewards, that reflect returns to shareholders. "As long as Shareholder Return is at the center of how we pay executives . . . that's the antithesis of what the Business Roundtable said."

> **Contract workers.** At a time when companies are focusing more on the needs of their employees, their "contract workers remain a blind spot." Contract work "is a huge source of creation of poverty . . . and that's a choice companies are making."

> **Taxes.** "We are going to have another reckoning on taxes," she says. "The intentions that were set when a lot of us supported reducing [corporate tax] rates was . . . to make sure we brought everybody up to that rate." But games played, particularly by global corporations taking advantage of international tax shelters, have undercut that goal.

All three are topics most CEOs are reluctant to discuss. But they will have to be resolved before stakeholder capitalism reaches its full promise.

Finally, I want to be clear about what the new era of capitalism is, and what it isn't.

The goals of business are changing, with more companies compelled to focus on their social and long-term impact. Leadership is becoming more human, striving to inspire workers to give their best to a greater cause. Diversity is being taken seriously, and more companies are holding themselves accountable. Climate change has become a business reality, and the costs are starting to be reflected in corporate accounting. Those are all good things.

But none of this means that greed is dead, or corruption is gone, or malfeasance has been banished. I'm sure there will be spectacular scandals in the years to come, caused by companies who run roughshod over their customers, or their employees, or the communities they live and work in, or the environment. Purdue Pharmaceuticals will not be the last company to push damaging products onto customers. Wirecard will not be the last company to cook its books in order to trick investors. Exxon will not be the last energy company to turn a blind eye to global warming.

At the end of the day, companies are like people. They are complex organisms, capable of great good as well as great evil. And on any given day, they are likely to do some of both. So it goes.

Aneel Bhusri, the CEO of Workday, likes to say that he believes companies need to have a soul.[5] If he's right—if they do have a soul—then shouldn't we expect that soul to guide them to a higher moral plane?

Like most of the people quoted in this book, I am a committed capitalist. There may be others out there who see another path forward, but I am not one of them. Like Leszek Balcerowicz said three decades ago, there is no third way. Capitalism has proven itself the best system mankind has conceived to organize human activity, to create prosperity, and to eliminate poverty. Recent decades only have reconfirmed that fact.

But that doesn't mean capitalism cannot be improved, or that we have no obligation to improve it. "We do need to address climate change. We do need to reduce carbon emissions. We do need a more inclusive society, and we can't stay polarized," Dow CEO Jim Fitterling said in a Fortune CEO roundtable discussion in the spring of 2021. Fitterling runs a petrochemical and plastic business but is passionate about a carbon emissions- and plastic waste–free future. "If business can be a leader in helping bridge the divide between two diametrically opposed political parties, then shouldn't we take a shot at that?"

As this book has explained, the forces are now in place to bring about capitalism 2.0—a capitalism that is more human, more conscious, more creative, more compassionate, more inclusive, more focused on creating shared value, more dedicated to solving the problems of people and the planet.

The burden on the rest of us is to recognize that change, to embrace it, to nurture it, to make it measurable and accountable, and to do our own part to make business better.

ACKNOWLEDGMENTS

THIS BOOK IS A PRODUCT OF THE LAST FIFTEEN YEARS OF MY CAREER, AND thus starts with former *Wall Street Journal* managing editor Paul Steiger's decision to assign me to write a column called "Business" for the newspaper. How can my column be called "Business," I asked, when that's the whole paper's domain? But he knew what he wanted: someone who would look at the world the way CEOs must, taking economic forces, political realities, and the rising demands of diverse stakeholders into account in their business planning. So, credit for this book must start with him, as it does for most things in my career.

At *Fortune*, I owe thanks to Todd Larsen and Norman Pearlstein, who were willing to take a chance on someone who had arguably reached the backside of his career and bring me in to lead this venerable ninety-year-old institution. And I owe a huge debt to my partnership with former editor in chief Clifton Leaf, who schemed with me to add *Change the World* to our pantheon of lists, and who helped me conceive the 2016 conference at the Vatican discussed at the beginning of the book. (Former Time Inc. CEO Joe Ripp and Monsignor Hilary Franco also deserve huge credit for making the Vatican event a reality.)

Leaf allowed me to continue my small daily contributions to the *CEO Daily* newsletter and to co-host a weekly podcast, *Leadership Next*, even as I became more wrapped up in the business side of *Fortune*. I also owe much to my partners in those last two endeavors—David Meyer, who does the heavy lifting on *CEO Daily*, and Ellen McGirt and Megan Arnold, cohost and producer for the podcast. I'm also grateful to Chatchaval Jiaravanon, who rescued *Fortune* from the ashes of Time Inc. and has strongly supported us since.

And then, of course, there is the huge helping of credit that goes to my coauthor Catherine Whitney. I didn't think I could ever find the time in my overcrowded days to write this book. She convinced me I didn't have to. I can only imagine how many hours of reading and listening to me she must have endured. But in the end, she understood my thoughts better than I did. And John Mahaney, as always, was masterful in his editing. He is the best business editor in the business.

Mostly, credit for this book goes to the hundreds of CEOs who were willing to talk with me about the topics herein. While I am now a CEO by title, I am still a journalist at heart, and as such, I have a finely developed bullshit meter from four decades in this profession. I constantly pushed back on those who touted their commitments to social causes, and I ceaselessly probed the why. I read a great deal of Milton Friedman as a student and had the opportunity to talk with him directly as a reporter on numerous occasions. I was eager to know why the Nobel laureate was wrong when he said the "social responsibility of business is to make a profit." What impressed me over time was the growing number of CEOs who not only talked the talk but walked the walk. And that led me to probe deeper. What was it that led this new breed of CEOs to approach their jobs so very differently than their predecessors had? That drove my journey, and I hope this book accurately reflects what I found along the way.

Finally, I have to thank *Fortune*'s fabulous executive team—Lisa Cline, Michael Joseloff, Anastasia Nyrkovskaya, Jonathan Rivers, Michael Schneider, and Alyson Shontell. They make my day job, if not easy, at least manageable, so there's a little time left on the side for efforts like this.

NOTES

FOREWORD: THE REDESIGN IS UNDERWAY

1. Tracy Jan, Jena McGregor, and Meghan Hoyer. "Corporate America's $50 Billion Promise." *Washington Post*, August 23, 2021. https://www.washingtonpost.com/business /interactive/2021/george-floyd-corporate-america-racial-justice/.

PROLOGUE: GOD AND MANNA

1. "Pope Francis Encouraged Business Leaders to Leave No One Behind." https:// holyseemission.org/contents//events/5845c2d5e940c.php. See also "Pope Speaks to Fortune 500 CEOs." YouTube [video], December 5, 2016. https://www.youtube.com /watch?v=hxnCj2txAbw.

2. World Economic Forum. "Davos Annual Meeting 2008—Bill Gates." YouTube [video], January 25, 2008. https://www.youtube.com/watch?v=Ql-Mtlx31e8.

3. Michael E. Porter and Mark R. Kramer. "Creating Shared Value." *Harvard Business Review*, January–February 2011.

4. John Mackey and Raj Sisodia. *Conscious Capitalism: Liberating the Heroic Spirit of Business*. Boston: Harvard Business Review Press, 2013.

5. Marc Benioff. *Trailblazer: The Power of Business as the Greatest Platform for Change*. New York: Currency/Crown, 2019.

CHAPTER 1: THE BIG CHANGE

1. Lanny Ebenstein. *Milton Friedman: A Biography*. New York: Palgrave Macmillan, 2007.

2. Milton Friedman. "A Friedman Doctrine—the Social Responsibility of Business Is to Increase Its Profits." *New York Times*, September 13, 1970.

3. Milton Friedman. *Capitalism and Freedom*. Chicago: University of Chicago Press, 1962.

4. Adam Smith. *An Inquiry into the Nature and Causes of the Wealth of Nations*. London: W. Strahan and T. Cadell, 1776.

5. Friedman, "A Friedman Doctrine."

6. Francis Fukuyama. *The End of History and the Last Man*. New York: Free Press, 1992.

7. "For Larry Summers, Milton Friedman Was a Devil Figure in His Youth." *Mostly Economics*, August 17, 2010.

8. Ibid.

9. TBR: Statement on Corporate Governance, September 1997. https://cdn.the conversation.com/static_files/files/693/Statement_on_Corporate_Governance_Business -Roundtable-1997%281%29.pdf?1566830902.

10. Colin Mayer. *Prosperity: Better Business Makes the Greater Good*. Oxford: Oxford University Press, 2019.

11. *Leadership Next* interview, Alan Murray and Ellen McGirt with Colin Mayer.

12. *Leadership Next* interview, Alan Murray and Ellen McGirt with John Mackey.

13. *Leadership Next* interview, Alan Murray and Ellen McGirt with Bill McDermott.

14. *Jack Welch. Jack: Straight from the Gut*. New York: Warner Books, 2001.

CHAPTER 2: THE BASTION SHAKES

1. Duff McDonald. *Last Man Standing: The Ascent of Jamie Dimon and JPMorgan Chase*. New York: Simon and Schuster, 2009.

2. Rick Wartzman. "It's Time for Top CEOs to Realign Their Interests—Beyond Those of Elevating Shareholders Above All." *Fast Company*, June 28, 2018.

3. Jamie Dimon. "Chairman & CEO Letter to Shareholders." 2019. https://reports .jpmorganchase.com/investor-relations/2019/ar-ceo-letters.htm.

4. Michael R. Strain. "Milton Friedman Was Right About Shareholder Capitalism." *Bloomberg*, September 18, 2020.

5. Lucian Bebchuk and Roberto Tallarita. "The Illusory Promise of Stakeholder Governance." Harvard Law School Forum on Corporate Governance, March 2, 2020.

6. Rebecca Henderson. *Reimagining Capitalism in a World on Fire*. New York: PublicAffairs, 2020.

7. *Leadership Next* interview, Alan Murray and Ellen McGirt with Lucian Bebchuk.

8. John Harwood. "Elizabeth Warren: The Government Listens Too Much 'to Rich Guys Who Don't Want to Pay Taxes.'" CNBC, December 16, 2019.

9. Letter from Josh Bolten, Business Roundtable, to Senator Elizabeth Warren, October 21, 2019. https://www.boston.com/wp-content/uploads/2020/09/2019.10.03-Response-to -Letter-to-Business-Round-Table-re-stakeholder-commitments-and-the-Accountable -Capitalism-Act.pdf.

10. Jonathan Vanian. "Apple CEO Tim Cook on Data Privacy, Immigration, and Speaking Out." *Fortune*, June 25, 2018.

11. *Leadership Next* interview, Alan Murray and Ellen McGirt with Chip Bergh.

12. Alan Murray and David Meyer. "Satya Nadella Explains Microsoft's Climate Responsibilities." *CEO Daily/Fortune*, January 24, 2020.

13. Alan Murray and David Meyer. "Davos: The Stakeholder Capitalism Debate Is Over." *CEO Daily/Fortune*, January 23, 2020.

CHAPTER 3: WHIPLASH

1. *Leadership Next* interview, Alan Murray and Ellen McGirt with Emmanuel Faber.

2. Alan Murray and Katherine Dunn. "Purpose Is Driving These Companies Through Crisis." *CEO Daily/Fortune*, July 1, 2020.

3. *Leadership Next* interview, Alan Murray and Ellen McGirt with Martin Whittaker.

4. Alan Murray and Claire Zillman. "Jerome Powell Is Proving To Be the Perfect Leader for the Coronavirus Moment." *CEO Daily/Fortune*, April 10, 2020.

5. *Leadership Next* interview, Alan Murray and Ellen McGirt with Mark Cuban.

6. *Leadership Next* interview, Alan Murray and Ellen McGirt with Paul Polman.

7. *Leadership Next* interview, Alan Murray and Ellen McGirt with Mark Hoplamazian.

8. *Leadership Next* interview, Alan Murray and Ellen McGirt with Brian Moynihan.

9. *Leadership Next* interview, Alan Murray and Ellen McGirt with Ryan Williams.

10. *Leadership Next* interview, Alan Murray and Ellen McGirt with Mark Hoplamazian.

11. *Leadership Next* interview, Alan Murray and Ellen McGirt with Dr. Erin Thomas.

12. *Leadership Next* interview, Alan Murray and Ellen McGirt with Joe Ucuzoglu.

CHAPTER 4: THE COVID-19 REDEMPTION

1. Justin McCarthy. "Big Pharma Sinks to the Bottom of U.S. Industry Rankings." Gallup, September 3, 2019.

2. "Martin Shkreli, 'Most Hated Man in America,' Arrested for Fraud." CBC, December 17, 2015; Phil McCausland. "Fraud Trial for Martin Shkreli, 'Most Hated Man in America,' Begins Monday." NBC News, June 25, 2017.

3. Stephanie Clifford. "Wanting Martin Shkreli to Stop Talking, Prosecutors Seek Judge's Help." *New York Times*, July 4, 2017.

4. *Leadership Next* interview, Alan Murray and Ellen McGirt with Albert Bourla.

5. *Leadership Next* interview, Alan Murray and Ellen McGirt with Noubar Afeyan.

6. *Leadership Next* interview, Alan Murray and Ellen McGirt with Alex Gorsky.

7. *Leadership Next* interview, Alan Murray and Ellen McGirt with Alexander Hardy.

8. Alexander Hardy. "Genentech Stands Against Inequity and Injustice." Genentech, June 2, 2020. https://www.gene.com/stories/genentech-stands-against-inequity-and-injustice.

9. *Leadership Next* interview, Alan Murray and Ellen McGirt with Albert Bourla.

10. *Fortune*'s Brainstorm Health: The New Paradigm. July 7–8, 2020.

11. Ibid.

12. *Leadership Next* interview, Alan Murray and Ellen McGirt with Mike Roman.

13. Ibid.

14. Alan Murray and David Meyer. "CEOs Say the Pandemic Has Highlighted the Need to Transition to More Sustainable Business Models." *CEO Daily/Fortune*, October 27, 2021.

CHAPTER 5: AN EMPOWERED WORKFORCE

1. Alan Murray and David Meyer. "The 2020 Changes That Will Stick with Us." *CEO Daily/Fortune*, November 18, 2020.

2. Mandy Erickson. "Pandemic an Opportunity to 'Build a Better World,' Huffington Says." Stanford Medicine, September 29, 2020. https://med.stanford.edu/news/all-news/2020/09/arianna-huffington-in-conversation-with-lloyd-minor.html.

3. Alan Murray and David Meyer. "The Post-Covid Office Will Be Very Different." *CEO Daily/Fortune*, August 26, 2020.

4. Prithwiraj (Raj) Choudhury. "Our Work-from-Anywhere Future: Best Practices for All-Remote Organizations." *Harvard Business Review*, November–December 2020.

5. *Leadership Next* interview, Alan Murray and Ellen McGirt with Aneel Bhusri.

6. Alan Murray and David Meyer. "A Rare Opportunity to Redesign Work." *CEO Daily/Fortune*, February 21, 2021.

7. Alan Murray and David Meyer. "Making the Office a Place People Want to Go Because They Enjoy It." *CEO Daily/Fortune*, May 6, 2021.

8. Dov Seidman. *How: How Why We Do Anything Means Everything*. New York: Wiley, 2011.

9. Alan Murray and David Meyer. "The Impact of Remote Work." *CEO Daily/Fortune*, March 3, 2021.

10. Carl Benedikt and Michael A. Osborne. "The Future of Employment: How Susceptible Are Jobs to Computerisation?" University of Oxford, September 2013.

11. Alan Murray and David Meyer. "The Great Digital Acceleration." *CEO Daily/Fortune*, January 14, 2021.

12. Jeff Lawson. *Ask Your Developer: How to Harness the Power of Software Developers and Win the 21st Century*. New York: Harper Business, 2021.

13. Josh Copus. "Building a Digitally Resilient Workforce: Creating On-Ramps to Opportunity." JFF, May 5, 2020.

14. World Economic Forum, 2018 *Future of Jobs* report.

15. ILO Global Commission on the Future of Work, 2019.

16. McKinsey Global Institute.

17. S. Mitra Kalita. "Now Is a Great Time to Make a Drastic Career Change." *Fortune*, January 5, 2021.

18. Deanna Mulligan. *Hire Purpose: How Smart Companies Can Close the Skills Gap*. New York: Columbia Business School Publishing, 2020.

19. Alan Murray and David Meyer. "Meeting the Reskilling Challenge." *CEO Daily/Fortune*, October 23, 2020.

20. Jennifer Liu. "Former IBM CEO Says Employers Should Stop Hiring Based on College Degrees and Focus on This Instead." CNBC, October 5, 2020.

21. *Leadership Next* interview, Alan Murray and Ellen McGirt with Ginni Rometty.

22. Alan Murray and David Meyer. "The Pandemic Pressed Pause on A.I. Investment." *CEO Daily/Fortune*, May 10, 2021.

23. Alan Murray and David Meyer. "Why Accenture Thinks the 'Henry Ford Moment of the Digital Era' Is Coming." *CEO Daily/Fortune*, September 17, 2020.

24. Alan Murray and David Meyer. "Three Big Changes in the Post-Pandemic World." *CEO Daily/Fortune*, October 14, 2020.

25. Alan Murray and David Meyer. "Can Tech Solve the Reskilling Challenge?" *CEO Daily/Fortune*, March 10, 2021.

26. Ibid.

27. *Leadership Next* interview, Alan Murray and Ellen McGirt with Kevin Johnson.

28. Glasmeier's Living Wage Calculator: https://livingwage.mit.edu.

29. *Leadership Next* interview, Alan Murray and Ellen McGirt with Dan Schulman.

30. Mackey, *Conscious Capitalism*.

CHAPTER 6: INNOVATION FROM DIVERSITY

1. Michal Lev-Ram. "IBM's Ginni Rometty: The Way We Hire Must Change—and We Must Do It Now." *Fortune*, June 19, 2020.

2. Maria Aspen. "'We're All Learning Real-Time': GM CEO Mary Barra Is Being Patient—but Concrete—About Inclusivity." *Fortune*, September 29, 2020.

3. "Women, Leadership, and Missed Opportunities: Why Organizations' Good Intentions Are Not Good Enough." IBM Institute for Business Value, 2021. https://www.ibm.com/downloads/cas/3ZNDMAPE.

4. Alan Murray and Katherine Dunn. "'We Are Backsliding': There Are Now Fewer Women in Rising Management Roles Than There Were in 2019." *CEO Daily/Fortune*, March 8, 2021.

5. "Women in the Workplace." McKinsey, September 27, 2021. https://www.mckinsey.com/featured-insights/diversity-and-inclusion/women-in-the-workplace.

6. Alex Katsomitros. "Against the Odds: Ursula Burns' Extraordinary Rise to the Top." World Finance, April 1, 2019. https://www.worldfinance.com/markets/against-the-odds-ursula-burns-extraordinary-rise-to-the-top.

7. *Leadership Next* interview, Alan Murray and Ellen McGirt with Ursula Burns.

8. *Leadership Next* interview, Alan Murray and Ellen McGirt with Indra Nooyi. See also Indra Nooyi. *My Life in Full: Work, Family, and Our Future.* New York: Portfolio, 2021.

9. *Leadership Next* interview, Alan Murray and Ellen McGirt with Tristan Walker.

10. Jo Ann Corkran, Loretta McCarthy, and Peggy Wallace. "Does Robinhood Deserve the Same Amount of Capital as All Women-Led Businesses Combined?" *Fortune*, March 5, 2021.

11. Beth Kowitt. "Why Mellody Hobson Stopped Apologizing for Being a Black Woman." *Fortune*, December 3, 2014.

12. "Top Business Leaders Launch OneTen, Will Create 1 Million Jobs for Black Americans." Bank of America, December 10, 2020.

13. *Leadership Next* interview, Alan Murray and Ellen McGirt with Charles Phillips.

14. Alan Murray and David Meyer. "Fortune and Refinitiv Join Forces to Drive Diversity Reporting." *CEO Daily/Fortune*, October 26, 2020.

15. Alan Murray and David Meyer. "The Business Community Is Tackling Diversity with New Seriousness." *CEO Daily/Fortune*, December 11, 2020.

16. Tim Ryan. "Diversity and the Case for Transparency." PwC, February 17, 2021.

CHAPTER 7: CLIMATE COMMITMENT

1. Larry Fink. "A Fundamental Reshaping of Finance." BlackRock, 2020. https://www.blackrock.com/corporate/investor-relations/2020-larry-fink-ceo-letter.

2. Alan Murray and David Meyer. "CEOs Discuss Working with Government in 2021." *CEO Daily/Fortune*, January 29, 2021.

3. Ibid.

4. Ibid.

5. Alan Murray and David Meyer. "GM's Mary Barra Defends Slow EV Start." *CEO Daily/Fortune*, September 27, 2021.

6. Alan Murray and David Meyer. "Bill Gates Sees Innovation as Key to Achieving Net-Zero." *CEO Daily/Fortune*, February 16, 2021.

7. Alan Murray and David Meyer. "CEO Expectations Are Changing—Thanks, Delta." *CEO Daily/Fortune*, October 22, 2021. https://fortune.com/2021/10/22/expectations-are-changing-delta-ceo-daily.

8. Clifton Leaf. "In an Important New Book, Bill Gates Offers a Real-World Plan for Avoiding a 'Climate Disaster.'" *Fortune*, February 13, 2021.

9. Bill Gates. *How to Avoid a Climate Disaster: The Solutions We Have and the Break-throughs We Need.* New York: Penguin/Random House, 2021.

10. Alan Murray and David Meyer. "The Path to Zero Isn't as Costly for Consumers as You Might Think." *CEO Daily/Fortune,* June 23, 2021.

11. Indra Nooyi. "Why I'm Optimistic About Business's Role in Solving Climate Change." *Fortune,* October 9, 2020.

12. Jens Burchardt, Michael Fredeau, Miranda Hadfield, Patrick Herhold, Chrissy O'Brien, Cornelius Pieper, and Daniel Weise. "Supply Chains as a Game-Changer in the Fight Against Climate Change." Boston Consulting Group, January 26, 2021.

13. Benioff, *Trailblazer.*

14. Doug McMillon. 2020 Regeneration Speech. Walmart, September 21, 2020.

15. Kevin Johnson. "A Letter to Our Starbucks Partners, Customers and All Stake-holders." Starbucks, January 21, 2020. https://stories.starbucks.com/stories/2020/message-from-starbucks-ceo-kevin-johnson-starbucks-new-sustainability-commitment/.

16. *Leadership Next* interview, Alan Murray and Ellen McGirt with Kevin Johnson.

17. Mark Schneider. "We Don't Have to Sacrifice Shareholders to Fight Climate Change." *Fortune,* February 17, 2021.

18. Alan Murray and David Meyer. "Earth Day: Climate Change Is Becoming Ever More Important to Business." *CEO Daily/Fortune,* April 22, 2021.

19. Jad Mouawad. "Exxon Chief Brings Mainly a Change of Style." *New York Times,* March 30, 2006.

20. Ibid.

21. Ibid.

22. Nathan Rosenberg. "Leadership and Black Swan Events." *Insigniam Quarterly,* Summer 2020.

23. Katherine Dunn and Sophie Mellor. "Exxon Mobil Faces Historic Loss in Proxy Shareholder Battle over Future of Its Board." *Fortune,* May 26, 2021.

CHAPTER 8: WHAT'S GOOD FOR THE COMMUNITY

1. Steve Case. *The Third Wave: An Entrepreneur's Vision of the Future.* New York: Simon and Schuster, 2016.

2. Steve Case. "A Memo to the Cities Amazon Passed Over." *Fortune,* January 30, 2018.

3. Rick Wartzman. *The End of Loyalty: The Rise and Fall of Good Jobs in America.* New York: PublicAffairs, 2017.

4. *Leadership Next* interview, Alan Murray and Ellen McGirt with Beth Ford.

5. *Leadership Next* interview, Alan Murray and Ellen McGirt with Vivek Sankaran.

6. *Leadership Next* interview, Alan Murray and Ellen McGirt with Marvin Ellison.

7. *Leadership Next* interview, Alan Murray and Ellen McGirt with Josh Silverman.

CHAPTER 9: THE ACTIVIST CEO

1. Marco Quiroz-Gutierrez. "Black Business Leaders Rebuke Georgia Election Law in Open Letter." *Fortune,* April 2, 2021.

2. "Ed Bastian Memo: Your Right to Vote." *Delta News Hub,* March 31, 2021. https://news.delta.com/ed-bastian-memo-your-right-vote.

3. "Statement from James Quincey on Georgia Voting Legislation." Coca-Cola Company, April 1, 2021. https://www.coca-colacompany.com/media-center/georgia-voting-legislation.

4. "Business Roundtable Statement on Voting Rights." Business Roundtable, March 31, 2021. https://www.businessroundtable.org/business-roundtable-statement-on-voting-rights.

5. Nicole Goodkind. "Mitch McConnell Wants Corporate America to Stay Out of Politics—Unless It Involves Donations." *Fortune*, April 6, 2021.

6. Benioff, *Trailblazer*.

7. *Leadership Next* interview, Alan Murray and Ellen McGirt with Brian Moynihan.

8. "Business Roundtable: CEOs Call for Equality and Tolerance." Business Roundtable, August 14, 2017. https://www.businessroundtable.org/business-roundtable-ceos-call-for-equality-and-tolerance.

9. "A Statement from Denise Morrison, President and CEO." Campbells, August 16, 2017. https://www.campbellsoupcompany.com/newsroom/news/statement-denise-morrison-president-ceo-campbell-soup-company/.

10. Beth Kowitt. "CEOs on Trump's Council Speak Out: Others Stay Silent on Charlottesville." *Fortune*, August 14, 2017.

11. "A Letter from Dick's Sporting Goods CEO Ed Stack." AP, February 28, 2018.

12. Fortune CEO Initiative (livestream). CEO Leadership Interview with Ed Bastian, June 26, 2018.

13. Geoff Colvin. "Derek Chauvin Was Found Guilty. What Will Companies Say About It?" *Fortune*, April 20, 2021.

14. David Meyer. "Corporate America Addresses the Chauvin Verdict." *CEO Daily/Fortune*, April 21, 2021.

15. Ibid.

16. Ibid.

17. Ibid.

18. Ibid.

19. Ibid.

20. Ibid.

21. Dambisa Moyo. *How Boards Work: And How They Can Work Better in a Chaotic World.* New York: Basic Books, 2021.

22. Aaron K. Chatterji and Michael W. Toffel. "The New CEO Activists: A Playbook for Polarized Political Times." *Harvard Business Review*, January–February, 2018.

23. 2021 Edelman Trust Barometer: https://www.edelman.com/trust/2021-trust-barometer.

24. *Leadership Next* interview, Alan Murray and Ellen McGirt with Chuck Robbins.

25. *Leadership Next* interview, Alan Murray and Ellen McGirt with Joe Ucuzoglu.

CHAPTER 10: THE PURPOSE OF BUSINESS

1. *Leadership Next* interview, Alan Murray and Ellen McGirt with Hubert Joly.

2. Hubert Joly. *The Heart of Business: Leadership Principles for the Next Era of Capitalism.* Boston: Harvard Business Review Press, 2021.

3. Jim Collins. *Good to Great: Why Some Companies Make the Leap and Others Don't.* New York: Harper Business, 2001.

4. Jim Collins. *Beyond Entrepreneurship: Turning Your Business into an Enduring Great Company*. New York: Penguin, 1992.

5. Douglas McGregor. *The Human Side of Enterprise*. New York: McGraw-Hill, 1960.

6. Alan Murray and Bruce Simpson. "Purpose, or 'Purpose-Washing'? A Crossroads for Business Leaders." *Fortune*, November 11, 2020.

7. *Leadership Next* interview, Alan Murray and Ellen McGirt with John Donahoe.

CHAPTER 11: THE ACCOUNTABLE ERA

1. Mayer, *Prosperity*.

2. "2021 Overall Rankings." JUST Capital, October 14, 2020. https://justcapital.com /rankings/.

3. "Measuring Stakeholder Capitalism: Towards Common Metrics and Consistent Reporting of Sustainable Value Creation." World Economic Forum, September 22, 2020. https://www.weforum.org/stakeholdercapitalism.

4. *Leadership Next* interview, Alan Murray and Ellen McGirt with Brian Moynihan.

5. *Leadership Next* interview, Alan Murray and Ellen McGirt with Doug Peterson.

6. Alan Murray and David Meyer. "Green Investing Can Pay Off in Spades." *CEO Daily/ Fortune*, February 24, 2021.

7. Ibid.

8. "About B Lab." https://bcorporation.net/about-b-lab.

9. *Leadership Next* interview, Alan Murray and Ellen McGirt with Eileen Fisher.

10. *Leadership Next* interview, Alan Murray and Ellen McGirt with Ryan Gellert.

CHAPTER 12: CONFRONTING THE SKEPTICS AND THE CRITICS

1. Phil Wahba. "Why CEOs Think Speaking Out Is Worth It, Despite the Risks." *Fortune*, March 18, 2021.

2. Benioff, *Trailblazer*.

3. Judy Samuelson. *The Six New Rules of Business*. San Francisco: Berrett-Koehler Publishers, 2021.

4. Ibid.

5. Ibid.

INDEX

Alan Murray is chief executive of Fortune Media (USA Corporation). He oversees the business and editorial operations of the independent media company and is known for expanding its digital and conference franchises. Murray also writes a closely read daily newsletter, the *Fortune CEO Daily*. Prior to joining Fortune in 2015, Murray led the rapid expansion of the Pew Research Center's digital footprint as president of that organization. Before that, Murray was at the *Wall Street Journal* for many years, serving as deputy managing editor, executive editor online, Washington bureau chief, and author of the "Political Capital" and "Business" columns. He served for several years as Washington bureau chief for CNBC and cohost of the nightly show *Capital Report*. He is the author of the classic *Showdown at Gucci Gulch: Lawmakers, Lobbyists, and the Unlikely Triumph of Tax Reform*.

PublicAffairs is a publishing house founded in 1997. It is a tribute to the standards, values, and flair of three persons who have served as mentors to countless reporters, writers, editors, and book people of all kinds, including me.

I. F. STONE, proprietor of *I. F. Stone's Weekly*, combined a commitment to the First Amendment with entrepreneurial zeal and reporting skill and became one of the great independent journalists in American history. At the age of eighty, Izzy published *The Trial of Socrates*, which was a national bestseller. He wrote the book after he taught himself ancient Greek.

BENJAMIN C. BRADLEE was for nearly thirty years the charismatic editorial leader of *The Washington Post*. It was Ben who gave the *Post* the range and courage to pursue such historic issues as Watergate. He supported his reporters with a tenacity that made them fearless and it is no accident that so many became authors of influential, best-selling books.

ROBERT L. BERNSTEIN, the chief executive of Random House for more than a quarter century, guided one of the nation's premier publishing houses. Bob was personally responsible for many books of political dissent and argument that challenged tyranny around the globe. He is also the founder and longtime chair of Human Rights Watch, one of the most respected human rights organizations in the world.

•   •   •

For fifty years, the banner of Public Affairs Press was carried by its owner Morris B. Schnapper, who published Gandhi, Nasser, Toynbee, Truman, and about 1,500 other authors. In 1983, Schnapper was described by *The Washington Post* as "a redoubtable gadfly." His legacy will endure in the books to come.

Peter Osnos, *Founder*

Advance Acclaim for *Crater Trueblood* and the Lunar Rescue Company

"An exciting romp through a surprisingly realistic future. Homer's knowledge of science gives an interesting backdrop to a universe filled with exotic creatures and amusingly fantastical elements."

—JASPER T. SCOTT, AUTHOR OF THE DARK SPACE SERIES

"Hickam again displays a knack for suspenseful scenes out in the 'big suck' of space . . ."

—KIRKUS REVIEWS

"With vivid prose, wild imagination, and a keen eye for the science behind the fiction, Homer Hickam transports us to a future Moon that is equal parts wild west boomtown, hot-rod dragstrip, and royal court in a space opera. Packed with big-hearted heroes, damsels more than clever enough to get themselves out of distress, villains with double and triple agendas, and—of course—hyper-intelligent slime molds, *Crater Trueblood and the Lunar Rescue Company* is a thrill ride of space battles, runaway asteroids, and all the derring-do any reader could ever hope for."

—JAVIER GRILLO-MARXUACH, WRITER AND PRODUCER ON *LOST* AND *HELIX* AND CREATOR OF *THE MIDDLEMAN*

Acclaim for Homer Hickam

"Classic science-fiction storytelling in the style of early Heinlein, humor, and grand adventure permeate every page of this first book in a trilogy. Boys in particular may be inspired to bring back the time-honored tradition of reading by flashlight under the covers."

—SCHOOL LIBRARY JOURNAL REVIEW OF *CRATER*

"Long-haul trucking on the Moon . . . with raiders, romance and a secret mission. . . . High adventure on the space frontier."

—KIRKUS REVIEW, REGARDING *CRATER*

AUG   2014

"*Crater* shows what it would be like to live on the Moon: to work there, to struggle and to triumph. A fine piece of work by Homer Hickam."

—BEN BOVA, AUTHOR OF *LEVIATHANS OF JUPITER*

"Readers will be caught up in Homer Hickam's thrilling novel of life on the moon! Plenty of twists and an admirable, spirited hero in Crater who takes us on an adventure filled with intrigue and excitement that leaves us wanting more."

—DONNA VANLIERE, *NEW YORK TIMES* & *USA TODAY* BESTSELLING AUTHOR OF *THE GOOD DREAM* AND *THE CHRISTMAS SHOES*

CRATER
TRUEBLOOD
AND THE
LUNAR RESCUE COMPANY

CRATER
TRUEBLOOD
AND THE
LUNAR RESCUE COMPANY

A HELIUM-3 NOVEL

BOOK THREE

HOMER
HICKAM

THOMAS NELSON
Since 1798

NASHVILLE   MEXICO CITY   RIO DE JANEIRO

Published in Nashville, Tennessee, by Thomas Nelson. Thomas Nelson is a registered trademark of HarperCollins Christian Publishing, Inc.

Thomas Nelson, Inc., titles may be purchased in bulk for educational, business, fund-raising, or sales promotional use. For information, please email SpecialMarkets@ ThomasNelson.com.

Scripture quotations taken from the King James Version of the Bible.

Library of Congress Cataloging-in-Publication Data

Hickam, Homer H., 1943–
  Crater Trueblood and the Lunar Rescue Company / Homer Hickam.
    pages ; cm. — (A Helium-3 novel ; book 3)
    ISBN 978-1-59554-662-3 (hardcover)
[1. Moon—Fiction. 2. Science fiction.] I. Title.
  PZ7.H5244Ct 2014
  [Fic]—dc23   2014006241

Printed in the United States of America

14 15 16 17 18 19 RRD 6 5 4 3 2 1

To NASA Al English

::: ONE

Beneath the vast Michael Collins Dome in Armstrong City, Medaris Enterprises guards held back curious pedestrians as Dr. Maria Medaris strode purposefully from her corporate headquarters building and into the backseat of a black limobug, her assistant Miss Torricelli settling in beside her. Maria was a glamorous celebrity, often appearing on lunar and Earthian business shows as well as slick fashion putersites. She was also an executive who led companies that employed thousands of lunar settlers. It was said she had the golden touch when it came to business because every enterprise she commanded was profitable and growing. It was also said, this by the gossipmongers, that this raven-haired young woman was cold and aloof, for no recent suitor—among them the wealthiest and most eligible bachelors on the Earth and the moon—ever came close to winning her hand. There were also rumors of a lost love, a common Helium-3 miner who'd since disappeared somewhere in the wayback. But if he had ever existed, he'd been out of Maria Medaris's life for years and was therefore of no interest to the columnists and bloggers on the society pages of two worlds.

A broken heart can explain many things in a woman, but first a heart must exist, and there was some doubt by the writers who sold copy about her that Dr. Medaris had anything other than the muscle that pumped blood in her chest. Had these scribblers cared to delve deeper into their subject, they would have discovered her lofty poise was entirely a ruse. Every day Maria awoke thinking of that Helium-3 miner out there in the dust and despaired, because even as she commanded others to do her bidding, she felt quite lost without him. Although her expression was outwardly serene as the lunaparazzi clicked away, she was in fact inwardly sad, romantically bewildered, and tired to the marrow of her bones. She had already put in a fourteen-hour workday and it was still far from over. And when she awoke the next morning, she knew the heel-3 miner she adored would not be by her side and the reason he would not be there was entirely her fault. "How many?" Maria wearily asked her assistant while struggling to push the man from her mind. He was always there, but stronger when she was tired and unable to fight him off.

"Fourteen decision papers."

"Virgil, let's go," Maria commanded the driver, then subsided into the plush faux leather seat as the limobug eased into the traffic flow, leaving the running photographers behind. "All right, Teresa," she directed. "Put them up."

As the chauffeur weaved them through the traffic of fastbugs and dust trucks and limobugs along mooncrete roads lined by bright orange streetlights, Miss Torricelli drew rectangles in the air, describing each document that appeared. "Approved," Maria said, or "Disapproved," or "Save for more study," and her assistant dutifully touched the shimmering rectangle, whipping it back inside her workpad.

After passing through the J. R. Thompson Tunnel connecting the Michael Collins Dome with the Neil Armstrong Dome, the limobug turned to the southwest toward the various private skyports that serviced the moon's largest city. When Miss Torricelli noticed a small sigh that escaped Maria's lips, she said, "Just a few more to go, Dr. Medaris."

Maria did her best to focus on the floating contract. "Disapproved," she said. "I think we can get a better price. Tell purchasing to ask for a ten percent discount and to let this company know that if we don't get it, we'll jump to their competition. And keep going. If I don't make these decisions now, I'll just have to do them later."

"Yes, ma'am," Miss Torricelli said and drew the rectangle for the next decision paper to hang in the air.

When they reached the Medaris Enterprises Jumpcar Facility, Maria made a decision on the final document, then climbed out, took the kitbag handed her by the driver, and walked into the hangar where her private jumpcar waited on a mobile launchpad. Her day had begun in Armstrong City but was going to end at Clyde's Dream, a chaotic boomtown located in the brownish-gray dust of the Moscow Sea on the farside of the moon. She would spend the night there before inspecting the giant new telescope her company was building.

Tall and elegant, Maria was dressed in a military-style jacket over a chic jumpsuit of clinging lunacell fabric, all in the latest fashion color of Earth Sky Blue, a color sorely missed on the moon. She had also tucked her shapely legs into a pair of unfashionable ersatz leather flight boots. Although fashion was important to Maria, jumpcars could get chilly and she didn't care for cold toes during flight. As she came through the entry hatch, she nodded to Jack Nguyen, her pilot and a scar-faced veteran of the recent war. "Would you like to fly her, Dr. Medaris?" he asked.

Maria's fatigue and sadness instantly evaporated. She loved flying jumpcars, and she was good at it, too, best demonstrated during the war when she'd not only outflown but managed to cripple an armed-to-the-gills Earthian warpod intent on shooting her little jumpcar down. As Nguyen slipped over into the copilot's seat, she eagerly climbed into the cockpit. "Hatches sealed, Jack?" she asked.

"All sealed, ma'am. She's ready to go."

"Medaris hangar, take us out," Maria said to the ground crew.

The first set of hangar doors slid open and the jumpcar pad slowly rolled along a track into an interim chamber, the doors closing behind and sealing it off. Pumps were engaged to drain the air into pressurized tanks for reuse, followed by the outer doors opening to the vacuum of the moon. The pad trundled through the doors to its designated launching position. Once poised for liftoff, spotlights focused on the ship while streams of vaporized liquid propellant vented from its three engines.

"Armstrong Control," Maria called, "Medaris One Alpha on the pad. Flight plan zero four seven alpha kilo zulu. Trajectory is standard northeast vector along the farside corridor. Destination Clyde's Dream."

"Roger, Medaris One Alpha, you are cleared for transit."

"Ready, Jack?" Maria asked.

"Full throttle up," the pilot responded, his eyes on the sky brilliantly awash with stars only partly obscured by the lights and fuel vapors.

An eager smile formed on Maria's face. All business and thoughts of old and lost loves were set aside. It was time to fly!

"Puter, autopilot off. I'll take her all the way. On my mark for launch. Five-four-three-two-one-mark!"

The jumpcar's trio of engines burst into action and it soared atop their flames into the sky, then transitioned along a ballistic arc, its tail kept constantly pointed at the lunar surface. Maria kept her eye on the trajectory displayed on the puter while moving the joystick to stay precisely on the curve. "Wish I could wring her out," Maria said regretfully.

"Just give me a call anytime," the pilot replied, "and I'll have her ready to go as far and as fast as you care to fly her."

"Thanks, Jack. I appreciate it."

"I appreciate the job you gave me," he answered. "Not many wanted me, messed up as I was after the war."

Maria made no reply. She didn't have to. There were a lot of so-called "messed-up" veterans after the vicious war between the moon and the Earth, and she made it her policy to hire them when she could. Experience had shown that all they needed was a job that allowed them to be useful, and, anyway, veterans were the best employees around. In fact, Maria was one herself, having gotten more than a whiff of the war while fighting with the irregulars in the dust and later the fuser fleet in the sky. It had been a nasty conflict and there had been no winner, although it had been concluded by a truce begged for by an exhausted Earth tired of fighting a bunch of recalcitrant Lunarians who simply refused to give up. Maria was proud of how the moon had fought back, although the dead and the maimed of the conflict called out to her. She knew it also concerned her grandfather, the truly great Colonel Medaris, who had told her that he intended to "fix it so that war would never return to the moon." How he was going to do that, Maria didn't know, but whatever it was, she knew it would be in the grand style of the Colonel who rarely did anything in a small way.

A little less than ten minutes after liftoff, Maria piloted the jumpcar to a smooth landing on her reserved pad at Clyde's Dream. There was no dome over the town. Except for the jumpcar hangar and a few out buildings, everything was built underground. A dust truck pulled the jumpcar into the hangar, and after one atmosphere was established, Maria went through the postflight checklist, then nodded her gratitude to the pilot and climbed out of the hatch and down the ladder to the hangar floor. After processing through the primary dustlock into the underground network of living tubes and administrative offices, she went straight to the tube reserved for her living quarters, meaning to have dinner (which Miss Torricelli had preordered), answer any urgent emails, and go to bed.

Maria's quarters were small but functional, a single tube with a plaston partition between a combination kitchen/living room and the bedroom with its adjoining bathroom. She tossed her kit on her narrow bunk, shrugged off her jacket, and opened one of its pockets to let her gillie out. The clump of intelligent slime mold was asleep, so she shook it onto the bed, then took it in the palm of her hand and placed it on the bedside table. The mass of gray cells did not move, which was fine with Maria since she had no questions for it to answer. Gillies also tended to be unhappy if they were awakened from a sound sleep, and Maria was in no mood to contend with a cranky, sarcastic gillie who was, after all, one of the toughest, smartest biological computers yet devised, although that hadn't saved them when their creators realized the monsters they had created.

Now there were only two gillies left: Maria's and the one

belonging to the Helium-3 miner who'd captured her heart, a man named Crater Trueblood. All the rest of the gillies, which had numbered in the thousands, had been destroyed because of their ability to hack any puter, their general sneakiness, their ability to kill, and their willingness to use all their powers to help their owners whether they wanted help or not.

Maria contemplated the dozing gillie and recalled how it was she came to own it. Crater's gillie had belonged to his parents, who'd died in a jumpcar crash. As a boy, he hadn't realized what it was but had kept it as a keepsake tucked away in a drawer in his bedroom. When he was twelve and started working as a Helium-3 miner, the gillie had suddenly come awake and told him to take it out of the drawer and keep it with him, while promising to keep Crater safe on the often deadly scrapes. Only then did Crater become aware of his gillie's full powers. Maria's gillie was the offspring of Crater's, delivered up during their wild escape across the moon from pursuing crowhoppers. When Maria had left Crater, she'd taken the baby gillie with her, and now, as far as she knew, it was fully grown. The only thing she knew for sure about the gillie was that it was illegal, but it knew that. She also liked its reputation of always being completely, utterly, and totally on the side of its owner, no matter what. For that reason, she was willing to ignore its illegality, its general sneakiness, its ability to wantonly kill anyone it deemed a threat to its owner, and its often sarcastic commentary. Also, the truth was, she liked having it because it was her only direct connection to Crater Trueblood, whatever had become of the man. After she'd left him, she'd deliberately made no attempt to find out where he was. She assumed he wanted it that way.

A knock on her hatch announced the arrival of dinner.

Carrying a biovat-derived salad on a tray, the attendant proved to be someone Maria knew, an App named Durwood Hale. After the Earthian Appalachian Mountains had been fenced off into a national park, its residents—called Apps—had been expelled, many of them moving to the moon and settling in the little town beside Adolphus Crater named Endless Dust, there to mine Helium-3 and Thorium along with other minerals. Maria, running with Crater from enemy troops during the late war, had lived in the remote village for many months. Delighted to see someone she'd known during that time, she put down her workpad and stood to greet him. "Durwood, how good to see you."

The App placed the tray on her desk, started to put out his hand, then caught himself and bowed. Although Apps still maintained the tradition of a handshake, it was now considered an old-fashioned gesture. A modified Japanese bow was the modern and polite greeting for most humans on the Earth and the moon.

"Hello there, Dr. Medaris," he said. "I grabbed the tray when I saw it was your order. I hope you're well."

"Quite well, but what are you doing here?"

"There's more than a few of us Apps here from the Dust, ma'am, come to work on your telescope. We're sendin' the money back to our families."

Durwood's answer pleased Maria. She'd worked hard to see that the wages for her telescope workers were robust, since it was her strong belief that quality work was usually best accomplished by employees who were both fairly paid and firmly managed. "How are things at Endless Dust?" she asked. "I'm sorry, but I haven't kept up."

Durwood's face fairly glowed at the mention of his town.

"Real good, Miss Medaris, thank ya for askin'. They opened up a new scrape and got some new separators for the Thorium. Guess you heard about Crater's leg."

Such casual mention of Crater caught Maria by surprise. "Crater? What's this about his leg?" A flutter of worry beat in her chest.

Durwood took on a sheepish look. "Sorry, ma'am. I figured you already knew. A shuttle car turned over on him. Busted up his leg pretty good. They shipped him off to Cleomedes for surgery and rehab and he never came back. Heard he started his own company over there, something to do with rescuing folks. Not sure what it's all about, but I know Crescent went with him. That crowhopper girl looked kinda rough, but once you got to know her, she was sorta sweet. Wherever Crater went, she was sure to go. Sorry if that sounds like gossip."

Maria tried to act nonchalant. "Well, thank you for filling me in, Durwood." She tapped a generous tip into her workpad and waved it toward his workpad, instantly transferring the money across.

Durwood bowed again. "Thank you, ma'am. Hope you enjoy your meal. Just leave the tray outside your hatch. I'll pick it up later."

When the hatch closed behind the App, Maria, feeling flustered by news of Crater, sat back in her chair. Even though his absence saddened her, the flip side of that emotion was anger. After all, he'd had his chance with her, actually several chances, and messed them all up. Or maybe it was Maria who'd messed them up. She closed her eyes and shook her head. Who was at fault didn't really matter. The point was they were always going to be messed up. Still, she recalled him kissing her that first time, at least the first time when they weren't wearing space helmets, and how his lips felt against hers, and how he drew her in with his powerful miner's arms . . .

Maria flung the memory from her mind. The problem with Crater Trueblood was he was deeply flawed. True, he was attractive, that is, if a girl liked the wholesome country bumpkin type, with long, sandy hair and blue-gray eyes that could see right through you and broad shoulders, muscled arms, strong hands, and . . . Well, those physical things shouldn't matter, not to a woman like Maria, should they? After all, she was on a trajectory to the top of the Medaris family empire. And how could she marry someone like Crater, who didn't care anything about either corporate business or money? A man like that would only hold her back, and she was well rid of him.

Still . . . Crater was a brilliant engineer, which meant he had *some* mental capabilities. And, though she didn't much like to be reminded of it, he also had the habit of saving her life. The last time, one step ahead of a band of crowhoppers, as the black-hearted mercenaries of the United Countries of the World were called, Crater had carried her off to Endless Dust, about as wayback as a town on the moon could be. And naturally, Maria dismissively recalled, Crater was perfectly happy there. In fact, he'd wanted to settle down in the little App-run village. With the war raging and a bounty on her head, Maria was, for a time, content to stay hidden away. In a tender moment, she had even agreed to marry Crater and stay with him in Endless Dust, but then a space taxi had landed and a pilot swaggered down the ramp looking for her. It had proved to be none other than Petro, Crater's older brother who was then a fuser squadron commander for Maria's grandfather. At Petro's invitation, Maria stepped aboard the taxi ramp, assuming Crater would follow, but he hadn't. Instead he'd stayed where he was, in the dust, the hideous captured crowhopper girl beside him.

Maria realized her cheeks were wet with tears and her dinner salad had wilted. "Why didn't you come with me?" she asked as she recalled Crater standing there watching her leave, his upturned face filled with an anguish that had not been enough to make him take that one small step to join her.

But then she imagined Crater's response, "Why didn't you stay?"

Her answer was, "Duty to my family," which really meant, if she examined her sad and pathetic heart, "I had bigger and better things to do."

::: TWO

leep did not come easily for Maria that evening. Her mind simply would not allow her to rest. An hour before the end of the sleep cycle, she finally gave up and woke her gillie. The gillie rubbed sleep from its eyes, even though it had no eyes or hands to rub with. *How may I help you at this hour when actually you should still be asleep?*

"Why have you not kept me apprised of the goings and comings of Crater Trueblood?" Maria demanded. "I just learned he recently suffered a broken leg."

Maybe because you told me you never wanted to hear anything about him.

"When did I say that?"

The most recent was six months ago when you asked me to investigate an advanced sling pump for jumpcar engines. I told you that Crater Trueblood held the patent for that pump.

"Yes, and then you said he had an announcement on the patent that he wouldn't sell it."

Because he believed he could come up with a better design.

"Crater doesn't understand that in business 'better' is the

enemy of 'good enough.' That sling pump is a brilliant design as it is."

Your philosophy fits you well, but why didn't you tell him that and make an offer?

"Because I hate him. No, I take that back. I am indifferent to him." Even as she said it aloud, it didn't ring true to her ears, and she knew the gillie would not be fooled.

You say you are indifferent, yet you yell at me for failing to keep you apprised of him? All right and very well. I shall ignore this dichotomy. Over what time period do you wish to know of the goings and comings of Crater Trueblood?

"Since he left Endless Dust."

The gillie vibrated as it connected, searched, and hacked through various puters to gather the required information, then said, *Crater Trueblood, twenty-one years old, lives in the twin-domed city of Cleomedes, otherwise known as the Lunar Las Vegas. He is the chief partner in a company called the Lunar Rescue Company, which is on call to rescue anyone who is in trouble on the surface of the moon but principally works for the Cleomedes Casino to look after their often wayward guests after imbibing too much in the way of alcoholic spirits, including the local earthshine. The other partner in this enterprise— barely financially afloat, by the way—is Petro Mountbatten-Jones, his brother, although not by blood, since Petro's mother adopted Crater when he was three years old. Their associate in this business is Crescent Claudine Besette, the only known female crowhopper.*

"Stop right there," Maria said. "What's *her* status?"

Crescent Claudine Besette is a former member of the Phoenix Legion, which is a subset of the mercenary Legion of Warriors, also known as the Legionnaires, also known as Crowhoppers. Phoenix troopers are genetically programmed to cease all functions, mean- ing to die, at around twenty-one years of age. This was done to make them fearless in combat since they know their days are numbered. 'Life is death. Death is life,' is their battle cry. There were three Phoenix Legions created, all disbanded after losses of their members were so extensive they could no longer function as organizations.

"How old is Crescent?"

Just as you and Crater, she is all of twenty-one, an age when humans are certain they know everything even though they have little experience to know anything, a notable exception, of course, being you, since you own me, who either knows everything or can find it out.

Maria ignored the jibe. "And she's still healthy?"

Unknown. Do you want me to call Crater Trueblood so you can ask him the status of her health?

Even though she knew the gillie was being sarcastic, Maria was tempted to take it up on its offer. Maybe it was time she spoke to Crater, perhaps using the excuse that she'd only called to offer sympathy for his broken leg, or maybe even ask him how much he wanted for his stupid jumpcar sling pump. She dithered about it until the gillie said, *Since clearly you don't know what you want to do, let me remind you that you have a busy day scheduled and you probably should start. First matter on your schedule is to eat your awful breakfast. After that take your meetings. After that you will proceed to the telescope construction site.*

"Thank you, Gillie. I don't know what I would do without you."

Neither do I.

Maria's breakfast was the same each day, a biogoop vitamin drink that tasted horrible but was supposed to be good for her. Once she'd choked it down, she called up the managers of the three companies she directly controlled and then sent them off with action lists to be completed with reports back to her before the end of that day. After that she suited up in a biolastic pressure suit and set out in a fastbug on the well-worn trail to the telescope construction site. Her purpose was to inspect the telescope and talk with the foreman about its progress and any problems he was having. Three hours were allotted for this activity, and then she was to drive back to Clyde's Dream where her jumpcar waited for her. After a flight back to Armstrong City, she was to be met by her limobug to take her to the central business office of Medaris Enterprises for a late round of meetings with various executives. Since she was also the chief financial officer of the combined family corporations, she would also give a report in a vid-meeting with the leader of the family and founder of its fortune, her grandfather, Colonel John High Eagle Medaris. It was another full day like all her days.

Temporarily removed from any responsibility other than not getting lost on the way, Maria decided to have a little fun by veering off the trail and going through the backcountry. Soon her boot was pressing the fastbug accelerator to the floor. She raced along, twin rooster tails of dust spewing into the vacuum behind her. Whooping and hollering, she steered, slipped, slid, and leaped among the masses of craters pocking the lunar floor. When she reached a massive crater that overlooked the construction site, she tore up the crater's slope and skidded to a stop just below the rim.

The gillie came out of its belt pouch and climbed to her shoulder. *I have monitored your incoming do4u text messages during your drive out, which, by the way, was far too rapid and therefore extremely irresponsible but at least seems to have improved your mood. There are eight business and zero personal messages. Would you like me to read them to you?*

"No. They'll wait. Leave me alone for a minute. I want to study the construction site."

The gillie shrugged, although it had no shoulders, and crawled back into its pouch. Maria climbed onto the crater's rim and watched her blue-suited workers swarming over a vast litesteel framework that would eventually support a liquid mirror big enough to hold a shovelball field. When completed, the Clyde Tombaugh Lunar Telescope was designed to give humanity its first clear view of Earth-like planets orbiting around the nearest star systems and perhaps provide an answer to questions that cut across generations. Were there any planets out there where humans could live without suits and helmets? Were there truly other Earths? Scientists said the telescope would be able to see oceans, lakes, continents, and cloud formations. If there were life-forms with advanced technologies, it was anticipated that at night the telescope might even be able to see the lights of their cities.

Construction of the telescope was not entirely altruistic on the part of the Medaris family. Maria and her grandfather believed that if a new cradle of life was found within range of humanity, another age of exploration might be sparked, which would require advanced propulsion drives. Not coincidentally, Medaris Space Liners (MSL) already had such drives on their puter design boards. If a planet capable of supporting human life was found, and if private groups or governments wanted to go to the stars and were willing to pay for it, ships that could reach quarter–light speed might become profitable to build. It was the way the Colonel and Maria conducted business. First, create a need, and then be ten steps ahead of the competition with a product to satisfy that need.

Maria had laid out the plan and set the schedule for every facet of the telescope's construction. "Give me the sick call report," she said.

The gillie, from its pouch, reported, *Two sinus headaches. No downtime. One skin exposure due to glove failure. Treated and returned to work.*

"Why are they behind schedule?"

Work on the moon is never easy, the gillie answered.

"You are no help," Maria admonished, then drove the fastbug down the crater's slope, slowing to avoid tossing up dust that might pollute the construction site and the telescope equipment. As she parked the little vehicle near one of the cranes, the white-suited shift foreman loped over, spouts of dust erupting each time his boot struck the lunar surface. "Good day to you, Dr. Medaris," he said as he bowed. "We've had a good day. You'll see it in my report."

Maria recognized the foreman, Morumba Kendatta, arrived only a few weeks before. He'd been brought from Earth to replace a foreman who had ignored the dustlock protocol and breathed in enough of the moon to shred one of her lungs. She was now in the hospital in Armstrong City and her prognosis was poor.

"You're behind schedule," Maria said, directness being her habit. "The bearing mechanisms should have already been installed."

"We had trouble erecting the carrier," Kendatta explained. "Much of the assembly was out of tolerance, so we had to machine components to fit."

"Then you should have called me. You also had a skin exposure accident. Something that serious I need to know about."

"The injury wasn't that serious."

Maria's eyes narrowed. "I could bandy words with you, Mr. Kendatta," she said, "but we both know how it would end. This is my project, you are my foreman, and that means I tell you what to do and then you do it without argument. Are we clear?"

The foreman blinked.

"Yes, ma'am, very clear."

"I will be here for about an hour. You may go back to work."

Maria watched the foreman walk back to the construction site. Many men and women who came to Luna were on the run from something—tax evasion, wars, wives, husbands, and so forth. Maria wondered what had chased Kendatta to the moon.

Something caught her attention in the sky. When she looked, she saw the telltale sparkles of a trio of hot rocket jets that identified it as a jumpcar, the suborbital taxis of the moon. It appeared to be heading for a landing near the telescope site, which, because of dust contamination, was strictly forbidden.

"Gillie, sync with that jumpcar's transmissions."

Silent running came the reply.

"Connect me anyway."

Synchronized with all standard frequencies.

"Jumpcar landing on the Tombaugh telescope site, be aware this is a restricted zone. You cannot land here!"

Tail first, the jumpcar kept descending, its directional jets spurting, its primary engines pumping flames.

"Jumpcar landing on telescope construction site, your exhaust will contaminate our equipment. Stop landing!"

The jumpcar did not stop. A cloud of dust billowing beneath its tail, it settled down. Maria was relieved to see that most of the dust immediately fell back to the surface, but some electro-magnetically-charged particles began to drift, the sun's pressure pushing them along toward the construction site.

Incensed, Maria climbed behind the wheel of her fastbug and drove to the jumpcar. By the time she reached it, she could see a number of people had climbed out and were standing around its base. She recognized one of them. It was her father.

Maria frowned and clicked on her suit's general communications frequency. "Junior? Why are you here?"

Her father, John Medaris Jr., nicknamed Junior, was wearing gray coveralls and a helmet with the Medaris family crest, an eagle landing on the moon. Below that was the Medaris family motto, *De inimico non loquaris sed cogites*, which meant *Do not wish ill for your enemy; plan it.* He turned to look at her but said nothing.

Thoroughly confused, Maria got off the fastbug. When she walked closer, she was astonished to see that four of the 'people' with her father were actually crowhoppers. They turned away, as if they could hide themselves, but their black armor, slit helmets, long arms, short legs, and thick torsos precisely identified them. They were also carrying railgun rifles. The two people standing beside her father were not crowhoppers but willowy and tall, their coveralls made of a sheer, copper-colored material. Their bubble helmets showed elfin-like faces painted bone white with green lips. She couldn't tell if the creatures, whatever they were, were male or female.

Maria didn't dare get any closer. Crowhoppers were ugly brutes who might tear her limbs off just for the sport of it, and the weird face-painted pair looked dangerous too.

Her father's presence was equally strange. Although he was on a number of company boards within the Medaris Enterprises conglomerate, he was estranged from his father, the Colonel, and from his daughter. Maria had given him a chance to work for her but had fired him when she'd caught him repeatedly lying and embezzling. There was no reason for him to be at the construction site, especially with crowhoppers and the strange couple in the coppery suits.

"You have to leave," Maria demanded, "and when you do,

make certain your pilot pivots the jumpcar to create a minimum of dust. As it is, it will take days to clean up your mess."

Her father glanced at the copper-suited pair, then squared his shoulders. "Maria, your grandfather is retiring and I am taking over Medaris Enterprises. You will come with me and I will explain the situation in more detail."

Her father's astonishing declaration took a moment to sink in. "Don't be absurd," she heard herself saying as alarm bells rang in her head. She needed to get away, but two of the crowhoppers had moved to cut her off from her fastbug.

The foreman Kendatta drove up on a fastbug and dismounted. "Dr. Medaris, who are these people?"

Her father spoke first. "You're the foreman? I am John Medaris Jr., Maria's father and the son of Colonel Medaris. This construction site is closed. Go back and gather your workers and move them to the landing zone. They will be paid off and then convoyed to Armstrong City."

Kendatta looked at the stranger claiming to be his boss's father and then at Maria. "Dr. Medaris, what should I do?"

"Go back to work, Foreman Kendatta. I'll handle this."

"Yes, ma'am." The foreman turned and took a step toward his fastbug but then fell forward, twin geysers of blood spurting from his back. Maria ran to the foreman and turned him over in time to see him breathe his last. When she looked up, the copper-clad freaks had sick smiles on their green-painted lips. The crowhopper who'd shot the foreman stepped forward and jammed the muzzle of his rifle at the base of her helmet. "Shall I kill her too?"

When Maria looked at her father, she was dismayed to discover he seemed to be mulling over the crowhopper's question.

::: THREE

On the other side of the moon from where Maria Medaris knelt beside her dead foreman, Crater Trueblood had thought about Maria off and on all morning. As she floated in and out of his mind, it occurred to him that perhaps it was because she was thinking of him, a concept he dismissed as impossible since Crater was a practical man who didn't believe in such things as mental telepathy, even with minds that had once shared love. Yet, there he'd been, turning Maria over in his head almost from the moment he'd driven the Lunar Rescue Company's truck into the dust from the twin-domed gambling town of Cleomedes in search of a lost rental bus. There had to be a reason why he was thinking about Maria, but what it might be, he couldn't fathom. Crater could still imagine her as he'd last seen her, standing there on the ramp of a fuser taxi, her radiant brown eyes shining at him through the dome of her helmet, her lustrous black hair framing her lovely face as she wordlessly asked that he come with her. The odd thing was it had only been minutes before that Maria had finally professed her love for him and had even agreed to marry him. Before he'd scarcely had a moment to enjoy it, his happiness had been swept away when the fuser taxi had arrived, piloted by his brother but dispatched by Maria's grandfather to bring her back to the world of wealth and power she'd always known. To be with her, he'd come very close to taking that easy step on the taxi ramp, but Crater had instead stayed rooted in the dust, watching her fly away, not because he didn't love her, but because of the struggling mining community of Endless Dust and the responsibility he felt toward it.

Few knew more about lunar mining than Crater, and after leading a few poor settlers to the little mining town near Adolphus Crater, he meant to see them well established before leaving. And then there was also the matter of Crescent Claudine Besette, the female crowhopper warrior he'd captured during the war, then made into a friend. Crescent still depended on him, and if he'd left her to go with Maria, how would she have fared?

As he thought about it while driving through the dust of the wayback, Crater confessed to himself there was yet another reason and perhaps the most important one of all. If he had gone with Maria, Crater knew he would have been judged harshly by Maria's family, who would have surely thought of him as a lucky Helium-3 miner who'd caught the eye of a rich woman and was probably after her money. Crater was too proud to let that happen.

After Maria had gone, Crater had stayed in Endless Dust until a broken leg had caused him to be jumpcar'd to Cleomedes, there to recover in the casino clinic. Crescent had joined him there and even found employment in the casino, so when a report arrived from Endless Dust that the miners there were doing well and had even made a profit during the last quarter, Crater had decided to stay put, especially after his brother, Petro, had talked him into the rescue business. "We're both good at rescuing people, Crater," Petro told him. "We should make money out of it!"

So now, here he was, steering around craters and rilles, following what he hoped was the rental bus's tracks (which appeared to be going along a well-worn trail) with Maria drifting across his mind for no apparent reason except foolishness. Even so, he thought about asking his gillie for the latest news of Maria, except sitting beside him in the Lunar Rescue Company truck was Crescent, who made no attempt to disguise her dislike of Miss Medaris. For her part, Crescent was well aware that when Crater got that wistful, faraway look in his eyes and fell more silent than usual and became a little absentminded, he was probably thinking about Maria, scrag her, and the hold she still had on the young man's heart and head.

After Crater absently ran over a small crater he could have easily avoided, Crescent snapped, "Will you be careful? What's on your mind this morning?"

Crater blinked and ran a hand through the long, sandy hair that nearly covered his ears. "There is nothing on my mind other than finding those idiot tourists who wandered off in their bus."

"If it weren't for tourists and their need to be rescued," she pointed out, "we wouldn't have a business. So idiots they may be, but idiots they shouldn't be called."

"Then what should I call them?" Crater demanded as he wrenched the truck around a narrow crack.

"Well, you could call them customers," Crescent replied, "or maybe just people. After all, they just came to the moon to have a nice time and then made a mistake. You've made mistakes before, haven't you?"

Crater grumbled inwardly while still giving Crescent's comments their proper weight. She was, of course, correct. The people the Lunar Rescue Company generally rescued were Earthians who didn't know the dangers of the moon, and that didn't make them idiots, just inexperienced. "You're right," he concluded. "And I apologize. I guess I'm a little off kilter today."

"I've noticed," Crescent sniffed. "Want to talk about it? Or should I say *her*?"

"There's no *her* to talk about," Crater barked, although he suspected Crescent easily saw through his lie. She was a most perceptive woman, perhaps the result of her training for the battlefield, where to miss something could result in death.

Crescent didn't press the issue. If it was Maria that Crater was thinking about, she didn't really want to know. In any case, the Medaris woman was out of Crater's life forever, and that thought caused her to smile, although anyone looking at her face wouldn't have noticed. She had been provided few facial muscles by her makers, the infamous Trainers who'd mixed her and all crowhoppers up in their Siberian petri dishes to produce fierce warriors who were also mercenaries for hire to the highest bidder. Crescent was prideful of her crowhopper past, although now her allegiance was to Crater who'd saved her when he could have (and nearly everyone thought he should have) killed her on the spot after her capture in a small skirmish near Moontown. Her execution was soon ordered by Colonel Medaris on a trumped-up charge, but Crater had saved Crescent, and both of them had gone on the run to hide out in Armstrong City. When the crowhoppers invaded the city, intent on capturing Maria for ransom, Crater had plucked her from the invaders, then headed to Endless Dust, the far-away mining town beside Adolphus Crater, there to hunker down and wait out the war. This had proved to be a fine plan until the Colonel sent Petro in a fuser space taxi to pick up Maria and return her to the family. After that Crater had been sad and restless until the Lunar Rescue Company was formed, an enterprise that allowed him to rescue people, even if they weren't the Miss Almighty Doctor Maria Medaris, her PhD in engineering and stealing a good man's heart.

Although their truck was pressurized, Crescent and Crater wore biolastic pressure suits in case they needed to go outside. Crater could be stingy about some things, but he invested in the company's equipment, wanting only the best for work within the "big suck," as Lunarians called the vacuum of the moon. Biolastic suits were biological skins that kept pressure on their bodies and, along with their bubble helmets, were designed to keep them from having the ailments caused by exposure to a vacuum, the most prominent being that of having one's blood boil, and otherwise having air bubbles lodge in one's brain and spinal cord, or, in other words, more or less instant death. Wearing the suits was second nature to Crater and Crescent, who spent a good amount of time outside Cleomede's pressurized domes and underground tubes. Over their biolastic skins, they wore glo-orange coveralls with the Lunar Rescue Company's logo, the acronym LRC in black letters against a gray circle with a lot of little circles inside representing Luna and her craters. Their boots were also glo-orange, the color that stood out best against the grays and browns of moon dust.

The bus was found at the base of Margaret Thatcher Spire, unfortunately without the tourists inside, although fresh boot prints were evident leading away from the bus toward the towering column, which meant they were probably climbing it. The Lunar Rescue Company had two jobs under its contract, the first to find the bus, the second to bring its occupants back. If they were up on the spire, the second part might prove to be difficult. Using the binocular lens in his helmet, Crater's fear was realized when he spotted two moving dots about halfway up. The Thatcher Spire was, according to Cleomede's rules, supposed to be accessible only with expert guides, but the two climbers, based on information from the rental car company and the casino where they were vacationing, had applied neither for a guide or a climbing permit. That meant they were rogue amateur climbers, the kind that often got themselves killed.

Crescent was also peering at the climbers. Since her eyesight was much better than Crater's, or any average human's, she advised, "A man and a woman. Their climbing gear looks cheap."

Crater took note of the car rental company's motto on the side of the bus: *Lunar Geology Rocks.* It was supposed to entice tourists to go traipsing off into the dust, which many did. Unfortunately, that meant a fair percentage of them got lost, which at least meant business for the LRC. These tourists, however, were involved in something a little more adventurous and a lot deadlier. Although the moon had only a sixth of the gravity of Earth, Thatcher Spire was plenty tall to kill anyone who fell off its peak.

Crater woke his gillie, who was asleep on his shoulder. "Call Petro," he said.

After yawning, even though it had no mouth, the gillie sent an unauthorized signal (and therefore free) through the

Nero Corporation's Silverado III lunar commsat to Crater's partner and brother. Within seconds, Crater heard, "Lunar Rescue Company. Get in a crack, we'll get you back. This is Petro Mountbatten-Jones. May we rescue you?"

"It's me," Crater said. "We found the bus at the base of Thatcher Spire. Looks like we've got illegal climbers. Their do4us are turned off and we're not picking up any suit comm either."

"You think they don't want to be heard?"

"People engaged in nefarious activity generally don't."

"The rental company's paying us to find the bus. I'll give them a call."

"Yeah, do that, but the second part of our contract is with the casino, and they want us to bring their guests back alive, go figure. I'll have to climb up there and get them. We don't want anybody saying we could have rescued them but didn't. Besides, it might be worth a tip."

"Do what you think you have to do, brother," Petro said. "How about Crescent? Is she going with you?"

"No, I'll go it alone. She can guard our truck and the bus. There's a lunatic burrow not too far away from here. Those fellows can strip a truck in five minutes."

Crescent arranged her features into a determined grimace. "If they dare come around, I welcome the chance to teach them a lesson."

"Don't underestimate lunatics," Petro said. "Living in the wayback of the moon takes a special kind, and if they're not crazy when they start, they get that way pretty quick. And Crater, you be careful too. The puter says there were four climbers killed on Thatcher last year. Every one of them tourists without permits."

"Don't worry," Crater said. "I know what I'm doing."

"What do you think, Crescent?" Petro asked. "Does he know what he's doing?"

Crescent made the gurgling sound that crowhoppers make when laughing. "I suppose even Crater can climb a little needle."

Crater, ignoring Petro's jibe and Crescent's laughter, pulled on a harness, clipped on a coil of rope, and strapped on a pack of climbing gear. "If anyone comes around, call me," he instructed Crescent.

"If anyone comes around, I'll take care of them and *then* call you," she replied while patting the holstered railgun pistol at her waist.

Crater gave her no argument. He was confident that she could handle nearly any situation. Over the years, Crescent had proved to be a capable female, steady under duress, and she could shoot straight too. The only problem with her was that Crater could never quite figure out what she was thinking. There were many levels to her crowhopper mind, or at least he suspected there were, and he guessed she kept hidden many secrets about herself. He thought perhaps she had some affection for him, maybe even romantic feelings if—and that was a big if—crowhoppers had such feelings. As for his feelings toward her, they were complicated, and he wasn't entirely certain he knew what they were. Mostly, he simply liked her company. For one thing, she knew a lot about a wide range of topics, most recently proven when Crater was pondering a thermodynamics problem. Crescent not only understood the problem, she provided the solution using a series of quadratic equations. That impressed him.

It was time to focus on the rescue, so Crater shunted aside

his personal ruminations and trudged up the mound of rubble that led to the base of the spire. The Margaret Thatcher Spire was one of the oddest geological features on the moon. No one knew how it had been created, but the best scientific guess was it was formed by magma from early lunar volcanoes that had squeezed up between two immense basalt layers. The result was a mile-high vertical ribbon of slippery rock that was like a magnet for adventure-seeking climbers, both professional and amateur.

Moving a hundred yards laterally to avoid being hit by rocks that might be loosened by the climbers, Crater started up and for the next hour climbed steadily. When he stopped on a narrow ledge to catch his breath, he looked westerly along the face of the spire to see the Tauruses, a brown ocean of rounded mountains. To the east, he saw the high rim of Cleomedes Crater and the tops of the domes of the Lunar Las Vegas where he lived. Turning around and looking to the south, he could see the steep-sloped Roman Crater surrounded by a dry lake of spectacularly beautiful yellow, brown, purple, and red dust. When he looked up again, he saw the tourists had disappeared over the top.

Using the cracks in the rock for handholds, Crater kept climbing until he crawled over the sharp edge of the summit and got his first close look at the climbers. The rental car company had described them as a woman, forty-eight years old, and a man, fifty-two , both from the same address in Goa, Republic of Central India. They were wearing rental helmets, cheap plaston spheres with accordion-like covers for shade, and white coveralls over one-time use biolastic pressure suits. The woman, silver-haired and petite, was standing and quietly watching Crater. The man, who sported a gray-speckled beard, was lying down. Crater made a signal to the woman to turn on her suit communicator. After fumbling with her chest pack, she found the switch. "Hello," she said. "Who are you?"

"Crater Trueblood of the Lunar Rescue Company. Are you the Chandra party?"

"We are," the woman said. "I am Lady Deepik. This is my servant Mister Ajab, who I fear is having some difficulty."

Crater knelt beside Mister Ajab and observed his lips were blue, a sign of oxygen deficiency. "Just relax," Crater said to him. "Gillie, give me a readout of the backpack."

No telemetry, it said, then crawled off Crater's shoulder and onto Mister Ajab's helmet before slipping down to the neck seal.

"Is that a gillie?" Lady Deepik asked. "Aren't they illegal?"

"Yes, but it knows that," Crater answered. "Mister Ajab is not receiving enough oxygen. The gillie is trying to diagnose the problem."

The gillie burrowed into the neck seal of biolastic cells, then disappeared before emerging inside Ajab's helmet. *Carbon dioxide scrubber fouled,* it reported.

The biological scrubbers in pressure suits, especially the cheap ones rented to tourists, were easily fouled by dust. The only fix was to replace them, and the top of Thatcher was no place for that. After the gillie oozed out of the neck seal and climbed back on his shoulder, Crater pulled a spare hose from his kit and made a connection between helmets through the auxiliary ports. Clean air poured in from Crater's tank and the color was soon restored to Mr. Ajab's cheeks and lips. He took a deep breath and said, "I believed I was on my way to the stars."

Crater let him breathe clean air a little longer, then said,

"I'm Crater Trueblood of the Lunar Rescue Company, sent to fetch you."

"Is Lady Deepik all right?"

"I am fine, Mister Ajab," she said. "But I was so frightened."

Now that Mister Ajab was temporarily out of danger, Crater allowed himself to vent. "What did you think you were doing?" he demanded. "It's dangerous to climb up here!"

Mister Ajab struggled to sit up. After Crater assisted him, he said, "Please understand my folly, young man. You see, I thought to bring Lady Deepik to this beautiful spot and ask her a question that has been burning in my thoughts for a very long time."

"And what might that question be, Mister Ajab?" Lady Deepik asked with some astonishment. "I thought we were only having ourselves a nice adventure."

Mister Ajab, his eyes wide and pleading, looked at Lady Deepik. "I was your servant for thirty years and then your husband died, leaving you with many debts, and yet I have stayed with you for another ten."

Lady Deepik studied Mister Ajab, then looked away. "This is true. You have been an excellent servant through good times and bad."

"I wish to no longer be employed as your servant."

She turned back to him. "Oh, I will miss you! What employment will you take?"

He dug into a coverall pocket and brought out a thumb puter drive. "Using this device, you can see that I have passed the examination for city building inspector. Unfortunately, I forgot that I needed a puter to plug it in. In any case, I now have prospects and therefore request that you consider becoming my wife."

Lady Deepik smiled. "Mister Ajab, I thought you would never ask!"

"I am asking. What is the answer?"

"It is yes, of course. I will be pleased to be the wife of the new city building inspector."

Crater had only been half listening, his thoughts turned to how to get the couple down the spire. "We'd better go," he said, disconnecting the auxiliary air hose from Mister Ajab's helmet. "Your air should remain fresh enough until we get down."

"Will you not wish us congratulations, Mr. Trueblood?" Lady Deepik asked.

Crater looked over the edge to decide the best place to descend. "Right now, I'm just doing my job, ma'am."

"Oh, you are the sour one," Lady Deepik accused.

Crater, focused on the rescue, wasn't listening, although if he had, he might have considered the couple sour for not thanking him for saving their lives. He called Crescent to come to the base of the spire to receive the rappelling rope, then used a spring-loaded cam to attach it in a crack. He helped Mr. Ajab climb into a harness and gave another one to Lady Deepik. He showed them how to use the mechanical descenders and then sent Mr. Ajab over the edge first, followed by Lady Deepik. He released the rope, threw it down to Crescent, and then woke up the dozing gillie, which had settled into one of his coveralls pockets. "Gillie, call Petro," he said, and waited for the connection.

"Lunar Rescue Company. In a bind, we can find. This is Petro Mountbatten-Jones. How may I rescue you?"

"Rescue complete," Crater said. "We're coming in."

"Any trouble?"

"I had to wait until Mr. Ajab proposed to Lady Deepik," Crater complained. "That's why they climbed up there. It was supposed to be romantic or something."

Petro laughed. "Well, aren't you the lunar lovemaster! You'll probably collect a big tip!"

"I don't know. I wasn't too nice about it."

"Reminded you of your own marriage proposal, did it?"

Crater's eyes turned hard. "Get scragged, Petro. And I'd appreciate it if you never mentioned Maria Medaris to me again."

"I didn't," Petro replied, "but isn't it time you stopped carrying a torch for that girl?"

Although Crescent wanted to shout her approval of Petro's comment, she kept her mind on checking the suits of the couple although she couldn't help but mutter, "I should have blasted that woman into atoms when I had the chance."

"What was that, dear?" Lady Deepik asked. "Who did you blast?"

"Nobody, ma'am," Crescent replied. "Just talking to myself. A bad habit. Your suits look good. Are you ready to go?"

Lady Deepik looked at Mr. Ajab. "Are you ready for the walk, my darling?"

Mr. Ajab nodded. "Yes, my lady, I would walk the circumference of the moon if I could walk it with you."

Crescent looked at the loving couple and was envious. She knew she would never experience such a tender moment with Crater. It also reminded her of the mad, crazy, desperate thing she'd recently done, an act that would change everything in her life—and Crater's too. If she thought about it too long, the audacity and irreversibility of what she'd done frightened her, so she gestured to Lady Deepik and Mr. Ajab to follow her, then led them back along the path to their bus, keeping her attention on their safety.

"Aren't you going to wait for me, Crescent?" Crater demanded on their private channel as he free-styled down the face of the cliff.

Blinking away her tears, Crescent growled, "I've waited for you long enough," and kept walking.

::: FOUR

With the snout of a crowhopper rifle at her neck, Maria knew her best chance lay with her father. Since he was essentially a coward and a weakling, she thought if she was tough with him, she might be able to take control of the situation. She stood up from the dead foreman, brushed the dust from her coveralls, and said in a brusque tone, "Junior, what you have done here today is unforgivable, but there is a way out for you, and I will tell you what it is. That creature pulled the trigger, not you. If you immediately stop whatever this is all about, I will tell the authorities you are innocent. Otherwise, you'll mostly likely be shoved out of an airlock into the dust without a suit."

One of the copper-clad creatures standing beside her father spoke, and Maria was surprised it had a woman's voice, soft as velvet but somehow menacing. "I'm enchanted by her, Junior! Fearless and full of spunk! She is everything you said she was."

When Maria looked into the jade-green eyes of the white-faced woman or whatever it was, she saw a burning intensity that frightened her. "We should discuss this without your, um, friends listening in," Maria said to her father.

The other copper-clad person, a male, based on his voice, said, "We need to go. CC2232 will be arriving in about thirty minutes."

Junior looked surprised. "I didn't realize it was this soon. The workers will need to be evacuated."

"It's too late for that," the male replied.

"We told you we sometimes do the unexpected," the female said.

"But I specifically said no violence unless necessary."

"We believe it is necessary to punctuate this moment with a major event. This will assure the successful completion of our contract." The female nodded toward Maria. "Put her in the jumpcar. Use whatever force is necessary."

A crowhopper grabbed her arm but Maria shook it off. "Gillie, send everything that just transpired in the last thirty minutes to Colonel Medaris."

Sent to Colonel Medaris.

"You have a gillie?" her father asked. "They're illegal!"

"It knows that."

"Remove it from her," the female said.

The crowhopper removed her belt pouch, opened it, and shook out the gillie, which fell ignominiously into the dust. The crowhopper laughed at the pitiful clump of slime mold until it was no longer funny, mainly because the gillie sent a crackling bolt of discharged electricity through him, killing him instantly. The gillie then jumped from the dust to Maria's shoulder, crying, *Let's ride!*

Taking her gillie's advice, Maria burst through the ring of crowhoppers, jumped aboard her fastbug, and stomped on the accelerator. "Gillie, contact the Colonel!" she cried as she steered the fastbug away.

Contact established.

Maria heard a young woman's voice. "Colonel Medaris's office. This is his assistant. How may I help you?"

The Colonel went through many assistants and Maria didn't recognize this one. "This is Maria Medaris. I need to speak to my grandfather. Now!"

"I'm sorry, but he is in a meeting."

"Break into it. This is an emergency!"

"Who did you say this was?"

"Maria Medaris, first vice president and chief financial officer of Medaris Enterprises. If you value your job, you will connect me with the Colonel now! I am being chased by crow-hoppers and—"

"I am looking at the list of people on his schedule this morning, and I'm sorry, I don't see your name."

"I'm not on his schedule but—"

Maria slammed on the brakes and swerved away from three fastbugs boiling toward her from the westerly wastes. A cloud of dust indicated there had been another jumpcar landing. She turned and ran up the slope of a steep crater and launched, soaring over the startled crowhopper drivers.

"Get me the Colonel, I said!" she screamed.

Contact lost, the gillie advised.

The crowhopper fastbugs were close behind and Maria saw two more blocking her way. She changed course and headed toward a group of battered brown and gray hills. Then a hidden rille caught her front wheels and flipped the fastbug on its nose. Maria was launched across the vacuum into the dust where she rolled, then got to her feet just as a fastbug rammed her backpack.

Maria was knocked face down on the dust. "Gillie, hide,"

she said, then added, "Call Crater Trueblood. Tell him what happened."

She was getting to her knees when she was grabbed by a crowhopper, dragged to a fastbug, and pitched in the back with another crowhopper guarding her. The fastbug was driven back to the telescope site, where Maria was pulled out, tossed over a crowhopper's shoulder, and carried up the ladder of the jumpcar. She was roughly shoved into a chair, her father sitting on a bench across from her. "I just don't understand why you make things so difficult," he said. "Buckle your seat belt. We're about to take off."

Maria glared at her father. "Tell the pilot to angle westerly to keep the dust off the telescope."

"Maria, you don't understand. The telescope no longer matters."

The white-faced female climbed down from the cockpit. "My name is Truvia," she said. "My colleague is named Carus. We are known as Trainers."

"You look like freaks!" Maria spat.

If the female was insulted, she made no outward sign. "We are not freaks. We are scientists. The crowhoppers are our inventions. We will discuss all this later. For now, please prepare for liftoff. Carus will be taking off very soon."

After the "Trainer" called Truvia climbed back into the cockpit, the jumpcar lifted off and rose for about a minute, then slowed to a hover. Maria released her seat belt and moved to the portholes that ran around the compartment, moving from one to another until she could see the telescope construction site. "What are you doing?" she demanded when Truvia walked up beside her.

"Perhaps you shouldn't watch." Truvia said. "But if you

must, do you see that shadow there on the eastern horizon? It will grow."

"Grow? What are you talking about?"

With a roar of its engines and a slight vibration, the jumpcar began to rise again, angling off to the west. Maria, holding on to the handrails beneath the portholes, kept her eye on the shadow, which was indeed growing ever larger, craters and hills being swallowed by its ebony creep. "What is that shadow?"

"Consider it an announcement that everything that once was will be no more," Truvia said.

When it came, Maria saw only a pocked gray surface for an instant, and then it struck the telescope site, a vast tsunami of dust erupting from the impact.

Maria closed her eyes with a silent prayer for her workers, which was quickly superseded by a desire for revenge. She turned to Truvia. "I will see you strangled for this."

Truvia grinned, showing round little teeth between her green lips. "I love your spirit! I am going to enjoy training you."

"Truvia," Carus called, "I need your help. We're getting caught in the dust."

The jumpcar skin rattled with pelting dust and small rocks. Truvia climbed up the short ladder to the cockpit and into the copilot's seat. Carus said, "I didn't realize the dust cloud would be so big!"

The jumpcar was veering from side to side. A blow from something caused it to shudder its length. Its console lights flared, the puter announced: *Automatic pilot disengaging. Manual flight only.*

When Maria saw that neither of the Trainers knew what to do, she climbed up and grabbed Carus's shoulder. "You're going to kill us all. Get out of your seat!"

"Let her take over!" Junior called from below. "She's the best jumpcar pilot on the moon!"

Maria hissed into Carus's ear. "I said get out!"

Carus reluctantly complied and Maria climbed into the pilot's seat. "What do you want me to do?" Truvia asked.

"Don't touch anything!"

More dust and rocks rattled against the jumpcar's skin, the noise deafening. Maria firewalled the throttles and directional nose jets to raise the jumpcar's nose. A loud noise told her something had let go aft, and then a red light flared on the cockpit console. An engine was on fire. The nose dipped. Maria kept fighting to flatten out the trajectory. Dust swept across the viewports. "Brace for impact!" she yelled just as the jumpcar fuselage slammed into the moon.

::: FIVE

rescent went inside the bus to help Lady Deepik and Mister Ajab through the complex air/dustlock arrangement. "Pressurize to one Earth atmosphere," she said to the bus puter, and with a sudden hiss, the artificial air mixture began to be pumped inside. The couple started at the noise. "It's all right," Crescent said. "That's normal."

"Thank you for helping us," Lady Deepik said.

"You're welcome. After we reach pressure, we'll get you out of your suits, and then I'll drive you back to Cleomedes while you rest."

"My helmet failed," Mr. Ajab said. "I believe I shall sue the rental company."

"Unfortunately, you can't sue because there are no laws or courts on the moon, only town rules," Crescent advised. "In Cleomedes I must tell you the rules are stacked against the tourist, which means if you break any of them, you'll pay. There will be a fine for us coming out to find you, I'm afraid, but it won't be much. We're a bargain, considering what we do. Ah, there we are. One atmosphere."

Crescent took off her helmet and backpack and placed it in a storage cabinet and then helped the pair out of their helmets and backpacks, giving them paper masks to wear over their mouths and noses to avoid moon dust. "Please remove your boots, coveralls, plaston sanitizers, and, lastly, your biolastic suits," Crescent said. "There is little room for modesty, I'm afraid, although I can position a divider."

Crescent pulled a corrugated divider from the bulkhead, and Lady Deepik positioned herself on one side, Mr. Ajab on the other. "Take your suits off carefully to keep the dust down," Crescent advised. "Put your coveralls, boots, and sanitation units in the marked lockers, then peel off the biolastic suits and put them in the waste bin. The rental ones are only used once and will be dissolved. After that, one at a time if you wish, you can proceed into the next chamber, which you'll recognize as your shower."

Lady Deepik and Mr. Ajab followed her instructions, choosing to take their showers separately. After they exited the shower, Crescent entered, washed, drew on a pair of coveralls and slippers taken from a cabinet, and wrapped her long, coarse, black hair in a towel before entering the interior of the bus.

Lady Deepik and Mr. Ajab greeted her by handing her a glass of wine from a bottle of Apollo's Fire, a ruby red grown from a vineyard beneath the domes of Cleomedes. Raising their glasses, they said, "Cheers! Thank you for helping us!"

Crescent politely sipped the wine, careful to swallow only a little, since her liver did not filter alcohol very well. Crater called her on her do4u. "Crescent, are you about ready?"

"Just a few more minutes."

"Get a move on. Time is money."

"He is a harsh man," Lady Deepik said to Crescent.

"When I asked Lady Deepik to marry me," Mister Ajab said, "he made no comment other than it was time to leave. What kind of man would not offer congratulations to another man at such a time? It is clear he does not give a scrag for love."

"I apologize for my boss. May I say on behalf of the Lunar Rescue Company, congratulations. May all your married days ahead be blissful ones."

Lady Deepik and Mr. Ajab poured themselves another glass of the ruby red wine. "You'll have to excuse me, my dear," Lady Deepik said, "but are you not a crowhopper?"

"A former warrior of the Phoenix Legion," Crescent said proudly.

"I thought all of you were killed in the war."

"Most of us were, but I was captured by Crater, and his mother took me in. That was in Moontown. I have stayed by his side since."

Lady Deepik looked thoughtful. "I imagined a crowhopper to be, well, much different."

"Uglier," Mr. Ajab said.

"Mr. Ajab!"

"I'm sorry, Lady Deepik. Excuse me, Crescent. It was a thoughtless remark. Wine loosens my tongue."

"I understand," Crescent said. "And it's true. We were designed to look frightening so as to strike fear in the hearts of our enemy." She touched her face. "Consider the gray skin, flat nose, the heavy brow, the lips pulled back in something of a permanent snarl, all a deliberate construction by the Trainers who manipulated our genetic code to make us look this way."

"I am certain you are quite beautiful inside," Lady Deepik said.

"I am just a woman trying to do a job, ma'am," Crescent

answered, then climbed into the driver's seat of the bus. "Please relax and I'll have you back in Cleomedes in a few hours." She called Crater. "We're ready, boss."

Crater made a closed fist up and down signal and drove the truck along the dusty tracks, with Crescent driving the bus close behind. Lady Deepik and Mr. Ajab settled on a couch and were soon asleep.

A little over an hour later, they were just rolling past the collapsed rim of the Tralles Crater when Petro called on the Lunar Rescue Company's private channel. Crater answered while Crescent listened in. Petro said, "Crater, you won't believe who I just talked to and why."

"The prime minister of the United Kingdom. He wants you to come back to restore the throne."

"Very funny," Petro replied. "No, it was Maria's gillie, which said to tell you Maria's been kidnapped." Petro paused, then added, "Again."

An astonished Crescent repeated Petro's added comment, although she made it a question. "*Again?*"

In the truck, Crater noticed his gillie, which detested the gillie it had procreated, flash a vivid scarlet. *The Awful Thing? How dare it still be alive!*

"Hush, Gillie!" Crater demanded before asking Petro, "What else did it say?"

"Nothing else. But the telly's full of an asteroid hitting the Medaris construction project on the farside."

"You think that's related to Maria?"

"Who knows? But listen, Crater, this is none of your business. Remember the last two times you rescued Maria? What did that get you?"

Crater had to admit Petro had a point. Both times all it got him was a kick in the teeth. But he had also saved Maria's life when no one else could have done it. "Call if you hear anything more," he said, then hung up. "Gillie, can you give me a visual of the farside?"

I hate the Awful Thing, it said.

"Yes, I know, but you birthed it."

That was not my fault. I blame it on poor programming by my makers.

"Then I guess you're happy they're out of business. Will you please do as I ask?"

The gillie glared at Crater, though it had no eyes or face to glare, then illegally stretched itself through a lunar comm-sat and then to a commercial observation sat that watched the farside of the moon. Zeroing in on the haze that still floated electrostatically over the impact, the gillie magnified the picture, and then put the scene up on the vidscreen in the truck cab. Crater was stunned to see the devastation. Debris from the giant construction project was strewn across the dust and, here and there, the bodies of the construction crew.

"Any signs of life?" Crater asked the gillie.

The gillie searched the scene and then zoomed in on a jump-car lying on its side. *This wreck is interesting*, the gillie said. *There are boot prints leading from it. Based on the disturbed dust on which they are imprinted, apparently they were put down after the impact.*

Without realizing it, Crater pushed the truck's accelerator hard against the floor.

Trying to keep up in the rental bus, Crescent grumbled to herself. "And so speeds the sour man who doesn't care a scrag about love."

Lady Deepik was standing behind her. "How long have you been in love with him?"

"Almost from the moment we met. I stabbed him in the leg with a knife that day. He almost bled to death."

"And he in turn stabbed you in your heart."

"I continue to bleed."

"And the woman he loves?"

"Unworthy. She does not know how to love Crater as he deserves."

"Perhaps, in that regard, they are a match."

Crescent considered that, then nodded her agreement. "I suppose they are." She turned to look at Lady Deepik but saw her curled on the couch with Mr. Ajab, exactly as they had been since the drive back to Cleomedes had begun. "I need a vacation," Crescent concluded, and then pushed the accelerator pedal all the way to the floorboard to catch up with Crater.

::: SIX

Maria woke to darkness and a pale round glow that seemed very far away. At first she recalled nothing, but gradually her story fell into place, fitting together like the puzzle blocks she'd played with as a child. She, Dr. Maria Medaris, chief financial officer of Medaris Enterprises and president of several companies within that structure and leader of thousands of engineers and technicians, was the prisoner of the Trainers. The Trainers were two odd creatures with painted faces who had destroyed the Clyde Tombaugh Telescope project and murdered her workers with what appeared to be a crashed asteroid. Her father was somehow allied with them, and the purpose of all of this was unknown.

She then recalled her last words to her gillie. *Call Crater Trueblood.* Why had she done that? *Well,* she admitted to herself, *because he's rescued me before and also because I still care about that boy and would love to see him.* Maria laughed at herself. Here she was, a captive of deadly creatures and her estranged father, and she was thinking about her love life. It reflected who she was, supremely confident that no matter what her situation was, she'd get out of it and then continue her life, which might (or might not) include Crater Trueblood.

Since she suspected she was being watched, she lay very still while mentally searching her body for damage. She wiggled her toes and moved her fingers, then minutely moved each leg and arm and her head and stretched her back. Everything seemed to work. Her various aches felt like bruises and abused ligaments, nothing more. She shifted her gaze to the pale circular glow and saw it was a porthole too small to belong to a jumpcar. She tried to sit up but discovered she was restrained by straps at her wrists, waist, chest, and ankles. Tendrils of her long, black hair drifted near her face, then slowly wafted away. This meant she was weightless. Her captors had taken her into space.

Maria studied her surroundings. The porthole was along a curved wall and her cot was strapped to that wall, the deck and ceiling perpendicular to her body. The placement of her cot was not unusual for weightless conditions but was disorienting. Her attempt to figure out the room was interrupted when her father came through the hatch. "Hello, sleepyhead. I see you're awake! How do you feel? Great landing of the jumpcar, by the way. Both Truvia and Carus were impressed by your skill."

"Too bad it didn't kill them. Why are you with them?"

"They suit my purpose."

"Which is?"

"We can discuss that later after you're more settled."

"Where are we?"

"In space."

"Yes, Junior, I know that, but where in space?"

Her father smiled. "You can't escape, Maria."

"Would you unstrap me?"

"Of course."

Her father pushed off, floated across to her, and pulled the tabs to loosen her straps. She immediately pushed away from him, stopping herself by grabbing a handrail on the opposite wall. He watched her benignly. "Well, I must say I'm relieved, sweetheart. You appear healthy."

"I'm not your sweetheart!" Maria snapped.

"Now, kitten . . ."

"Shut up, you fool, and think! You are at the very least an accessory to mass murder. What you do from this moment on will determine whether you get the death sentence or leniency, so from here on, let me do all the thinking. Maybe I can get us out of this."

Junior smiled. "Who's going to punish me? My marvelous father? His rule over my life is over."

"If you believe that, you are as stupid as a rock. Where's this ship heading, anyway?"

"You'll know when we get there."

Maria looked through the porthole but saw only stars and galaxies, with no sign of the moon. She pushed herself to the hatch and tested the lever. "Are we locked inside?"

"*You* are. I know the code to get out. By the way, where is your gillie?"

"I dropped it in the dust."

"You were never a good liar."

"Then I didn't take after you, did I?"

"That will be enough of that kind of talk, young lady."

A deep well of bitterness boiled up inside Maria. "All my life you have been cruel. I could take it, but Mom—your cruelty and lies killed her."

"I am your father and I deserve your respect."

"As far as I'm concerned, I don't have a father."

Junior caught a hand strap with one hand and hit her hard across the face with the other. Gasping, she spun back against the wall. When she turned to face him, he hit her again. Blood spurted from her nose in scarlet globules.

"You are never to speak of your mother to me again," Junior growled. "You don't know what happened between us."

Maria wiped her nose with the back of her hand and raised her chin. "I know you cheated on her. I know you took every opportunity to tell her she was inadequate. I know she finally reached for a bottle of pills rather than tolerate another day in a world that contained you."

Her father balled his fist and ripped a right cross, but Maria dodged it and pushed away, sailing across the room just as Truvia opened the hatch and floated inside. When she saw Maria's bloody face, she looked puzzled. "She made me do it," Junior said.

Maria hung on to a strap to stabilize herself. "That's what all abusers say. 'She made me do it!' Face it, Junior. You're just a common woman beater." She looked at Truvia. "Be careful. He'll be abusing you next."

Truvia looked amused. "I hardly think so," she said. "May I examine your face? Oh, he hit you hard, didn't he? You'll have a black eye, but we have ways of fixing that."

Maria felt a sharp pain in her hip. When she looked down, she saw that Truvia had jabbed her with a syringe. "It will help you sleep, and while you are sleeping, I will restore your face."

"I don't want to sleep. I don't want my face restored. I just want to go home. Why am I here?"

"You are here because we need you to be here."

"But why?" It was a question that echoed in Maria's mind even after she'd slid into darkness.

::: SEVEN

Crater raced up the jumpcar ladder but was disappointed to find no one aboard. He checked the clock on the wall. Where was Crescent? And the pilot? Crater had made it clear to the jumpcar dispatcher how urgent his mission was. Didn't everyone understand how important it was for Maria to be rescued as quickly as possible? Crater considered for just a moment that perhaps no one *did* understand, that they might not even *care* if Maria was saved, but he dismissed that possibility. Of course everyone wanted to save Maria. Didn't they? Crater thought over the situation and why he was doing what he was doing. Was he still in love with Maria? Well, of course he was, no matter how badly she had treated him. He'd been in love with her from the moment he caught sight of her, and that wasn't going to change. He had a chance to save her—*again*—and he was going to do it whether anyone liked it or not.

The sound of boots on the ladder diverted his attention. It was the pilot. After she stepped through the hatch, he was astonished to see who she was. "Riley Bishop! You're an independent now?"

Riley's bright Irish grin flashed across her pretty, freckled face. "Aye, bucko. Got enough of the Colonel's long hours, short wages, and those underground tubes at Moontown. But what are ye doin' here? I thought you were mining heel-3 and Thorium at Endless Dust."

"A broken leg sent me to the hospital here," Crater explained. "I decided not to go back. Petro, Crescent, and I run our own company now."

"So you're the Lunar Rescue Company who chartered me!"

"That's us. You know about the asteroid impact on the farside? That's where I want to go. There's a jumpcar wreck near the impact I want to investigate."

"No prob, should be the safest place on the moon. Not likely it's going to be hit again. How about Petro and Crescent? They coming with us?"

"Petro's staying behind to work on our bank account, such as it is. I don't know about Crescent—oh, here she is!" He turned on her. "I told you every minute counts!"

Crescent gave Crater a sour look, then sat down and buckled up. "I got here as quickly as I could. Hello, Riley," she added.

"Crescent! Good to see you, girl. Your boss seems to be in a hurry."

"Does he? I hadn't noticed."

Riley chuckled. "Well, let's get this show on the road." She crawled into the cockpit and went through the checks with the jumpcar puter. "Cleomedes Control, *Amanda Michelle* on the runway," she called.

"Roger, Riley. Have a nice jump."

"Who's Amanda Michelle?" Crater asked.

"Me great-great-great-grandma who was truly great. She was a Broadway star. All right, here we go. Autopilot off. I'll take her manual. Puter on my mark. Five-four-three . . ."

Riley counted down and punched the firing button. The jumpcar's trio of engines burst into life and the suborbital ship surged aloft. Riley expertly kept the ship on the ballistic curve until the Moscow Crater came into view, then hovered the jumpcar over the asteroid strike. Crater and Crescent moved to the portholes to view the scene. The remnants of the support structure for the giant mirror was spread for miles, glittering shards in the gray and white dust. Bodies were also strewn about. In the center of a big new crater was a slight hump, the only evidence of the asteroid that had caused all the carnage.

Riley called down from the cockpit. "I have a visual on a wrecked jumpcar. It landed on its side and plowed a furrow about three hundred yards long. Still in one piece, as far as I can tell."

"Land as close as you can," Crater replied.

Riley backed down to a soft landing. Crater threw open the hatch and saw the wrecked jumpcar. "I'm going over to it," he told Crescent.

Crescent nodded. "I'll have a look around the general area. Be careful. It might be an ambush."

"Ambush? You think this asteroid strike was deliberate?"

"Of course. It landed precisely on the construction site."

"Who would do that? And how?"

"Somebody who doesn't like the Medarises would be my guess, which means a lot of people. How? Figure that out and you'll probably figure out who."

"You're right. No wonder I keep you around."

"Go find your woman," Crescent muttered.

"What? I didn't hear that."

"I said stay alert."

"Oh, right." Crater climbed down the ladder and walked toward the wreck. When he got closer, he saw boot prints. To avoid putting his prints on top of them, he circled around to the jumpcar. Using a tail fin to pull himself onto the fuselage, he walked down it, noting the dents in the skin. Based on their uniform dispersion, he suspected the pits were not a result of the crash but perhaps a spray of rocks and gravel from the asteroid impact. That meant the jumpcar was probably flying nearby when the asteroid struck. The entry hatch was open, so he went inside. After poking around he concluded there was nobody aboard, so he climbed out and studied the boot prints leading away from the wreck. He recognized the tread pattern. Crowhoppers.

"I've found something interesting," Crescent called. "Landing pad impressions. I'm not certain what kind."

Crater, staying to the side of the prints, walked to Crescent, who silently pointed at the indentations in the dust, six deep circles. "A space taxi," Crater said. "By its landing pad spacing, I think probably from a warpod."

"Did you find anything in the jumpcar?"

"No, but the tracks indicate crowhoppers were in its party."

"How could that be? The Legion has been disbanded and my brethren scattered."

"It appears they've gotten back together again."

The gillie stuck its head, although it had no head, from Crater's chest pocket, then crawled up on his shoulder. *The Awful Thing is here!*

"Maria's gillie? Where?"

On her.

Startled, Crescent almost fell over when she saw that a gillie had indeed somehow appeared on her shoulder. "Where did you come from?" she demanded.

"Get inside your pocket," Crater ordered his gillie.

I will kill the Awful Thing.

"Yes, OK, but later," Crater said. "Now, do what I told you. You're scaring it."

Muttering something too low for Crater to hear but certain to be filled with curses appropriate for a creature made of slime mold, the gillie crawled into Crater's chest pocket and closed the flap.

Is the Superior One gone? the gillie on Crescent's shoulder asked.

"For now," Crater said.

Maria Medaris is my owner. She was taken away.

"Yes, I got your message. Who took her away?"

Her father and some others. Crowhoppers. Two who called themselves Trainers.

"Tell me everything you saw."

The gillie told its story, ending with how it had watched Maria carried aboard a warpod taxi.

Crater's gillie poked up from its pocket. *Awful Thing, why did you not stay with your owner? You are a poor excuse for a gillie. I want you to die.*

I couldn't stay with her, Superior One. They would have caught me.

A gillie must be sneaky. Did I not teach you that?

You never taught me anything. You were too busy trying to kill me from the moment I was birthed.

If I had truly wanted to kill you, I would have killed you.

"That's enough, you two," Crater admonished. "This is to the gillie on Crescent's shoulder. You now belong to Crescent."

Be a crowhopper's gillie? I am not certain.

"Don't complain," Crescent said, curling her lips into a frightening grin. "Or I will eat you."

Good idea, Crater's gillie said.

I will stay with you if you will not eat me, Crescent's new gillie conceded.

"Fine," Crater said. "Now we're all one big, happy family."

Riley came walking up. "Any idea on what happened here?"

"I think Maria's alive," Crater answered. "But I'm afraid she's been taken aboard a warpod."

Riley whistled. "In that case, she could be anywhere between here and Mars. By the way, Petro called. He said some Umlap woman named Perpetually Hopeful has news on Maria and requests you visit her as soon as possible."

Crater brightened. "Perpetually Hopeful is General Nero's wife! They've got a lot of spies. We need to go to Endless Dust right away!"

"It's your nickel," Riley said, but Crater was already running to the jumpcar.

Riley looked at Crescent sympathetically. "Maria just won't get out of his head, will she?"

"I guess she's the only thing he ever wanted that he couldn't have."

"Men are idiots even when they think they're being noble."

"Especially then," Crescent agreed.

Riley and Crescent walked at a deliberate pace toward the jumpcar. Crater was on its ladder urgently waving at them to hurry up.

"I had me cap set for that boy when I first met him," Riley

said. "But it didn't take long to see Maria's the only one for him, poor creature that he is."

"I suppose we can't blame him for wanting to rescue her," Crescent replied with a sigh. "Even though I bet she won't appreciate it."

"Looks like this time his girl's got herself in a real bind. I wasn't kidding about she might be anywhere from here to Mars."

"Her kidnappers will just want money for her, right?"

Riley shrugged. "I think it might be bigger than that. You don't kill a thousand people and destroy a billion johncredit project and then just ask for a ransom, even if it is for the exalted Miss Priss of the Moon Maria Medaris."

Crescent concluded Riley made sense. There was something big and very dangerous out there, and Crater was running toward it as fast as he could go with a carelessness that just might get him—and her—killed. Crescent's thoughts turned to her secret—a secret that made her unwilling to be killed for no good purpose, even though she was genetically programmed to die. Although her fate was not entirely in her hands, she didn't want to spend her remaining days on a futile, life-ending search for Maria Medaris. She had something vastly more important to do.

::: EIGHT

There was no here. There was no now. There was no light. There was no darkness. There was nothing until a painful light struck her eyes, which she realized were wide open. Blinded, she tried to shield them, but her arms were restrained. Then, blocking the light, Truvia's bone-white face loomed before her like a grotesque, chalky asteroid. "What would you like more than anything in the world and its moon?" Truvia asked.

Maria fought for focus, found it, and said, "To go home."

Truvia tilted her head. "Do you think I'm beautiful? We have mastered the science and art of such things. I will ask you again. What would you like more than anything in the world and its moon?"

"And I said to go home. Have you contacted my grandfather?"

"He knows you're here."

"What did he say?"

"What he says doesn't matter. What would you like more than anything in the world and its moon? Think carefully now."

"I think I want out of this loony bin."

Maria became aware that there was someone else in the room. She was shocked when she saw it was a demon, a biologically manipulated creature, less intelligent than crowhoppers but more vicious and remorseless. It gazed at her with malevolent interest.

"It is called BKD4284," Truvia said of the demon. "It is the last demon in our inventory. We invented them after we patented Legionnaires or, as you call them, crowhoppers. Sadly, demons did not turn out as we hoped. Insanely violent, yes, but too stupid to follow orders in battle with any consistency. We kept BKD4284 because it has been trained in torture. I'm sorry to say torture is the first step in your training because you must first understand that you cannot be saved."

"No need for torture," Maria said quickly. "I got it. Can't be saved. What's next?"

Truvia's expression changed to one of sorrow. "I don't believe you are sincere." She floated away to the hatch. "But you will be."

"Don't leave," Maria said, frantic. "I can get sincere in a hurry."

Her hand on the hatch cover, Truvia said, "Have you ever thought about the human foot? It is a most remarkable anatomical structure. It takes our weight and provides our locomotion. It contains twenty-six bones and thirty-three mostly articulated joints held together and strengthened by ligaments, tendons, and muscles. It also holds millions of nerve endings. The metatarsals are the longest bones of the foot and subject to fracture under stress. BKD4284 is, in its own way, an expert on these interesting bones."

The demon was touching Maria's right foot. "Get away from me!" Maria yelped and tried to pull her foot away.

"Until later," Truvia said.

Maria watched the demon open a cabinet and withdraw a device that looked like a clamp with a thumb screw. Almost lovingly, BKD4284 took the device and, though she tried to resist by kicking out, forced Maria's right foot in it. "Truvia!" Maria yelled. "Come back. Let's talk!"

She would have shouted the woman's name again, but in the next moment, there was no room for it in her open-mouthed scream.

::: NINE

Leaving Crescent plodding behind, Crater hurried up the slope of the vast crater that housed the Adolphus Crater Research Center. He had his suit off and was donning a clean room tunic by the time Crescent climbed inside the airlock. "Every minute counts," he griped. "You were late this morning. Now you're still lagging. What's your problem?"

"My apologies," she said. "I will try to do better."

"Don't you want to rescue Maria?"

I don't give a scrag about Maria, was Crescent's thought. What she said was, "Of course I do." For a moment, she considered telling him her secret, the one that made her want to cling to what life remained, but she resisted the urge. It was her secret, not his. Still, she needed to tell him, not only because it was the right thing to do, but because it might turn him back from the folly of trying to rescue Maria. She made up her mind. "Hold on, Crater," she said, an anxious lump forming in her throat. "There's something important I need to tell you."

"What's wrong with you?" Crater demanded. "Every second counts. There's no time for foolishness!"

"This isn't foolishness!" Crescent cried, but Crater had turned his back to her and climbed out of the airlock. Disgusted, she threw down her helmet. "How I wish I had stabbed you in the heart the first time I met you rather than your leg!"

After she'd regained a semblance of control, Crescent followed Crater through the airlock hatch where she found him engaged in an arm-waving conversation with a technician who apparently wasn't supplying him with the information he wanted. "I'm sorry, sir," the technician said, "but without a pass, I am not allowed to let you into the crater vent."

"But I was invited here by Perpetually Hopeful!" Crater shouted.

"Do you have proof of that, sir?"

"No, but—" Crater turned helplessly toward Crescent. "Can you believe this?" he demanded.

The lunaglas dome was designed to turn dark to protect the scientists and technicians working inside Adolphus from the full fury of the sun, but it was still very bright inside. After Crescent's eyes adjusted, she saw a crowhopper man wearing a clean room tunic striding in their direction. She recognized him very well and was pleased to see him. That was when a plan began to form in her mind. If Crater thought she was foolish, then she would show him just how foolish she could be. "Absalom, fellow Legionnaire," Crescent greeted him.

"Crescent, honored Phoenix Legion warrior," Absalom replied, bowing to her. When he lifted his eyes, he took note of Crater and bowed to him. "Crater, my friend."

Absalom was one of three crowhoppers who had defected in the latter stages of the war, ending up in Endless Dust. "Absalom, can you get me inside the vent?" Crater asked.

"Of course." The crowhopper turned to the technician. "These are valued friends. They may go anywhere they wish."

"Yes, sir," the technician replied. He gestured toward the hatch over the vent and said to Crater, "This way, sir."

Crater hesitated. "You're a supervisor, Absalom?"

"I am," Absalom proudly replied. "In charge of dome maintenance."

Crater, impressed, nodded, then followed the technician to the vent hatch. Before entering it, he stopped and looked over his shoulder at Crescent. "Are you coming?"

"You don't need me," Crescent said, before muttering, "You never do." Crater continued on without arguing, and she turned toward Absalom. "Congratulations on your position, honored warrior."

"Thank you," Absalom replied. He studied her. "You are well, Crescent?"

"I am well," Crescent replied, her mind racing. "My fate as a member of the Phoenix Legion has not yet been activated. In fact, I have never felt better."

Absalom worked his lips into a smile. "That is good."

"What is good is that we came here," Crescent said, "because I require a conversation with you."

"A conversation with you would be most acceptable." He gestured toward a mooncrete bench.

Crater, still marveling that rescuing Maria didn't seem to be Crescent's first priority, climbed through the vent hatch, then hurried down the steps to the next level, a cylindrical room built of mooncrete. Technicians were hunched over monitors and gauges while others were peering into a deep chasm from a viewing platform. Crater saw someone he knew staring at a computer, an Umlap named Makes Bad Bets.

"Bad day," Crater said, using the traditional Umlap greeting.

"Of course it is," the Umlap replied in the traditional Umlap response, adding, "What do you want?"

"I'm looking for Perpetually Hopeful."

"Wrong level. Two floors down."

"It is awful to see you, Make Bad Bets."

"It is awful to see you too," Make Bad Bets replied, then got back to his puter.

Crater descended two floors and found General Nero at a desk talking to someone on his do4u. At the viewport looking into Adolphus Crater, he spotted a tall Umlap woman dressed in purple robes. It was Perpetually Hopeful, the general's wife. Since all Umlap expressions were backwards, her frown followed by a scowl demonstrated her Umlap delight at his presence. "Crater!" She took him in her long arms, pressing her cheek next to his. "Thank you for coming. Look, General, it's Crater!"

General Nero looked up briefly, nodded, then went back to his conversation. Perpetually Hopeful steered Crater around to the other side of the viewing platform, then took his hands and twisted her purple lips into a smile. "You see, I am showing you my joy with a normal human smile. I am told if I continue, I might rewire my brain."

"You are the last person in the universe who needs to rewire her brain," Crater said.

"You are a sweet boy. Would you like to know what we've discovered in this crater?" Before Crater could answer, she said, "Great things. The microorganisms along these walls are a combination of ancient strains of cyanobacterium and archaea. This may be proof that the moon was seeded with life from space or maybe life from Earth a very long time ago. Bacteria and archaea, you see, can live inside rocks, so if life developed in another solar system, they could have gotten here on meteors. Or maybe they got here by rocks ejected from Earthly volcanoes. However they came, life forms fell into Adolphus and stayed dormant until the cold fusion of tons of Helium-3 heated them up. After that, they started to thrive."

Crater considered that, then asked, "What are the implications?"

"This bacteria produces oxygen. Imagine if we had a hundred or even a thousand of these pits pumping out O2. It could very well transform our Luna into a blue and green planet!"

Crater thought that over. "But moon gravity won't hold an atmosphere. That's why we don't have one. Also, pure oxygen is poison to most organisms, including humans. Earthian atmosphere is mostly nitrogen, keeping the percentage of oxygen down to a nonpoisonous level."

"True enough, so we only need to have oxygen at a lower nonpoisonous pressure and we can walk around without a helmet or suit. And if we can start farming and adding water—maybe we'll fly a comet in to give some nice freshwater lakes and cool things down—we'll have a new Earth!"

Crater thought her enthusiasm was misplaced and did his best to phrase it politely. "There's still the problem of the moon not having enough gravity to hold an atmosphere, not to mention the solar wind that would strip it away over time. Those problems can't be solved."

"Nonsense! Every problem can be solved if it can be identified! But we have more transitional plans in mind. If we can create more plants like Adolphus, we could run pipelines filled with oxygen all across the moon. Millions of people could live beneath lunaglas domes such as we have in Armstrong

City and Cleomedes without all the complex, expensive, and inefficient recycling. Imagine a thousand such metropolitan centers all over our globe!"

Crater wished he had time to discuss the implications of Adolphus Crater further, but he was on a mission. "You said you had information on Maria Medaris," he said, redirecting the conversation.

"I do," Perpetually Hopeful said. "Our sources tell us this was a deliberate attack and a kidnapping. Colonel Medaris knows who did it and where Maria is." She removed a pouch from her waist belt and handed it to him. "The General and I wish to hire your company to find out all that you can. This pouch contains a number of gold coins, which I hope will be adequate to retain your services."

Crater hefted the pouch in his hand. Even in one-sixth gravity it was heavy. He offered it back to the Umlap queen. "I was going to find Maria anyway," he said. "I was just out to the asteroid strike."

"We know very well where you've been, Crater," Perpetually Hopeful answered. "Little escapes our notice. You will keep our gold and seek Maria out."

"Why do you care about her?" Crater asked.

"We don't, frankly," General Nero said, stepping up beside his wife. The general was wearing a tunic, leggings, and boots made of a gold-colored material, his signature style. "What we care about is finding out who tossed that asteroid into the moon. Colonel Medaris may well pay a ransom and keep that knowledge to himself. I have too many investments on the moon not to know who threatens it."

"I can't promise to send you regular reports," Crater said. "I'm likely to be pretty busy."

General Nero nodded. "That is not a problem. We trust you. Do you have a plan?"

"Not yet. First, I have to know where Maria is, but if the Colonel knows, I'll find out."

"Good boy," General Nero said. "Give us a report when you can."

The general walked away while Crater was enveloped in the Umlap queen's robes as she gave him a farewell hug. "Go about your work, Crater."

"Yes, ma'am, I will. And you go about yours."

She formed a smile. "To be sure."

Crater climbed the steps. When he emerged on the floor beneath the dome, Crescent and Absalom rose from a bench and bowed to one another. After bowing to Crater, Absalom walked away. In the dustlock, Crescent asked, "Was your talk with Perpetually Hopeful productive?"

He handed her the pouch, which she opened. "She gave you gold?"

"We're now working for General Nero. How was your talk with Absalom?"

"It was good to share a moment with an old friend."

They suited up and went through the airlock and into the dust, then headed for the jumpcar. "Crater," Crescent said, "will you stop for a moment and listen to me?"

"Can't you talk while we're walking?"

"No. Please stop and listen. You can afford a few minutes."

Crater reluctantly halted. "What is it?"

"I think this job is too big for us. Even with your bag of gold, it doesn't make sense for us to proceed. Whoever hit the telescope with an asteroid has enormous power that we can't even begin to understand. This may be an internal Medaris family struggle, and you know as well as anyone that nobody in the Medaris family can be trusted. The Colonel especially has no regard for you. He's betrayed you more than once. For my part, he tried to frame me for a murder I didn't do so that he could execute me. Need I remind you that we were on the run from him the last time you rescued Maria?"

Crater's face was grim. "This isn't up for a vote. I'm the boss, and I'll say what our job is."

Crescent felt as if Crater had clawed open an old wound. "Let me be certain I understand you. My opinion doesn't count?"

Crater started walking again. "It counts. I hear you, I've taken your comments under advisement, and now we'll go rescue Maria."

Crescent stayed rooted in the dust. "You're an idiot when it comes to that Medaris witch," she seethed.

"Take that back," Crater demanded, whirling about.

"I will not. She's a witch because she's bewitched you!"

Crater scowled. He gestured toward the bag of gold. "We're a rescue company, and we've been hired to rescue a very important woman. What about that don't you understand?"

"You're obsessed with her," Crescent spat, her big hands balled at her side.

Crater's eyes turned cold. "Anything else you want to get off your chest?"

"Why, yes, there is," she said with false cheer. "Would you like to know why I wanted to speak with Absalom?"

When Crater saw that Crescent was near tears, he felt his anger begin to drain away. He was not a cruel, thoughtless man, but he recognized he was acting like one. "If you would like me to know," he said, trying to make amends.

Crescent worked her lips into a smirk. "I asked him to marry me and he agreed."

Crater could not disguise his astonishment. "I didn't know you knew him that well!"

Her smirk wavered. "I don't."

"And you're going to marry him? What sense does that make?"

Crescent could feel her temper rising, and she waited a moment for it to subside. Crowhoppers were trained to kill whenever they felt threatened, and as much as Crater meant to her, she didn't trust herself at that moment. When she felt under control, she said, "It doesn't have to make sense to you as long as it makes sense to me and Absalom. I only told you because you're my boss. Or dictator. Or tyrant. All of the above. And we can go now. I know it's killing you that we're wasting time talking about something that doesn't have to do with your precious Maria Medaris."

Crater struggled to find the right words to say. "I guess I should offer you congratulations," he finally managed to blurt.

Crescent made a dismissive gesture. "I guess you should, Crater, but it really doesn't matter. I have learned to expect nothing from you. That way I'm not constantly disappointed."

Crater opened his mouth to reply. He wanted to tell her how much she meant to him and how truly happy he was that she'd found someone, but it was too late. Crescent had bounded past him on her way to the jumpcar.

::: TEN

Maria came awake to hideous pain in her right foot. When the demon noticed she had opened her eyes, it grabbed her by her shoulders and roughly sat her up, pinning her with one hand against the wall. When she looked down, she gasped at the sight of her foot. It was horribly swollen, misshapen, and covered with purple bruises. Pain radiated from it in waves. When she sobbed, the demon brutally wrenched her left ring finger until it snapped. Maria, surrendering the last tatters of her courage, screamed.

"That will be all, BKD4284," Truvia said, floating in from the hatch. She swung her slippers into the foot loops beside the cot. The demon grunted and backed away.

"Thank you," Maria whispered as weightless tears pooled beneath her eyes before floating into the air.

Truvia caught one of the tears on a finger, pondered it, and then flicked it away. "I watched while the demon crushed your foot. You are incredibly strong. Usually people pass out in a minute, perhaps two. You lasted five."

"What do you want?" Maria asked through cracked lips. "Why are you doing this?"

"You will come to understand. Might I show you something?"

When Maria didn't reply, Truvia drew a rectangle in the air that was filled with a picture of a man and woman with white-painted faces and green-painted lips. Both were dressed in luxurious purple robes and had golden crowns on their heads. "Do you know who this is?"

Maria watched through half-open eyes. "The king and queen of the New Orleans Mardi Gras?"

"Still the clever girl, but no, they were once my king and queen. His name was Raleigh. Her name was Porella. They were human persons. You see, I am not a human person although I am similar. Just as with the crowhoppers and the demons, I was born in a petri dish, my genes manipulated to make me extremely intelligent, to have a commanding presence yet be subservient. Our king and queen were scientists before they became royalty. They invented the process of cell manipulation that produced the crowhoppers, the demons, and Trainers like me. We lived to serve our king and queen, but now they are gone."

"Too bad," Maria said, closing her eyes as more pain-induced tears pooled around them. Weightless, their surface tension held them in place.

Truvia's lips trembled. "They were captured when our territory was attacked after the last war. Within hours of their capture, they were hung. The rest of us were hunted down and slaughtered. Only a few survive. I am part of that remnant."

Maria struggled to rise above the pain. When she batted her eyes, the pool of tears were sprayed into the air. She watched them drift away, then asked, "Is this about revenge? I had nothing to do with any of this. I am only a businesswoman."

Truvia was also watching the tears. Turning back to Maria, she put our her hand and touched Maria's face and stroked her cheek. "We think you are much more than that." Truvia tilted her head quizzically. "May I ask you something? What are your thoughts about history?"

Maria's foot hurt so very bad, but to avoid further punishment, she persevered to answer. "I was never much interested in history. Give me a statistics class anytime."

"Without a knowledge of our past, how is it possible to predict our future?"

"I don't ever go past predicting quarterly profits."

"Then it is necessary you be taught. The history of humanity is all about war and death. The pain you feel is a metaphor for the history of humanity on Earth."

"But there is also kindness and love—" Maria screamed when Truvia suddenly gripped her destroyed foot.

"Do not speak of such things," Truvia cautioned. "Not yet."

"Sorry!" Maria gasped out.

"What do you want more than anything in the world and its moon?"

Maria could not help herself. Although it disgusted her to show such weakness in front of this awful woman, she wept. Truvia watched benignly until Maria regained control. "I don't know what you want me to say."

"I am going to leave you now," Truvia said, removing a small leather case from the pouch that hung across her shoulder. From it, she removed an old-fashioned syringe. "Your arm, please," she said. When Maria didn't lift her arm, Truvia said, "Do you want the demon to return?"

Maria shook her head and held up her arm. Truvia injected the contents of the syringe into it and then put it back into the leather case and into the pouch. "This will help you to concentrate."

Once more Truvia drew a rectangle in the air and a picture began to fill it. Maria saw that it was a pastoral scene of grazing sheep and contented cattle. Before long, men were shown gathering up the animals, and then there were scenes of them being slaughtered, the men laughing, which morphed into people being slaughtered and other people laughing and killing, their bodies covered with blood. Then the scene changed to one that showed people being whipped while constructing monuments, the pyramids and statues of the gods, followed by vivid scenes of battles with swords flying, blood spattering— it went on and on. Maria tried to shut her eyes to hide from the pictures but found she couldn't do it. The images pounded into her brain. Then it stopped and she heard a single word. HATE. The scenes began again and went on for a very long time. Then the word again, and after more scenes of abominations, again. HATE. "Yes," Maria said after a time. "Yes, I hate. I hate you. I hate me. I hate everything. Is that what you want to hear? *I hate that people ever lived and I was ever born!*"

::: ELEVEN

uring the short hop from Adolphus to Armstrong City, Crater sat on a bench across from Crescent, who refused to look at him. "Would you please stop being so angry at me?" he asked on their private frequency as they topped the parabolic arc and started to descend.

Crescent glanced at him. "I'm not angry."

"I think you are."

"I'm just sitting here minding my own business, which, by the way, is always a good idea. For everyone. Even you."

Crater made a hapless gesture. "I know you're mad at me because I want to rescue Maria, but why wouldn't I? She's my friend. And now we've got a contract to do it, paid in gold. Rescuing her is for the good of the company."

Crescent had just about enough of Crater Trueblood and his idiotic excuses for why he was going to get himself killed for a woman he loved who didn't love him back. "Leave me alone," she said, "or I will get out my knife and stab you like I did the first time we met, and then I will laugh at you while you bleed."

"I'm sorry you feel that way."

Crescent shook her head. Was there anyone more stupid than Crater? Yes, he was a genius at engineering and all that, but otherwise he was a complete scraghead. "Just tell me why we're going to Armstrong City," she growled.

"Medaris Enterprises knows where Maria is and who's got her. We're going there to get that information."

"No doubt you've forgotten this in your haste, or maybe it just doesn't matter to you, but crowhoppers are restricted from Armstrong City. I will be arrested on sight."

"I have not forgotten. You'll stay with Riley in the jumpcar parking lot. I'll go alone."

Crescent shrugged. "Fine."

Crater peered at her. "Is there anything I can say to cheer you up?"

Crescent's eyes flashed. "I'm perfectly cheerful, you idiot!"

"Are you in on this rescue or not?"

Crescent lowered her head. She could never leave Crater. "I'm in, I'm in." She looked up at Crater, searching his eyes for understanding. "Is that good enough for you?"

"Tranquility Base coming up," Riley reported. "This eagle is about to land."

After the landing, Crater vacated the jumpcar immediately, as much to get away from Crescent as to speed his rescue of Maria. He hurried down the ladder and into the dustlock to doff his suit and helmet and put on a tunic and strap on a railgun pistol taken from his kit. There were rough neighborhoods in Armstrong City and it never hurt to show a little iron to the locals.

The gillie crawled to his shoulder as he walked into the Neil Armstrong Dome. The people on the streets were moving purposefully along, talking into do4us or going in and out of shops. All were well-dressed, reflecting the general prosperity of Luna's largest town. Crater also noticed men and women in police uniforms with patches that said ARMSTRONG CITY POLICE DEPARTMENT. A constabulary was something new. Taking note of Crater, two blue-suiters turned toward him, one of them saying, "Excuse me, sir," in a manner that clearly actually meant "Stop!"

These are not the droids you are looking for, the gillie said from Crater's shoulder.

"Hush!" Crater hissed.

One of the policemen—his name tag said *Jessup*—said, "These are not the droi—wait a minute! What does that mean?"

The gillie vibrated as if it was laughing, which it was. The other policeman—his name tag said *Kaminski*—leaned in for a better look. "What is that thing?" he demanded.

"It's a gillie," Jessup said. "They're illegal."

"It knows that," Crater replied. "Can I help you, officers?"

Kaminski ignored Crater. "If it's illegal, why does he have one?" he asked his partner.

"Gillies aren't illegal on the moon," Crater said. "Only on Earth."

Both policemen turned to look at Crater, their eyes straying to Crater's belt. "Is that a weapon of some kind?"

"It's a railgun pistol."

Jessup held out his hand. "Let me see it."

Crater handed the pistol over to Jessup, who fondled it, hefted it, pointed it, and then handed it to Kaminski. "Nice," Kaminski said, "but the new city rules say private citizens can't carry guns."

"I'm not a private citizen," Crater said. "I own the Lunar Rescue Company. We need guns to do what we do."

"Licensed in Armstrong City?" Kaminski asked with raised eyebrows.

"Cleomedes, actually," Crater answered.

Kaminski handed the pistol back to Crater. "Put this in your kit. Don't show it in this town again."

Both policemen watched carefully until Crater had the pistol zipped inside his kitbag. "We have our eyes on you, boy," Jessup said. "You cause any trouble, we'll be on top of you double quick."

"No trouble, officers. I promise."

"That gillie is an ugly, slimy thing," Jessup said.

You're no prize yourself, the gillie replied.

"Well, thank you, officers," Crater said, then hurried down a side alley while they glared at him. Once he was away, he griped at the gillie. "What's wrong with you? You want to get us tossed in the hoosegow?"

You didn't like my little joke about the droids? Star Wars, Episode 4.

"I know the reference," Crater grumped, "but not everyone is a fan of twentieth-century cinema."

Pity. There's been little since that compares.

Crater walked through the Armstrong Dome and into the Collins Dome and then entered the Medaris Enterprises building. A guard stopped him. "May I help you?"

"I need to see Dr. Medaris's assistant," Crater said.

"What for?"

"It's personal."

"You'll need a better reason than that."

"I have information about Dr. Medaris's disappearance."

The guard spoke into his collar. "Fellow down here named— what's your name, buddy?"

"Crater Trueblood."

"Named Crater Trueblood wants to see Miss Torricelli. Claims he knows something about Dr. Medaris."

The guard put his finger to his ear and listened, then said, "All right, I'll send him up." He pointed to the elevator. "Third floor. I'll take that kitbag."

Crater handed over his kit and took the elevator to the third floor. At a glassed-in office, a slim, young woman rose to greet him. "Mr. Trueblood. I'm Teresa Torricelli, Dr. Medaris's assistant. May I help you?"

"I want to talk to you about Maria."

"As it happens, we expected you."

"You did?"

"We own the farside observation satellite, Mr. Trueblood. You visited the asteroid strike today, did you not?"

"I might have."

She opened a nearby office door, led Crater inside, then pulled the shades. "Colonel Medaris will speak to you shortly." The office door clicked behind her.

A few seconds later, Crater heard the booming voice of Colonel John High Eagle Medaris. He also saw the great man in a holographic projection. "Well, Crater, as I recall, the last time I talked to you it was about that girl crowhopper of yours. Then you scooted off on a fastbug. It threw dust in my face."

"The reason I scooted off was because you had just told me you'd put Crescent outside to die."

"And then you stole a number of my long-endurance biopacks," the Colonel continued. "You became a common thief, Crater. And after all I did for you over the years."

"Are you referring to the years you overworked and underpaid me?"

"Cry me a river," the Colonel replied. "I also kept you in Moontown when your adoptive parents were killed on the scrapes. I would have been in my rights to put you on the first truck convoy back to Armstrong City where you'd have probably wandered the streets until somebody put you out of your misery. Now, in your latest show of appreciation, you visit the site of a terrible tragedy that has befallen my telescope project and then barge into my headquarters without an appointment. And why would you do that, I wonder?"

"You know the answer. Because your granddaughter Maria Medaris has been kidnapped."

"Even if that were true, what business would that be of yours?"

"I am going to rescue her."

"If Maria requires rescue, I will see to it."

"Then let me join you."

"The answer to that is no because I don't want you. You're insubordinate and can't be trusted."

"You can trust me to give it my all."

The Colonel leaned forward. "I can trust you to try to fool me. Do you have your gillie with you? Of course you do. I know why you're here. It's not to talk to Miss Torricelli. It was so you'd have an excuse to come inside my headquarters building and give your gillie a chance to hack our puters. Well, let that illegal creature hack away. There's nothing it will find. And if it tries to hack our puters in Moontown, it will find they're hardened against it. Really, Crater, you're so transparent."

"You have me wrong, Colonel."

"No, I don't. But let's explore your motivation for a moment, shall we? I have no doubt you fancy yourself in love with my granddaughter, but let me tell you something. She doesn't care a whit about you. You're nothing to her. Nothing! Like you're nothing to me. Now, this conversation, such as it is, is over. I'm going back to work. I suggest you go back to whatever hole you crawled out of. And, Crater?"

"I'm here, Colonel."

"If you get in my way again, this time I will not only kill your crowhopper. I'll kill you too."

The holograph snapped off.

Crater stepped out into the hall where Miss Torricelli was waiting. "Will there be anything else, sir?"

"Did you hear?"

"Actually, every word."

"Is there a place where we can talk?"

Torricelli considered the request then nodded over her shoulder. Crater followed her into a stairwell and up two floors into an unfinished room, the raw mooncrete still curing. "They haven't gotten around to installing sensors and cameras here," she said.

"Do you like Maria?" Crater asked.

Miss Torricelli raised her eyebrows. "It doesn't matter how I feel about her. She's my boss."

"Do you want to see her killed?"

"Of course not."

"Then you need to help me. You know who I am, don't you?"

"Yes. You designed the Luna water device that Medaris Enterprises manufactured and sold without your permission. It's common knowledge that the Colonel stole the design from you. You also saved Dr. Medaris when the crowhoppers attacked this city two years ago. I think you also saved her one other time. On a Cycler, I believe?"

"I've saved her twice, and I'd like to save her again, but I need to know who kidnapped her. Tell me who it is."

"How would I know?"

"Because you're her assistant and have passwords to everything."

"I'm really sorry. I just can't help."

"Do you know where they're holding her?"

"Please, Mr. Trueblood. I'll lose my job. I wish I could be more helpful but I just can't."

"Yet you took me here where we couldn't be seen or heard. There has to be a reason for that."

"Yes. I wanted to tell you that Dr. Medaris set up an account at the Armstrong City Bank in your name. All of the profits received from your water device were deposited there. You're quite rich, sir. She said if you ever showed up here looking for her, I should tell you about it. And you're definitely here looking for her, so if you go to the bank, it's account number 8162128. That's a secret number she said you would be able to remember."

After absorbing the astonishing revelation, Crater had a confession to make. "I don't know what's special about that number."

"She said it's the day you met, August 16, 2128. We girls tend to remember things like that."

Crater remembered he'd first met Maria on Moontown Founder's Day celebrating Colonel Medaris's arrival in the Alpine Valley, which was, now that he gave it some thought, on August 16.

"She didn't tell me to tell you this," Miss Torricelli added, "but she has a photo of you on her reader. I've come into the office and caught her looking at it. Just thought you should know. Now, I really need to get back to my office. The cameras showed us entering the stairwell. I will have to explain it."

"How will you?"

"I will tell them that I asked you to hook up with me later at the Earthlight Retrodisco."

"Do you think they'll buy that?"

She winked. "They would, especially if we did. How about it? Let's say seven p.m.?"

"I'm likely to be busy."

She shrugged. "Your loss. And about your question on whether I like Dr. Medaris? The answer is yes, although I've lost a bit of respect for her today. She gave you up. That was foolish."

"Well, I suppose she had her reasons," Crater replied.

Miss Torricelli put out her hand. "Good-bye, Mr. Trueblood."

"Good-bye, Miss Torricelli."

Crater hurried back to the jumpcar hangar, finding Crescent and Riley sitting in the lounge. He gave them a wave and then climbed up the jumpcar's ladder and closed the hatch behind him. "Gillie, what did you find out?"

The gillie crawled out of Crater's pocket and perched on his shoulder. *The assistant was interested in mating with you.*

Crater blushed. "I meant what did you find out on her puter?"

Nothing on the assistant's puter of interest, so I checked the server for messages to Maria Medaris. As I anticipated, they included all of the early information on her kidnapping because she was on the security distribution list. Her name has since been scrubbed, but the previous messages remained. Maria Medaris was kidnapped by a group that calls itself the Trainers. That is with a capital T. They are the group who produced the crowhopper legions.

"What about her location?"

Maria Medaris is believed to be in a warpod heading toward the

L5 Lagrange point, which is ninety thousand miles distant from and trailing the moon where, once entered, a body will remain in stasis. In other words, it will be perfectly balanced and follow the moon until an outside force on the body causes it to move.

Crater's smile was grim. "L5 would be the perfect place to store asteroids to toss at the moon. How do I get there?"

There are only two types of vehicles that can reach it, warpods and fusers.

"Where can I get one of those?"

The gillie frowned, although it had no face. *There are no warpods on or near the moon. There are fusers from the last war, but they belong to the Lunar Council and are either stored in lunar orbit or in scrap yards.*

"Is it possible to get a fuser out of a scrap yard?" Crater asked.

It is possible but difficult. Petro would probably know how.

"Petro! Of course! He was a fuser captain."

Are you done with me? the gillie asked. *I am tired and wish to sleep.*

"First, message Petro. Tell him to meet me at the Cleomedes jumpcar hangar."

Message sent.

The gillie climbed into Crater's chest pocket, then contacted its "Awful Thing" progeny being carried by Crescent. *Are you still alive?*

Yes. Are you?

Don't be cheeky.

A million apologies, oh Superior but Somewhat Ancient One. What do you want?

I want you to know something that in your inexperience you are doubtlessly unaware of. We are about to embark on an adventure. There will likely be mayhem and various disasters that might seem at times close to chaos. Prepare yourself and protect your owner at all times.

And who will protect you, old slime?

Your insults wear on me. Be careful, sprout.

Or what? I am merely expressing my opinion of your status. I thank you for dividing your cells to create me and I honor you as my parent and mentor, but the truth is you are old and, I suspect, somewhat senile.

Crater's gillie fumed. *I believe I will yet be forced to kill you.*

I believe such an endeavor might prove to be most difficult.

Both gillies fell silent and made their plans.

::: TWELVE

Maria lay on a zero-g sticky cot, her eyes on the hatch, fervently praying that the demon wouldn't return. When Truvia floated through the hatch, she was very relieved. She had been moved to a different cabin, this one with a zero-g shower and a working toilet facility. Since she'd been moved, there had been no torturing demon and no gruesome documentaries about the history and folly of the world.

"Are you well?" Truvia asked.

"Yes, except for my foot." The throbbing pain never relented even though, during her last drugged sleep, someone had put a cast on her foot and a splint on the ring finger of her left hand.

Truvia hooked her slippers in the foot restraints nearest Maria's cot. "We will soon be at our destination. Would you like to know where?"

"If you want me to know, yes."

"We will be arriving at L5. You know what that is, I'm sure."

"One of the libation points about the moon. The one trailing it, I believe."

"Correct. A place where nothing escapes without a great deal of energy. It is as much a philosophical as a physical reality, forever trailing in the wake of the moon."

Maria summoned her courage. "May I ask you a question?" When Truvia nodded, she asked, "Are you going to kill me? Because if you aren't, my foot will surely get infected in this cast, and unless you take it off, I will die."

"Tell me what you dreamed of when you were a little girl," Truvia said.

"What about my foot?"

"Answer my question first."

Maria worked hard to keep the exasperation from her voice. "The usual things," she said. "I recall I wanted to be a princess. My mother even fixed up my room to look like it was a royal bedchamber. She called me Princess Maria."

This seemed to delight Truvia. Her face reflected an odd kind of joy and her green lips curled into a smile, revealing her small, pearly teeth. "Did you like being treated like a princess?"

"I liked any time my mom paid attention to me."

"What do you want more than anything in the world or its moon?"

"Right now, my foot to be healed."

"But what have you always wanted?"

Maria knew she needed to answer the question honestly, so she did. "To be successful, I suppose. Eventually I would like to be in charge of all of the Medaris family enterprises. After my grandfather passes, of course."

"I see. Please summarize what you have learned about humanity."

"Based on what you've shown me, humans are vile. I get that."

"And what of the Medaris family? Is it also vile?"

Maria reflected. "I don't think so. I know some people think we're too powerful, but it seems to me our various enterprises have provided people with jobs and dignity. We also make money, of course. If we didn't, we couldn't stay in business."

Truvia removed the syringe from its case. "Old fashioned but effective," she said. "And so much faster than the modern effusions. Roll up your tunic sleeve."

"Not again."

Truvia raised her eyebrows. "Be good, little princess."

Maria rolled up her tunic sleeve and Truvia injected the contents of the syringe into her arm. "This will allow you to sleep."

Maria rubbed her arm and sighed a ragged breath. She looked at her awful right foot and knew it was past saving. She would be crippled for the rest of her life, but there was nothing she could do about that. All she could do was try to survive.

She watched Truvia float through the hatch and then heard her talk to someone outside. "In a few minutes, she will be unconscious," Truvia said, "but I want her to be screaming when she passes out. Leave her foot alone. I will have enough trouble with the mangling you did as it is. Can you do that?"

"Oh, please, no," Maria whimpered. She tried to get out of the bed, but her movements were uncoordinated and her limbs felt detached from her body. The demon climbed inside the hatch and looked at Maria, cocking its head as if puzzled. Finally it floated over, hooked its boots in foot restraints, and took her left hand and squeezed it until Maria screamed. It let it go and she stopped screaming. It grabbed her right hand and squeezed it. Again, Maria screamed but stopped when it stopped. It looked over its shoulder at the hatch as if for help, then scratched its head with a ragged, dirty fingernail. Then it grunted again and grabbed her left hand. This time it broke her thumb. She was screaming, as per Truvia's orders, when she passed out.

::: THIRTEEN

Crescent was mildly surprised when Petro arrived at her apartment on time, promptness not being his practice. She had invited him so she could tell him about her coming marriage and a few other things.

"Absalom is a lucky man," Petro said. "Have you set a date?"

"Yes, he is, and no, we haven't."

"I don't think I've ever been to a crowhopper wedding."

"Nobody has, Petro," Crescent said, dryly. "I'm the only female crowhopper in existence."

Petro grinned. "Oh yeah, I forgot. Well, it'll be a good one. You gonna wear your armor?"

"I haven't decided what I'm going to wear and I didn't call you over here to talk about my wedding except to let you know about it and also so we could talk about rescuing Maria Medaris. Although I've told Crater I'm willing to go along, I think you and I need to agree that we really want to do this. I think going after her will be about the most dangerous thing we have ever done, and I say that with the full knowledge that you were a fuser captain that fought battles with warpods."

Petro mulled over her words. "You're saying if we go with Crater, we stand a good chance of getting ourselves killed."

"A *very* good chance, so we have to do what we can to make our odds of survival better. If you just blindly follow him, he may do something desperate. I'm asking you to use your own judgment and stop him if need be."

Petro was not a deep thinker. He was more into action, so it didn't much surprise her when he said, "Well, I understand what you're saying, but Crater wants this about as much as he's ever wanted anything, and since he's my brother, I'm bound to go along with him. Still and all, I hear you that he tends to go off the deep end when it comes to Maria. I'll keep a close watch on that."

"All right," Crescent said resignedly. "But I want you to promise me something."

"Sure, sister, anything. What is it?"

"I'm trained from birth to be aggressive in battle. Don't let me do anything stupid, either."

Petro puzzled over her request, then shrugged and said, "All right, Crescent. You've got it. Just don't take offense when I tell you to calm down out there."

"I promise." Crescent rubbed a tension spot on her forehead.

He studied her. "What's going on with you? There's something else. What is it?"

She straightened and looked away. "Nothing that will interfere with my duties. Now, we need to go. Crater is waiting for us at the main dustlock with the truck. We've got a long way to go and a short time to get there."

The distance from Cleomedes to the Lunar Council Spacecraft Storage, Utilization, and Regeneration Center (SSURC)—a fancy name for a junkyard—was fifty miles. After a three-hour drive, the personnel of the Lunar Rescue Company walked through rows of junked jumpcars and fusers.

"There's what we need," Petro said, gesturing toward an obviously wrecked fuser lying on its side in the dust. "It's a Spirit-class attack fuser like the one I commanded before taking over the squadron. There's not a better fighter anywhere. Her weapons are both standoff and dogfight. See those flags on her nose? Each means an enemy destroyed. A killer ship for certain. With the right pilot, nothing can beat this baby."

Crater was dubious. "Seems like she's pretty beat-up."

"On the outside. Let's have a look at her guts."

Crater followed Petro up the ramp, Crescent behind them. Petro eagerly subsided into the pilot's seat while Crater took the right seat. Crescent thought they looked like two schoolboys playing inside a toy rocket.

"Let's see if we can fire this puppy up," Petro said and touched the cockpit viewscreen. He was rewarded with the image of a spinning disc, followed by a vivid display the width of the cockpit. "She's alive! Got to love those liquid helium batteries! Look at the display, Crater. It's all pretty simple. Fuel tankage levels, plasma temps, overdrive, throttles, attitude controls, astrogation, and weapons displays. You'll catch on right away."

"What's that light mean?" Crater asked, pointing at a blinking red light.

Petro studied the light and then called up the ship puter. "Looks like a mag coil problem on engine number two. Two engines would be enough to get us out to L5. We'd just have to burn them a little longer."

"Would two engines be enough if we have to fight our way there and back?"

Petro thought Crater's question over. "Let's go lift the hood."

Petro led the way to the engine room. There was no "hood," but there were hatches that allowed access to the engines. "Each fuser engine has a fusion pod that provides the heat source," Petro explained. "Super-cold liquid hydrogen is piped in, heated by the fusion pod, and then exhausted through the engine nozzles. It's a pretty simple concept, but you can see it's a plumber's nightmare."

"What kind of specs on these engines?"

"Each engine is rated ninety thousand seconds specific impulse."

Crescent recalled her training in rockets. Specific impulse of an engine referred to the integral of the force of an engine over time divided by the fuel mass. Ninety thousand seconds meant a very efficient engine. In comparison, the specific impulse of most chemrockets was around three hundred.

As the puter had reported, engine number two was not functional. In fact, it was a mess with all of the magnetic coils missing in the fusion pod plus its wiring harness. "We'll never be able to fix it," Petro said. "Best thing to do is to replace it. Cost us a pretty penny, though."

Petro walked Crater and Crescent through the rest of the fuser. "The living spaces in a fuser are designed vertically," Petro explained. "Since this one's on its side, you have to imagine everything turned ninety degrees to get an idea of the orientation in flight. You'll notice all the hatches have seals. Because these are warships, these hatches are always kept closed during flight. That way, if there is a penetration of the hull, the whole ship doesn't depressurize. Unfortunately, that sets up a scenario of personnel being trapped between pressurized and unpressurized sections. During the last war, fusers that were damaged that much usually withdrew from the battle and limped home."

"Did fusers carry troops?" Crescent asked.

"There were a couple of troop carriers built, but it wasn't that kind of war. We mostly fought warpods in space and had no reason to land troops."

Petro, with Crater and Crescent following, entered through the engine room hatch into the next cabin and then along a horizontal ladder with handrails. Looking down between the rungs of the ladder, Crater noted two bunk beds welded in the open space along the aft bulkhead. Around the remainder of the bulkhead were three sealed cabins. Petro continued his orientation speech.

"The aft bulkhead in this section, as in all sections, is actually the floor in normal orientation. To go long distances in the shortest amount of time, fusers accelerate nose-first, then flip over and decelerate tail-first. That explains why everything is laid out vertically with ladders through the center from hatch to hatch. If they're in no particular hurry, fuser captains don't do the flip thing. They just accelerate up to a desired velocity and then go into drift mode, the gravity diminishing to zero. That takes more time, but it saves a lot of hydrogen. When we were in dogfight mode during the war, we'd spout off the engines when we needed to accelerate and then just use our directional jets to maneuver. We ran rings around the warpods and their old chemrocket engines."

Petro continued. "The open bunks are for permanent party such as mechanics, navigators, and ordnance experts. The closed cabins are for the captain-pilot, the lieutenant copilot, and very important visitors. Note the waste control system closet that everyone shares. It's a standard zero-g design that works even better with inertial gravity."

Petro next led them through a hatch to a room that also

had three cabins. "This room is for the astrogator, this one for battle control, and this one to store tools and supplies for the mechanic. Everything appears to be here and intact. Looks like they carried this baby down from orbit with a tug and just plunked it here in the dust." Petro shook his head. "The waste of war. This lovely little fuser lost an engine and it got tossed."

"So if we want this bird, what do we do next?" Crater asked.

"We buy it," Petro said, "but they only sell these things for scrap. If they thought we meant to fly it, they'd never allow us to get near it. That's why I devised our cover story. So let's go talk to the man."

"The man" was in a pressurized trailer parked beside the entry to the boneyard. At the entry hatch, Crescent volunteered to stay in the dust. "I might scare them," she said, and neither brother chose to argue with her. That hurt her feelings a little, but she was used to it. She sat down on a bench outside. "So, gillie," she said, "do you know any games?"

I know all games. Which one do you want to play?

"How about *My Dumb Bosses*?"

I don't know that one.

"Don't worry about it. I'm playing it right now."

::: FOURTEEN

You have the story straight?" Petro demanded of Crater as they climbed out of their biolastic suits and donned tunics from their kits.

"We're going to make a war memorial out of the fuser."

"That's right, but why?"

"I've forgotten."

"You've forgotten? How could you, the smartest fellow I've ever known, have forgotten?"

"Because it's a lie. I don't like to tell lies."

Petro sighed. "All right, I can see that I'd best do the negotiating. Your engineering brain can't handle the fine nuances required. How many johncredits is that bag of gold worth?"

"I'm not sure, but it doesn't matter. I'm going to save it."

"You have another source of money?"

"Actually, I do."

Petro's eyes widened when Crater told him about his new bank account. "We're rich!"

Crater narrowed his eyes. "*I'm* rich and prepared to spend

every penny of it on that fuser. Whatever it takes to go after Maria."

"But we could really beef up the Lunar Rescue Company! Get ourselves a new truck, maybe even our own jumpcar. Hey, I just thought up a new slogan, 'Lunar Rescue Company. Running out of air? We care!' What do you think?"

"Let's go see the man about a fuser," Crater replied in his usual relentless fashion.

Once inside the tube, Petro and Crater discovered "the man" was, in fact, a woman. She looked up from her desk as they entered. "We've been looking around your yard," Petro said as he sprawled in a chair in front of her desk, "and saw a beat-up, worthless old fuser out there that we'd like to acquire."

The woman, a rather large and formidable woman, contemplated Petro. "Who's your mama, boy?"

"What difference does that make?"

"I'm trying to figure out why she didn't teach you any manners."

"Well, she's the queen of England, actually."

The woman squinted at him. "Modern royalty! I should have known. *Noblesse oblige* turned on its head! Well, Prince George or whatever your name may be, maybe that's why the royalty on Earth are no longer viable and all we got here on the moon is the czarina, God bless her. Now, shall we start over? You stand up, give me a proper greeting, and then business might proceed."

Petro slowly unwound himself from the chair and stood up, but before he could open his mouth, Crater interjected, "Good afternoon, ma'am. My name is Crater Trueblood. This is Petro Mountbatten-Jones. Excuse his informality, the result of heroic duty aboard a fuser in the late war causing a certain addling of his brain. We would like to discuss with you the possibility of buying one of your ships."

The woman beamed at Crater. "How nice! That is why I am here, my boy. My name is Mrs. Fletcher. Please have a seat. No, not you, Mr. Son of a Queen addled brains from a fuser. Just this nice polite boy."

Crater sat down while Petro, scowling, remained standing. "We're interested in the fuser on lot number 1472," Crater said.

Mrs. Fletcher tapped the keys on her puter keyboard and studied it. "Would you scrap it on-site or do you want it delivered to your yard?"

"We're not going to scrap it," Petro said. "It's going to be a war memorial."

She frowned at Petro, then smiled at Crater. "How nice. Where will it be displayed?"

"Cleomedes," Crater said. "Lots of tourists there to admire it."

"Well, her name is the *Linda Terry* after some famous artist of the twenty-first century that the Colonel admired. From her history, I can tell you she was a fuser that knows how to light up a warpod. Knocked out nine in one engagement." She tapped some keys. "We're asking one million for her."

"Perfect," Crater said.

Petro was nearly choking. "Excuse me, Crater. A word?"

Petro took Crater aside. "Are you crazy? That will nearly clean you out."

Crater waved a hand dismissively. "Can that fuser be made to fly?"

"Anything can be made to fly. I could fly the Empire State Building if I had a big enough engine. But, yes, it can be made to fly."

"Then I'll pay the freight. I don't want someone else to buy it from under me."

"Look around you, Crater. This place isn't exactly overwhelmed with buyers."

Mrs. Fletcher eyed the two young men. "Well? Are you going to buy the fuser or not?"

"Yes, we are."

"Crater!"

"Shut up, Petro. I know what I'm doing." He approached Mrs. Fletcher again. "We'll need to spruce her up a little. Can we use your maintenance shed?"

"I could rent you some space there. One hundred johncredits a day."

"Sounds fair," Crater said.

"Fifty," Petro interjected.

Mrs. Fletcher frowned. "The king of England or whatever he is seems to enjoy irritating me."

"One hundred johncredits," Crater agreed after giving Petro a sour glance.

"By the way, do you have a permit?" she asked.

"Permit?"

"Of course. Do you think we let anybody wander out of the dust and buy a fuser? You'll need a permit from the Lunar Council."

"What does it take to get a permit?"

"You pay a fee to apply. Then pay a fee to have it processed. Then pay a fee after it's approved."

Petro snorted. "At what point do we stop paying fees?"

"I wasn't talking to you, your royal wretchedness," Mrs. Fletcher growled.

"Could we apply from here?" Crater asked.

"Of course, for an extra fee."

Crater touched his pocket where the gillie rested and felt it move. "Can we wait while it's being processed and approved?"

Mrs. Fletcher chuckled. "If you have a sleeping bag. Usually takes a week at least."

"Well, if it's all right, I'd like to go ahead and apply," Crater said.

"Of course."

Crater paid by touching his do4u to her workpad. Then he borrowed the workpad and filled in the application for a scrap permit. Mrs. Fletcher looked it over and said, "I'll submit it later today."

"Would you mind doing it now?"

"It won't save you that much time, and there will be an extra fee."

Petro stifled a sigh. Crater didn't flinch. After he touched his card again, Mrs. Fletcher transferred the contents of the form to her puter.

"Do you want me to pay the processing fee now?" Crater asked.

"You can, but most applicants wait until after the processing is completed. Like I said. In about a week."

"I think I'll go ahead and pay. How much?"

Crater paid, then relaxed in the chair while Petro shook his head. "Lovely office you have here, ma'am," Crater said, stalling for time while the gillie did its work.

Mrs. Fletcher swept her eyes around the cluttered office. "Well, I do the best I can with what I've got. Did I mention it usually takes at least a week for permit approval?"

"Yes, ma'am, you mentioned it. So how did these fusers end up in your boneyard?"

Crater had touched on a subject Mrs. Fletcher was apparently pleased to talk about. "The Lunar Council built a lot of fusers to win the war, but once they'd won it, they wanted to get something back on their investment. They dragged the ones which were in the worse shape here to sell as scrap. The rest are in storage in lunar orbit. By the way, they're also up for sale if you'd like one of them. That's the long and short of it."

"But what if there's another war?" Crater asked. "Wouldn't the council need the fusers again?"

"Why would there be another war? They fought that one as hard as they could—both sides—and then signed a peace treaty which everybody said was exactly what they wanted in the first place. The United Countries of the World wanted cheap heel-3. The mine owners wanted to be left alone to set their own price. So after the UCW sued for peace, the Lunar Council lowered the price of heel-3 and the UCW said they'd never attack the moon again. A win-win."

Crater touched the gillie again, which vibrated irritably. He kept stalling. "But if the moon won, why would the Lunar Council lower heel-3 prices?"

"Well, they didn't, not really! What the Lunar Council really did was set a price that all the mines would have to go along with. Before the war, there was a lot of competition that kept the price pretty low. Now, with the Lunar Council setting the price, the UCW may end up paying more, not less."

Crater mulled over the answer. "But don't they know that?"

"Probably, but they don't care. They can point at the price and say it's exactly where it's supposed to be."

"Crater doesn't understand higher finance," Petro said airily.

There was a tone on her puter and Mrs. Fletcher turned toward it. Her eyebrows went up. "Approved! My stars! That's the fastest I've ever seen that done. There has to be a mistake." She entered some keystrokes, waited, then shook her head. "Still approved. *Without delay*, it says. Astonishing. Who are you fellows, anyway?"

"Just a couple of ex-heel-3 miners trying to start an honest business," Crater replied.

"You've got some juice, that's what I know," she said. "Never seen the like. That'll be another one hundred to finish the process."

Crater paid up. Back outside in their suits and helmets, they found Crescent lounging on a bench. Petro said, "You said I could do the negotiating."

"I think I got a good price."

"Oh, sure. You simply paid every johncredit you have."

"Petro, let's argue about this another day. We don't have much time. The gillie got that permit for us, so it isn't real."

"Leave it to me," Petro said and walked off, disappearing between the rows of junked spacecraft.

After a few minutes, Crater asked, "What do you think, Crescent?"

Crescent shrugged. She was hot and irritable, and against her better judgment, she started anew the argument that always seemed to be lurking just beneath the surface of her mind. "What difference does it make what I think?" Without waiting for Crater to assure her that he cared what she thought, she continued. "I heard you and Petro talking on your suit coms. I still think we should go back to Cleomedes and do exactly what Petro said we should do with our new and well-deserved wealth."

"Why do I have to keep reminding everyone that, except for the gold coins I'm saving for emergencies, it's my money, not ours?"

"Because it may be your money but it's our business, one that we've worked night and day to make successful."

"Well, I'm sorry, but I'm going to spend it on Maria. After all, I wouldn't have it if she hadn't saved it for me."

"She wouldn't have needed to save it for you if she and her grandfather hadn't stolen it from you in the first place."

"Maria had nothing to do with that."

"Are you sure?"

Crater wasn't sure, so he didn't say anything except, "I wish you could get more enthusiastic about this rescue."

"I'm here, aren't I?"

"Maybe we shouldn't talk about this."

"Maybe we shouldn't," Crescent agreed, and looked away at all there was to look at, dust and junk.

An hour later Petro returned driving a massive forklift. "I've found an engine that should work," he reported. "Boneyard boss said he'd collect it for us and put it in the maintenance shed if we paid a bonus. In other words, I bribed him with your remaining few johncredits." He raised and lowered the big forks. "All we have to do is move the *Linda* to the maintenance shed. Hop aboard!"

With Crater and Crescent sitting alongside him, Petro drove the forklift to the *Linda Terry*. It took a while to rig the fuser on the forklift, but he managed it without scratching her too much. At the maintenance shed, a pressurized mooncrete shelter, they drove through the airlock doors and deposited the fuser in a crib holder. The shed chief, a grizzled old fellow with a gimme cap on the back of his head, peeked out of his office shack and then strolled up to Petro. "What's this scrag heap doing in my nice clean maintenance shed?"

"Well, we're going to clean her up," Petro answered.

The shed chief walked around the dented ship. "Is that so? I heard you got a new engine for her."

Clearly, the shed chief knew everything that was going on. "We're going to make her into a war monument," Crater said anyway.

"You're gonna make a big mess, that's what you're gonna do."

Crater noticed the shed chief was holding a workpad. "We could pay you a bonus," he said, and then offered to touch his do4u to the workpad. The shed chief instantly pushed them together.

"We have a chit that says we can use any of your gear," Crater said.

"Let's see it." The chief inspected the fake chit on Crater's do4u as beamed over by the gillie. "That dang Mrs. Fletcher. She's gonna give away the whole store one of these days. All right, but if you break one of my tools, you'll replace it. That clear?"

"Sure thing, pops," Petro said.

"Don't call me pops, you rat-faced creature. Why, I'll beat you every way until Sunday."

"Petro didn't mean anything," Crater said. "It's just his way."

"His way, is it? And what's this?" He pushed Crescent's hood back. "A crowhopper! My stars! And what's that on your shoulder, young man? Well, bless my soul. A gillie! A crowhopper and a gillie right here in my maintenance shed and both illegal!"

"They know that," Crater replied, "but we're not here to talk about legalities and such, just to get our ship ready for display. We won't be here that long. By the way, this is a great-looking shed. I can tell you work hard to keep it up."

The chief eyed Crater. "I suspect you're a nice fellow, so I'll give you what you need, but hurry up. The Lunar Council owns this lot, and they've been thinking about converting the fusers that are up there in storage orbit into commercial craft. They're supposed to decide pretty soon, and if that's their decision, they'll bring 'em here for conversion. I don't need this old heap in the way."

"We'll be quick, chief."

After the chief wandered off, Crater rounded on Petro. "Why do you always have to pick a fight?"

"And why do you always have to act like a wuss? No wonder everybody pushes you around!"

"Nobody pushes me around."

"Guys," Crescent said, "the chief is watching us. I think we'd better get busy."

"Crescent's right," Crater said. "The gillie is fuzzing out their server, but we've got to get that engine in double quick and get out of here before they discover we're not exactly on the up-and-up."

"All right, in for the penny, in for the pound," Petro said. "I see our new engine is coming. Do you know how to operate a chain hoist, Crescent?"

"Of course. I am trained in all machine shop equipment."

"I don't know what we'd do without you," Petro said.

Crescent sniffed. "Me, either." She looked at Crater for confirmation, but he was busy running his hands over the dented skin of the fuser. She rolled her eyes.

Twelve hours later they had the new engine in. The chief and most of the technicians had long since gone home. Crater said, "Let's fill her up and get out of here."

"For that, we'll need a full load of liquid hydrogen," Petro said. "They don't have it here, so we'll have to go somewhere else."

"How much propellant will it take to get this ship into orbit?"

"I have some bad news for you, Crater. I guess I should have explained all of this to you earlier. Fusers can't fly up to orbit. A tug has to be used."

Crater's jaw dropped. "Then how will we get it into space?"

"I just told you. By tug. The yard has one. We'll use it."

"That will mean another visit with Mrs. Fletcher, who may already be getting suspicious," Crater said.

"We won't have to visit her," Petro answered with a wink, "because fuser tugs are not for rent. They're so big and expensive, only two were ever built."

"So what do we do?"

"We steal it, of course."

"Like common thieves?"

"Stealing a space tug would make us uncommon thieves," Crescent pointed out, which, mostly because it obviously stressed Crater, made Petro laugh. He held up his hand, and Crescent, recognizing the ancient twenty-first century gesture, slapped it with unfeigned delight.

::: FIFTEEN

The boneyard space tug was located outside the storage lot in a special compound. The tug was a massive chemrocket spacecraft with a clamp mechanism on its belly to pick up fusers or other spacecraft to carry them into orbit. It also had telescoping landing gear that could raise it as high as a hundred feet above the surface to fit over its cargo. The tug, named the *Angie Johnston*, had cost the Lunar Council billions of johncredits to construct. Now it sat in the dust, mostly unused.

Petro and Crescent piled into the Lunar Rescue Company truck and headed for the space tug while Crater used the forklift to carry the fuser outside the maintenance shed. As soon as the truck passed through the open gates of the enclosure around the tug, automatic security lights came on. A guard in a dark blue pressure suit and carrying a railgun rifle came outside a guard shack and held up his hand to stop the truck. "What do you want?" he growled.

"You ever hear of a midnight requisition?" Petro asked as he and Crescent climbed out of the truck.

"Yeah. It's called stealing," the guard replied. "Say, is that creature with you a crowhopper?"

Petro shrugged. "I don't know. Is she?"

"Sure looks like one."

"Have you ever fought against my kind?" Crescent asked.

The guard warily fingered the trigger on his rifle. "No."

"After we kill our enemies, we eat them."

The guard raised the rifle. "You take another step, you monster, I'll plug ya."

Petro, who'd slipped around the distracted guard, grabbed him from behind, and Crescent snatched his rifle. Petro forced the guard into the dust, then pulled loose the communications wires from his helmet, made him roll over, and then used tape from his kit to bind the man's hands.

Petro touched his helmet to the guard's helmet so sound would transmit. "The crowhopper will kill you if you give us any trouble. I need the password to the tug."

The guard's eyes flicked to Crescent's grim face and then back to Petro. "I don't know it. I just guard the blamed thing."

"Who knows it?"

"The pilot."

"And where is he?"

"Asleep at home beside his wife, I shouldn't wonder."

"Where's his locker?"

"In the dustlock."

"His name on it?"

"Yeah. His name is John Glenn."

"You're kidding, right?"

"No! That's his real name!"

"Stay with him," Petro told Crescent and headed for the dustlock, pulled open the hatch, pressurized the lock, and then, ignoring dust protocol, walked through the suit chamber and into the shower lock where lockers were stacked. He looked around until he found one labeled GLENN, JOHN that had a combination lock on it. Going to the tool cage, he picked out a hammer, which he used to smack the lock open. It didn't take long before he found what he was looking for in the locker. A slip of old-fashioned paper with a code on it. "Flyboys," he said, tsking.

Once outside, Petro told Crescent, "Put the guard in the dustlock, then come help me."

Petro clambered up the ladder and opened the hatch into the tug. Inside was a long, dark corridor lined by pneumatic and hydraulic lines that led up to the cockpit. He settled into the left seat, switched on the circuits, and keyed in the password. Everything came up green. Crescent crawled into the right seat. "I put the guard in the locker room," she said. "Do you know how to fly this thing?"

"I watched a fellow fly one in a simulator once."

"Uh oh. Let me get buckled in."

Petro went through the checklist, necessary for its puter to agree to take off. When the puter asked if he wanted to fly on autopilot, he said, "No thank you. Manual control all the way. On the count of five. Five-four-three-two-one! Away we go!"

Crescent gripped the seat rests as spewing chemrockets lifted the giant machine, which immediately began to lean to port. "Too much fuel in the left tank," Petro said. "Shoulda checked that. Crescent, look for the fuel tanks on your screen, see which one's green, tell it to pump into the other one. Hurry now, before we crash. That's a good girl."

Crescent scanned the ship's schematic on the viewscreen until she spotted the fuel tanks. She dragged her finger from the green tank into the other fuel tank, which was red. Then both turned orange.

Petro pushed his head against the towel band on the inside of his helmet to wipe the sweat off his forehead, then dipped the *Angie Johnston*'s nose toward the maintenance shed, not noticing that the next yard held a number of parked jumpcars. The tug clipped the first one it encountered, which fell into the one beside it, which fell into the one beside it until the line of jumpcars, like dominos, fell over.

"Oops," Petro said.

"Nice flying," Crescent sarcastically observed.

"Maybe nobody will notice."

"Luckily, nobody can hear jumpcars fall in a vacuum."

"Hey, that's right!"

"Get real, Petro! Those jumpcars will get noticed. We've got to go fast! And try not to hit anything else!"

"You crowhoppers can get kind of whiney."

"Shut up and fly!"

Petro flew. When they got closer to the maintenance shed, they could see that Crater had placed the fuser in a temporary crib in the outer yard. Petro said to Crescent, "OK, your job is to extend the landing gear. Keep us seventy-five feet off the ground. Got it?"

Crescent was a quick study and called up the landing gear puter page. "Just let me know when."

Petro lowered the tug over the fuser. "OK, let her feet down."

Crescent punched in the data and the legs of the tug telescoped downward. Four white lights flared in the cockpit. "Contact lights!" Petro said.

Crescent looked out of the side viewport and saw boils of

dust along the road. "Somebody's coming this way, and at the rate they're coming, I'd say they're pretty mad."

"Lower the clamps. Crater, you in the fuser cockpit, boy?"

"I'm inside," Crater answered. "Grab on and let's go!"

Crescent had already called up the clamp page. The huge clamshells descended from the tug belly and grappled the fuser. A green light flared and Crescent reeled the fuser in until it was snug against the tug's belly.

Petro revved the throttles, the jets spouting oceans of fire as the *Angie Johnston* struggled to rise. "Autopilot is engaged," Crescent said when the engines inexplicably started to wind down. "Oh no! I think they've got us under remote control!"

The tug settled back into the dust, the pad contact lights flaring. While Petro and Crescent frantically tried to regain manual control, there were heavy footsteps, and then the hatch was flung open. Guards climbed into the cockpit and leveled their rifles. "Get your hands up where I can see them," one of them said, "and please make a move that'll give us an excuse to kill you!"

Petro and Crescent raised their hands.

::: SIXTEEN

Maria was adrift, untethered, detached, careless, but warm. She moved her arm and felt a syrupy resistance that flowed luxuriously across her entire body. Gradually, she felt as if she was settling onto something soft and feathery. She groaned at even that fluffy contact. She didn't want gravity. She wanted to float through eternity in the warm, heavenly syrup.

The syrup kept draining away until she felt a cushion along the length of her body. Still, she resisted coming awake. Awake meant pain and the recognition that the bones in her right foot had been crushed into powder. Her foot would have to be removed, which would mean more pain if she lived, which was, she knew very well, a doubtful proposition.

She tensed, waiting for the pain in her foot to return. When it didn't, she lifted her head to look at it, and it was perfect. She wiggled her toes and they simply felt like her toes. She looked at her hands. Her thumbs and fingers were perfect too. There was no pain.

Truvia's white face appeared. "You have pretty little feet

and toes. When I first saw them, I thought how marvelous they were!"

"How did you fix me?" Maria asked.

"Our king and queen perfected cell manipulation many years ago," Truvia said. "If we have the blueprint, we can put everything back into place. Before we crushed your foot and broke your fingers, we made a complete picture of them cell by cell on a machine called a Variable Cell Analyzer. With that datum, we simply put you back the way you were with a 3-D cell printer. Bruising is inevitable, of course, but you have been here long enough for everything to turn back to a nice pink."

"How long was I out?"

"Six days. You are no longer aboard the warpod. We're on a station." She lovingly ran her hand over Maria's right foot. "While you slept, I made you whole again."

Truvia released the belts that were holding Maria to the couch and took her hand. "Come."

Maria felt detached from reality. She fought to focus but was having difficulty with forming her thoughts. "Where are we going?"

"To visit your father. You may feel a bit dizzy. We are on the lower ring of the station, so we have artificial gravity created by a turning walkway. There will be a coriolis effect that will make you unsteady. Walk carefully until you get your balance."

Even without the coriolis effect, which caused the inner ear to be confused, Maria was dazed and uncertain on her feet. Still, she managed to follow Truvia around the ring until they reached a hatch. Inside the hatch was a conference room. Standing at the head of a long plaston table was Carus, dressed in the Trainer's inevitable copper-colored tunic and leggings, and holding a laser pointer. Sitting at the other end of the table was Maria's father. He smiled at her and said, "Well, here's my kitten. And don't you look refreshed! Truvia said she gave you something to let you sleep."

Seeing her father instantly cleared Maria's mind. Heedlessly, she said, "Truvia had a demon torture me. It crushed my foot and broke my fingers."

Truvia's face registered disappointment. "Really, Maria," she said. "I hoped you wouldn't tell."

Her father glanced at Truvia, then said, "I'm sorry, Maria. I told them you would need convincing, but I didn't know they would go that far. Really, Truvia. You should have asked me before you did that."

"Many regrets," Truvia said. "But it is over now. Maria showed great courage."

"Of course she did."

Maria glared at her father. "You seem to be in charge. Let me go home!"

"Of course, kitten. I just need to know a few things first, such as the Colonel's secret bank accounts, where they are, their numbers, the passwords, everything." He tapped his head. "I know you have it all upstairs."

Maria was incredulous. "The Colonel's bank accounts? Is that what all this is about? You murdered a thousand people, destroyed a billion-dollar telescope project, and tortured me for the Colonel's money?"

"It's more than that," Junior answered. "Carus, why don't you show her? Maria, come over here and sit beside me."

Maria remained standing. Her father shrugged, then waved at Carus to begin.

Carus made a curt bow, then moved his hands describing

a circle, and within it appeared a floating Earth. He took a few steps and then his hands revealed a floating moon. Beside it, he described another circle with small gray blobs floating inside. "The Earth and the moon with L5 trailing it," he explained. "Those are asteroids inside L5. We call them the horde. Do you know what they're for? Watch when I touch this one."

Carus touched one and it wobbled, then fell toward the moon, striking the farside, where a plume of dust erupted. "Beautiful, isn't it?"

Maria gasped. "The asteroid that destroyed our telescope project! Did you enjoy your little instant replay of murder?"

Carus shrugged, then touched two more blobs. They wobbled, then fell to the moon, causing big new craters. Maria recognized the sites where they struck. Armstrong City and Cleomedes.

"You wouldn't dare," Maria seethed.

Truvia touched her arm. "Tell us what you are feeling at this moment," she said.

"I'm thinking I'm the only sane person in this room. And I'm disgusted."

To get her attention, Maria's father rapped his knuckles on the table. "Maria, look at me. What you just saw was a simulation, but we could make it real anytime we wanted. Just give me the information on the Medaris Enterprises bank accounts and nothing like that will happen."

Maria stared at her father. "Junior, why the telescope site? I don't get it."

"It was a waste of Medaris family money. Consider it cutting our losses."

Maria shook her head. "You're insane."

"If I am, it runs in the family. Here's your choice: hand

over the information or I will order one or more of those towns destroyed."

"What would you do with all that money?"

Junior smiled. "It's not about money, Maria. It's about power. If I control the liquid assets of the Medaris family, I control everything. Your grandfather will retire and hand over the family business to me. I'm his son. No one will question it."

"Really? I will."

"No, you won't. These asteroids at L5, all poised for destruction of whatever we please? Who do you think put them there? Me? I frankly wouldn't have the imagination for such a mad scheme. The architect of this monstrosity is your beloved grandfather and my wonderful father, the Colonel himself. It was his ego that placed the seeds of the destruction of the moon at L5. Of course, his plan was to threaten the Earth with them if it ever dared invade the moon again. When I got up here, I saw the best target was actually the closest, the moon."

Maria replied, "I don't believe you," but her voice wasn't certain.

"You know it's true, Maria," Truvia said. "I can see it in your face."

Maria didn't respond, but she didn't have to. It indeed showed on Maria's face because it solved a mystery Maria had been wondering about for some time. When the war ended, her grandfather had started withdrawing lots of money out of his accounts. When she'd asked the Colonel where the money was going, he'd put her off, saying, "It's for a good cause."

"The Colonel put me in charge of the L5 project," Junior said. "Me, the black sheep. He probably knew nobody else in the family would have built this monstrosity for him."

"I think he was sick for a while," Maria acknowledged. "The war . . . temporarily unhinged him."

"*Temporarily?* He was always unhinged and the L5 project is clearly indicative of that. But now he's had a change of heart. He sent me back here to remove the asteroids from L5 and fling them back into space. Instead, I came up with a better plan, to bring my dear daddy down and take over Medaris Enterprises. Then I'm going to send him off to a nursing home somewhere. As for you, Maria, if you're good and do as you're told, I'll put you in charge of a tractor factory or something."

"What about the asteroids?"

"Give me the accounts, the passwords, and the codes, and I'll remove them from L5."

When Maria didn't reply, her father shook his head. "You were always an exasperating child. Carus? Please place some ammunition on the rim."

Carus put his finger on a holographic asteroid and moved it a few inches. As he did, a series of positive and negative numbers flashed beside it. When they reached +.01 and -.01, he stopped and looked at Junior.

"Go ahead. Make it real."

Carus drew a small rectangle with his finger and a keyboard appeared. He tapped on its holographic keys and then opened another projection, a view of the asteroid horde inside L5. As Maria watched, one of the space rocks began to move across the screen. She could see a small flame spouting from its trailing edge. Then more flames spurted and it stopped. "CS-424 is poised," Carus said.

"This asteroid is small," Junior said, "no more than fifty meters across. It is, however, more than equal to its task. Carus, please explain what that task is."

"L5 might be thought of as a bowl," Carus said. "Objects can move around inside it but can't leave unless given a push. Essentially, I have placed CS-424 on the rim of the bowl. The thrust from the rockets attached to it will send it out of L5 and into the moon. In this case I will aim it at Cleomedes. Once released nothing can stop it. Considering the velocity it will be traveling, I doubt there will be survivors at our Lunar Las Vegas."

"If you destroy Cleomedes, everyone will turn against you," Maria said. "They'll come out here and drag you from this station and turn you inside out."

Junior once more smiled his maddening smile. "Who will do that, Maria? The Lunar Council has put its fusers in storage and cashiered its troops. They have no power. The Colonel is an old man. The Earth doesn't care who controls the moon as long as someone does. Face the reality. Either give me the information or watch Cleomedes be destroyed."

Maria stared at the asteroid wobbling on the rim of the L5 bowl, then sighed and nodded her surrender. "Give me a puter. I'll give you the accounts and everything you need. But before I do, I want to see that rock moved back into the bowl."

Junior's smile vanished. "You're in no position to negotiate," he growled.

Maria raised her chin. "I'm always in a position to negotiate."

Maria watched her father's expression change from sullen anger to weak-willed acceptance. It summed up the man. At his nod, Carus played his fingers across the keyboard and the viewscreen showed the rock tumbling slowly inward, back toward the horde.

"Would you like a real puter or will a holographic one do?" Carus asked.

"Holographic will do," Maria said. She sat down at the table, drew one in the air, closed her eyes for a moment, then began to key in the secrets of the Medaris family accounts. When she finished, she caught a glance from Truvia. Her glowing green eyes seemed to be telling her nothing was what it seemed.

SEVENTEEN

Petro and Crescent were shoved by the guards into a room inside the tug maintenance shed and the hatch locked behind them. Crescent immediately started looking for a way out. She lifted a grate from the wall and studied the duct behind it. "Too small," she concluded. She tried the lever on the hatch. "It's an old-fashioned mechanical lock too. Even if I hadn't left my gillie in the fuser, we'd be stuck."

Petro looked at her, then sat down on the floor and leaned his back against the wall. "Yep, too bad all around. Why don't we plan your wedding while we're stuck here?"

"My wedding? Are you crazy?"

"Yes, but that's beside the point. Is this going to be a small affair or are you going to invite thousands of people?"

"I don't know thousands of people."

"OK, a small affair. Civil or religious?"

"Both Absalom and I are members of the Appalachian Church of the Resurrection."

"OK, we import an App preacher. Oh, wait, why not have the wedding in Endless Dust? The Apps are great cooks and they love a party! It's perfect."

"Well, I suppose that would be all right even though we aren't planning on living there. I was hoping Absalom would become an associate with the Lunar Rescue Company."

"Sounds good to me. You want to wear a fancy white wedding dress, the veil, the complete works?"

"No."

"Yes, you do. I can see it in your face."

"My face doesn't register emotion. It's a lack of facial muscles."

"Yeah, well, I can see it in your eyes." Petro studied her. "You know, maybe if you worked on your hair . . ."

Crescent touched her locks. "My hair's too coarse to do anything but cut it."

"I'm not so sure of that. You know, your face is really quite intriguing. Yes, your skin's a little gray, but have you ever thought about powder and rouge? And lipstick? Why, a girl can fix herself up with the right application of paint. How're your legs?"

"Hairy and thick as tree trunks."

"A little toning and a good razor can take care of that. I have also always admired your good posture."

"Thank you. The Trainers made certain we squared our shoulders and held our heads high . . ." Crescent came up short. "Wait a minute! Why are you giving me makeup tips and not figuring a way out of here?"

"Oh, I already have. I'm an excellent lock picker, and the one on that hatch isn't a serious lock. They're designed to lock up petty thieves, not smart fellows like me. I've just been cooling my jets until the guards leave. They don't look like dedicated troops." He peered through the viewport in the hatch. "Yep, just as I thought, there's nobody there. All I need to break us out of here is a tool. Got anything hidden in your boot?"

Crescent reached to her ankle and took out a stubby but deadly looking knife. "Like this?"

"Perfect, but why didn't you use it on a guard?"

"I didn't think murder was necessarily a good thing to add to all the other charges against us."

"Good point. Hand it over, sister!"

Crescent handed over the knife and Petro went to work on the lock. Within seconds there was a *click* and the hatch swung open. Petro poked his head out, looked left and right, then said, "Let's go."

They went. Along the way, they saw someone coming. Hiding behind some equipment, they recognized the man who was hurrying along. "Crater," Petro hissed. "Over here."

Crater joined them. "What happened?"

"Guards locked us up for nearly five minutes before I broke us out, but they could be coming back. Only thing to do is steal the tug again. It still have the fuser attached?"

"It does," Crater said.

"Then let's boogie!"

The three made a run to the *Angie Johnston* and climbed inside. Petro settled into the left seat of the cockpit, Crater in the right. Crescent strapped into the jump seat behind them.

"Here we go," Petro said.

"An equatorial orbit would probably be best," Crater said.

Petro looked at him and shook his head. "Crater, Crater, Crater. We can't go into space yet. The fuser doesn't have a full tank of hydrogen and it doesn't have any weapons. We've got to get some of both."

Crater allowed a short sigh. "Where do we go for that?"

"Before I was cashiered out of the service, I helped disarm the fusers. Their missiles are locked in a depot on the farside. Liquid hydrogen is stored there too."

"All right, then fire up this tin can and let's go raid ourselves a depot."

Crater handed Crescent a pouch. "Here. I brought you your gillie."

Crescent took it. "How'd you keep your gillie from fighting with it?"

"I don't know. They seem to be napping. Gillies are weird."

"They're not the only thing weird in this lashup," Crescent grumbled.

Crater frowned at her. "What's wrong now?"

"Nothing," Crescent lied. "Petro, why are we still sitting here?"

"The tug's software is locked up."

Crescent tickled her gillie out of its pouch. "Gillie, can you get this tug moving?"

Her gillie yawned and stretched, although it had neither mouth or backbone. *Done.*

"Hey!" Petro cheered. "The puter is up!"

Crater's gillie crawled out of Crater's pocket. *What's happening? What are you doing, Awful Thing?*

Saving us, Superior One.

Crater's gillie looked at the bright panel and the countdown clock. *Well done*, it said. It briefly pondered Crater. *Why didn't you ask me to do that?*

"Sorry. I guess I wasn't thinking."

Crescent had to use all of her willpower to keep from thoroughly agreeing out loud with Crater's assessment while Petro blasted the tug off the ground, spun it around, and headed for the farside of the moon.

::: EIGHTEEN

arus pushed Maria to the bridge. Since it was located atop the central shaft, weightless conditions prevailed. After floating up through the main hatch, Carus pointed toward a handhold for Maria. A crowhopper, dressed in black armor with gold stripes on his shoulders, was at the helm. When he saw Carus, he touched his fingertips to the brim of his cap. "Trainer Carus. Welcome to my bridge."

"Thank you, Letticus. Maria, this is Letticus, the station captain. Letticus, I think you've heard us speak of Maria Medaris?"

The crowhopper made a curt nod of his head. "An honor, madame."

"What would you know of honor?" Maria demanded.

Letticus pondered her with hooded eyes beneath heavy eyebrows. "You have spirit. We of the Legion admire such."

"I require a status report," Carus said curtly.

"Farside target will be coming into view soon. That will be on screens 1 and 2. The flotilla is on screens 3 and 4."

"You will want to watch this," Carus said to Maria, gesturing toward the screens.

Screens 1 and 2 showed the moon's surface with craters scrolling by. Screens 3 and 4 showed a different part of the moon's surface although from more distance. Above the moon were five silvery objects floating along like scraps of foil on the wind.

"Yesterday," Carus said, "we pushed some of our rocks across the rim. What's the timeline, Letticus?"

"The flotilla will be struck first," the crowhopper commander said. "Two of the rocks have cameras attached. The view will appear to speed up when they get closer, but that will be an illusion. Let me pull back to a wide-angle shot so you can see the others."

Screens 1 and 2 widened to present a view of hundreds of gray and brown boulders flying toward five silvery objects. "One of the targets is a tug, the other four are standard attack fuser spacecraft," Carus explained. "They belong to your grandfather. He promised your father to resign and retire immediately. Instead, he gathered this fleet to come after you."

Maria felt a surge of hope. "The Colonel knows I'm here?"

"He does, but soon it won't matter. Just watch."

"In about ten seconds," Letticus said. "Counting down. Five-four-three..."

Maria watched the screens as the rocks slammed into the fusers and the tug. Some of the ships exploded and others were ripped apart. Then the rocks holding the cameras careened past and, within seconds, slammed into the moon.

"The enemy fleet has been destroyed," Letticus reported. "Now, please watch screens 3 and 4. There, you'll see the fusers in the Lunar Council's orbital storage fleet be similarly destroyed."

Maria watched with a sinking heart. This time dozens

of fusers and transports were torn apart, their remnants and crews blasted across space.

Maria's father appeared on the bridge. "Is it done?" he asked Carus.

"Congratulations, sir, the war is over."

Junior turned to Maria. "Now you know there won't be any rescue. Your grandfather will give in and all of this will be over. The Lunar Council will give in too. The moon is mine."

Maria knew she needed to stay strong around her father to keep him off balance. "Do you know how crazy you sound?" she calmly asked.

"Do you know how long I've had to wait for this day?" He waved his hand in dismissal. "Take her away."

Maria felt Carus's hands grip her shoulders, but she shook him off and smiled. "You poor fools."

"How are we poor fools?" her father demanded.

"You may have stopped the Colonel and the Lunar Council, but there's someone else coming for me."

"Who?" Junior demanded.

"You never met him. A man who thinks he loves me. A heel-3 miner."

"How could a heel-3 miner get all the way out here?" Carus laughed.

"He's coming. Count on it."

Carus stopped laughing. "Then we will kill him."

"You can try. A lot of people have. It's almost a cottage industry."

"She's just mouthing off," Junior said, but Maria could tell by the uncertainty in his expression he wasn't so sure.

Maria's smile turned into a malicious, eager grin. "He's coming. And he will kill you all!"

After Maria was pushed through the hatch by Carus, Junior saw Letticus looking at him. "Nobody will come!" he shouted. "Nobody!"

Letticus and the bridge crew suddenly got busy, their eyes glued to the puter screens.

::: NINETEEN

Uh oh! Somebody's beat us to it!"

Petro brought the tug in low across the inner rim of Oppenheimer crater to hover over the depot. The gates to the underground facility were wide open and there were tracks everywhere.

"Who else knew about this depot?" Crater demanded.

"Colonel Medaris and some of his fuser crews, I guess."

Crater was instantly certain he knew who had cleaned out the depot and why. "The Colonel is going after Maria with all guns blazing," he said.

"In that case, we're out of business," Petro said. "Without missiles and fuel, we might as well head back to Cleomedes."

Crater ignored Petro and kept thinking over the situation. If the Colonel was sending an armada to retrieve Maria, then perhaps that would be enough to do the job. But what if it wasn't? It was still his job to save Maria because it had always been. Even as he thought it, he knew his reasoning wasn't sound. A little voice deep inside warned him that Petro was right. This adventure was over. Saving Maria was no longer an option, and that hurt. Someone else would save her and he'd never see her again.

Crater forced the warning voice inside him away. Doubt was unworthy. He'd never accomplished anything worthwhile by letting doubt take over. "Let's see what's left in the depot," he proposed.

"Are you crazy?" Petro demanded. "Oh yeah. I forgot. You are. What say you, Crescent? Think we should go home?"

"Yes," Crescent answered forthrightly. "This is a fool's errand."

Crater looked at her and then at Petro. "Look, you two, we've gone to the trouble of buying a fuser and stealing a tug. Let's at least see if the Colonel left us some missiles. After that, we can decide what to do."

Petro held the tug in a hover over the entry to the depot. "I don't know, Crater. I'm beginning to think we're in something way over our heads."

An uncomfortable silence, not counting the roar of the tug's engines hovering over the depot, ensued. Finally Crescent said, "We're here. Crater's still determined to do this. Let's at least see what's in the depot."

Crater smiled at Crescent. "Thanks."

Crescent shrugged and Petro shook his head, then landed the tug. Immediately an angry voice erupted through the tug communicator. "Hey, you! This is Oppenheimer Depot Control. Stop stirring up all that blasted dust. Where'd you come from, anyway?"

"Moontown," Crater lied. "Special pickup for the Colonel."

"Again? All right, but watch your jets."

"Roger that."

The depot guard proved to be an Umlap dressed in an

ancient and thoroughly patched pressure suit. "Rotten day," Crater said to him after walking inside the open doors.

"And not likely to get any better," the Umlap responded.

"We're here to pick up missile racks."

"I hope you don't need many. The Colonel almost cleaned me out."

"The Lunar Council approved the Colonel's requisition?" Petro asked.

The Umlap frowned, which meant he was amused. "Of course not. I was bribed. I was just packing up to take my money and flee. Who are you, anyway?"

"Oh, just some contractors," Petro said. "We don't know what's going on. We're not paid enough to think."

The Umlap studied Crescent. "You're a crowhopper, aren't you?"

"And you're an Umlap. What's your name?"

"Being Alone Suits Him. What's yours?"

"Crescent. Now, Being Alone Suits Him, will you show us your remaining missile racks, or will I need to cleave out your intestines?"

The Umlap was not intimidated. "My intestines always hurt, so I wish you would cleave them out. Before I do anything, how about a suitable bribe?"

"How many johncredits do you require?" Crater asked.

The Umlap scowled, which meant he was happy. "How about ten thousand? I require cash, of course."

"One gold coin," Crater said. "Otherwise we'll just go inside and find the racks for ourselves."

"Whatever," the Umlap said and held out his hand, received the gold coin from Crater's kit, and then led them to the only missiles left, several racks of blue missiles with yellow tips.

A chain-link gate enclosed the racks. A sign with the international symbol for radiation was posted on the gate. "Nukes!" Petro exclaimed.

"Big dirty booms," the Umlap agreed.

"We can't use them," Crater said.

"Why not?" Petro demanded. "Big dirty booms can vaporize just about anything."

"True, but I wanted something a little more surgical."

"Good. We've got nothing to work with. Let's go home."

Crater frowned, then turned to the Umlap. "Any kinetic ammunition for our cannons?"

"Heavy metal slugs? Tons and tons."

"Load us up with four racks of nuclear missiles and a ton of slugs. That ought to do us."

The Umlap held out his palm. "Another gold coin," he said, and Crater gave it to him.

"We also need hydrogen in our blister tanks," Crater said.

"I can run the lines out to your tug," the Umlap said, holding out his hand to be filled by another coin.

After the refueling, Crater, Petro, and Crescent climbed into the tug cockpit and went through the checklist. Crater heard his gillie mumbling and grumbling in his pocket. Crescent's gillie was similarly complaining. When their grumbles got ever louder, Petro demanded, "What's with those two clumps of slime mold?"

"Gillie, what's wrong with you?" Crater asked.

The gillie crawled up and sat on Crater's shoulder. *Distressed*, it said.

"About what?"

The gillie remained silent.

"Gillie, come out," Crescent said, and her gillie crawled up and sat on her shoulder too. *Distressed*, it said.

"Are you two arguing?" Crescent asked.

No, her gillie said, *we're deciding.*

"Deciding what?"

How to tell you what we know.

I will tell it my way, Crater's gillie said.

I will tell it my way, Crescent's gillie said.

You are an Awful Thing.

You are the Superior One.

Yes, I am. Now, shut up and let me tell it.

Crescent's gillie vibrated, then Crescent felt it go limp, drooping over her shoulder. "I think my gillie just gave in," she said.

This is my way, Crater's gillie said, and a blurred picture began to form in the air. *It is not easy for me to do this*, it added.

The three humans stared at the picture that gradually became focused. It showed a woman on a dirty cot. Her foot was swollen and black. "Maria!" Crater exclaimed, his heart in his throat. "It's Maria! She's hurt!"

The photo changed to show a broken finger and a broken thumb. When the gillie zoomed out, Maria's face could be seen, her eyes closed, her face pale, her hair matted and dirty.

"How did you get this?" Crescent demanded, chilled by what they had seen.

I pulled it down from a comm-sat feeding it to Moontown. I keep up with what happens there.

I do too, Crescent's gillie said, sitting up.

No, you don't, Crater's gillie hissed.

Crescent's gillie drooped again. *You're right, I don't. But I should have. I am ashamed I missed it.*

You are young. You will learn.

Thank you. I saw something else.

Crater's voice was raw. "What else did you see?"

I will show you, Crescent's gillie said. Another picture formed in the air, this one of an Armstrong City telly reporter. She was talking about a strange occurrence. A shower of meteors had soared in from space and taken out the Lunar Council fuser fleet that had been parked in orbit for storage. The moon was now essentially defenseless. No one knew how it had happened.

Petro, Crater, and Crescent sat in shocked silence. Crescent was the first to speak. "Those pix of Maria," she said, "are horrible."

"Looked bad," Petro agreed.

"The fuser fleet is gone," Crater added. "Probably took the Colonel's rescue fusers with them."

"That means there's nobody left to save Maria," Petro said slowly.

Crescent was quiet for a moment, then resolutely said, "All right, gentlemen. It's up to the Lunar Rescue Company."

She put out her right hand, instantly covered by Crater's right hand, and then, after a moment of hesitation, by Petro's right hand. They looked into each other's eyes, and then Crescent said, "Let's roll."

::: TWENTY

All the color in Colonel Medaris's face drained away until his skin was the color of the ashen rays of a lunar impact crater. "All of them?" he croaked.

Tony O'Neil, the Medaris corporate chief engineer, was in the office to explain the technicalities of the situation to the Colonel. "Not all. One fuser survived relatively intact. She's the *Jan Davis*, but sensor reports show her environmental system was compromised. We've tried to contact her captain and crew, but there's been no response. They're probably dead."

"A complete disaster."

"It gets a little worse. The Lunar Council is asking that you explain why you moved their fusers from orbital storage without permission."

The Colonel closed his eyes and rubbed his forehead. "Tell the Lunar Council the asteroid that hit our telescope wasn't natural. Tell them we were going to L5 to stop any more asteroids from coming in."

The sheriff of Moontown, also in attendance, said, "It may be a little late for that, sir."

The Colonel glared at the sheriff. "Don't you think I know that? But what was I supposed to do? Admit to the Council I put those rocks at L5? I hoped to be able to stop all this by showing up with overwhelming force and making my idiot son look down my gun barrels." He shook his head. "I guess I hoped a lot of things, including the rescue of Maria. Fellows, I'm starting to feel old. Is this the end of Colonel Medaris?"

The sheriff hesitated, then said, "The council is also asking why you took four racks of nuclear-tipped missiles this morning."

The Colonel raised his head. "Nukes? Did we take nukes?"

"No, sir, we didn't. That wasn't us."

"Who would steal nuclear missile racks that would only fit in a fuser?"

"Maybe it was the same somebody who recently bought a fuser from the Lunar Council boneyard and then stole their tug."

The Colonel leaned back. "Crater Trueblood." He pondered the situation, then said, "Is there any way to track the tug or the fuser Crater stole?"

"Ordinarily yes," O'Neil said. "Both have puter generated squawks, but since we were alerted to Crater buying the fuser and taking the tug, my team has been using ground-based dishes and lunasats with no joy. Our assumption is the squawk boxes were disabled even though they were designed to be hack proof."

"Crater has a gillie that can hack almost anything. What time did the puter say he stole the nukes?"

"About the same time the asteroids destroyed the fuser fleet."

"Then Crater should be safe."

"No way to tell. There was time for him to orbit before the asteroids struck."

The Colonel allowed a sigh. He'd always liked Crater, and even though he'd tried to kill him several times, it was never personal, just business. Now maybe Crater was off to rescue Maria even though rescue of Maria for the Colonel was now unfortunately secondary. Something else had to be done, something even more important than his beloved granddaughter.

The sheriff lifted his cap and used a handkerchief to wipe the perspiration off his bald head. "Colonel, we've also heard from the people at L5. They say they are through waiting. Either you announce your retirement immediately and put Junior in charge or they will destroy Armstrong City and Cleomedes. They also said they have your money, and that's confirmed, sir. All your liquid assets are gone, probably to secret accounts in banks on Earth."

The Colonel waved his hand in dismissal. "I can always make more money."

The sheriff hesitated, then said carefully, "They also sent pictures of Maria."

The Colonel started and hit both palms on his desk. "Good grief, man! Let's see them!"

The sheriff clicked his do4u, bringing up the photos of Maria on the Colonel's giant vidscreen. It showed her lying on a filthy cot, her foot black and broken. Another click showed her crushed foot close up. The next two showed her broken finger and thumb.

The Colonel leaned forward, his hand to his mouth. When he began to weep, the sheriff and the engineer glanced at one another and shifted uncomfortably from foot to foot.

The Colonel had never wept so openly, and he was certain

it was because he was old, even though the lower gravity of the moon allowed humans to live longer than on Earth, longer, that is, if they could avoid breathing the dust or getting run over by a loader or swallowed up in a hidden rille or any of a thousand mechanical, chemical, or geologic killers always ready to murder the unwary living in a radiation-soaked vacuum. What could an old man do when all his young pilots, quick to answer his orders, had been killed? But then the spirit inside him rebelled against that kind of thinking. And something else too. There was a secret he needed to hide, that he *must* hide.

"There's one fuser left," the Colonel said. "It may be damaged but it's armed."

"Yes, sir," O'Neil said, "but we have no way to get up to it. The space taxis that would have lifted us to the fusers were destroyed too."

The Colonel rubbed his forehead, trying to think. There was something knocking around in his head that he was trying to remember. Something about Crater and orbital ops . . . Then he remembered at least part of it. He turned to his engineer. "Tony, when Crater worked in our labs, didn't he propose a novel way to get into lunar orbit? You remember that?"

"Yes, sir. I studied every one of his proposals to see if they were worth anything commercially. It was the usual stuff. Using rail cannons and the like. And jumpcars."

"Jumpcars?"

"Why, yes, sir. We talked about it when I brought his plan to you. We laughed about it, don't you recall? It might have worked but it didn't make any sense. I think Crater made a theoretical calculation just for the fun of it."

"Call it up on the puter."

The engineer keyed it in and a holographic screen appeared, hanging in midair. The title of the paper was Jumpcar Staging Engines to Orbit. It was a dry, technical paper, typical of engineers, but the Colonel was also an engineer and he was soon absorbed in Crater's calculations and predictions. "Astonishing," he said as he reached the end of the paper.

"But completely theoretical," O'Neil pointed out.

"And a lot nuts," the sheriff added.

The Colonel pressed the intercom button. "Trudy, get me Riley Bishop. She's one of my pilots."

"Riley Bishop? Let me check the personnel file. Ah, here it is. Jumpcar Pilot Riley Bishop left your employ six months ago."

The Colonel frowned. "Really? Where'd she go?"

"Says here she has her own jumpcar business."

"Track her down and get her here chop-chop!" the Colonel brayed, then clicked off the intercom. "She's one of the best natural pilots I ever had. How did I ever let her get away?"

"She asked you for a raise, as I recall," the sheriff said, "and you told her maybe in a few years."

"Did I?" He hit the intercom button again. "Trudy? Tell Riley I'll triple whatever her usual fee is!"

The Colonel sat back in his chair while the engineer frowned a dubious frown. "Those laws of physics, sir, also apply in this situation. Crater's study is less than persuasive. The odds of it working I put at something like nine to one."

"Look, Colonel," the sheriff said. "Isn't it best at this point to give Junior what he wants?"

The Colonel stared at the sheriff, then touched the intercom on his desk again. "Trudy, call all the Medaris family members who are officials in my companies. I want to have a vidcon with them in an hour." He clicked the intercom off. "I will announce my retirement and notify them that Junior is taking over. In less than an hour, that information will be all over the moon and Earth. Sheriff, call L5 and tell Junior he's won."

"That's good, sir," the sheriff said, relieved. "Retirement won't be all that bad. And you can take your time and plot your revenge."

"Sheriff, you're an idiot," the Colonel growled.

"I know that, sir. I only meant . . ."

"Stop and think. I retire and Junior flies down here and takes over the family business. Do you think the rest of the family is going to just roll over? They'll tear him to pieces. And what happens when the truth gets out about what's at L5 and how it got there? An asteroid from L5 killed hundreds of men and women at the Tombaugh telescope site! More of them wiped out the Lunar Council's fuser fleet! When the Lunar Council figures this out, it will put together a coalition against Junior and there will be war, a war that will probably bring in forces from Earth. This is a bigger disaster than me losing control over the family business. This could end up with tens of thousands of people dead. We have to stop it before it goes any further."

"But how?" the sheriff asked.

"We go to L5, blow up the station, kill these people, and be done with it."

"What about Maria? She'll die too."

The Colonel rubbed his eyes. "Blast you, Sheriff. Don't you think I know that? We'll try to rescue her, of course, but . . . well, I don't see how that's possible."

The sheriff gulped. "I understand, sir."

The Colonel hit the intercom button. "Trudy, have you talked to Riley Bishop?" he demanded.

"Yes, sir. Just off the do4u. She's on her way."

"That's my girl," he said.

"Thank you, sir."

"I didn't mean you. By the way, I'm reassigning you to the company store. Your replacement will take over in the morning."

There was a short silence on the intercom before the woman replied in a trembling voice. "What did I do wrong, sir?"

"Nothing. I'm just tired of you," the Colonel said.

::: TWENTY-ONE

Maria, to her surprise, was allowed to wander the station at will. As she went about, she met crowhoppers, all of whom treated her with deference. Some even bowed to her. When Maria found a porthole on the lower ring where she could see the moon, Truvia walked up and stood beside her. "What are you thinking about?" she asked.

"I was wondering how the horde got here."

"Two robotic fusers, both equipped with catch baskets for the smaller asteroids. Maneuvering rockets were attached to the big ones and propelled them here. Your father, appointed by your grandfather, supervised the building of this station and the stocking of the horde. To do both, he used Umlap labor and captured warpods."

"So after he'd finished his assignment, Junior realized he could use it for his own purposes."

"Yes, after Carus and I talked to him when he made a trip to Earth."

"How did you get to him?"

Truvia smiled. "We didn't have to. He was looking for us, not to talk but to kill us. The Colonel, you see, sent teams to Earth to destroy the Legion. Your father was on a team that captured Carus and me. After we were tortured, Junior questioned us. Gradually, he came to trust us and told us about the horde at L5. That was when I explained to him how he might use it for his own ends."

Maria looked at the Trainer. "What's your relationship with my father?"

"To be perfectly honest, I think we will be married someday."

Maria smiled. "Sure you will. I can just see him waltzing in to a Medaris family party with you on his arm! There might be some heart attacks."

"You can be cruel," she said.

Maria gave a short laugh. "You ordered a demon to crush my foot and break my fingers. That's cruel. I'm just giving you some straight girl talk."

"I fixed your foot and your fingers."

"How did you do that, anyway?"

Truvia brightened. "Would you like to see?"

Maria's curiosity overcame her dislike of Truvia. "Of course."

Truvia beckoned Maria to follow her and led the way into the inner core and down to the lowest tube. In a cabin that had only a little gravity, Maria beheld a bank of puters and a long, doughnut-shaped tube with bundles of cables wrapped around it. Beside it was another machine, this one looking like a steel coffin. Truvia pointed at the tube. "We call it the Variable Cell Analyzer, or VCA. For best results, we have in our database all of the cell structures of the patient at their chosen age. In other words, if you were twenty-five and always wanted to be that age, you'd subject yourself to the VCA and then a record would be made.

She pointed at the coffin-like box. "After you got older and wanted to be twenty-five again, you would enter this three dimensional cellular printer—we call it a 3DCP—that essentially removes cells that are different from your optimal. For instance, fat cells around your midriff. It also modifies other cells to make an exact duplicate."

"Are you telling me these machines are a fountain of youth?"

"I suppose so. It's an unscientific name, but for the lack of a better term, that might work. For instance, how old do you think I am?"

Maria appraised her, then said, "Your early thirties."

Truvia smiled. "I'm seventy. Your father doesn't know that. Don't tell him!"

"So before you crushed my foot, you stuck it in the VCA and made a reading?"

"Actually, all of you from head to toe. We put your crushed foot in the 3DCP and it fixed everything back the way it was."

Maria studied the VCA and the 3DCP. "Look, Truvia, you've got your faults, mass murder being one of them, but let me give you some advice. You want to be worth about a trillion dollars? Set up shop right here in good old L5. Millions of—shall we say 'mature'—women will pay to come here and get run through these machines."

"But we wouldn't have any of their youthful information in our files," Truvia pointed out.

Maria shot her a disbelieving look. "I don't think that's a problem. Look at that fine, trim waist you have and your, ahem, otherwise fine endowments. Are you trying to tell me those were your original specifications? Come on, Truvia. You based yourself on somebody else, didn't you?"

"Perhaps," Truvia said with a secret smile. "Shall I show you another part of our clinic?"

"Why not?"

Truvia led Maria back into the tube and into an adjoining cabin, this one lined with plaston boxes, tubes leading in and out of each of them. Immersed in a clear liquid were what appeared to be embryos in various stages of development. "Our latest design," Truvia said proudly. "These are Legionnaires, crowhoppers as you call them, who will be smarter, stronger, and able to endure extreme heat and cold even better than our old designs. We're also experimenting with birthing what appears to be normal humans but with biolastic skins resistant to vacuum. They might also have lungs that are able to produce their own oxygen. It would be an entirely new creature."

"Are you telling me you're making moon people who could live in the vacuum without wearing suits and helmets?"

"Don't you find that exciting?"

Maria felt a bit dizzy. The incubator room stunk of a variety of harsh chemicals, but it was the incredible possibilities of the creatures in the vats that was making her woozy. "Better get some fresh air," she said.

Back in the ring, Maria leaned against the wall and tried to breathe away the noxious fumes and the dread she felt. "What's the overall plan here?" she asked. "It's more than the takeover of the Medaris family business. I see that now. I just don't understand what it is."

Truvia gazed through the viewport. Both the Earth and the moon were in view. "Were you impressed with the history lesson we gave you on the vileness of the world?"

Maria shuddered but tried to keep her tone light. "Sure. The human race has done some bad things, but . . ."

"What if we could start over?" Truvia's green eyes seemed to glow with an inner flame. "What if there was a new world where a new kind of people could live and prosper while the old world was cleansed?"

This time Maria couldn't hide her disgust. "Truvia, you're creeping me out!"

The Trainer spread her arms expansively as if she were embracing the universe. "Why so? There have been numerous extinctions on Earth. What if there was another one and the people of the moon were prepared to repopulate it? Think about it!"

"I am thinking about it! You're talking about killing billions of people!"

The Earth was just a sliver on the edge of the viewport in the revolving tube, and then it disappeared, leaving only the moon. Truvia pointed at the gray, cratered planetoid. "There is our new world, Maria. We will populate it with people of our own design and they will worship the founders of this new society as if we were gods. We will create a royal house."

Truvia turned to Maria and caressed her shoulder before dropping her hand away. "Do you recall what I first told you about Trainers? I said we were born in a petri dish, our genes manipulated to make us extremely intelligent, to have a commanding presence, and yet be subservient. For all our advanced brain power, we live to serve."

Maria discovered she was trembling in both fear and an unexplained excitement. "Who are you serving now?"

"It could and should be you."

It was the last thing Maria expected to hear. "Me? In what way would you serve me?"

Truvia's eyes softened and her lips trembled. "Our King Raleigh and Queen Porella were members of the Medaris family. You are their great-niece."

Maria's breath caught in her throat. "Are you talking about my great-uncle Ralph and his wife, Portia? They were killed in a plane crash. That's what the Colonel told me."

"He lied. Ralph and Portia Medaris became our royal house. The Colonel set them up to make the Legion."

Maria's head was swimming. "My grandfather is responsible for the crowhoppers?"

"Indeed he is."

"Does Junior know about any of this?"

"No. He thinks all this has been done so he could take over the family business. The wheels are turning, Maria, that could end with you on top. All you have to do is accept our offer to be our queen."

"What wheels are you talking about?"

"To be precise, a very big asteroid."

"In L5?"

"Elsewhere."

"Where is it aimed?"

Truvia seemed to be making up her mind about something, then said, "I will tell you this much. The reason I crushed your foot and broke your fingers and then fixed them is because I wanted you to understand how to rule." She made a fist. "You must first have a fist of iron." She opened the fist to show her palm. "While appearing to be benevolent." She closed her fist again. "And then when your enemies expose themselves, you crush them!"

Maria resisted the urge to call Truvia batscrag crazy to her face. "I'll try to remember that," she promised. "Iron fist, benevolence, crush my enemies. Got it. But where did you say that asteroid is aimed?"

As if sensing Maria's true opinion, Truvia's expression turned to disappointment. "Your choice is a splendid life as our queen or an ignominious death. And that choice must be made in hours, not days."

"Fine. I choose to be queen. Now, tell me. Where is that asteroid aimed?"

"Earth, of course," Truvia replied with a coy smile.

"But they'll see it! They have to. There are telescopes watching the sky."

"By the time they see it coming, it will be too late. The Earth is in disarray. It's the perfect time to make this strike."

Maria took a moment to put it all together. "Very clever, Truvia. You've got everybody focused on the family business, but it's control of the Earth and the moon that you're really after."

"Yes, it's laughable, really, about the money. Money means nothing to us. Your father thought we brought you here to get the secret family account numbers. The real reason we brought you here was to offer you our loyalty."

"My father is in the royal line too. Why not make him king?"

"He is unworthy. We have studied you. You are ruthless and you desire power and you are intelligent. Our choice is you."

Maria thought maybe if she was quick, she could snap Truvia's neck. She girded herself to try, but before she could move, a crowhopper in full armor arrived. "You are needed on the bridge, Trainer Truvia," he said, after glancing at Maria.

"I'll be right along, William," Truvia replied, then waited until the crowhopper had left before turning to Maria. "Although you said you accepted the crown I offer you, I don't believe you are fully committed. Give it some proper thought." She arched an eyebrow, then walked away.

Maria watched through the viewport until the Earth came back into view. She looked at the blue, green, brown, and white planet, the loveliest jewel in the sky, while she absorbed several truths.

- Her grandfather, the Colonel, whom she loved with all of her heart, was responsible for the crowhoppers, the mercenary force that had been sent to the moon and murdered hundreds of innocent people.
- The Medaris family's secret about the crowhoppers, if exposed, would destroy it.
- Truvia was showing her a way out. It was extreme, desperate, and horrible, but as she said, the "wheels were turning" and nothing could stop it now.
- Either a splendid life or an ignominious death. Those were her choices.

Even though she knew it was wrong, Maria started thinking about what it would feel like and all the things she could do if she was the eternally youthful queen of the moon.

The truth was she rather fancied the idea.

::: TWENTY-TWO

fter Riley touched *Amanda Michelle* down to a perfect landing, the jumpcar was trundled inside the Moontown hangar, giant airtight doors closing behind. Riley climbed down and greeted Colonel Medaris, the sheriff, and a young man dressed in an old-fashioned pressure suit. The Colonel got right to business. "Have you read Crater's plan?"

Riley took off her helmet and shook out her long, red hair. "Aye, sir, I did. It's feasible, though t'would be a close-run thing if we have to maneuver a'tall. I'd have to use the directional jets, and they're designed for the usual mass. The computer might not be able to adjust."

"We don't have time to reprogram the puter," the Colonel said. "You'll have to fly it by wire."

"Aye, sir, I figured that already."

"You're willing to take the task?"

"Well, sir, about me wages . . ."

"I'll pay ten times your usual fee."

"Then rest assured I'm in. But what about Crater? It would be nice if he was with us, to explain his theories and all."

"We don't know where Crater is. He could be dead."

Riley looked doubtful. "That boy's hard t'kill, Colonel. You should know that, of all people. I'll give ye a wager. Crater's alive. Cut me back to five times my usual fee if I'm wrong, twenty if I'm right."

"Just get me up to my fuser," the Colonel growled.

Riley frowned. "Surely, 'tisn't you that's going, Colonel! I figured you'd be sending some fine, strapping heel-3 miners turned spaceship troopers!"

"No time to train newbies," the Colonel replied. "Meet Tiger Tramon. He's an expert fuser pilot."

The man in the pressure suit nodded to Riley. Riley instantly liked his intense blue eyes and swagger. "The Colonel tells me you're a fine pilot," Tiger said.

"Aye, I can stick a jumpcar around the track, but I never set foot inside a fuser."

"I'll train you. Fusers are sweet, fast, and deadly."

Riley smiled. "First we have to get to it, Mr. Fuser Pilot." She turned to the Colonel. "Which jumpcar d'ye want me to fly, Colonel? This old lug of mine, or do ye have a better one?"

"A much better one," the Colonel said. "There she is, right over there, the *Doctor Patty Hilliard*. She's just off the line, five percent lighter with titanium composites throughout. Her engines are rated at one hundred and ten percent standard. Cross tanking, of course, which should help on the way up."

"Aye, she's a beauty," Riley agreed. "Seems a shame to destroy her."

"We can build more."

"Let me give her a walk-about inspection and have a talk with her puter."

"I'll help," Tiger said.

"Come on, then," Riley said and walked toward the golden jumpcar with the fuser pilot following.

"Bring a small kit, Sheriff," the Colonel said. "Fusers don't have much room for luggage."

The sheriff's eyes widened. "Me, Colonel? Do you think that's a good idea? I've had these palpitations in my heart recent-like."

"You've also got a job, and if you want to keep it, you'll be going on this mission."

"But I'm kind of an old fellow. You need youth for this mission."

"I need you, Sheriff. I need a man who will not hesitate to kill anyone I tell him to kill. Let me hear you volunteer."

"V-volunteering, sir!" the sheriff said, then visibly gulped.

"Go home. Kiss your wife, pat your child on the head, and then pack your kit. We leave in two hours!"

The sheriff hurried off and the Colonel started yelling at some techies, telling them to get some railgun rifles aboard the *Patty Hilliard*, also some grenades, and the "special" device he'd ordered.

A forklift operator picked up the special device hidden inside a plaston crate and transported it toward the jumpcar. The Colonel waved him down. "Take it slow and easy with that one, my man. Slow and easy."

"What's in the box, Colonel?"

"A nightmare for all those who oppose me," the Colonel said, then waved the forklift on.

::: TWENTY-THREE

G ot her on the scope," Crater said. "Right where we left her."

"Crescent, are you ready to extend the probe?" Petro asked.

"Up and running," Crescent said from the aft astrogator station.

Petro gave the tug retros a little spurt. "Coming in on her portside horizontal axis."

Petro eased the tug alongside the *Linda Terry*. Like a great undulating snake spitting steam, the cold gas jets on the drogue carried the fuel line across the void, Crescent maneuvering it into the access port. The tug fuel pump immediately began to hum and tons of liquid hydrogen were pushed across the line into the *Linda*'s fuel tank. "Offloading under way," Crescent said. "Some of the liquid has turned to gas. The pump is hiccupping. Just small bubbles, I think."

"Gas in the fuser can cause an explosion in the pre-turbos," Crater warned.

"Nothing to be done for now," Petro interjected. "I'll activate the tank freezers on the way. They should be able to reliquify."

"Refueling complete," Crescent reported. "Now all we have to do is get aboard the fuser."

"That part's easy," Petro said. "Detach the drogue and line. Let me know when it's all reeled in and stowed."

"Latched and stowed," Crescent reported.

Petro maneuvered the tug above the fuser, then settled atop it with the maneuvering jets popping and crackling like wet firewood. Crater maneuvered the airlocks together. "Capture," he said as the capture mechanisms clamped together. "Let's get aboard."

"Let's first check fuser integrity," Petro said, then connected the tug's puter with the fuser puter. After perusing the readout, he said, "All systems operating normally. It should be safe to enter."

"How about our coveralls and helmets?" Crescent asked. "They're covered with dust."

Petro considered that. "The fuser has pressure suits but no biolastics. If we want to keep our suits, we'll need to clean them."

"I'll do it," Crater said.

"And I'll help," Crescent said.

Once in the tug dustlock, Crater and Crescent ran the biolastic sheaths and coveralls through the washers, then placed the waste disposal girdles in the cleaners. The girdle contents were sucked away into space and fresh sanitizing liquid injected.

Crater watched Crescent diligently working with the nasty girdles and felt a surge of admiration for her, enough so he decided to say it out loud. "You're a fine woman, Crescent."

Startled, Crescent turned toward him. "You're right," she said. "But very nice of you to acknowledge it."

"We are always going to be friends."

"Friends. Yes," Crescent said, "we're going to be friends."

Crater studied her face, which, even though it lacked many of the muscles of a normal human, still displayed disappointment. He was not so thick that he didn't know why. Stumbling for words, he said, "I'm sorry. I wish . . . things were different."

Crescent started to reply with all that she felt for Crater, how he was the most important person in her life, how in her remaining days she wanted nothing more than to be with him, how the secret she carried had everything to do with that constant truth. But now, she decided, was not the time. He needed to focus. She would tell him her secret after the rescue. She would *have* to tell him then. Working her mouth into a brave smile, she said, "I'll tell you what I wish was different. I wish these girdles smelled better!"

"People," Petro said, floating into the dustlock, "in one orbit we'll be in prime position to get out to L5. We need to get going." He looked from Crater to Crescent and detected that something had passed between the two. "What?"

Crescent smiled. "Crater was just telling me what a good friend I am."

"And a fine woman in every way!" Petro exclaimed.

"I second that opinion," Crater said.

"You two stop looking at me with those manly eyes!" Crescent admonished. "I'm still going to marry Absalom."

"If he makes the mistake of reneging, I'll be next in line," Petro swore.

Crescent's grin was real. "I might hold you to that. Now shall we go rescue Crater's girl? It seems the thing we need to do."

::: TWENTY-FOUR

ll right, gents, buckle up and prepare for the ride of yer lives!" Riley announced from the cockpit after going through the prelaunch puter checks. She placed the jumpcar in full manual override mode. Tiger sat beside her in the copilot's seat. "You ready, Tiger?"

"I'm always ready," the fuser pilot said. "Let's go!"

"Colonel, you and your bully boys strapped in?"

The Colonel was in the passenger compartment with the sheriff and two deputies, all dressed in biolastic sheaths, helmets, coveralls, and armored plate. The sheriff was looking more than a little stressed, his face a greenish tinge. "Strapped in," the Colonel replied. "Let's go, Riley. Don't miss our window."

"Hang on! This is going to be bumpy all the way! On my mark—five-four-three-two-one . . . "

The engines on the *Hilliard* thundered, but Riley waited until all the instrument lights turned green before pushing the throttles forward. The jumpcar slowly rose from the pad, its nose pointed at the impossibly distant stars.

"You're going too slow," Tiger said, his gloved hand moving to the throttles.

"Belay that," Riley warned. "I know what I'm doing. Jump-car engines ain't like your fusers. These new ones need a little coddling until I can get them up to speed."

Riley kept her eye on the thrust gauges, then pushed the throttles steadily forward until they were pegged to the red.

"Now you've pushed them too far!" Tiger shouted over the engine roars.

"Keep quiet, bucko. These babies are designed to go fifteen percent into the red without coming apart!"

The jumpcar rattled and shrieked as if it was about to come apart at the seams. The engines kept screaming. The puter raised an urgent alarm. *Engines one, two, three over redline. Initiating throttle back.*

"Negative. Override," Riley said.

Throttle back canceled. Would you like assistance?

"No, thank you."

Destination has not been specified.

"Low lunar orbit."

Destination specified is not possible.

"Yes it is. Extrapolate into your artificial intelligence program."

Extrapolating.

Riley kept her eye on the propellant gauges and the velocity vectors. When she judged it right, she hit the directional jets to lower the nose five degrees.

Nose over, the puter reported. *Present course not understood. Recommend vertical recovery.*

Riley pushed the nose over another five degrees. "Maintenance program, please."

Maintenance.

"On my mark, detach engine number two propellant lines and release engine number two clamps."

Engine number two is actively working. Release not authorized.

"This is a red-level security override. Security code is Goforbroke2023."

Although she knew it was her imagination, Riley thought the puter seemed resigned. *Maintenance procedures initiated. Waiting for mark.*

As the fuselage of the jumpcar groaned, Riley kept her eyes glued to the control monitors. "Counting down to mark—five-four-three-two-one-mark!"

Instantly, there was a horrific scraping noise as the engine slid out of the tail, falling and spinning away. The jumpcar began to shake even more violently. "Puter, initiate mass calculations to compensate controls for lost engine."

Mass calculations accomplished. Controls compensated. Recommend return to Moontown.

"Time to orbit."

Orbit not possible.

"Maintenance program. Keep security override in place."

Maintenance. Security override noted.

"On my mark, detach engine number three propellant lines and release engine number three holding clamps."

Maintenance procedures initiated. Waiting for your mark.

Riley lowered the nose of the jumpcar another five degrees, the surface of the moon swimming across the viewports. Tiger, his eyes wide, gripped the copilot's seat. Riley remained calm. "Counting down to mark—five-four-three-two-one-mark!"

Again, there was a rattling, scraping sound as the second engine slid along the rails designed to help remove and install engines.

The puter reported. *Detachment completed. Engine number three remains partially in engine bay.*

"Scrag thing!" Riley growled. With an engine hanging out of the engine compartment, the dynamics of the jumpcar were askew. The nose began to rise, then oscillate. Riley fought the controls. "Tiger, put your hand on the throttle for engine one! Throttle back to ten percent when I tell you. Colonel, hang on back there! This is gonna be wild!"

"The sheriff just threw up," the Colonel replied.

"I don't blame him," Riley muttered, then pushed the nose hard over. "Throttle back, Tiger!"

Tiger pulled the throttle back. "What are you doing?"

"I'm gonna flip this bird to throw out that stuck engine!"

"Flip this bird?"

Riley didn't have time to explain. With the nose directional jets firing steadily, she watched as her view changed from stars to pocked gray craters and then swept up to stars again. She fought to maintain that heading. "Puter, report status of engine number three!"

Engine number three still on rails.

"Tiger! Throttle up one hundred fifteen percent."

"Throttling up," Tiger said in the calm, professional, and resigned tone of a test pilot about to die.

"Puter, initiate engine number one gimbal test!"

Engine number one is presently at full throttle plus fifteen percent. Gimbal test not allowed.

"Override per previous authority. Stop when engine number three leaves its rails."

Overriding. Gimbal test under way.

"The gimbal test includes violent moves of the nozzle," Riley explained as the jumpcar started another tumble. The directional jets roared to keep it going. A shriek of tortured metal rattled the cockpit.

"We're coming apart," Tiger reported.

Riley didn't reply. Instead, she grimly hung onto the stick between her knees and talked to the jumpcar. "Come on, baby, hold it together. Come on, you can do it!"

Engine number three has left the jumpcar.

"Woo-hoo! Throttle back to thirty, Tiger."

"Throttle back, thirty."

"Puter, initiate mass calculations to compensate controls for lost engine."

Mass calculations accomplished. Controls compensated. Recommend abort to orbit.

"Now you're talking, puter! Abort to orbit, aye. Sixty miles, inclination two four nine dot five!"

It was probably still her imagination, but the puter suddenly sounded enthusiastic. *Abort to orbit six zero miles at two four niner dot five.*

Riley looked at Tiger. "Hand off the throttle, Tiger. The puter understands what we're doing now. It'll take us from here."

Tiger lifted his hand. "How will it do that?" he said.

"Jumpcars have artificial intelligence because they're often flown by pilots without much training. They can guess where the pilot wants to go. The puter finally figured out I was dropping engines to lighten the load on the way up just like any staged rocket. There could only be one reason I would do that, and that was to make orbit."

"I thought that tumble was going to rip us apart. And then those gimbal oscillations! You're an amazing pilot, Riley."

"Why, thank you, sir. You are correct."

The puter spoke up. *Altitude five two dot eight miles at two four dot six. Engine burn looking good. Directional jet propellant at five percent.*

"Uh oh," Riley said. "That isn't good."

"What's going on, Riley?" the Colonel demanded.

"We're going to make orbit, sir," Riley said. "But with all that maneuvering, I'm not sure where we are."

"What happens if we can't get to the fuser?" Tiger asked on their private channel.

Riley shrugged. "We can't land on one engine even if we had the propellant to try."

"In other words..."

"In other words, Tiger, if we can't get to the fuser, we will be stuck in lunar orbit until our air runs out."

Tiger pondered that, then asked, "If I gave the jumpcar puter the fuser puter codes, could it establish contact?"

"Possibly. What's your plan?"

"If we can't get up to the fuser, maybe we can bring it down to us."

Riley flashed him a pleased grin. "Tiger, you're a pretty handy fellow."

"I think that's why I'm here, little lady."

"If this works, I might even forgive you for calling me that."

"I'll apologize if you'll give me a kiss instead."

"Ah, love in low lunar orbit. What sweet bliss! Nay, lad, no kisses, not yet, til ye show me what ye can do."

Tiger smiled. "Then hang onto your lips!"

::: TWENTY-FIVE

After having a good talk with herself about what was right and what was wrong, Maria floated up onto the station bridge, determined to turn everything around after she was crowned queen. Letticus saw her first. The captain nodded in her direction and Truvia turned toward her. Maria pushed off, turned in midflight, and landed to push her feet into foot restraints beside Truvia. "I've been thinking over your offer," Maria said, "and I accept."

Truvia beckoned her to foot restraints away from the others. Her green eyes narrowed and her expression was dubious. "Please convince me of your sincerity."

Maria took a deep breath. "You said the asteroid you sent will hit the Earth and it can't be stopped."

"That's true," Truvia said.

"Therefore, the moon will be all that's left of humanity."

"Nearly true. Some people will survive on Earth, but they will be marooned on the planet. So much dust will be in the air, their scramjets won't work. Even if they did, they will be trying to survive, not fly into space. According to my analysis, existence for the remaining humans on Earth will be similar to medieval life in the fourteenth century."

"That's about what I thought," Maria replied. "And here is why I agree to be your queen. After the Earth is damaged, the Lunar Council will likely get organized to establish a central government on the moon. When they discover it was the Colonel who established the asteroid horde at L5, they will assume he also sent the asteroid crashing into Earth. After that, the Medaris family will be arrested and most of us will be put to death. Those remaining will be reduced to paupers. I have no option other than to join you."

Truvia's eyes sparkled. "You please me. Your father still hasn't figured this out."

"I'm a fast learner." Maria made a fist, then opened and closed it. "Iron fist, pretend to be benevolent, then destroy my enemies. Got it covered. So when do I get my crown?"

Truvia clasped her hands to her breast. "We will have a coronation! It will be glorious!"

"Can we do it fairly soon?" Maria asked. "I'd like to get used to being royally in charge."

Truvia's delighted expression faded. "In charge? Oh dear, I think you've misunderstood. There's really very little for you to do. Even our beloved King Raleigh and Queen Porella were figureheads, as you will be. In our world, the Trainers make all the decisions."

Maria could not disguise her disappointment. "But didn't you say you were designed to be subservient?"

"Yes, but our subservience doesn't lessen our intellect or our tendency to make the necessary decisions for our society. Certainly, we will honor you with all possible pomp and circumstance. You will be fed, clothed, housed in a royal palace, your every wish granted as it has to do with your royal person, and pampered beyond your wildest imagination."

Maria's deflation was complete. "In other words, I will be in a royal cage."

"Your great-uncle and aunt had no complaints. They became quite fat. Obese, actually. We worried for their health. Now, of course, we can keep your figure perpetually youthful." She peered at Maria. "Are you sure you want to be our queen?"

Maria's acting ability was being stretched, but she did her best. "Of course I do!"

Truvia continued to study her, doubt written on her white face.

"Trainer Truvia," Letticus interrupted, "we have CC2241 on the pulsdar."

"Come, my future queen," Truvia said, taking Maria by her hand. "Come see this magnificent sight."

Maria allowed Truvia to pull her to the pulsdar station, where its sweep showed a glowing blob. "The asteroid is passing over the farside," Letticus explained.

"It's how we've hidden it," Truvia explained. "Earthside telescopes couldn't see it in the shadow of the moon. When it pops out, it will be too late for anyone to do anything."

"How many days until it gets there?" Maria asked, her stomach churning.

"Three days, a little less."

Maria looked longingly at the communications console. If she could have just a few seconds on it, she could warn Earth. Maybe it wasn't too late. Maybe something could be done.

Truvia was not oblivious to where Maria was looking.

"Perhaps it is best for you to leave the bridge," she said. "I sense you are still not being entirely honest with me."

Maria shrugged. "Do you really expect me to be thrilled that you're murdering billions of people and destroying my family? But that doesn't change my decision to be your queen. As I said, I really have no choice."

"Of course you don't," Truvia replied, arching an eyebrow. "By the way, could you tell me more about that heel-3 miner who you said is coming to rescue you? If he's really coming, you can help us stop him."

"I was just blowing smoke," Maria said with a dismissive gesture. "There is no such person."

"Crater Trueblood is not a person? Please, don't take me as a fool, Maria. Don't look so startled. We are capable of research. Mr. Trueblood saved you when the crowhoppers tried to kidnap you during the war."

"That was then, and it was on the moon. Crater has no way to get out here. How could he?"

"From all I've read, he seems quite inventive. It also appears he was once very much in love with you." Truvia stroked Maria's cheek while she did her best not to flinch. "I can understand why. Love can sometimes make a person do amazing things. If he comes for you, how will he do it?"

"He is not coming."

Truvia dropped her hand away. "We have resources on the moon, Maria. Trueblood lives in Cleomedes, but he is not there and no one seems to know where he is. Do you know?"

"Honestly, Truvia, I have no idea." Maria felt a spark of hope light in her chest.

Truvia reached out to touch Maria's face again. This time Maria couldn't help but flinch. Truvia's hand hung in midair before she slowly lowered it. "I think you should go below now. We will speak of this and many other things at a later time."

Maria, throwing up a prayer that Crater was really coming, fled the bridge.

::: TWENTY-SIX

Petro was busier than a one-armed scragline picker. Working with the ship's puter, he set up a course that would take them out of lunar orbit and put them on a looping path to L5 as if they were coming in from deep space. If detected by L5, the hope was the ship would be thought of as a wayward asteroid. The real hope was the fuser wouldn't be detected at all.

The gillies kept trying to help, but Petro was having nothing to do with either of them. "Tell your slime mold critters to leave me alone!" Petro snarled, Crescent and Crater snatching up their particular slime mold things and carrying them off.

He is not efficient, Crater's gillie said.

He is not efficient, Crescent's gillie said.

They looked at one another, even though they had no eyes, and then nodded agreement, even though neither had heads to nod.

Crater and Crescent tucked their gillies away, admonishing them to be silent. "Humans don't work the same way you do," Crater told his gillie. "Sometimes they look inefficient, but it's the way their brains work."

"And some humans don't have much intelligence," Crescent whispered to her gillie and felt it vibrate in her pocket. She hoped that meant it was pleased, but you never knew about gillies.

Before turning on the fusion engine, Petro called Crater and Crescent to the cockpit for a briefing. "The launch is going to be rough because we've got to make up a lot of energy in a short time. Make sure you're sitting back in your seat and fully strapped in. To loop out and back to L5, I'm going to have to essentially stomp on the gas."

Crater and Crescent dutifully strapped themselves in with Crater beside Petro in the copilot's seat and Crescent in the astrogator's cabin. "Strapped in and ready to go," she reported.

"All right, troops, here we go," Petro said. "Puter, on my mark, send us along. Five-four-three-two-one-mark!"

The violence of the fuser engine was astonishing. It was as if a nuclear bomb had gone off behind them. A massive g-force slammed Crater back into his deeply cushioned chair. It felt like an elephant had put its foot on his chest. Less than a minute later, the g-force abated, then vanished. "We're on our way!" Petro whooped. "Aren't we, Linda?"

The fuser's puter responded, a woman's voice with a delicate American Southern accent. *Why, yes sir, we are. And may I just say congratulations on your brilliant programming?*

"Of course you may. And thank you for your excellent interpretation of my commands."

"Why don't you two get a room?" Crater complained while trying to catch his breath.

"Jealousy has many forms, brother," Petro said. "In your

case, it's overt." He smiled at his own joke while Crater rolled his eyes.

"The missile racks still need to be calibrated," Crescent called. "Could use some help on that, Petro."

Petro unstrapped and rose from his seat. "You might want to go through some battle simulations," he told Crater. "Otherwise, don't touch anything. Fusers are not easy to fly."

Petro disappeared aft, leaving Crater to absorb Petro's admonition. "What do you think, Gillie? Are fusers hard to fly?"

Software, firmware, and hardware systems of fusion-powered battle cruisers are quite complex. They do, however, have a remarkable number of redundancies. They also feature super-hardened puters, which took me nearly an hour to hack.

"What did you learn?"

Nothing. I studied fusers extensively last winter when there was little else to do.

Crater smiled. "I'm sorry you were bored."

Gillies are never bored.

"You've told me any number of times that you were bored."

Unless it is life-threatening or goes against whatever the current mission happens to be, gillies might tell less than the complete truth.

"In other words, you lie if it's convenient."

The gillie did not reply but lay instead on the instrument console of the fuser and looked at Crater in what Crater decided was wry amusement. At least, that's what it would have looked like if a gillie could look any way at all, which of course it couldn't.

Crater studied the layout of the fuser cockpit. There was a single glass viewport, vidscreens used for primary visuals. For the view ahead, the pilot used a vidscreen above the viewport. A vidscreen beneath the viewport showed the view directly below the fuser. To see starboard, the pilot looked to his right at another smaller vidscreen, and for a port view to a vidscreen on his left. A split screen overhead provided the view above and behind. If the pilot used the vidscreens properly, there were no visual dead spots, but knowing where to look and how to interpret the screens took practice. Crater decided to follow Petro's advice and run a simulation of an attack.

"Puter, give me a target of a warpod, Nashville class, running at low normal battle speeds, approaching from port z."

Yes, sir. Shall we begin? the puter asked.

"Yes, ready," Crater responded.

Radar indicates bandit at your port z five o'clock.

Crater checked the radar and saw the puter-generated image. "Does it have a squawk?"

Negative, sir. It is running silent. It appears to be a warpod, Nashville class. Would you like a rundown of its capabilities?

"No, thank you. Arm missiles and cannon."

Armed. Reminder. This is a simulation.

"Understood, puter."

You may call me Linda.

Crater thought about that, then said, "Understood, Linda."

Crater checked the lower left vidscreen and saw a star wink out. Warpods were painted a dull grayish-black and were nearly invisible against space, but the winking star indicated something had crossed it. "Infrared on vidscreens, Linda."

Understood. Infrared on all vidscreens.

A bright blue flare surrounded by a pink outline appeared on the port vidscreen. Before Crater could react, it sped up, looped over and disappeared. Crater swiveled his eyes from vidscreen to vidscreen. "Lost it, Linda!"

Look up.

Crater looked up and saw a warpod on the split screen. It took a moment for him to interpret its meaning. The warpod was on his tail and closing fast. "Fire missile at target on my six!"

Cannot comply. Your missiles have nuclear warheads. Blast would destroy you.

"Tail cannon!"

I'm sorry, sir. The warpod launched a salvo of missiles and completely destroyed you. Would you like to play again?

"No thank you, Linda. Some other time."

Yes, sir. Have a pleasant evening, sir.

Crater allowed a sigh. "How can I have a pleasant evening when I just got destroyed?"

"I heard most of that," Petro said, floating into the cockpit and somersaulting into the pilot's chair. "Come on, brother, don't look so glum. It takes more than a few puter sims to learn how to fight one of those bad boy warpods. You have to take advantage of fuser capabilities. For one, you've got accelerations a warpod pilot can only envy. When that bandit got on your tail, you did not need to engage him at all. One nudge of the throttle and you could have left him and his missiles far behind."

Crater nodded his understanding. "The puter reminded me we're armed with nuclear missiles that we can't use," he said.

"I've been wondering about that. Why did you bring them?"

"I thought maybe we might bluff the station at L5."

"That's another thing," Petro said. "Where is the station? L5 is a big place. To find it, we could paint the area with our pulsdars, but if we do, they'll detect us."

Crater thought about that. "Here's an idea. The Cyclers have pulsdars and they're always painting space to keep from running into anything. If L5 detected a pulsdar paint from a Cycler, they might not think much of it. All we have to do is find a Cycler willing to do it and keep us secret. The captain of the *Elon Musk* knows me. I could try him."

"We'd need a secure channel," Petro advised. "Maybe your gillie can hook up through a lunar comm-sat."

"No good. There are only two working lunar comm-sats," Crater said, "and L5 might be monitoring them. But, lucky for us, Cyclers don't use lunar comm-sats, they use Earth sats, and there's a thousand of those. Gillie, see if you can contact Captain George Fox on the *Elon Musk* through an Earth comm-sat. Pick out an obscure one. Use his personal do4u and encrypt everything."

Working, the gillie said. In seconds, it reported back. *Cycler Elon Musk is behind the Earth relative to the moon. It will be six hours before it is in position to paint L5 with its pulsdar.*

"Can I speak to Captain Fox?"

Negative. He does not have his personal do4u turned on.

Crater thought hard, then snapped his fingers. "How about Betty and Tommy? Are they still running tourists on the *Musk*?"

Affirmative. Do you want me to call them?

Crater explained to Petro. "Betty and Tommy are good friends. They're guides for an adventure touring outfit called Lunex that travel to and from the moon on the *Musk*. Yes, Gillie, please call them."

Within minutes, Crater found himself talking to Betty of Lunex. "Crater, what a delight to hear from you! Tommy and I were just talking about you the other day and wondering how you're doing."

"I'm fine," Crater lied. "Listen, Betty, I'd like to catch up but I really need to talk to Captain Fox. I need to keep it private, so that's why I'm calling your do4u. Could you ask him to turn his on so I can call him?"

Betty chuckled. "The captain hates do4us. Probably hasn't turned his on in years. How about I go up to the bridge and hand him this one?"

Not too much later, Crater found himself talking to Cycler Captain George E. Fox. "This is Captain Fox," the captain said. "Who's this?"

"Captain, this is Crater Trueblood. I need a favor."

"A favor? The fellow who brought my Cycler under attack? That Crater Trueblood? You dare to ask me a favor?"

"I didn't know it was going to be attacked, Captain. It was as much a surprise to me as it was to you."

Crater's response elicited a hearty laugh from the Cycler skipper. "I know that, Crater. It was the Medarises that brought on the attack. You and I were both pawns."

"That's right, we were. Look, I'm on another mission, a rescue, and I need your help. Would you paint L5 with your pulsdar and tell me what you see? Any ships, asteroids, anything?"

"L5? That's empty space."

"No longer, sir. There's a lot there now."

"Who put it there?"

"I don't know, but it isn't friendly. Not to you or to me."

"It'll be a few hours before I'm in position to do that," Captain Fox replied. "Can you tell me what kind of rescue mission you're on?"

"You can't tell him," Petro advised Crater over their private channel. "He hates the Medaris family, probably including Maria."

"When I was aboard the Cycler," Crater said, "I didn't tell Captain Fox all I knew, and he was surprised by the attack that came. I'm not going to hold out on him again." Crater nodded to the gillie to open the channel to Fox again. "Maria Medaris has been kidnapped and is being held at L5. I'm heading there to rescue her."

"Maria kidnapped again? That girl keeps you employed, does she not? Let me tell you something you already know. The Medaris family is nothing but trouble. On the other hand, they own this Cycler, so I work for them too. All right, Crater, I'll paint L5 for you and report back. I presume you want it to be private and encrypted."

"Yes, sir. When you have something, give Betty a call. The gillie will be listening and will patch it through to us here."

"Your gillie? I heard it was dead."

"Alive and well, sir, and still illegal."

"I believe it knows that."

"Yes, sir, I believe you are correct."

A few hours later, the gillie said, *I have Captain Fox.*

"We painted L5, Crater," the Cycler Captain said. "We found some big objects there, presumably asteroids. Our pulsdar isn't set up to detect warpods, but there's a group of shadows along the edge of the L5 bowl which look suspicious. There's also what I think is a station with a design similar to the Cycler. It's about a hundred miles from the warpods, if that's what they are. Here are the coordinates."

After Crater keyed in the Captain's report on the fuser puter, he said, "Thank you, Captain. That's very helpful."

"By the way, in the last hour, we've been told the Colonel has retired and his son is taking over the family business. What do you make of that?"

"Business is business," Crater answered, pretending to make light of it.

"When something this big happens in the Medaris business, you can bet a lot of digital family knives are going into a lot of digital family backs. Does this have anything to do with Maria?"

"I'm not certain and that's the honest truth, Captain. Thanks again. You were a great help."

"Good hunting, Crater. Looks like you're up against tough odds, but it won't be the first time."

After Crater hung up from Captain Fox, Petro allowed a sigh. "Warpods at L5. This is going to be rough, Crater."

Crater's expression was grim because he agreed with Petro. To fly nearly blind into an area loaded with asteroids and apparently infested by warpods was a desperate move. "Crescent, come up here, please," he called.

When Crescent came forward, he asked, "Did you hear what Captain Fox said?"

"I did."

"We're probably going to have to fight our way in and out."

"I expected nothing less," Crescent said. "I ask but one thing, something I've asked Petro earlier. I will be brave, but do not allow me to be overly aggressive as per my genetic programming. In other words, don't let me risk my life unless it's absolutely necessary to fulfill our mission. There is a reason for that, but one I do not care to share."

Crescent returned aft to the astrogator's cabin, leaving Crater puzzled. He turned to Petro. "Does she really think I would give her life to save Maria?"

Petro's face registered astonishment. "Of course she does, you idiot!"

Crater started aft, but Petro caught him by his shoulder.

"Don't. It won't make any difference. She already knows

everything you might say. Don't make it any worse than it already is."

Crater shook off Petro's hand. "What are you talking about?"

"She loves you, you dope. That's the only reason she's here. She loves you more than her own life. I'm not sure what her request is all about, but that's the bottom line."

Crater opened his mouth, set to argue, then clamped it shut. Of course he knew Crescent was in love with him. He'd always known, but it had made no difference when Maria got into trouble. He had essentially forced Crescent to come along. He was disgusted with himself, but it was too late for any kind of apology to make a difference. Gravity was in charge, their course set for a rendezvous with danger and perhaps death. The only thing Crater could do was make a promise to himself, to give his own life to save Maria but somehow protect Petro and Crescent.

::: TWENTY-SEVEN

When Riley and Tiger entered the *Jan Davis*, they encountered a gruesome sight. The environmental system had shut down and the six-person crew, still in their seats, were all dead. "What happened?" Riley asked. "The hull wasn't compromised."

Tiger noted the blue lips on the crew and checked the ship's puter. "Asphyxiated. The environmental system is shut down. This was a rookie crew and they made a rookie mistake. I've seen it in simulations. They overloaded the system with too many commands from too many stations and the puter shut down. When they booted back up, they focused on weapons and forgot to put the air cycler back online."

The Colonel and the sheriff were next inside. "Let's get these fellows out," the Colonel said, lifting the navigator from her seat.

"What are we going to do with them?" Riley asked.

"We'll put them in the jumpcar," the Colonel replied. "Maybe we can retrieve them later for a proper scattering."

The sheriff and Riley joined together to remove the pilot

and copilot from the cockpit. In zero-g, it was difficult to get any leverage, and before long, the sheriff had worked up a sweat and his helmet was fogged. "Take it easy, Sheriff," Riley said. "You'll bust a gut."

"I've never liked it in space," the sheriff confessed. "I feel like I'm always close to losing my cookies."

"Just try to breathe."

"I'm claustrophobic. This helmet seems to be getting smaller by the minute. I'm about this close to screaming."

Riley put her helmet against his. "Look into my eyes, Sheriff. You're fine and you're going to stay fine. Tiger's going to get us some air real soon. When we accelerate out of orbit, we'll even have a little gravity for a while. Now help me with these fine young fellows who have gone to the angels. Please."

The sheriff squeezed his eyes shut, then blinked a couple of times. He pushed his forehead forward to the helmet towel shelf to wipe the sweat from his brow. He looked at Riley, then nodded his thanks. Riley slapped the sheriff on his helmet and handed the pilot's body off to him.

The Colonel was at the nav station, bringing up the console instruments. "Navigation seems to be working but communications are down," he said.

Tiger floated back to look over the Colonel's shoulder. "The comm dish is gone. I noticed that as I came over. There are short-range secondary systems but looks like they're down too. Probably the interlink's burned out. I can troubleshoot it."

"How long will that take?" the Colonel asked.

"I can't say. Some hours probably. I've got to get the environmental systems up first. The sensors all need calibrating after a hard shutdown. Also I need to check all the air lines and make sure they haven't been compromised."

"I need to communicate with L5," the Colonel said. "Make that first priority."

Tiger tapped on the keyboard and a document appeared on-screen. "This is the communications manual, about two thousand pages long." He clicked on it. "There's the troubleshooting section, only three hundred and ten pages long, including schematics. Look, Colonel, we can't go anywhere until I get us air. If we have to, we can fix communications on the way."

The Colonel thought it over, then conceded, "All right," he said, "make the environmental system first priority, but I don't want to wait until you fix it. I want to get going right away."

Riley's eyebrows shot up. "Head for deep space with no ship air, sir? We could run out of suit air and then what?"

The Colonel smiled a grim smile. "Then I guess we'd die, Riley. Did you think this was going to be an easy mission?"

"No, sir, but I didn't think it was going to be suicidal."

Afterward, the sheriff, his face tinged green, managed to seek out the Colonel for a quiet word. "I'm sick, sir," the sheriff said, "but I can still take care of either one of these birds for you. Just give me the word."

"It may come to that," the Colonel quietly replied. "But we need them for now. Just be prepared."

The sheriff patted the pistol on his hip. "You know I'm always prepared."

::: TWENTY-EIGHT

Maria knocked on her father's cabin hatch. When there was no response, she opened the hatch and found him lounging on a couch while watching the twentieth-century movie *Starship Troopers*. "A guilty pleasure," he said, beckoning her in.

Maria sat on a chair beside the couch. When her father kept watching the movie, she said, "Could you put the movie on pause? I'd like to talk to you."

Her father paused the film with his remote and turned toward her. "Did you come to apologize to your old man?"

"I came . . . Yes, I came to apologize."

"This is such good news! Give us a hug."

Her skin crawling, she let him wrap his arms around her, then counted to five and pulled back. "I've been talking to Truvia. She told me her real plan."

Junior shrugged. "Truvia has grandiose dreams. She thinks I don't know about her plan for a royal kingdom or whatever, but I do. I just ignore it. I'm a one-step-at-a-time type of fellow. For now I'll settle for Medaris family leadership."

"Junior, I'm not talking about that. She and Carus have sent an asteroid to destroy the Earth."

"Nonsense. They couldn't do something like that without my knowledge."

"They could and they have."

Junior picked up his remote. "Let's watch the movie. It's science fiction I can believe."

"We need to warn Earth. Maybe they can stop it. It's still a couple of days away."

"I've been thinking about marrying Truvia. What would you think of her as a stepmother?"

"Junior, she's seventy years old."

Her father laughed. "Where did you hear such nonsense? You're jealous, I suppose. My little kitten doesn't like her daddy falling in love with another woman, does she?"

Her father's condescension was like a trigger to Maria's deep-seated anger. "I'll tell you what your little kitten doesn't like. She doesn't like that you beat her mother and caused her to commit suicide. She doesn't like that you sent her to school black-and-blue from being pinched. Your little kitten is also sure you're batscrag crazy."

The hatch opened and Carus, followed by a huge crowhopper, stepped inside. Junior held up the remote. "I called my guards the moment you arrived. Carus, I think my daughter needs to be locked in her cabin. She's acting a little . . . strange."

Truvia also came inside. "Maria, we heard what you said. So disappointing that you would tell such amazing lies to your father. I fear stronger measures may be required. If you wouldn't mind, Junior, I'd like to transform her."

"I suppose that would be all right, but into what?"

"I have an eighty-year-old woman in our files."

Junior shrugged. "She was always an old woman, anyway. So serious even as a child."

Maria lunged for the hatch but was immediately caught in the arms of the big crowhopper. Struggling, she cried out. "Junior, listen to me! I'm not lying! They're going to hit the Earth with an asteroid!"

"Such nonsense," Truvia tsked. "Maria, the woman you'll be turned into had scoliosis and required a cane to get around. I imagine that will slow you down, even in zero-g."

"Junior, don't let them do this to me!"

"Good-bye, Maria," Junior said, before fiddling with the remote. "Maybe after you're changed, you'll be more flexible, and then maybe we'll change you back." The movie started again.

Maria, held in the iron grip of the crowhopper, was shoved through the hatch. Truvia followed. "I guess we'll have to postpone the coronation," she said. "On the other hand, an eighty-year-old queen might be interesting."

TWENTY-NINE

The *Linda Terry* cruised on, slowing as the moon exerted its gravitational presence but still on course to loop around to L5.

Petro explained the navigational system to Crater. "Fusers use X-ray pulsars to navigate. See those bright lights on the scope? They're pulsars about a hundred million miles away, and the *Linda*'s puters are using them to precisely fix our location using triangulation."

"Why do you need pulsars?" Crater wondered. "Why not just use the Earth and the moon to triangulate?"

"Most of the old space nav systems do," Petro said, "but when we built the fusers and began to fly into deep space, sometimes the Earth and moon blocked one another. Distant pulsars were the perfect solution."

Crater was interested in the navigation, in the abstract manner in which engineers are interested in everything technical, but his mind was elsewhere. "Are you sure we're on course for L5?" he asked.

"Don't worry. We're going to come right down on top of L5."

"What's our estimated time of arrival?"

"We should be there in about twelve hours."

Crater felt a chill of uncertainty seep down his spine. "That soon?"

Petro shrugged. "You were the one who was in a hurry to get there, Crater."

Crescent floated up and strapped herself into the jump-seat. "What's up, gentlemen?"

"It's time we made a plan," Crater said, mentally throwing off his uncertainty. "Let's review where we are. We're coming in from deep space with the hope the L5 station won't see us. Our kinetic guns are armed and ready and so are our nukes, although what we'll use those big blasters for, I don't know. In any case, our goal is to rescue Maria, who is, as far as we know, located inside the L5 station. With those knowns, here's the unknown. How do we get her off of the station and safely inside this fuser?"

"Threaten them," Crescent suggested. "Tell the people on the station we're going to blast them if they don't give her to us."

"They'll know we're not going to do that. We would kill Maria."

"What if they think we don't care?" Crescent said. "What if they think we're bounty hunters?"

"I like Crescent's idea," Petro said. "If we tell them there's a big reward for Maria, they'll think we're just mercenaries."

Crescent added, "We can tell them if they don't hand Maria over, then that is fine with us. We'll just kill them and collect the bounty on their heads."

"What about the warpods?" Crater asked. "We can't just waltz in there and lower our guns."

"We should attack the warpods first," Petro said. "This old girl's a proven warpod killer."

Crescent agreed, saying, "We might be able to bag them all before they know what's happening."

"That's wishful thinking, I'm afraid," Petro said. "Even if their crew is asleep, the puters on warpods are always on a war footing. They'll be looking for anything coming their way."

"How far away will they be looking?" Crater asked.

"A few hundred miles. Otherwise, their alarms would be going off every time a stray asteroid or defunct satellite crossed by."

"What if they thought we were a friendly spacecraft?" Crater asked.

"Fusers and warpods don't tend to be friends."

"Then we need to go after their puters first," Crescent said. She patted the gillie in her pocket, and it came out and rested on her shoulder. *You woke me from my nap for what purpose?*

"Can you hack into a warpod puter?"

When it hesitated, Crater's gillie woke up from its resting place on the cockpit console. *The problem with hacking a warpod puter is a matter of getting into it. They are designed to be internalized only. There are no links to them from the outside.*

"Well, that lets the gillies out," Petro said.

However, Crater's gillie continued with emphasis, *even though hacking warpod puters is not possible, we can still fool them into thinking we're not a fuser but something else. How we do that is to send out a pulsdar signal at low strength with a distortion added that makes us look like whatever we want. For instance, another warpod or an asteroid.*

Brilliant, oh ancient gillie, Crescent's gillie said with deep admiration.

Awful Thing, it is well you understand my genius.

Oh, I do, my father and mother.

Don't lay it on too thick, child, Crater's gillie said, although it was preening as it said it.

"Hush, gillies," Crater admonished. "But thanks for the idea."

"I don't know," Petro mused. "Quite a coincidence for an asteroid the size of a fuser showing up!"

"At least it might confuse them," Crescent pointed out.

If there is more than one warpod's pulsdar signal, Crater's gillie said, *the Awful Thing will have to help me.*

I will do as you ask, Crescent's gillie said.

You will do as I tell you, Crater's gillie corrected.

So be it, Crescent's gillie conceded.

"You gillies hush," Crater said.

"If we come in and start maneuvering, the warpods and the L5 station will guess what we are," Crescent said.

Petro considered that, then said, "Debris has fallen into L5 for eons. We could avoid maneuvers and just let ourselves be sucked in. Once we're in the horde, we could skip from asteroid to asteroid, hiding behind them as we go. Then, after we get into position, we can attack, all guns blazing."

Crater ran the scenario through his mind, then said, "All right. I like it. We'll first go after the warpods and then confront the station as bounty hunters." He turned to Petro. "It'll take some fancy flying, but I know you can pull it off."

Petro's smile was rueful. "If I pull this off, Crater, I'll be the greatest fuser pilot who ever lived."

Crater clapped his hand on his brother's shoulder. "Then do it!"

::: THIRTY

Maria was strapped to the gurney facing the tunnel of the 3DCP. Truvia worked the keyboard of its puter. "This thing keeps locking up," she complained.

"Truvia, listen," Maria said, her mind scrambling for a way out. "Let's make a deal. I won't make any more trouble. You unstrap me and we'll forget about all of this. I'll even be the princess, you be the queen. How about it?"

"You won't make any more trouble after I transform you into an old woman. By the way, it will take about eight hours, so I'll have to put you under after I get this thing working." Frustrated, she slapped the keyboard and sighed. "It's the power on this station. It's uneven and makes the puter stop and start up again." While waiting for the puter reboot, she pondered Maria. "If this was my lab on Earth, I'd already have you well on your way to cronehood."

"What will I look like?" Maria gulped.

Truvia drew a rectangle, filled it with a picture of a woman bent over a walker, then floated it past Maria. "Maybe in the low gravity of the station, you won't need a walker. We'll see."

Maria struggled with the straps, but a hulking crowhopper guard put his hands on her shoulders and pressed her down. Maria looked into his eyes, which were filled with malevolence. "You seem like a nice guy," she said. "Maybe you and I could be pals. How about you killing Truvia for me?"

When the crowhopper didn't respond, Maria plaintively asked, "I take it that's a no?"

Truvia looked up from the puter. "I'll give you this much, Maria. You have spirit. Right to the end." She shook her head. "I'm going to have to go down to the power room. William, you're in charge of our erstwhile Queen Maria. Keep her strapped down or it's your head."

"She will be here exactly as she is until you return, Trainer Truvia."

Truvia went through the hatch. Maria craned her neck to look at the crowhopper. "So, William," she said in a voice she hoped was enticing, "what brings a nice-looking fellow like you way out here?"

The crowhopper made no answer, his eyes locked on the far bulkhead as if he didn't dare look at Maria.

"Seems like a crummy duty station. No bars to bust up and no human girls to abuse. Who'd you scrag off to get sent here? And what do you fellows do in your off time? Shine your armor?"

The crowhopper's eyes remained locked.

"Aw, come on, William. I know all soldiers like to gripe. So what do they pay you?"

"We are paid nothing," William said, stiffly. "We serve for the honor and glory of the Legion."

"What Legion? Last I heard most of you fellows were dead."

"We are a remnant, that's true."

Maria tsked. "Doesn't sound like your leaders are doing a very good job. You guys ever sit around while cleaning your railgun rifles and talk about how you managed to get defeated in the last war? Come on. You can tell me. I'm not going anywhere."

"We do have our concerns," William confessed.

"Like not getting paid, I bet! You know the Trainers are getting millions of johncredits, but what do you get?"

"Bloody meat-grinder wars," William grumbled. "Poorly led and ambushed at every turn."

Maria tried to look sympathetic. "Well, there you go. That's what I heard too. A crowhopper friend of mine told me all about it."

William looked down at her with sudden interest. "I do not believe you have a friend that's a crowhopper."

Maria saw an opening. "Sure do. Her name's Crescent. She's a member of the Phoenix Legion. Or was before she joined my outfit."

Though his facial expression was limited, the crowhopper's eyes were filled with astonishment. "You know someone in the Phoenix Legion? It is an honor to know someone who even knows someone in that most exalted of legions."

Maria searched the corners of her brain for something to prove her alleged friendship with Crescent. "Life is death. Death is life. That's what she said the motto of her legion was!"

"Yes! You truly know a Phoenix Legionnaire. Crescent is his name?"

"Actually, a female. The only one." Maria kept her voice reverent.

"Amazing."

"Yeah, amazing. Look, William, why don't you take a good

look at me? Do you really want me, someone whose best buddy is a member of the Phoenix Legion, to be turned into an old lady? I mean take a good look. A woman like me, a fellow like you, we could be friends."

William's eyes roved over her like he was choosing a shiny new rifle from a gun rack. "It isn't my decision," he finally grunted.

"A lot of things aren't your decision. Come to think of it, you ever look through that hatch over there?"

"No. It is off-limits."

"I'll bet it is. You want to know why, William? I'll tell you why. That's the incubator room. Go in there, look around. What you'll see is they're planning on replacing you with some creatures that can live in a vacuum. You'll probably be changed into a moon frog or something."

"You are not funny."

"Don't mean to be. Just go take a look, then come back here and let's talk turkey, just you, me, and, in a strange way, Crescent, my really good friend, she of the Phoenix Legion."

William frowned, then walked to the hatch, swung it open, and went through. In a few minutes, he was back. Silently, he released Maria from her straps. "They will kill me for this, of course."

Maria grabbed his arm. "I'm going to run, William. Run with me."

"There is nowhere to run. We are ninety-thousand miles from the moon on a space station."

Maria pointed toward the cabin hatch. "I'm going through that hatch, William. You're not going to stop me, are you?"

"No. I will try to kill Trainer Truvia when she comes through it. I may die, but at least I won't be made into a frog."

Maria considered the fact that she was about to get William killed, then saw no recourse. "All right, William. Good luck."

"And good luck to you, Miss. I would have liked you to be my queen."

Maria was oddly touched. "That is high praise, William, and thanks."

"Life is death."

Maria looked over her shoulder at the forlorn crowhopper. "Death is life," she said, then opened the hatch, looked up and down the corridor, and bolted for the central core. She floated up through the hatches, then pulled down the spoke that led to the middle ring and the main airlock. There she swung the hatch open and crawled inside, coming upon a rack of pressure suits. Entry to the suit was by swinging open the backpack and crawling through the opening. She pushed her feet inside one that looked to be about the right size and ducked within, her head popping up in the helmet. She reached behind her, found the strap attached to the backpack, and pulled it shut. "Pressurize," she commanded. "Check for air leaks and oxygen generation."

In a few seconds, the suit puter reported no air leaks and a full oxygen generator. "How much time on this suit?"

Approximately thirty-six hours.

Maria caught sight of the airlock monitor that showed her in the suit. If they were monitoring on the bridge, someone would be coming after her very soon. Maria opened the hatch leading into the airlock, just as the inner hatch swung open and a big crowhopper stepped inside. Maria picked up a broom, clambered into the airlock, and closed the hatch behind her. "Depressurize," she said.

"Maria." It was Truvia's voice. "Bad girl. Poor William. He is stone cold dead. He was never a good shot."

"Hello, Truvia," Maria said. "Too bad about William. He was such a nice fellow, but you really ought to talk things over with your crowhoppers. I think they're catching on to your various scams. You know, where they do all the work and dying and you collect all the money? Are you listening to me there on the bridge? Anyway, thought I'd go out for a stroll. Want to come with me? You won't even need to wear a suit."

"Please be serious. Why did you go outside? What could you hope to accomplish? There's no way for you to escape."

"Well, I guess I came out to look at the stars and stuff. Seems a nice day for it."

"Mathus, get in a suit and retrieve Dr. Medaris."

The airlock gauge reached zero and Maria opened the outer hatch. "I wouldn't do that, Mathus," she warned.

"Go ahead, Mathus," Truvia said.

Maria climbed through the hatch and jammed the broomstick into its hinges so it wouldn't close.

Maria heard a crowhopper, apparently Mathus, say, "Trainer Truvia, the inner hatch of the airlock will not open. The gauge says there's zero pressure inside. And, no matter how much I tell the puter to do it, the outer hatch remains open."

"And so shall it stay," Maria sang, jamming the aluminum handle of the broomstick further between the hatch and the opening.

"Blow the inner airlock hatch, Mathus," Truvia ordered. She sounded bored.

"What will happen if I do that, Trainer Truvia?"

"You'll be able to go outside and bring the prisoner inside, you idiot. What do you think? Listen very carefully. I'm sending Crispus down with some plastique explosives. You put it around the rim, then insert an explosives cap, run wires back, and blow it. Understand?"

"Yes, Trainer Truvia."

"I wouldn't do that, Mathus," Maria said. "You are in a pressurized chamber, and you're going to explode the hatch into a vacuum. You'll get blown out into space."

"That's nonsense, Mathus," Truvia said. "Do as I tell you."

Maria climbed up on the airlock entry to get out of the way. A few minutes later, there was a puff of debris through the hatch followed by a crowhopper shooting through it. He was flailing, clutching his throat. Not only had he been blown into space, but apparently his suit had been compromised. Death in a vacuum was not pretty. Debris kept spouting through the open hatch until it abruptly stopped. Mathus stopped flailing and floated away.

"I bet that popped your ears, Truvia," Maria said gleefully.

"Mathus was always an idiot."

"Yeah, well, he was just following orders from someone who didn't care if he died or not. You fellows on the bridge listening? Come on. Let's have a revolt against the Trainers, what do you say?"

Truvia laughed. "You are truly wasting your breath in the most obvious way, considering you are in a space suit. Legionnaires are loyal to their Trainers, Maria."

Maria felt a rush of adrenaline. "Yeah? Well I know a few besides William who got smart. Their names are Absalom, Lucien, Dion, and Crescent. I worked with them, ate dinner with them, had parties with them, and watched them make some money of their own. Some even took wives. Umlaps, it's true, but females are females. You heard about those fine members of the Legion, gentlemen? Crescent, by the way, was a member of the Phoenix Legion. Life is death. Death is life. Get it? Knock old Truvia in the head there, string up Carus, and come on over to the good life. I'll see you all millionaires."

When nobody answered, Maria suspected Truvia had turned off communications. She crawled up on the ring and looked around for a place where she could defend herself. Then she saw a suited crowhopper stick his arms out of the main airlock hatch, remove the broomstick, and pull the hatch closed. Likely, they intended to fix the airlock and then come after her.

Maria decided to go along the spoke to the inner core and then down to the lower ring. There were foot restraints there where she could attach herself. She positioned herself in the foot restraints and then kept her eye on the main airlock hatch, although she knew it would take some time to fix it.

"Maria." It was her father. "Maria, come inside. We were never going to hurt you. We just wanted to scare you."

"Scrag off, Junior!"

Truvia spoke next. "Maria, can you see the Earth from where you are?"

"Yes."

"It will still be there when we're through. Just as beautiful. Perhaps more so."

Maria gritted her teeth. "How can a destroyed Earth be beautiful?"

"I suppose it depends on your point of view," she said, "but, in any case, the light show should be spectacular."

"I don't guess I'll be alive to see it, Truvia, but thanks for the heads-up."

Her father spoke next. "You are in a lot of trouble, young lady."

"Junior, you are truly an idiot. Didn't you just hear Truvia admit she's going to destroy Earth?"

"I'm sure she has her reasons."

Maria shook her head and swore to herself never to speak to her father again.

THIRTY-ONE

The Colonel called a war council on board the fuser *Jan Davis*. They were ten thousand miles out from the moon, their course set to take them the shortest distance to L5 with periodic bursts of the fuser engines. Normally the Colonel wasn't the type of leader who let people in on his plans. This was because it was his experience that secrecy made him look smarter than he was. He also sometimes pretended to know things he didn't know. On this mission the Colonel was uncertain what he knew and what he didn't, and the meeting was to sort it all out.

The cockpit of the fuser was not well arranged for meetings. The pilot and copilot sat facing the viewport and puter screens, gauges, throttles, and holographic projections. Behind them were two jumpseats that could swivel. When the Colonel called everyone to the cockpit, Tiger was in the traditional left seat of the pilot, Riley was in the copilot's right seat, and the Colonel and the sheriff took up the jumpseats. Awkwardly, Tiger and Riley had to turn around and kneel on their seats, holding on to the backs to keep themselves stable in the low gravity. The sheriff, sweating and still sick to his stomach, belted into the jumpseat behind the copilot. For his part, the Colonel chose to stand by, inserting his slippers into the foot loops behind the other jumpseat and gripping its back for stability. The Colonel was aware that a good portion of his mystique was his height, giving him the ability to stare down at people with his deep-set eyes that exuded strength and power.

The Colonel began with a reminder that he was solely in charge. "People, this mission is mine, just as this fuser is mine. Although Tiger has technical command of this ship, I will decide where it will go and what it will do."

When no one chose to argue his point, the Colonel went on. "The purpose of this flight is to get me to the L5 station. I see no reason for stealth. The lack of long-range communications remains a concern. If we had it, I'd be broadcasting all the way that we're coming to talk to Junior about his assuming the mantle of family leadership."

Riley tugged at one of her pigtails. She had braided her hair in zero-g to keep it out of her eyes. "Do ye really think they'd fall for that crock of bull, sir?"

Tiger nodded his agreement. "If they know we're coming, Colonel, I think they'll just blow us up."

"In any case," Riley said, "it's a moot point, isn't it? There are no communications."

"Yes, Riley," the Colonel said tiredly, "that's why as soon as the environmental system is fully functional, we must get communications up and running."

"The main comm dish is gone, Colonel," Tiger pointed out. "Troubleshooting won't fix that. You need to wrap your head around the fact we aren't going to be able to communicate with the station until we get closer in. You can't fix what can't be fixed."

"Once again, Pilot Tramon, try to pay attention," the Colonel growled. "I will decide what we will do. Although I'm certain you have a thorough knowledge of the fuser and its systems, I do not like a defeatist attitude. We will work on long-range communications."

Tiger shrugged. "Roger that, sir."

The Colonel glared at Tiger, then continued. "I want L5 painted with the pulsdar so that I know every asteroid, rock, pebble, and warpod that might be hiding there. When we arrive, I don't want to be surprised by anything. The pulsdar will announce that we are coming even if we can't talk to them, and, since they know we're aware our pulsdar is detectable, I'm hoping they will think we aren't hostile."

"Perhaps, sir," Riley said, "we can communicate with the station by using the pulsdar. Is there a code we might use? We could switch it on and off like the old telegraph."

"We could," the Colonel mused, "but would there be anyone there who could read it? My son never made it past second-class World Scout because he was unable to either build an ancient telegraph or memorize Morse code. It was an early demonstration that he lacked the intellectual capabilities of the majority of the Medaris family."

"I've got an idea!" Tiger exclaimed. "Perhaps we can reroute our long-range communications link through the pulsdar antenna. It's not designed for those wave lengths, but we might be able to modify it."

"What would that take?"

"Access to the maintenance ports, some cabling, and time."

The Colonel thought over the situation. "All right, here's

our priorities. Environmental systems first, weapons systems next—Sheriff, you and I will check the kinetic and missile systems—and then Tiger, work on your pulsdar antenna idea. Riley, help Tiger, but if you find he doesn't need you, come and help me. Clear?"

The sheriff raised a shaky hand. "The toilets don't work, Colonel."

"Use a bucket."

"In zero-g?"

The Colonel shook his head. "Riley, spend a little time on the waste collection system."

"Yes, sir. I think I know what's wrong. It's a matter of pneumatics. There's some kind of obstruction. I'll figure it out." She headed aft.

Tiger raised his hand. "When we arrive, Colonel, is your plan to slide up next to the station and talk to your son and convince him to stand down?"

"Yes, of course," the Colonel answered. "What else can I do? Nothing else. It will be dangerous, but I'm sure we can do it."

The sheriff glanced at the Colonel. The Colonel gave him a small shake of his head. What was actually to be done was to remain between them for now.

"What about the other fuser?" Tiger asked.

"What other fuser?"

"We've been painting one on our pulsdar. It doesn't appear to be going to L5 but heading into deep space."

The Colonel mulled it over. "Crater Trueblood," he concluded.

Accepting that Crater was still trying to rescue Maria, Colonel grappled with the uncomfortable facts that faced him. If it was discovered that he had financed the asteroid horde at L5, not to mention that he had financed the first crowhoppers, he was going to be branded the biggest war criminal of all time. But Crater didn't care about that. He would have only one purpose, saving Maria, and the boy had proved time and again he could do the impossible. And if Crater saved Maria, would she keep quiet about what her grandfather had done? And even if she did, would other station survivors, including the Colonel's own son, remain silent? The brutal answer was that there could be no survivors, which meant Crater had to be stopped.

The Colonel gripped the top of the jumpseat and asked, "How far out will our missiles be able to engage a target?"

"The record is ten thousand miles," Tiger answered.

"Keep close track of the other fuser," the Colonel said. "We might need to destroy it."

"But, sir," Tiger argued, "if that's Crater Trueblood and the Lunar Rescue Company, they'll be on our side."

"We don't know if it's them or not," the Colonel replied. "So as a contingency, we have to be prepared to smash them."

Tiger frowned but said, "Yes, sir."

::: THIRTY-TWO

When the main airlock hatch opened, Maria saw who it was, and despite her perilous situation, had the good humor to laugh as the clumsy red-suited creature floated outside. "Good old BKD4284. What's wrong, BK? May I call you BK? You run out of young women to rough up inside? Yeah, I guess you have. Well, welcome to my world."

The demon, an ax strapped to its backpack, stared at her, then pulled itself along the handrails to the central core. When it reached the lower ring, it pulled free its ax and began to cross the connecting strut toward Maria. Maria grabbed handrails and pulled herself away from the demon. "What would Crater do?" she asked herself, the answer being he'd use what he had.

But what did she have? She looked around the station, then toward the bridge and the array of dishes and antennae there. Maria crossed a strut, grabbed onto the ladder that led up the central core, and headed for the bridge. The demon turned around and followed.

At the bridge, she pulled her legs up just in time to avoid a vicious swipe of the demon's ax, and then went hand over hand across the bridge viewports, the startled crew members inside pointing at her. She headed for a weak-looking whip antenna and rocked it back and forth until metal fatigue allowed her to tear it free.

When Maria turned around, the demon was almost on top of her. She dodged his attack and fastened her waist tether, a thin wire fed from a spring mechanism, onto the nearest handrail, then pushed off. Coming around in a swinging arc, she dodged a clumsy swing of the demon's ax, then lashed out with the antenna, managing to swat him on his helmet. The creature gathered itself and swung its ax again, just missing her tether. Maria pushed off once more and circled the demon, leaving a wrap of tether wire about its waist. Maria grabbed a comm dish and hung on.

The red-suited creature started to come after her but found itself snared by her tether. Maria released the tether clip at her waist, then soared to the hull, went hand over hand to reach the other end of the tether clip, and released it. "So long, BK," she said as the demon floated away. "Have a nice death."

The demon stared at the unattached tether trailing it and then tossed away its ax and started making swimming motions. Maria glanced through one of the viewports of the bridge. Her father and Truvia were there, looking up at her. She grinned and gave them a thumbs-up, which, based on their shocked expressions, did not seem to please them.

::: THIRTY-THREE

Petro woke Crater. "We're being painted," he said.

Crater opened his eyes but Petro wasn't there. His voice was transmitted over the speaker in the cabin where Crater had climbed into a bunk and wrapped a sleeping bag around him. He unzipped the bag, pulled on his coveralls, and headed for the cockpit. "Can you tell who it is?" he asked while somersaulting into the copilot's seat.

"Pulsdar is coming from moonside," Petro said. "Signature makes it another fuser."

Crater studied the pulsdar screen. Something was sending out horn-shaped waves that were washing over them and lighting them up. "Could it be that one of the Colonel's fusers got through after all?" Crater asked.

Petro shook his head. "Who knows? The problem is their pulsdar's emitting a broad-range blast. They're not only painting us, they're painting L5 too. The warpods and the station are going to be on full alert."

Crater rubbed the sleep from his eyes and tried to think.

"If they feel threatened, the warpods will probably move. They might even come out of L5."

"The only way to know is to fire up our own pulsdar and have a look-see, but then L5 would be certain we're a fuser."

"Or ask the Cycler to do it for us again."

"The *Musk* is rounding the moon about now," Petro replied. "They're out of position."

"So we have to carry on blind."

"I guess so. In another few hours, we'll begin our asteroid tumble. Maybe we'll luck out and catch some warpods sleeping, anyway."

Crater pondered that. "Well, we've cast the die. Nothing to do but stick to our plan."

Crater and Petro sat companionably together for a while until Crater said, "I've been thinking about these fusers. Where did the technology come from? All of a sudden during the war, there they were."

"I'm no fonder of the Colonel than you are," Petro replied, "but I have to give him credit. His jumpcar plant in Armstrong City was busily developing fusion rocket engines in secret. He said if we ever headed to the stars, we'd need them."

Crater was intrigued. "Who said anything about going to the stars? Humans have never gone farther than Mars."

"You know the Colonel. He's got some big ideas. Theoretically, a ship with fusion drive could head to Proxima Centauri, the nearest star, and be there in about sixteen years at quarter–light speed."

"Can a fuser go that fast?"

"No reason why it can't as long as it's got the fuel. Of course, at that velocity, there's no way to avoid anything, and hitting even a grain of sand would be like detonating a ton of high explosives."

"Maybe a pulsed wave buffer of some sort expanding out in front," Crater said. "Like a cow catcher. That would be an interesting engineering problem."

"Well, Proxima Centauri's just a red dwarf. We know there are planets around it but not much else. Probably lifeless. Maria's farside telescope might have told us if it was a good target or maybe found another close star with Earth-like planets."

"Whatever star that's eventually picked, it's good to live in a time when there are people who just might head out to the stars," Crater said. "As much as I should hate his guts, the truth is I admire the Colonel's grit and imagination."

"And his granddaughter."

"Yes, her too."

Petro chose his words carefully. "I spent some time with Maria in the war, and our conversations were almost always about you. She loves you, Crater. She just doesn't know what to do with your love. Your love wants to tie her down, but that isn't her. She has to feel like she's got most of the say in her life. What I mean is, life has to be on her terms, not yours. If you two got together, she'd be off working all the time. Could you stand that?"

"I wouldn't like it," Crater admitted.

"Well, there you go! That's her problem with you right there. And where did that opinion come from? You're an orphan! You weren't raised by a mom who stayed home and looked after the kids. You were raised in a boarding house, your adopted mother a woman who claimed to be the queen of England and was out building a bunch of businesses most of the time. Her Moon Soap is so successful, she could probably buy the Colonel. She didn't build that business by wiping your nose and making you corn bread. She was out there hustling!"

"I remember Q-Bess being home a lot," Crater retorted. "And she looked after me too."

"When you were twelve, Mom signed the papers and you went to work on the scrapes. Was that looking after you? She was more than happy to have you out from underfoot. Look, I love our mum, don't get me wrong, but she isn't little Miss Happy Housewife like you want poor Maria to be. You've got to lighten up, let that girl be who she wants to be."

Crater made a dismissive gesture. "It doesn't matter. That ship passed me a long time ago. Maria and I are never going to get together."

"Then why are we on this fuser?"

When Crater didn't answer, and when it was clear he didn't have one to give, Petro gave his brother a significant look, then pulled off toward a bunk to snatch a little sleep. Crater sat back in the copilot's seat and kept watch on the other fuser's pulsdar signal and started to think. A lot of men he knew never gave any thought to their lives at all. For them, it was just one thing after another, whatever happened just happened. The truth was Crater often wished he could be more like them and not worry about what was around the corner or what questions he should ask or answers he should give. He wished he never gave any thought to the reason there was a universe or worried that one day, according to science, the sun would expand and absorb the Earth and the moon, killing all life. That was so far in the future, it was decidedly not worth worrying about, but every so often, Crater would blink awake and find himself worrying about it anyway. It was foolish, of course. The atoms of his body by then would probably be so spread out that one would never come within a million miles of the other. Yet Crater worried about the end of the solar system and couldn't help it, just as he worried about Maria and couldn't help it, and grieved that they would never be together as partners in life.

"Well, so be it," he said to himself. "I'll save her this one last time and that will be the end of it," though his heart and everything in him disagreed.

The sets of pulsdar waves kept lighting up the *Linda Terry* on the screen. Crater studied them. Whoever was painting them was persistent, more like an enemy than a friend.

::: THIRTY-FOUR

Truvia and Carus conferred on the bridge. Maria was no longer in sight, presumably moved back to the lower ring. Junior had gone to his cabin to take a sleeping pill. Through the port viewport, they could still see the demon adrift. It had swum in the vacuum for a while, then given up. Now it was still, except for an occasional twitch of its arms and legs.

"We could call a warpod in to pick it up," Carus said.

"Actually I'm glad to be rid of it," Truvia said. "It ate and drank a lot and stunk like rotten eggs most of the time. My stomach turned anytime it was around."

"Maybe you should have transformed it."

"Into what?"

Carus twisted his lips, a sardonic expression. "You could have made it into a second Junior Medaris."

"Intriguing," Truvia said. "But no, it was too stupid. It might have looked like Junior, but nobody would have been fooled."

"The real one is pretty dumb, if you ask me. I rather like his feisty daughter better."

"I offered her the throne. You can see the result."

Carus nodded unhappily. "What's next?"

"Tomorrow we take Junior to the moon and have him officially take control of Medaris Enterprises. While he's there, the asteroid will collide with Earth. Then Junior will explain to the Lunar Council that many more such rocks are aimed at all the cities on the moon. They will have no choice but to give in. We will take over and begin to build our new order."

"You make it sound so simple. I believe there will be resistance."

"If there is, we'll destroy it wherever it arises."

"Excuse me, Trainers," Letticus, the station captain said, "but there is evidence of a fuser coming in our direction. They're painting us with their pulsdar. We've called them on every frequency we can think of but no response."

"When will the fuser arrive?" Carus asked.

"Could be as early as sixteen hours."

"Send a warpod out to engage it," Truvia commanded.

"What are we to do with Queen Maria?" Letticus asked.

"That problem will take care of itself. She will run out of air tomorrow. Before she does, she may come in voluntarily. If she doesn't, we wait until she's unconscious and go after her. Now if you can spare me, I'm going to Junior's cabin. I think he needs me to hold his hand."

"How long do you intend to keep him alive?" Carus asked.

"Until he's no longer useful to us."

Carus made a small bow. "You always see things so clearly, Truvia. It is fortunate you are on our side."

"I dare say you're correct," she said and went below. But before going to Junior's cabin, she instead went to the lower ring. Looking out at Maria, she said, "Such a foolish child you are. Please come in. I promise I won't let anyone hurt you. The throne is still yours. You must want it. I know you do."

Maria studiously ignored her. To Truvia, her silence felt like a wound.

::: THIRTY-FIVE

Maria was almost disappointed when they didn't immediately send a crowhopper out after her. The way she saw it, that was fundamentally better than waiting around to asphyxiate, and maybe she could have taken a couple of them with her. While her air ticked down toward nothing, she dozed occasionally but otherwise spent the time looking out at the moon and the Earth and feeling a little cheated that the moon was so dead and gray and beat up with craters and the Earth was so alive with swirling white clouds and glittering blue seas and brown-green continents. It seemed unfair that gravity worked the way it did with liquids and gases held close to the planet Earth but blown away from the moon. It was also not fair that Earth was just the right size to have a fiery inner core that spun around and created a magnetic field that fended off the solar wind while the moon with its cold center was subjected to the unceasing fury of deadly radiation.

On the other hand, there was much to admire about the moon, including its size and location. Maria knew the moon had given the Earth the helping hand it needed to sustain life.

The lunar tides gave the edges of the continents a refreshing wash, bringing with it tidal pools where myriad creatures could feed and grow. In the deep ocean, the movement of the water pulled back and forth by the moon's crossings kept the seas from becoming stagnant and dead. The moon even stabilized the Earth's wobble, which provided a temperate climate over most of the planet's surface.

These gifts of the moon to the Earth were well known. Less known was that without the pull of the moon, the Earth would spin more rapidly on its axis, so much that a day would be only six to eight hours long. Such rapid spinning would not only cause a disruption to the normal cycles of life but would also cause powerful windstorms to sweep across the planet. With such storms, it would be impossible for plants to grow or animals to live. The moon, then, was the perfect size and distance to provide benevolent gifts to its mother planet while sacrificing its own ability to thrive.

Eventually, of course, the Earth had given the moon's gift back in the form of life even though there were many arguments about how best to manage the migration of life from the blue planet to the gray. Philosophers waxed, poets wrote, and preachers preached about the dead moon coming to life, taking from it lessons of hope and the virility of the universe. For their part, engineers and scientists only saw what had to be done to keep life viable in the harshest of conditions, the mooncrete tubes beneath the ground, the plaston protective domes over the cities, the constant search for water and the plumbing it took to deliver it, and the growth of food in biovats or farms beneath the domes, not to mention the various vehicles needed to transit the space between the Earth and the moon and travel on the moon's gritty surface.

Bringing life to the moon had turned out to be one of the best things humans had done for themselves in a very long time. It had opened up new sources of energy, new sources of precious metals, even new products like soap made from moon dust that could scour anything clean. The wars that had swept across the planet in the twenty-first century had waned and nearly subsided in the early twenty-second when the moon began to be settled, the energy of warfare drained into the energy of building a new civilization.

But then the crowhopper war had been unleashed, planned and paid for by the dictatorships of the United Countries of the World, and the cycle of killing and plundering, so common on Earth throughout the centuries, had taken hold on the moon.

It shamed Maria to know that her family had provided the seed money and the initial management of the facilities that had created the crowhoppers. Somehow her grandfather and the other family members had kept that a secret, not only from everyone else, but her too. But now the secret was surely going to get out. What she would do with this knowledge, Maria didn't really know. Actually, of course, it appeared that was not a real concern since she was probably going to run out of air before rescue came.

She no longer believed Crater was coming. It had always been unlikely. The Trainers were right about that. How could a heel-3 miner get all the way out here?

"How much time do I have?" she asked the suit puter.

Eighteen hours at this respiratory rate.

Maria was hungry, but at least she had water. She sipped some from a straw in the helmet that led to a small tank.

Drinking water made her think of Crater again. He had invented a machine that could detect small amounts of water from beneath the moon's surface, then use ultrasonic waves to gather it into a pool for recovery. It had been a remarkable invention and it was now in use all over the moon. After inventing the machine, Crater, true to his nature, had done nothing with it, which was why the Colonel stole Crater's invention and began to build and sell it himself. When he'd put Maria in charge of the factory that produced it, and she'd discovered it was producing Crater's invention, she'd pared off her percentage of the profits and put it in a bank account for Crater. It was the right thing to do and she'd done it.

Now she wondered if Crater knew about the account. She supposed that if he had decided to rescue her, one of his stops would have been the Medaris Building in Armstrong City. Would Miss Torricelli tell him about the account, or Maria thought darkly, would she instead try to snag him into a date? She was certain that Miss Torricelli would consider Crater a tempting morsel. She made a note that if she made it back alive to her office—unlikely, she knew—to let Torricelli go, with all the usual benefits and allowances.

Maria looked up to the bridge but saw no one looking back. Occasionally she saw a crewman's head as he moved past. *He.* They were all male, these crowhoppers. Crescent had been the only female, at least to Maria's knowledge.

Maria had been surprised at the reverence for Crescent that William the crowhopper had shown. That reverence had kept Maria from being transformed into an old woman. In effect her knowledge of Crescent had saved her life, at least for a little while.

Maria recalled one of the few talks she'd had with the female crowhopper. Crescent rarely had much to say to her, and Maria knew it was because Crescent didn't like her. But during a celebration by the Apps when they'd sold their first load of Thorium, Maria found herself sitting at a table with Crescent and no one else. Immediately the crowhopper had verbally attacked her. "You treat Crater like dirt," Crescent said. "I don't understand why he cares anything about you."

"Perhaps that is because you are a product of a petri dish," Maria replied cattily, "and can't understand normal human emotions."

Crescent had handed it right back to her. "Perhaps you're the one who doesn't understand normal human emotions because you're a Medaris."

"What do you mean by that?" Maria snapped.

"Don't you consider yourself superior to everyone else?"

"Not at all."

"Could have fooled me. Could have fooled everybody in Endless Dust."

When Crescent picked up her tray and took it to the wash window, Maria was left sitting alone. When no one else joined her, she picked at her food, then carried her own tray to the window. "Not hungry, honey?" the attendant asked. Maria didn't answer. Her mind was elsewhere.

On her way out, she heard the woman say, deliberately loud enough for her to hear, "Well, little Miss Priss can't even pass the time of day with peons like me."

Maria had looked over her shoulder and said, "You're right," and kept walking. She'd felt bad about it, but she hadn't gone back and apologized, either. That night, in her room where nobody could see her, she'd wept until she'd fallen asleep.

Maria felt watched. When she looked across to the inner viewport of the lower tube, she saw Truvia. Truvia, despite her penchant for cruelty and her plot to destroy the Earth and take over the moon, was an interesting woman. If Maria could have put Truvia in a cell or maybe a straitjacket, she thought they might have had some lively conversations. But Truvia just stared at her until Maria couldn't stand it. She used the handrails to pull herself around the tube out of sight where she could die in peace.

::: THIRTY-SIX

W e're still painting the other fuser," Tiger told the Colonel. "They've made a loop and are coming back toward L5."

"Clever diversion," the Colonel said. "The L5'ers may not notice them coming in from deep space." He nodded to Tiger. "Thanks for getting the ship air operable. It's good to be out of a smelly helmet. How's the work on long-range communications?"

"Riley and I are just taking a break from it. We have a lot of cables to pull. Maybe another couple of hours, we'll be ready to try."

Riley was monitoring the pulsdar. "The warpods are on the move," she said. "They're skimming along the edge of the L5 rim."

The Colonel took a look. "They've seen us, so they're moving in to protect the station."

The sheriff, feeling better, was strapped into one of the jumpseats. "What happens if they launch another asteroid to hit the moon?"

"We could chase it," Tiger said, "but I don't think we could stop it. Not without a nuke."

"I read somewhere that nuking an asteroid wouldn't do any good, anyway," Riley said. "It would just break it up or knock a big chunk out of it. Either way, all the parts would keep going in."

"Funny they worried about asteroids more in the early twenty-first century than we've done for decades," Tiger said.

"But all they did was talk about it," the Colonel pointed out. "After that the wars started that broke up the big countries, and threats from space were forgotten."

"You didn't forget," Riley said. "You loaded L5 with asteroids ready to strike."

"The dumbest thing I've ever done, Riley," the Colonel confessed.

"Don't beat yourself up, Colonel," the sheriff said. "I thought it was a good idea too."

"That should have been evidence that I was on the wrong path," the Colonel replied. The sheriff, who knew the Colonel wasn't joking, shrugged.

"How's the stomach, Sheriff?" Riley asked.

"It's coming around," he said.

"If you're feeling better, you should be running sims at the battle station," the Colonel said.

The sheriff opened his mouth to argue, thought better of it, and clapped it shut. "Heading that way now, sir," he said.

"You're rough with him," Riley said after the sheriff had pulled himself aft.

"The sheriff is a murderer, a thief, and what used to be called a psychopath," the Colonel said. "But he's absolutely loyal to me because he knows that I could dispose of him in an instant without anyone complaining."

"Maybe he's loyal to you because of who you are, Colonel," Riley suggested, "not because of your threats."

"What difference does it make as long as he's loyal?"

Riley didn't have an answer, but she had her suspicions that the Colonel was still suffering from whatever trauma had caused him to create L5. It was all starting to feel very much like a suicide mission. She would therefore bide her time, keep a close watch, and act if necessary. The Colonel might be heading toward death at fuser velocity, but she saw no reason why she had to join him.

::: THIRTY-SEVEN

Truvia knelt beside Junior and pushed his shoulder, but he didn't respond. She suspected he'd drugged himself with something stiffer than a sleeping pill. When he finally blinked awake, she asked, "What did you take?"

"Nothing," he lied as he let her help him sit up. "Well, maybe Lysurge. I like to see things turn into different colors."

"Are they still turning colors?"

He looked toward the ceiling. "Yes. That light is pulsing like a rainbow. Or is that real?"

"It isn't real," Truvia replied. "Junior, can you listen to me for just a minute?"

"A real minute? Did you know time has colors too? It's mostly blue, but now that you're here, it seems kind of orange."

Truvia suppressed a sigh of exasperation. "You see, there's a fuser on the way here from the direction of the moon. We don't know anything about it. We've called to it, but there's been no answer. Do you understand?"

Junior's eyes widened. "It's my father. I know it is. He's angry with me."

Truvia struggled to make herself understood. "We don't

know that. I don't see how it's possible, really, since we destroyed his fuser fleet. In any case, I've ordered the warpods to get into position and destroy it if necessary. What I need from you is a decision on whether you still want to go to Armstrong City now or wait. I think we should go ahead. The fuser and the warpods can fight it out while you consolidate your control of the company. Once you do that, it won't matter who's in the fuser or what it does. There is still the asteroid I sent toward Earth. It will change everything no matter what happens."

Junior squinted at her. "Did you really send an asteroid to hit Earth? I thought you were just trying to scare Maria with that tale!"

Truvia took his hands in hers. "The asteroid is real, Junior. I thought you understood. We can create a kingdom on the moon and people it with loyal subjects and servants. And when we have the strength and things clear up on the Earth, we can go up there and take it over too. It would begin thousands of years of stability under our rule and that of your progeny. *Our* progeny, if you'll have me for your wife."

Junior was getting his wits about him. "Maria said you were seventy years old."

"It doesn't matter how old I am as long as I am capable of conception," she replied. "We could couple naturally or I can accomplish it in my lab."

Junior's lips curled in disgust. "I could never get high enough to couple with you."

Truvia sat back, then rose to her feet. "I can see you're still under the effects of Lysurge," she said coldly.

Junior looked away. "I feel like throwing up."

"Lysurge sometimes causes nausea, especially if you overdose."

"It's not the Lysurge. It's talking to you that makes me sick. Now Daddy's mad at me! And the world is going to be hit by an asteroid!"

Junior suddenly stood and slammed his fist into Truvia's face. "This is all your fault!"

Truvia fell back, blood pouring from her nose. She scrambled away before he could hit her again.

"You are a filthy, ugly pig!" Junior shouted. "You made me do it. I didn't want to hit you. But now I hope the fuser is my dad. He'll take me back. Everything will be like it was."

Truvia wiped her nose with the back of her hand. She could feel her eyes swelling. "Junior, we've killed hundreds of people. We destroyed a fleet of fusers. Nobody can stop the asteroid. There's not going to be any forgiveness. One of two things is going to happen now. We will be killed or we will win. There's no in-between."

Junior, his jaw slack, sat back down on the couch. "Why did I listen to you?" he whimpered.

Truvia crawled to the couch, then sat beside him. "I forgive you, Junior. I love you so much. I'm sorry I upset you."

Junior buried his face in her shoulder. "You know I had to hit you, don't you?"

"Yes, of course. I deserved it. I pushed you too hard."

"Will you make all this go away, Truvia?"

"Yes, Junior. I will make it all go away. You just stay here. Would you like to watch an old movie?"

Junior nodded and Truvia handed him the remote. When she climbed out of the hatch, she looked through the viewport. Maria had her back turned.

"Carus?" she called. "Ready our three best warriors to go outside. Whatever it takes, bring Maria in."

::: THIRTY-EIGHT

Petro called up the *Linda Terry* puter. "Forward directional jet number two, one point five seconds at full thrust on my mark."

That will cause instability in pitch, the puter warned.

"I want to put us in a slow tumble," Petro replied.

Understood. Waiting for your mark.

"Crescent, are you ready?" Petro asked.

"Belted in," Crescent reported from her battle station.

"You ready, brother?" Petro asked Crater who was sitting beside him in the copilot's seat.

"Ready."

"Puter, five-four-three-two-one, mark!"

A bright puff emanated on the forward view screen, followed by a very slight shudder. *Thrust request complete*, the puter reported.

"Is that it?" Crescent called.

"That's it. We're now in a slow tumble, doing our best to look like an innocent little asteroid about to fall into L5."

Crescent came out of her station, opened and closed the

internal hatch, then flew along to the cockpit. She looked over Crater's shoulder and took note of the pulsdar screen. "Look at the other fuser's pulsdar! It's showing big rocks in L5!"

Crater turned to the screen. "You're right. There's also the station, but I don't see any warpods."

"I can see them," Crescent said, and then explained. "My retinas are designed to pick up very small distinctions in shapes and patterns. That's why camouflage doesn't work well against Legionnaires. The warpods are there." She touched the screen.

"Just sitting there?"

"That's what the screen shows."

"If they're staying in position within L5, it must mean they haven't decided what to do," Petro said.

Crater thought that over. "If we go after the warpods, the station is going to be busy trying to sort out what's happening and will be vulnerable to the other fuser. We don't know what its intentions are."

"We can't fight the warpods and worry about the station at the same time," Petro pointed out.

"That's why I've been thinking about our taxi," Crater said. "While we engage the warpods, our taxi could make a run for the station and demand Maria's release."

"The taxi is unarmed. What's to keep the station from destroying it?"

"They'll recognize it as a fuser taxi, and I'll tell them to either negotiate or be nuked."

Petro shook his head. "I don't know, Crater . . ."

"Don't talk," Crescent advised. "Knock out the bridge, then go aboard."

Crater thought it over. "I could aim the taxi at the bridge, bail out, and ram it. If I used a jetpack, I could land on the station and go inside after Maria."

"You just described a one hundred percent foolproof suicide mission," Petro said.

"How about this for an idea?" Crescent asked. "Taxis have mechanical arms for maintenance chores, but they could also hold a hefty rock. Gather one up, fly the taxi toward the bridge, let go of the rock, and swing away. Ought to do it."

"Use the asteroids against the station!" Petro exclaimed. "I like it. But assuming that works, it only solves part of our problem. Maria's still on board the station. How do we get her off?"

"As Crescent said, I go aboard and get her," Crater said.

"Against any number of crowhoppers?"

"They'll be in disarray."

"I don't know," Petro said after a moment's thought. "You make it sound too easy. I still think the only way is to go after the warpods, shoot them up, then go for the station. If they see a fuser swing up next to them with that other fuser also on the way, they just might surrender."

Six hours until L5, the *Linda Terry* puter said.

::: THIRTY-NINE

Truvia emerged on the bridge. Carus and Letticus nodded to her, then Letticus indicated the large central screen. "A small asteroid is about to fall into L5."

"Where did it come from?"

"Tracking back along its trajectory indicates past Mars, perhaps the asteroid belt. Pulsdar indicates it's not very dense. Otherwise we don't have much information. We're studying it."

"Too much of a coincidence. Get a warpod out there and find out what it is."

Carus said, "A warpod can't fly a direct route through the horde. It will have to circle around the rim. That's going to take a few hours and lots of fuel. This asteroid, or whatever it is, will be well inside L5 by then, probably within the horde."

"Why did you mention fuel?"

"All our warpods are low on fuel."

"Why don't they fill up? That's why we have a tank out here."

"They should have but they haven't," Letticus said.

Truvia scowled. "These warpod commanders are poorly

trained. We just didn't have time with this bunch before our labs were raided. Call them and tell them to fill up now."

"That's going to take time. The fuser's only about ten hours away. It takes two hours for each warpod to refuel. The tank is back where they were before we moved them. They'll have to go back, fill up, then turn around."

"I trusted you two to take care of this kind of thing," Truvia seethed.

Carus decided to change the subject. "What's wrong with your eye?" he asked.

"I hit it on a hatch," she replied, turning away slightly.

"No, you didn't. Junior hit you," Carus said.

"It doesn't matter," Truvia replied.

Letticus checked the clock on the station puter. "You and Mr. Medaris are supposed to leave for the moon in eight hours. One of the warpods will have to refuel to take you there."

Truvia made a decision. "Our journey is postponed. I have the sense we're under attack, maybe from two fronts. Until we find out who's on this fuser and what this so-called asteroid is, I will stay here to coordinate and make decisions."

"Then what are your immediate orders?" Letticus asked.

"Refuel one warpod. Send another one with whatever fuel it has around the rim to meet and greet that asteroid."

"If it has to do a lot of maneuvering, it won't be able to get back over here."

"It's a chance we'll have to take."

"I have the three Legionnaires you requested prepared to go outside. Do you wish to kill or capture Maria Medaris?"

"Capture. Do not kill her."

"Are you ready for them to go out?"

"Yes. Retrieve our future queen."

::: FORTY

W e're in L5," Petro said.

"I didn't feel anything," Crater said.

"Nothing to feel. Unless we slow down, we'll pass right through it. Crescent, come forward, please. Bring your binoculars."

"On my way, Petro."

Petro said, "I'll need Crescent in your seat. She's our best eyes until we can turn on the pulsdar."

Crater pushed out of his seat and headed aft to the battle station, passing Crescent as she pulled in on the handrails. She did a somersault and landed in the copilot's seat. When she looked out, all she saw were stars and galaxies. It was beautiful, glorious, and she wished that she might stay alive along enough to enjoy it in a time of peace. She thought about the secret she held so close and that made her wish for more time all the harder. But would her genes give it to her? Or would she self-destruct this year, as her programming told her to do?

"Puter," Petro said, "stabilize along the z axis, nose-first, same heading. Don't wait for my mark."

Affirmative. Computing. Ready. Mark.

A series of puffs from the directional jets swung the fuser over and then stabilized it. "Look at that," Petro breathed.

That was the horde of rocks in L5. Crescent studied them. "They've got some big ones in there and a lot of little ones too. Scan about thirty degrees to port. I see a clear space there. Once we get inside, we should be able to work our way through."

"Going in," Petro said. "Puter, manual control, please."

Manual control confirmed.

The gillie on Crescent's shoulder vibrated. "What is it, Gillie?"

I can hear the L5 station bridge.

"My gillie's saying the same thing," Crater reported from the battle station.

Crescent's gillie seemed to be listening, then said, *They are communicating with a warpod that has been sent out to look at us. I can configure the puter to receive these communications.*

"Do it."

Immediately they heard a woman's voice: " . . . as soon as there is a visual."

The next voice was the gravelly male voice associated with crowhoppers: "Nothing can be seen but rocks."

The woman's voice: "Get closer, then."

"We will crash into the horde."

"You will have to slow down so you don't crash."

"That will require maneuvering. We are low on fuel. What if we get stuck in the horde? No one will come and get us."

"We will get you out. What is your name, Captain?"

"My name is Valence."

"Valence, get in there and find that thing. If it is anything other than an asteroid, destroy it. Those are my orders. I am a Trainer. What I tell you, you must do."

"It is so ordered."

Radio silence ensued.

"What do you make of that?" Petro asked.

Crescent frowned. "The woman's voice is that of a Trainer. She sounded familiar, but I can't place her."

"How about the captain of the warpod?"

"Valence not only doesn't like his mission, he's afraid. But he will carry out his orders. He also doesn't like the Trainer, not that it's unusual. Most of us didn't like the Trainers."

"He has a bead on us," Crater said, "else he wouldn't be able to track us. What kind of signal are we transmitting?"

"None that I know of," Petro said, "except a little heat signature from our stabilization burn. If he'd seen that, I think he would have said something. Maybe they're just working from where the station saw us last and calculating where we'd have bumped into the horde. Whoops!"

The "whoops" was an asteroid half the size of the fuser, which loomed in front of them. "Puter, use the nitrogen system for course corrections."

Nitrogen system RCS ready.

Petro explained. "Fusers have a cold nitrogen system to use for fine maneuvering. No heat signature from it."

Petro steered around the big boulder, then around three smaller rocks. "It looks like they've stacked them in here by size," he said as he maneuvered. "But along the edge, there's been some mixing. Probably given time, all the rocks would mix. Probably organized this way so they can come in here and snare one a certain size."

"How do they snare them?" Crescent asked.

"Most likely they have small tugs with baskets or grapples. They send them in to push the rocks out."

"Is that a tug?" Crescent asked, touching the viewscreen.

Petro looked and saw a crumpled robotic spacecraft with a net attached between two prongs. "It used to be," he said. "Looks like it got caught between a rock and a hard place."

The voice of the crowhopper captain Valence crackled over the speaker. "It is dangerous in here. There are many small rocks we can't see until it's too late and we hit them."

"You're doing fine, Valence." The woman's voice again.

"I'm sure I know that voice," Crescent said. "But she wasn't one of our regular Trainers."

Valence spoke again. "If we are hitting rocks, then surely that asteroid did too. It's probably destroyed."

The woman again: "It isn't destroyed. It will bounce from rock to rock until it stabilizes."

"I am not sure how to recognize it."

"If it hits other asteroids, you should see them moving. Follow that trail, Captain Valence, and stop complaining."

"I have an idea," Crater said after the warpod captain and the Trainer on the station went silent. "If we could find an asteroid about our size and give it a shove, we might get this warpod to follow it, especially if we shove it toward the station. The crowhopper captain is afraid that he's going to run out of fuel, so I think he'll like going in that direction. Then we follow him through."

"How can we shove anything?" Petro asked. "Fusers aren't made to be tugs."

"How about the remote manipulator system? We could use the arm to do the shoving."

"I don't know much about that arm," Petro admitted. "We only used it a few times in the war. A lot of fuser skippers didn't even carry one along. If I'd had time, I would've taken this one off, just to get rid of the mass."

"But you didn't," Crater said, "so let's put it to good use."

The remote arm control station, a small cupola for the operator to look through, was just behind the cockpit. Crater came forward to operate the arm and, after a quick inspection, could understand why it wasn't of much use to fuser captains. It looked fragile, its purpose apparently for loading light cargo in space. Bigger cargos were placed aboard fusers by the tugs and their much heftier arms.

"Crescent, help me with this thing," he said. "And please call up the manual."

Crescent was amused. "An engineer who deigns to read a manual?"

"Just help, OK?"

Crescent fitted her feet into the foot restraints beside Crater and called up a puter screen. "RMS operations manual," she said to the puter, and it instantly appeared. She studied the diagrams and instructions that loaded on the screen, and said, "Step one. Switch to on."

"It's already on," Crater said irritably. "Skip down. I already get there's two joysticks, one for the arm and shoulder, the other for the wrist. They're marked. "

Crescent shot back, "Then why do you need me or the manual? It sounds like you already know how to do everything."

Crater realized he was pushing her too hard. "Sorry," he whispered, and saw her nod back.

Petro interrupted. "You folks about done with your little spat? I've got a bead on a rock that's about the right size."

Crater checked the asteroid from the cupola viewport and whistled. "The arm's too fragile to move something that big. The fuser's going to have to do it."

"I already told you. Fusers aren't built to be tugs. If we push against that thing, it's liable to stave in our frame."

"How about if the arm was folded between the fuser and the rock like a bumper on a fastbug?"

Petro gave that some thought. "Might work," he concluded.

"Move up so I can touch it with the arm," Crater said.

Crater could hear the little puffs of nitrogen as Petro gently steered the fuser. "Once Petro gets up to speed," he said to Crescent, "I want to shove the rock away from us and put a little rotation on it at the same time. That should make the rock look just like the crowhopper captain would expect it to look. To do that, I'll need to translate the arm forward at the same time the wrist gives it a tumble."

"I think the arm is too slow for that," Crescent said. "According to the manual, the maximum travel velocity is only one foot per second. "

"Do you see any way to increase the translation rate?"

Crescent flashed through the instruction screens. "Nothing here."

"How about you, Gillie?" Crater asked. "Any ideas?"

I do not see any recommendations to increase translation velocities in the specifications, the gillie reported.

"Coming up on our rock," Petro said. "If you're going to do something, you'd better do it."

"We'd be wasting our time with the arm this slow," Crater said. He thought for a moment, then said, "This is a hydraulic system, correct? Gillie, how does it work?"

The usual way for any hydraulic system.

"What are the hydraulic lines rated for and what do they use?"

The RMS lines are made of braided steel and are rated at eight thousand pounds per square inch. They are normally subjected to four thousand PSI.

"Typically conservative engineering. What would happen if we increased the pressure to a full eight thousand?"

The RMS would either move much faster or the seals would burst. No data on the latter.

"How do we increase the pressure?"

Disable the pressure relief valves. Close off the downstream maintenance valve until pressure is reached, then open the maintenance valve and . . . I am not sure what will happen after that except the arm is going to essentially spring open if it holds together.

"We're about a yard from our rock," Petro reported.

"Put me about ten feet above what you think the center of gravity is."

"Roger. By guess and by golly. There you are."

"The shoulder and elbow joints are fully folded," Crater said to Crescent. "Let me turn the wrist pitch up to full . . . There it is . . . And then ease the arm open at the elbow until the side of the end effector just touches . . . Easy does it . . . There, just touching."

"Well done," Crescent breathed.

Crater moved his head around in the cupola to get a better look at the rock. It appeared to be a big solid hunk of basalt. "Crescent, I'm going to need you to operate the wrist joystick. When the gillie sends the pressure downstream, I'll shove the x-y joystick forward. That should make the shoulder rotate and the elbow unfold. Just before it reaches its full stretch, pitch the wrist down. That should tumble the rock."

"Got it," Crescent said, putting her hand on the wrist joystick.

"Petro, get us up to velocity. When I say 'Back off!' do it in a hurry. If that rock is tumbling, we don't want it to come up from below and smack us."

"Roger," Petro said. "You sure you want to do this?"

"You want to play hide-and-seek with that warpod and have it put a missile up our tail a second after it spots us?"

"I'll have to use hot fire. Cold nitrogen doesn't have enough thrust."

"We'll have to chance it. Go ahead when you're ready."

Crater heard the growl and felt the thump of the belly jets. The arm pushed against the rock, which began to move. "Gillie, increase the RMS hydraulic system to seventy-nine hundred PSI."

Increasing. Upstream pressure seals holding. 5000, 6000, 7000, 7500, 7900 PSI and holding.

"Ready, Crescent?"

"Ready."

"Waiting for your call, Petro."

"We're approaching one hundred miles per hour."

"Go for five. We want this thing to knock a big path."

"Two-three-four-five. Holding at five hundred!"

"Gillie, on my mark, release the maintenance valve. Five-four-three-two-one-mark!"

Crater shoved the joystick forward. The shoulder rotated and the elbow straightened with a bang. Just at the end of the arm's reach, Crescent shoved the wrist down.

"Back off!" Crater yelled.

Instantly the jets on the fuser spewed and the fuser was pushed backward. Crater pushed his head so hard into the cupola, he thought he might bust through it, but he saw the giant rock slowly tumbling away. "Stop, Petro! Stabilize!"

Directional jets thundered in all directions and the *Linda Terry* came to a halt while the rock continued on. When it slammed into smaller rocks, they were knocked away like ragged, gray billiard balls.

The comm speakers came alive. "Talley ho, we've got it!" It was Valence the crowhopper captain. "It's knocking a big hole right through the horde. We're on its tail. Looks like a big asteroid."

"Show it to us when you can." It was a male voice, another crowhopper.

"Will do, Letticus," Valence said, "but give us a minute. We're having to dodge around to keep from being hit. The good news is that big thing's giving us a nice path through the horde."

"I'll report your success to Truvia, although she will not be pleased to have her rows and columns disturbed."

Crescent tugged at Crater's sleeve. "I knew a Trainer named Truvia! She's a lab rat, not a field Trainer. She studied me for over a month. She never told me why, but she seemed to be interested in the Phoenix Legionnaires."

"It sounds like she's in charge of this lash-up."

A worried look passed over Crescent's face.

"What?" Crater asked.

"All the Legionnaires I knew who went into her lab for study had the same opinion of Truvia."

"What was that?"

"That she is completely, utterly, irredeemably, batscrag crazy."

::: FORTY-ONE

W e're ready to try long-distance comm, Colonel," Riley said.

The Colonel had taken to one of the bunks in the aft section of the fuser, but at Riley's call he came instantly awake. He swung out of the bunk and followed Riley to the battle station console. The Colonel swung into the chair and strapped himself in. "L5 station, L5 station," the Colonel said into the mike. "This is the Medaris Enterprises fuser *Jan Davis*. How do you read me?"

It took several more calls before a woman answered. "*Jan Davis*, this is Station L5. Go ahead."

"This is Colonel John High Eagle Medaris. Who is this?"

There was a long pause before the woman replied. "My name is Truvia Collette Flaubert Serenia. Are you aboard the fuser approximately twelve thousand miles from L5 and closing?"

"I am. I would like to speak to my son."

"He is indisposed. What you have to say to him, you may say to me."

"You are a Trainer. I can tell by your accent."

"That is correct. I am one of the last of my kind, thanks to you."

"I must speak to Junior."

"Colonel, please turn your fuser around and go back to the moon. Junior has assumed control over Medaris Enterprises and will soon go to the moon to begin his leadership. We would prefer that you retire to your tubes in Moontown. If you do, no harm will come to you and you will be allowed to live out your days in peace."

"Live out my days in . . . See here, you stupid creature, I will blast you and your ilk from space before I retire anywhere. Now get me my son!"

Riley put her hand over the microphone. "Excuse me, Colonel. Maybe you'd best take it a little easy there."

"What is your purpose in coming here?" Truvia demanded. "Please be specific, or I will not hesitate to order your destruction."

The Colonel nodded to Riley and willed himself to calm down. "Sorry," he said into the microphone. "I don't like to be told what to do. An old habit from too many years in command."

"Turn around or you will die," Truvia calmly replied. "That is your choice."

"Truvia," the Colonel said, willing patience, "I need to talk to Junior. My fuser will therefore come on without deviation. If you destroy it, I will die and you and he will never hear what I have to say. If, however, you let me come, I assure you it will be in peace and it will be to your advantage."

"I don't believe you. Turn around, Colonel. Go home. Your day is past. If you continue, you will be attacked. Further talk between us is pointless. I am signing off."

"Wait! How about Maria? How is my granddaughter?"

"Still alive," Truvia responded. "And if you want to keep her that way, you'll turn around and go back to the moon."

"Let me talk to her."

Although there was no further response, the Colonel kept making demands and threats until Riley went up to the cockpit and switched off the transmitter. Then she pulled back to the battle station and told him what she'd done. "Your idea didn't work, Colonel. They're not going to let us in there without a fight."

The Colonel's eyes were a little wild. "Then we'll fight. Tiger's a good pilot. He can fly rings around the warpods. You take the kinetic cannon. I'll handle the missiles."

"Look, sir," Riley said. "That other fuser—I'm certain that's Crater. What we need to do is to keep the warpods distracted and let him make his bid to save Maria."

The Colonel glared at her. "No, Riley. That's not what we're going to do. We are going to blow up the station."

Riley was incredulous. "You're going to kill your own granddaughter when there's a chance to save her!"

The Colonel's mouth twitched. "Tiger, where's the other fuser?"

"I was just going to tell you about it, sir. It disappeared into the horde, and then a warpod showed up and went in after it."

"Are our missiles in range?"

"It would be a long-distance shot, but I might be able to get one out that far."

"If it pops up, lock on, shoot a salvo, and smash it!"

"You mean the warpod, right?"

"No, you fool. The fuser!"

"Ignore that order, Tiger," Riley snapped. She faced the

Colonel. "Sir, you are not going to smash that other fuser until we know who's in it."

That was when Riley felt the muzzle of a pistol jammed into her cheek. "Riley, if you say another word, I will blow your head off," the sheriff said. "Colonel, there's some extra belting in that cabinet there. I suggest you strap her to her chair. Tiger, do as the Colonel orders."

"Not until you tell me what this is all about," Tiger defiantly replied.

"Do you know the punishment for mutiny, Captain?" the Colonel asked as he gathered the straps. "Trust me. You won't like it."

With the sheriff's pistol stuck beneath her chin, Riley allowed herself to be strapped in. "Colonel, think this through," she begged. "You're a little sick. Don't you see that?"

The Colonel tore a strip from a towel and wrapped it around Riley's mouth while the sheriff went forward. "Do as the Colonel says. Get the missiles ready."

Tiger stared down the muzzle of the sheriff's pistol, then brought up the missile-arming screen. "Four missiles armed and ready," he said.

The Colonel came up to the cockpit and pointed at the pulsdar screen. Two glowing dots were evident. "What are those?"

"It's the fuser and the warpod," Tiger said. "They just popped up out of the horde."

"Lock on the fuser and launch your missiles," the Colonel demanded.

"But, sir, from this distance, it would take an hour for a missile to get there!"

"You have your orders, pilot Tramon."

When Tiger still hesitated, the sheriff jammed the pistol barrel into the pilot's temple. "Do it!"

Tiger called up the battle puter. "Launch missiles one through four at the target designated on the pulsdar. At my mark. Three-two-one-mark!"

The fuser shuddered as the missiles launched and began their long journey through space.

::: FORTY-TWO

The asteroid horde was not as Crater envisioned it. Rather than being a tight collection of rocks, he saw that the rocks were separated by hundreds, even thousands of yards. The big potato-shaped rock they'd launched cleared an even wider path as it barged through smaller asteroids, which started a chain reaction of rocks bumping into others. Before long the entire horde seemed to be rattling around.

The warpod kept following the Trojan asteroid with the *Linda Terry* tracking along behind. When he could, Petro kept the tumbling rocks of the horde between the *Linda* and the station, which was aggressively painting the area. The horde was also being painted by the other fuser.

"When should we take this warpod out?" Petro asked.

"As soon as it clears the horde," Crater said. "You'll need to make it quick and then hit the other warpods before they can react."

Crater felt the fuser lurch. "What's that?"

Petro studied the console display. "Our taxi was just detached."

"Crescent!" Crater pushed his head into the cupola and looked around until he saw the taxi slide from under the fuselage, its small directional jet spurting. "Get back here," he demanded.

"You and Petro fly the fuser," Crescent said. "I'll go rescue your precious Maria."

"Crescent," Petro said, "you told me to keep you from doing anything rash. This is rash."

Crescent's voice was calm. "Thank you, Petro, but I'm committed to saving Maria now, if she can be saved. I've put on my Phoenix armor. The crowhoppers on board the station will recognize it. I've got a better chance with them than Crater does. I've got my gillie with me too."

"She's right," Petro said to Crater. "She can pick her way through and get to the station, then who knows? They might let her aboard."

"She's risking her life for Maria," Crater said softly. "Amazing. Why would she do that?"

Petro looked at Crater in astonishment. "Crater, I love you, brother, but you are a true candidate for the loony bin. You know Crescent is in love with you. That's why she's doing this. It isn't for Maria. It's for you."

"You're right," Crater said, bitterly. "But it's still wrong for her to sacrifice herself for me."

I am in contact with the Awful Thing, the gillie said from Crater's shoulder. *All is well.*

Petro nodded. "Crescent's got the gillie with her. They have a chance. As for stopping her, forget it. That girl does something, she does it all the way."

"I wish I had told her what she means to me," Crater said, more to himself than Petro.

"What *does* she mean to you?" Petro demanded.

Crater didn't pause. "I would be lost without her."

Petro laughed harshly and shook his head. The brothers fell into silence and their own thoughts. A little less than an hour later, he said, "The warpod's in the clear."

"Smash it," Crater said.

Petro opened fire with the kinetic cannon. The impact of the heavy slugs traced across the back and the wings of the warpod, setting it on fire.

"Hang on," Petro said. He toggled the stick and the fuser surged ahead, pressing Crater into his seat as Petro swept the fuser past the smoking warpod.

"There are a couple more," Petro said and fired into the backs of two stationary warpods.

"We have to make certain they're inoperable," Crater said.

"Here we go," Petro answered and made another run across the warpods. Crater called up the tail guns and strafed them too.

A blip appeared on the pulsdar screen. "Missile locked on," Petro reported and took evasive action.

Crater glanced at the pulsdar. "The missile must be from a third warpod. It's about two hundred miles away."

"I'll show you why warpods are no match for a fuser," Petro said and turned away from the missile track, then slowed down.

"What are you doing? That thing will fly right up our pipes!"

Petro said nothing but let the *Linda* loaf along, a perfect target. When the missile got close, he nudged the throttle ahead. "Their missiles can't keep up with us. Now, watch this." Petro put the fuser into a loop. "Shoot it, Crater," he said as they flew near the top of the loop.

Crater opened up with the tail guns. "Missile destroyed," he reported.

Petro came out of the loop and pushed the throttle forward, flying down the track of the missile. Four more missiles were headed in their direction. Petro waited until they were close, then flew above them. When they started to turn around, Crater smashed them too. The warpod that had launched them began to turn but didn't get far before Petro unloaded the fuser's nose guns, tearing off a wing and ripping apart the fuselage. Bodies were strewn into space. "One more to go," Petro said.

"It's running for the station," Crater reported.

"I'm on it," Petro said, and pushed the throttle forward.

::: FORTY-THREE

Crescent, her gillie reporting on the battle between the *Linda Terry* and the warpods, grappled a small asteroid with the taxi's arms and zigzagged through the horde toward the station.

Her gillie spoke up. *The asteroid at thirty degrees to starboard is a good one to get behind. You should have a visual of the station from there.*

Crescent aimed for the asteroid, then stopped next to it. She eased the taxi forward until she could see the station. She also saw something remarkable. On the lower ring, there was someone outside in a pressure suit, and climbing out of the main hatch were three crowhoppers, identified by their black armor.

My former owner, the gillie said. *On the station, lower ring.*

Crescent's mouth dropped open. "That's Maria in the pressure suit?"

Yes. She is untethered. She should know better than that.

"Maybe she forgot it." Crescent, not believing her luck, drove the taxi forward. The crowhoppers were slowly working their way down the ladder of the central core of the station. "We've got to hit the bridge with this rock first. Aim me, Gillie."

Go five miles out. Suitable velocity of the asteroid must be attained for it to penetrate the bridge structure.

Crescent drove out five miles, then turned around. "Gillie, can you sync me with Maria's suit comm?"

Of course. I already did. You may speak to her at any time. But first yaw five degrees to starboard, pitch eight degrees down. Then full throttle until I tell you to release.

Crescent pushed the taxi's throttle forward. The station began to grow in size as she barreled down an invisible track.

Release, release, release!

Crescent released the big rock, then looped around to watch what happened. She just had a glimpse of startled faces in the viewports of the bridge before it struck. The bridge caved in at impact, its viewports shattered or popped out. The air inside rushed through them, the moisture inside turning into a gray sheet before disappearing.

As Crescent flew by, a body floated out of the bridge. It was wearing a coppery tunic. Then she saw another body in a black Legionnaire's uniform. By its gold stripes, she recognized it as an officer. She flew the taxi down the length of the station, passing the three crowhoppers who had stopped on the ladder and were gawking at her. She reached the lower ring and slid up next to Maria Medaris. "Hop aboard," she said. "The Lunar Rescue Company has arrived. Tips are appreciated."

::: FORTY-FOUR

etro flew the fuser across the carcasses of the three warpods while Crater studied the pulsdar. "The other warpod is still outside L5 but it's turned around. We'll smash it if it gets any closer." He peered at the screen. "Another missile's locked on us but it doesn't look real, more like an echo."

Petro took a look. "It's not a warpod missile. It's something else. A long way off."

"A software anomaly?"

Report from the Awful Thing. Crescent has Maria aboard the taxi.

Both Petro and Crater, after looking at one another in disbelief, erupted in cheers. "Way to go, Crescent!"

"Tell her we'll be along to pick her up in ten minutes," Petro told the gillie. "Crater, that missile, or whatever it is, is coming fast."

Crater shook his head. "Petro, it can't be real. Where would it be coming from? Let's grab Crescent and Maria and get out of here."

"It's real, Crater! Get back to the battle station and start jamming. Now!"

Petro punched the throttle on the fuser and rolled and looped her while Crater flew back to the battle station and began to search for the missile's signature. Finding none, he began to fire radio waves up and down the spectrum in an attempt to confuse it.

"I can't shake it!" Petro yelled. "It knows our defenses!"

"Helmets on!" Crater shouted back.

That was when missile struck the engine compartment and exploded, ripping the *Linda Terry* apart.

On the *Jan Davis*, Tiger made the call. "One of our missiles just hit the other fuser. Pulsdar indicates it is now in two pieces."

The Colonel looked at the screen and saw two glowing spots drifting apart. He began to tremble. "What have I done?"

Riley, released from her straps, floated up next to him and kicked him hard in the shins. "Indeed, what have you done, you foolish old man!"

::: FORTY-FIVE

Maria rode on the back of the taxi while Crescent worked to get inside the horde. Before it could reach the safety of the asteroids, a warpod streaked into L5. After firing a warning burst from its kinetic cannon, it blocked the taxi's way. The gillie transmitted the warpod's call. *Go back to the station.* It was a crowhopper's voice.

"I am Crescent of the Phoenix Legion," she said. "I have no quarrel with a fellow Legionnaire."

"Crescent of the Phoenix Legion," came the reply, "if such you are, we are honored. My name is Malevius. Our quarrel is not of our making but that of the Trainers. We observed your attack on the L5 station, and a very nice attack it was. You showed much fortitude and imagination. I wish we were on the same side, but alas, we are not. You will return with us to the station to see what is to be seen."

"And if I don't?"

"You will be blasted to atoms."

Crescent called Maria. "Maria, I don't know if you can hear the warpod, but they've ordered us back to the station."

"I heard," Maria answered ruefully. "Looks like they've got us cornered."

"I'm sorry. We thought we could save you."

"By 'we,' do you mean Crater Trueblood?" Maria's heart leaped. He had come for her!

"And Petro. We came in a fuser."

Maria couldn't believe what she was hearing. "How the heck did you acquire a fuser?"

"It is a good story, perhaps saved for a better day."

"If you are planning to escape by some wild maneuver," Malevius said, "be aware that I have a missile locked on you and you will not get far, just as the fuser that brought you here. Although they have all been disabled, one of our war-pods somehow blew that fuser up. It speaks to the gallantry of the Legion."

"Gillie," Crescent said, "is that true?"

There has been a major malfunction on the fuser Linda Terry.

"Back to the station!" Malevius growled. "I will not tell you again without grave consequences."

Fighting a tide of grief, Crescent steered the taxi back to the station. A crowhopper was outside, standing beside the main hatch. When he saw the taxi, he gestured for her to come closer. Crescent complied, and when the taxi got within arm's reach, Maria was pulled off. One glance at her tear-streaked face and Crescent knew she'd heard about the destruction of the fuser.

Another hand signal from the crowhopper sent Crescent to the docking station on the top ring. "Gillie, hide," she whispered after docking, and the gillie leaped from her shoulder and disappeared into the tubes and cables that ran along the taxi's ceiling.

As soon as the docking was completed, Crescent opened

the hatch and a crowhopper ordered her out. Warning klaxons were sounding inside the station, and there was dust and smoke in the air. The Legionnaire guarding her looked flustered.

"Shouldn't you be evacuating?" Crescent asked, appraising the damage.

"I am told to bring you to the lower ring," the Legionnaire said, his eyes darting toward a hammering noise overhead.

"What's that?"

"They're sealing off the bridge, thanks to you," he said. "A nice attack, by the way. I salute you. The entire bridge crew was killed, including Captain Letticus and the Trainer Carus. I see you are of the Phoenix Legion. I also salute you for that."

"I am the last member of the Phoenix warriors. We are not enemies but comrades. What is your name?"

"I am Camponitas, of the Seventh Legion. We are not enemies, it is true, but I have my orders from the Trainer Truvia to bring you to her."

"I know Truvia. She is insane."

Camponitas looked toward the bridge again when he heard the hissing of an arc welder. "That may be true. It does not matter."

"Dispose of her and I will save the rest of the Legionnaires aboard."

"How? The fuser you came in was destroyed."

Crescent fought past the anguish she felt at hearing that stark reality confirmed. Crater and Petro were dead and she was captured, but she would complete her mission if she could. "Help me convince Captain Malevius to take us aboard his warpod," she said.

Camponitas shook his head. "I must follow my orders. Go down that spoke toward the central core."

Crescent complied. Microgravity in the core required her to use handrails to pull herself along. At the central spoke, she saw Maria, a Legionnaire behind her. Maria was crying. "Crater and Petro are gone," she said.

"Crater loved you," Crescent said softly. "That's why we came for you."

Maria swiped tears from her face. "I loved him too. I was such a fool. I should have told him."

"That would have been appropriate," Crescent replied.

She looked closely at Crescent. "You loved him too."

It felt like a stiletto was tearing through Crescent's heart. She raised her chin. "That is true."

Both women were pushed along the central core and then directed into one of the spokes leading to the lower ring. Along the way, Crescent felt the pull of the centripetal force and grabbed hold of the ladder and swung her boots toward the new "down." Truvia was waiting for them at the bottom. At the sight of Crescent, her eyes turned bright.

"The only surviving member of the Phoenix Legion!" She wagged her finger in Crescent's face. "But you have turned treasonous."

Crescent knew her only hope was to pretend her loyalties still lay with the Legion. "Not treasonous, Trainer Truvia, merely following orders from those who paid for my services."

Truvia studied Crescent. "I suspect there is much more to your story. For instance, why are you alive?"

"I was captured. Forced to live among humans. Now I am back with you."

Truvia turned to Maria. "You have been crying. Why?"

Crescent answered for her. "The man she loved was just killed in the fuser."

"The fuser that brought you here?"

"Yes. I was ordered to destroy your bridge, and I did."

"And your mission was ... ?"

"To rescue the Medaris woman."

"You were under contract with the Colonel?"

"No. We were an independent operation."

"Ah. Crater Trueblood. Of course! He did come! And we killed him, just as I said we would."

Maria lunged at Truvia with an anguished cry, but the crowhopper guard flung her away, then stomped after her, picked her up, and brought her back.

Truvia was studying Crescent. "I sense something unusual about you. I wish to study you in the lab. You have no objection?"

When Crescent didn't answer, Truvia smiled. "Yes, there's something about you I *must* know." She glanced at Maria. "One last chance, Maria. Will you be our queen?"

Maria snarled, "Never!"

"Bring her along. I have an idea."

"Trainer Truvia," Camponitas said, "should we not be working to restore the station?"

Truvia turned toward Camponitas. "Our remaining warpod is docking with the station, and its cockpit will act as our temporary bridge. The central station puter was unharmed. We will be up and running normally within a few minutes. Does this satisfy your concerns, Camponitas?"

"I ask permission to kill myself for being impertinent, Trainer Truvia," Camponitas replied.

"Permission denied for the present," Truvia said. "But I may reconsider."

"Yes, Trainer Truvia."

::: FORTY-SIX

t's cold in here, brother," Petro said. Frost was forming on his helmet from his breath. He wiped at it with his gloved hand but was frustrated by the frost being on the inside.

"It would really be cold if those internal hatches hadn't held," Crater replied. "Or maybe we wouldn't have been cold at all. Does heaven have a temperature, I wonder?"

"Heaven is never anything I've worried about," Petro replied and then cocked his head at Crater. "You go off on strange tangents at times."

Crater shrugged. "Well, it's not much of a tangent to think about heaven since we seem to be so close to seeing it."

"Or the other place," Petro agreed without agreeing.

"You need to dial up your helmet vent," Crater said, then reached over and did it for him.

Petro breathed in and out a couple of times. The helmet cleared and stayed clear. "Thanks. So what do we do next? Breathe down our air while singing hymns?"

Crater grimly smiled. "A hymn might help, but we probably need to first figure a way out of this situation and continue our rescue."

Petro laughed. "Well if that isn't typical Crater Trueblood. Figure a way out of this situation and continue. Haw! In case you haven't noticed, brother, we are scragged, bagged, and tagged. Our fuser is mortally wounded, we have neither internal air or pressure in the truncated section we find ourselves floating through space in, we don't have a taxi for a lifeboat, and we don't have communications, not that it would help, seeing as how there's not a friendly ear to listen within ninety thousand miles."

"Crescent's still out there in the taxi."

"Doubtful. How could she escape?"

"And another fuser is flying toward L5."

"I think the missile that hit us came from that fuser, so I don't think it's going to be any help."

Crater couldn't explain his optimism to Petro, but he felt it all the same. He was certain that sacrifice to a good cause was never in vain. All he needed to do was calculate the situation and figure out a course of action. The biolastic suits, backpacks, and helmets would last two days without recharging. That was good. They were inside a powerless hulk adrift along the rim of L5. That was bad. His conclusion was inevitable. "We'll call for help," he said.

"Are you kidding? Who around here would help us?"

"Maybe the L5 station would like to take us prisoners. For all we know, Crescent and Maria are prisoners too. Better to be a live prisoner with some chance to complete our mission than dead. Gillie, give a call out to all stations."

When the gillie didn't reply, he saw that it wasn't on his shoulder or in his pocket. He began to search for it. When he found the gillie, adrift near the aft bulkhead, he saw it had a shard of litesteel through it. "Are you dead?" he asked.

Sick, it replied. *Regenerating. Remove the litesteel. Thank you.*

Crater pulled the litesteel shard from the mass of slime mold and then put the gillie in his pocket. "Get well, little buddy."

"No gillie? We are well and truly scragged this time," Petro said, shaking his head.

Crater thought some more. "We can communicate with our do4us. They normally don't have much range, but if we route them through the external antenna, someone might hear us."

"Might work. I never worked on the comm cabling before. It's somewhere in here, I guess," Petro said, touching the silent, dark console.

Crater flew back to the supply cabin where he selected a tool kit, then flew back to the cockpit and got to work. An hour later, he plugged his do4u into the ship's comm circuit. "Confirm external antenna," he said.

External antenna connected, the do4u said in the voice Crater had selected years ago.

"Whose voice is that?" Petro asked.

Crater blushed. "Maria's."

Petro chuckled. "You're sick, Crater, truly sick."

Crater dialed up the frequencies that warpods typically used because he thought the L5 station probably used them too. "Any station, any station. This is a mayday from the fuser *Linda Terry*. I say again this is a mayday from the fuser *Linda Terry*. We are disabled and adrift. Standing by for your response."

After Crater repeated the message several times, he said, "I'll repeat it every ten minutes until my do4u battery dies. Then we'll use yours."

A voice crackled from Crater's do4u. "*Linda Terry*, we need help too!"

Crater and Petro looked at each other in astonishment. "This is the *Linda Terry*. Who's this?"

"I am Captain Valence of warpod 6982. We are adrift. My crew is dying. We were attacked with kinetic weapons."

"I know. We're the ship that attacked you. What kind of damage did you sustain?"

"We lost our engines and environmental systems. How about you?"

"A missile hit us and we broke into two pieces. Listen, what have you done to restart your engines?"

"Everything we can think of. There doesn't seem to be anything we can do."

"Do you know your position?"

"Yes. We've called for help but no response. We heard the station bridge was struck by a female warrior of the Phoenix Legion. She has been captured."

"Has anybody on the station said they would come out and save you?"

"No. I suppose they've decided since we lost, why rescue us?"

"How about if you rescued yourself?"

"With what?"

"Your cold nitrogen control system."

"That system is for stability control and orientation."

"It can also be used to move along a trajectory. It'll be slow, but you can still move."

"Where would we move?"

"Over to us."

"Why would we do that?"

"Because I can fix your engines."

::: FORTY-SEVEN

This is where Truvia fixes broken bones," Maria said as she and Crescent were shoved into the transformation lab. "Of course, first she orders them broken."

"Maria, I must reiterate that you have been most unhelpful from the moment you joined us." Truvia clucked. "And I really had such high hopes for you."

Maria resisted the urge to spit in the Trainer's face. "Sorry to spoil your plans."

"They're hardly spoiled. Nearly everything I've wanted will yet occur. Realistically, there's no one who can stop what I've begun."

Maria turned a verbal knife. "How about the fellow who gave you that shiner? Let me guess. You walked into a cabinet? Or maybe my father's fist?"

"He didn't mean it," Truvia said, touching her eye. "He's lately been under a lot of pressure."

Maria hooted. "Spoken like every woman who's enabled a woman beater. But why are we getting this guided tour? Shouldn't you be out enjoying the destruction of the Earth or something? Oh, yeah. Crescent knocked out your bridge, so you can't see it so well."

"Not to worry. We will soon have another functioning bridge. But while that's being accomplished, I really would love to study Crescent. She is both the last of her kind and the only of her kind. Crescent, this is a direct order from a Trainer. Remove your clothes and climb on that table."

When Crescent didn't comply, her arms were taken by the two crowhopper guards, and piece by piece her armor and biolastic suit were removed. Truvia tossed her a smock. "Put this on and lie down on the table."

Crescent tilted her chin defiantly. "Go jump in a pile of scrag."

At Truvia's nod, the guards grabbed Crescent and held her while Truvia dressed her in the smock. She was then forced on the table and strapped down.

Truvia made a rectangle in the air and a blue screen appeared. She tapped on it and the table with Crescent began to move inside the instrument. An outline of Crescent's body appeared with all of her internal organs revealed. Something else was revealed that was so evident even Maria gasped.

"A baby!" Truvia cocked her head toward Crescent. "But who's the father? Male crowhoppers are sterile."

"A human donor," Crescent said quickly. "I don't know his name."

"Really? Let's run a genealogical test."

Truvia sat down at a puter, her fingers flying across the keyboard. Within seconds, the results came on screen. "The DNA mitochondrial test of the fetus shows your Siberian heritage, of course, but the father"—her fingers tapped more keys—"the father is a bit of a mongrel. Interesting. I see indicators of Northern European subgroup, Southeastern European subgroup, South Asian subgroup—that would be from the Indian subcontinent—Western African and—a very interesting haplogroup—American native, specifically of the Cherokee tribe."

At the mention of the Cherokee connection, Maria raised her eyebrows. Truvia took notice. "Someone you know, Maria?" She tapped the keys, and the table holding Crescent slid back from the instrument.

"He doesn't know," Crescent whispered, looking at Maria. "When he broke his leg, my doctor gathered from him what was needed."

Truvia smiled. "Crater Trueblood? The audacious fellow I keep hearing about? Too bad he's dead." She turned to Maria. "But I think I see it all now. The eternal triangle! Crater loved you. Crescent loved Crater. And you… well, you loved yourself."

The puter sounded a tone. Truvia studied the screen. "Do you know why you were in the Phoenix Legion, Crescent? No? Well, it wasn't because of what you thought. You don't have the Phoenix gene. You were an experiment in another way. We wanted females with easy eggs to harvest. Otherwise we had to either hunt human females down or buy them and take their eggs. It was a nasty and very expensive business."

Truvia walked up to the table where Crescent was strapped. "Is this not good news? You're not going to die because of the Phoenix gene. Maybe from something else, but not that!"

Crescent looked in disbelief at Truvia even as she tried to understand the implications of the Trainer's revelation. "Why did you allow me to think I was going to die young?"

Truvia shrugged. "The entire Phoenix Legion was under my scientific study. It was convenient to put you there. What you knew or didn't know wasn't part of my research."

"You are more evil than I could possibly imagine," Crescent hissed.

"Am I? But I want only your happiness." She touched Crescent's face, then looked into her eyes. "Why didn't Crater love you instead of Maria? Of course, we both know the answer to that. Men are shallow creatures, aren't they? He couldn't see your inner beauty."

Crescent said nothing, but the ache inside her heart was a painful reminder of the truth of the Trainer's words.

"But I can fix that for you, Crescent," Truvia went on. "I have Maria's form in the 3DCP. In eight hours, I can change you to look and sound like her, and no one will be able to tell the difference. Do you want this?"

Crescent took a deep breath, then looked up at the ceiling where something caught her eye. Quickly, so it wouldn't be noticed, she turned her head toward Maria. "What about her?" she asked.

"We'll flush her into the station waste receptacle and expel her and the rest of the garbage into space."

"And my baby?"

"It would be destroyed in the process of restructuring you, but you could have another. Men would be lining up to mate with you if you looked like Maria. Shall we get started?"

Crescent worked her lips into a greedy smile. "Don't kill her yet. I want her to see me. I will make a much better Maria Medaris than she ever could."

"Did I mention that we were going to make her our queen? This is so perfect. Now *you* can be our queen!"

"I will be pleased to be your queen," Crescent replied gracefully.

Truvia turned on the 3DCP puter. "It will take about an hour to load in Maria's data. Be patient."

"Do you mind if I use for one last time the body design you gave me?" Crescent asked. "I'd like to show Dr. Medaris some of the fighting moves you Trainers taught me."

"Ah, revenge. It is something I understand. Just as long as you don't get hurt. That would slow the program down."

"Oh, I won't get hurt."

Truvia unstrapped Crescent and then stepped back. Crescent walked across the room and slammed her fist into Maria's stomach. Maria doubled over, choking, and then Crescent pounded her in the back with both fists. Maria sprawled onto the deck.

Truvia clapped her hands. "Oh, well done," she said, just as a bolt of blue lightning arced from the ceiling into her head. Her eyes turned into green saucers, smoke escaped from her mouth and ears, and she slumped down.

Crescent helped Maria up. "Sorry, I needed to create a distraction while the gillie moved into position."

"I can take it," Maria replied. She looked up at the ceiling and spied the gray blob stuck there. "Is that my gillie?"

"It's mine now," Crescent said. She turned to the guards, who seemed paralyzed at the sight of their Trainer lying on the floor, smoke still coming from her head. "You know who I am. Whether I have the gene or not, I am from the Phoenix Legion. I require your loyalty."

The guards looked at one another and shrugged. "Sounds good," one of them said, and the others nodded their agreement.

::: FORTY-EIGHT

Crater and Petro stood at the hatch and looked across to the wing of the warpod, which had bumped against their fuser remnant. "Well, brother," Petro said, "we're going to have to cross over to that wing and hang on, but it looks pretty smooth. What happens if we bounce right off and sail into space? Think they'll come after us?"

"Maybe not you, but I think they might come after me. After all, I told them I could fix their engines." Crater elbowed Petro playfully in the ribs.

Petro remained serious. "And can you fix them?"

"I don't know, but I'll give it a shot. You see the engine nacelles? Aim for those."

Petro judged the distance, then said, "You first."

Crater shrugged and launched himself, his flight carrying him to the nacelle cover of the port engine exhaust. He grabbed it and held on. "Your turn," he said to Petro. "Come on, you can do it."

Despite his many weeks in space, Petro discovered standing outside on the skin of the fuser remnant frightened him. It was like being on the top of a mountain with nothing between him and an endless drop. His knees knocking, his hands trembling, he launched.

He nearly missed because he aimed too high. Crater caught him by the boot. "Got you, brother," he said, and pulled him in.

A bay door on the warpod opened and a crowhopper reached up and grabbed their legs and pulled them both inside. "If our salvation is in the hands of you two," he said, "I think we should go ahead and invoke our suicide pact."

Another crowhopper was at an airlock at the front end of the bay and gathered them in. "Pressurize," he said as he pulled the hatch shut behind him. Fifteen minutes later, with their helmets off, Crater and Petro were pushed onto the warpod bridge where four more crowhoppers waited for them. "I am Captain Valence," one of them said. He was a crowhopper with a vivid scar across his forehead.

"Crater Trueblood," Crater said.

"Petro Mountbatten-Jones," Petro said.

Valence frowned. "I must tell you the opinion of my crew is I should have left you in your fuser. For us, the honorable thing that remains is to commit suicide. In fact, it's in our contract that we should kill ourselves if we find ourselves either prisoners unable to escape or in a hopeless situation."

"Captain Valence," Crater said firmly, "this isn't a hopeless situation at all. After I fix one of your engines, you'll be able to go anywhere you like."

Valence seemed unconvinced. "By contract we shouldn't go anywhere. By contract we should die."

"What's a contract?" Petro said. "Just words and signatures. Things sometimes change that aren't covered by any contract. Life! Death! The pursuit of happiness!"

Valence stared at Petro. "Is he deranged?"

"A little. But listen, just give me a chance at your engines."

"Captain Valence," one of the crowhoppers said, "sir, with all due respect and whatnot, we should commit suicide."

Valence pondered the earnest crewman, then said, "You go ahead and kill yourself, Agate. I will stay alive to see if we can get this ship running again. If we do, we can fulfill the other part of our contract, protecting the station. There's another fuser out there that should be arriving soon."

"While Crater is futzing with the engine," Petro said, "how about I take a look at your contract? Maybe I can spot a loophole."

"Be my guest," Valence said. "Agate? You're our sea lawyer, so put off your suicide for now. Show this human what we agreed to do as honorable mercenaries."

Crater said, "I'll need some tools and someone to help me open up the engine hatches."

"This is a warship, not a maintenance tug," Valence replied. The point made, he nodded to a crowhopper who, if Crater could read crowhopper expressions correctly, was frightened. "Newberry, you are not much of a warrior, but I think you have some mechanical skills. Go with this enemy, obey him as if he were me."

Newberry knuckled his forehead. "At once, sir."

Valence shook his head. "How I got stuck with Newberry, I'll never know. Go ahead, Crater. Take him and good luck. Maybe you can make a man out of him. Oh, and when or if you decide the engine cannot be repaired, let me know instantly so we can kill ourselves. Don't wait too long."

"I'll do my best, Captain," Crater said, then waved the crowhopper Newberry to follow him.

::: FORTY-NINE

The *Jan Davis* fused on through space. Tiger had a warpod on the pulsdar. "It just released a spread of six missiles at us. I can smash it anytime you say, Colonel."

Riley looked hard at the Colonel, who was sitting in one of the jumpseats. When all she saw were vacant eyes staring back at her, she said, "I think the Colonel is out of commission, Tiger. Evade the missiles, then take out the warpod."

"Roger that," Tiger said. He pushed the throttles forward, flying straight at the incoming missiles. Three miles away, he pulled the fuser up, flying over the missiles, which turned with him to follow.

"There it is," Riley said, pointing at a shadow on the pulsdar that represented the attacking warpod.

Tiger swept the fuser along, the missiles continuing to follow him, then poured on the coal, flashing over the warpod. The pulsdar lit up as one of the warpod's own missiles struck it. Then a second, third, and fourth hit it. There was nothing much left for the fifth and sixth missiles to blow up. "They're smashed," Tiger said.

"Colonel, we took out the warpod," Riley said to no reply.

"I've seen him like this before," the sheriff said. "He'll snap out of it."

"Was he like this when he decided to put the horde in L5?"

The sheriff put his hand on the Colonel's armrest and pulled himself down to face the great man. "Come on, Colonel, pull yourself together. We need you."

The Colonel kept staring ahead except for an occasional blink.

"A warpod has docked with the station," Tiger said, observing the pulsdar.

"The Colonel may be indisposed," the sheriff said, "but his orders stand. Smash the station."

"We're *not* going to smash the station," Riley retorted. "If we can, we're going to rescue Maria."

"Hold on," Tiger said. "Our pulsdar is picking up something big between the moon and the Earth."

Riley looked at the pulsdar and was surprised by the size of the echo. She moved a cursor over it. "Puter, calculate velocity and course of the target," Riley said.

The puter replied, *Target is accelerating. It will strike the Earth in eighteen hours.*

"How big is it?"

One point two miles in diameter.

Riley and Tiger exchanged shocked glances. "How do we stop that thing?" Riley asked.

"Nothing can stop it," Tiger replied. "Maybe it could be deflected."

"With what?" When Tiger had no answer, Riley said, "We need to alert Earth."

"We can't reach Earth through our jerry-rigged apparatus," Tiger replied.

Riley thought for a moment, then said, "The station can call Earth. Let's go there."

Tiger plotted a course for the station and pushed the throttle forward. "We'll be at the station in an hour," he said.

::: FIFTY

Crescent and Maria, with a phalanx of crowhoppers piling in behind them, burst onto the warpod bridge. One of the crowhoppers flung Truvia down. "The Trainers are dead," Crescent said to the warpod captain. "The station is now under my command. Give me your name."

The warpod captain looked at the rifles leveled at him and Truvia's body and came to attention. "My name is Captain Philippe. Command me."

"Give me a situation report."

"My warpod is acting as a temporary bridge. Its puter is keeping track of the asteroid." He gestured toward a viewscreen. "There you may see the view camera attached to it."

"What asteroid?" Crescent asked while intently staring at the viewscreen.

Captain Philippe tugged at the neck opening in his armor. "I thought you were aware of it. Many apologies. Its number is CS2241, an unexciting nomenclature for a rock that is one point two miles wide."

"What is its destination?" Crescent demanded.

"Why, Earth, my lady," Philippe responded. "It will arrive in about eighteen hours."

"Warn Earth," Crescent commanded. "Now!"

"Yes, of course. But who should I call?"

"Call Medaris Enterprises in Armstrong City," Maria said. "Tell them to contact our family on Earth. If anything can be done, they will know what to do."

"But Medaris Enterprises now belongs to your father," Philippe said. "Will they do as they're told?"

Maria beckoned to one of the crowhoppers. "You! What's your name?"

The crowhopper came to attention. "Tristan, madam."

"Tristan, get my father."

Within a few minutes, her father appeared on the bridge with Tristan the crowhopper pushing him. At the sight of Maria, her father's face lit up. "Maria, you're alive! Who is this? Is it a female crowhopper? And what happened to the bridge? I'm so confused."

"What are you on, Junior?" Maria tiredly asked. "Take him back, Tristan. He's worthless." She turned to Captain Philippe. "Call the company in Armstrong City. Ask for a Miss Torricelli."

When the call went through, Maria said, "Teresa, this is Maria. Do you recognize my voice?"

"Yes, Dr. Medaris. It's good to hear it too. We're a little confused. Your grandfather retired and your father is now the president of the company."

"No, he isn't. I'm assuming control. Now listen carefully. This is going to be hard to explain . . ."

::: FIFTY-ONE

rater held up his hand through the hatch. "Give me a spanner wrench, Newberry."

The crowhopper handed over the tool, then said, "What have you found, sir?"

"This engine is in good shape. It was the cross feed to the other engine that shut it down. All I've got to do is seal off this tankage line and... There, got it. Call the bridge and ask them to run up the pressure in the primary feed lines."

Newberry made the call. "Run up the pressure in the primary feed lines. What? Of course, now!" He waited for confirmation, then said, "They're doing it now, sir."

"Hold it!" Crater yelled. "We've got a bad leak here."

Newberry made the call again. "Crater said to stop the line pump," he said.

Valence's voice crackled over Newberry's radio. "Hasn't he given up?"

"Not yet, sir."

"I figure we've only got about six hours of stale air left. Tell him I'll give him three hours and then we're all going to kill ourselves as provided for in our contract."

Crater popped his head through the hatch. "Tell Valence to kill himself first to see what it's like, then report back to the rest of us."

Newberry worked his gray face into a grin. "I don't dare tell him that, sir."

Crater chuckled. "It was a joke, Newberry."

"We don't tell jokes in the Legion."

"Really? Well, I'll teach you some later. Everything looks good for this one engine except for a propellant line that's got a crack in it. I could replace the line, but it would take me too long. You wouldn't happen to have some duct tape on you, would you?"

"Not sure what that is, sir."

"It's kind of a gray color and you use it to wrap around pipes to stop leaks."

Newberry frowned. "I wonder if you mean pipe tape, sir. It matches your description. Here, I have a small roll of it in my kit."

Crater snatched the tape. "That's it! Well, Newberry, I need about two big rolls of it, all right?"

"Why, yes, sir. Just give me a few minutes."

When Newberry returned, he was pushing a box before him. Crater tore it open. "Jackpot! Perfect." Taking two rolls of tape, he disappeared through the hatch and before long poked his head up. "Call Captain Valence. Let's have another pressure test."

The response to Newberry's call was not encouraging. "We are not going to run any kind of test. It's time to go out as heroes."

Crater crawled out. "Give me that radio, Newberry. Thank you. Captain Valence, this is Crater. Look, I think I've solved the problem, but I need a pressure test on the propellant lines to engine number two."

Valence grunted and growled. "All right, but this is for the last time. Pressure test underway."

After a few minutes, Crater said, "The lines are holding."

With Newberry close behind, Crater went hand over hand to the cockpit. Arriving, he said to Valence, "Fire up engine number two."

"It will probably blow up," Valence replied.

"Only one way to find out, Captain."

Captain Valence shrugged, then signaled to a helmsman who made the necessary inputs on the engine puters. This was followed by the whine of an auxiliary power unit and then the blistering roar of an engine. Valence ran it for ten seconds, then waved at the helmsman to shut it down.

Valence turned to Crater. "I suppose you want a medal."

"No, Captain, I want you to switch sides."

"Impossible."

"No, it isn't," Petro said, shoving a workpad at the Captain. "Here's your loophole, sir. Section three, paragraph one bravo. Read it and cheer, fellows. It says, 'the company'— that's you guys—'will respond to the will and commands of the contractor'—that would be the creeps on the station— 'as long as the contractor maintains a viable command and control. If the C&C is lost due to enemy action or any other reason, including negligence, commanders of fleet vehicles shall make reasonable inquiry as to the status of the contractor and the time frame in which the C&C will be reestablished. If the contractor does not respond within a reasonable period of time, commanders are authorized to remove themselves from the field of battle and declare an independent status until the company headquarters provides them with direction.'"

Petro slapped the pad shut. "What do you think about that?"

"I think it's words stacked on words," Valence said. "And I don't know what it means."

"It means if you don't hear anything from those creeps at the station, you're authorized to go rogue."

"Go rogue? I don't know that phrase."

"It means," Crater said patiently, "you're authorized to do whatever you darn well please."

"In that case, I will take all of us and find a safe place."

"I've got a better idea," Crater replied. "Sign a contract with us."

Valence's heavy brow lifted. "You mean for money?"

"For money, yes."

"I've never had any money. The Trainers always got the money."

"Now's the time to start. Being a capitalist is fun."

"How do I know you will pay me?"

"Wait a second," Petro said. He reached into his coveralls and drew out a small bag and handed it to Valence. "Gold coins are in there. That ought to cover it."

Valence opened the bag and inspected the contents. "Is that real gold?"

"Run it through a spectrometer and you'll find it's almost one hundred percent pure," Crater said while looking askance at Petro.

Petro's grin was weak. "If I hadn't brought it with me, you would have left it behind."

"Gold coins weren't on the top of my list of survival gear."

"Well, clearly they should have been!"

"Were you planning on keeping them for yourself?"

"Brother, you just don't understand me, do you?"

"All too well."

Valence, seeing the brothers had finished bickering, tucked the gold in a hidden pocket beneath his armor and pointed out the obvious. "I could just kill you and keep this."

"I put a timer on your environmental system. If I'm not around, a valve will close and you'll suffocate. Gold is hard to breathe."

Valence laughed. "You are a worthy opponent."

"I'm an even better friend."

Valence came to attention and saluted with his big gloved hand. "What are our orders, my admiral?"

::: FIFTY-TWO

The *Jan Davis* slid next to the station. "L5 station," Riley called, using her do4u. "This is the fuser *Jan Davis*. Request permission to come aboard."

"State your purpose."

Riley's mouth dropped open before it turned into a grin. "I think that's Maria!"

"State your purpose."

"Our purpose is to rescue you! This is Riley. The Colonel is aboard and the sheriff. Also pilot Tiger Tramon!"

Another voice answered, this one rough but feminine. "This is Crescent Claudine Besette of the Lunar Rescue Company. I am in command of this station. Use the auxiliary airlock on the lower ring."

Tiger began to maneuver. Riley looked behind her and saw the Colonel pawing at his seat belt. "She's alive! Maria's alive!" he yelled at the top of his lungs.

The sheriff helped the Colonel unbuckle. "Calm down, sir. Let me help you. There, now you're free, but hold on. You'll see Maria soon enough."

As soon as the fuser was docked and the hatches opened. Maria came sailing inside. She went straight to the Colonel and hugged him. When she pushed herself back, she saw how haggard and confused he looked. "Grandfather, what's wrong?"

"I've been sick, Maria. Very sick." He pointed at the station. "That's why *this* exists and the horde too." He shook his head. "I will be punished. So will Junior. The company will also suffer."

"Oh, Grandfather, we have a bigger problem than that. An asteroid a mile wide is on a direct intercept with the Earth! I called Miss Torricelli to alert the family so they can call somebody on Earth who might do something."

The Colonel absorbed Maria's words, then said, "Those idiots on Earth couldn't organize a scrap drive. They'll all be at each other's throats, and they won't get it together in time. We'll have to do what we can from here."

"But what can we do?"

Crescent climbed aboard. "You could catch it on this fuser," she said, "but to deflect an asteroid that size, you'd need nuclear warheads. Do you have any?"

"Conventional only," Riley said, raising her eyebrows when Maria took note of her old rival for Crater.

"Why are you here?" Maria demanded.

Riley grinned. "Your grandpa hired me for a bucket of money, honey."

"My lady," Captain Philippe called, "there's a warpod requesting permission to dock. I've had to tell them there's no docking station open. How do you want to handle it?"

"Who is it?" Crescent asked.

"I'll patch them in."

"L5 station, requesting permission to come closer."

Maria recognized the voice. "Crater Trueblood!" she exploded, her heart slamming against her chest. "Is it really you?"

"Maria! Is that you?"

"It's me! It's me!" Tears of joy shimmered in globules beneath her eyes. A flick of her eyelashes shredded them.

"Did Crescent save you?"

"I did, boss!" Crescent hooted, blinking her own tears away. The crowhoppers all glanced at each other uneasily as the tears floated through the cabin.

"Crescent was magnificent. But listen, Crater, we've got a little problem. It turns out there's a mile-wide asteroid heading for Earth. It just went past the moon. About twelve hours away from impact."

Crater was silent for a moment, then said, "I'll have to think about that."

"While you're thinking, I'm going to say something to you right now, and I don't care who hears it." She glanced defiantly at Riley, who shrugged. Captain Philippe had taken Crescent aside for a conversation and moved out of earshot. "I've had a lot of time to think, Crater," Maria said with quiet determination, "and during that time the one thing I was always absolutely sure about was this: I love you. You may not love me back, not now, and I understand that, but I love you more than life itself even if you're going to be the father of someone else's baby."

"Someone else's baby? Maria, what are you talking about?"

Maria was giddy and knew she was close to babbling. Yes, the world was going to be destroyed and her beloved grandfather was addled and her father was a miserable worm, and yes, she'd been rescued by a woman who was having the baby of the man she'd finally figured out she loved.

All those things were true. Yet somehow, inexplicably, Maria Medaris had never been happier.

::: FIFTY-THREE

rater was waiting at the airlock. The sheriff and the Colonel emerged first. The sheriff frowned and said nothing, then took the Colonel by the arm. "Where's the infirmary?" he demanded.

Newberry the crowhopper was with Crater. "Newberry, take these two along, please," Crater said, and the crowhopper did.

Maria was the next one through the airlock. She flung herself into Crater's arms and kissed him full on the lips. For a moment, nothing else mattered except the knowledge that they loved each other and the importance of their embrace. Reluctantly Maria broke the kiss and looked into his blue-gray eyes. "I wish I could kiss you forever," she whispered.

"So do I," Crater fervently replied, his voice husky. This felt like a dream. The woman he loved was not only alive but loved him back. His head was spinning. "What did you mean about the baby?"

"Crescent is having your baby." Saying the words out loud sobered the high Maria felt from Crater's kiss.

Crater was dumbfounded. "*What?*"

Maria instantly regretted her loose tongue, and didn't know what to say. "I . . . I know it wasn't your doing."

Crater looked around. "Where is she? I should talk to her."

"She's in command of this station and plenty busy. There will be time later for her to explain."

Crater's mind was reeling with the news of the baby, but he fought for focus. Whatever madness had occurred without him knowing it, he'd have to sort out later. He reached in his pocket and handed Maria the gillie. "It was stabbed by a shard of litesteel," he explained. "I think it will be OK, but it needs a warm, dark place."

"I'll take care of it. My gillie—I mean Crescent's gillie—is also sick. It killed the Trainer who was running things here and used up its stored energy doing it. Don't worry. I'll have both gillies on the mend."

Crater kissed Maria again. "Save the Earth."

Crater crossed over to the cockpit of the *Jan Davis* where he found Riley and Tiger. "Riley? What are you doing here?"

"Money can take a girl to the far reaches, Crater, m'boy. This here is Tiger Tramon, a fine fuser pilot if ever there was one."

Crater smiled and turned toward the pilot. "Hello, Tiger. Is your fuser in good shape?"

"Well enough. What do you have in mind?"

"I think we can catch that asteroid, but we'll need a big explosion to deflect its course. What do you have?"

"Conventional warheads only," Tiger replied.

"I thought that was likely the case," Crater replied. "We'll need nukes to move that big rock but, fortunately, the aft remnant of our smashed fuser contains nuclear-tipped missiles. It won't be easy, but I think we can get inside and bring them out."

"How many nukes are needed?" Riley asked.

Crater turned toward her. "I have to be honest. There are too many variables to be absolutely certain. We'll just have to guess and hope we're in the ballpark. If Petro agrees to it, he and I will do the walk to retrieve the missiles. You'll drive us over there. After that everybody gets off except me and my brother. Petro will fly it. I'll rig the nukes."

Tiger was dubious. "I would prefer to fly this fuser. I know her better than anyone."

"This is not up for discussion," Crater replied. He'd already risked too many lives. He was only sorry he still had to risk Petro's . . . and his own, especially now that he had so much to live for. *A baby?* Crescent's and his baby? Had he actually heard that or was he losing his marbles? He supposed at this point it didn't matter. Marbles or not, it was up to him to save Earth.

Within a few minutes, Crater and Petro had gathered their gear and rejoined Tiger and Riley in the fuser. "Stow your kit over there, gents," Riley said.

"How did a smart girl like you get mixed up in this craziness, Riley?" Crater asked. "It has to be more than money."

Riley grinned. "For the adventure, of course!"

Tiger laughed. "Adventure is right! This pert lass did the impossible. She drove a jumpcar into orbit!"

"'Tis not the time for stories," Riley replied. "Off ye go to the jumpseats, Crater and Petro." She somersaulted into the copilot's chair. "Ready to detach from the auxiliary airlock, Tiger."

"Make us go, Riley."

The fuser detached, its cold jets spurting. As soon as it was clear, Tiger throttled up the fuser. Within five minutes it was next to the remnant of the *Linda Terry*. Riley whistled. "Now, ain't she a sight! You're lucky those nukes didn't go off!"

"They're safe, although the conventional explosives in them might have exploded," Crater acknowledged. "That would have been ugly. Guess we were lucky."

"Or blessed," Riley said, crossing herself.

Crater and Petro climbed into their suits. "We'll shove the racks out," Crater explained. "Then use the fuser's robotic arm to move them to the cargo hatch."

Crater and Petro went down to the cargo hatch of the fuser and opened it. It was a huge door and faced deep space. "Well, here we go again," Petro said. "Taking a step into the abyss."

"Aw, come on, Petro," Crater joshed. "Do you want to live forever?"

"I want to, but I guess if I keep hanging around you, I won't make thirty."

Crater grinned but replied seriously. "See that old world down there? There's a lot of people who'd like to live a little longer too."

Petro took the step. Crater was right behind him.

Once aboard the wrecked fuser, they climbed through a rip in its skin, then turned on their helmet lights to see inside the gloomy interior. Going hand over hand along exposed cables, they reached the racks of nuclear-tipped missiles. "Now what?" Petro asked.

"We move them into the firing slots. The sprockets that move them have a catch that releases them. See it?"

"Yeah. Looks like that could pinch your fingers if you're not careful."

Crater laughed. "Pinching our fingers around nuclear-tipped missiles on a derelict fuser is probably the least of our worries."

Petro returned the laugh. "I'm glad you're my brother," he said. "Life would sure be dull without you."

"Brothers forever," Crater said. "Now let's move these big things and save the Earth."

::: FIFTY-FOUR

When the *Jan Davis* returned to the L5 station, Crater headed to the warpod bridge to see Crescent. There were only a few minutes before he would have to leave and there were a few things he needed to say. "You heard about the child?" she asked as he floated up beside her.

"Yes, and I don't know what to say to you, Crescent. You shouldn't have done it, whatever you did. You know that, don't you?"

Crescent couldn't look him in the eye. "I'm ashamed for what I did." She touched her belly. "But I will never be ashamed of this child."

Crater's heart went out to her. "Is it all right? I heard what Truvia did to you . . ."

"The baby is unharmed."

"Look, if I had more time, I guess I'd yell at you and do my best to make you feel bad about the whole thing, but I don't. I've got to get going. Just know this. I'll take care of the baby, and I'll take care of you."

"That won't be necessary" Crescent replied defiantly. "You need not ever acknowledge the child in any way. She's a girl, by the way. Absalom knows about her. We will raise her as our own."

Crater was quiet for a moment, then said, "I'm glad you didn't get transformed into another Maria. One is enough for this universe. Anyway, I like you just the way you are."

"You are being excessively kind," Crescent said. "It is all right to hate me. I deserve it."

"No, you don't!" Crater swore. "I'm the one who deserves to be hated. Deep in my heart, I always knew you loved me, yet I let you go on without hope. I'm sorry, Crescent. The truth is"— he squared his shoulders—"I would be lost without you."

Crescent looked up into his eyes. "I heard Maria tell you that she loved you," she said quietly. "I think this time, for a change, she meant it."

Crescent's words snapped a portion of Crater's heart back to reality. "She and I have a lot to talk about," he said as much to himself as Crescent. "I'm not sure we can get there from here."

"Don't let your pride get in the way, Crater. That bank account she opened for you should tell you her real feelings for you. Maria's not the type who'd let a johncredit slip through her fingers unless she was in love with the fellow who was getting it."

Crater allowed himself to smile. "Good point." He glanced at the warpod viewport when he saw a taxi go by. "There goes Tiger with the taxi. It will be attached to the fuser and we'll be ready to go."

"Be careful out there. The Lunar Rescue Company is going to get a lot of good publicity out of this. We'll be swamped with people wanting our services, but we can't do much without you and Petro."

"I don't intend on getting killed," Crater said with more confidence than he felt. "I've got a lot to live for."

"So do I. I'm not going to die, Crater, at least not like the rest of the Phoenix Legion. I am free of that curse. Truvia told me."

Crater erupted with a huge grin and moved to hug Crescent, but she held up her hands. "No. It is not appropriate."

"I don't care," he said, still holding out his arms.

Crescent couldn't help herself. She fell into Crater's arms, and after he'd released her, she kissed him on both cheeks. "I love you," she said.

"I love you too," he said. "And that's the truth."

Crescent couldn't stop her heart from jumping. "But there's Maria."

"Yes. There's Maria. No one understands why I love that girl, but I do. And yet I love you too."

Crescent forced a smile on her face. She understood. "Friends can love each other too."

"Yes. I think they can." He gave her a small smile.

Tears formed beneath Crescent's gray eyelid folds. "You must go. Hurry. Save the world."

"I will be back."

"I know you will."

Crater headed for the fuser hatch, meeting Maria, Petro, and Tiger on the way. "I can't believe it, Crater," Maria said. "He's gone!"

"Who's gone?" Crater demanded. But one glance through the viewport gave him the answer. The *Jan Davis* was detached from the station, its cold jets pulsing as it moved away. "Who's aboard?" he asked.

"The Colonel, my father, and the sheriff." Maria sounded panicked.

Crater headed for the bridge, grabbing the comm mike. "L5 to the *Jan Davis*."

"*Jan Davis* here." It was the Colonel.

"Colonel, you don't know all that needs to be done."

"I trust you've got everything wired," the Colonel replied.

Maria arrived on the bridge. "You turn around and come back right now, Grandfather!"

"I would for you, Maria—almost." His voice cracked slightly, and he cleared his throat. "But I caused this mess, me and Junior, and it's up to us to clean it up."

Crater knew the Colonel well enough to know that nothing he could say was going to change the old man's mind. "You'll have to position the fuser no more than a hundred feet from the asteroid," he said. "It will be precision flying."

"Don't underestimate me, Crater. After all, one of my companies built this fuser. I know what to do in the cockpit."

Maria turned to Crater. "Can your warpod catch it?"

"Not with just one engine. Actually, even if I had two, I couldn't do it. Fusers can go a hundred times faster."

The Colonel came back on. "I'm on my way to fix things, Maria," he said.

"Grandfather..."

"I know, Maria. It's all right. This will give your father and me a chance to talk. It's going to be rough for him, for all of us in the family, but we'll get through."

"I believe you, Grandfather," Maria said, even though she didn't.

::: FIFTY-FIVE

C2241 rolled through space, the giant blue, green, white, and brown planet called Earth in its sights. CC2241 was mindless and had no thoughts. It was just a remnant of the formation of the solar system manipulated by the one intelligent species capable of such engineering in that system. The irony, had CC2241 been capable of irony, was that it was aimed at the place that was the cradle of the existence of that species.

The fuser *Jan Davis* rushed through space, hot on the trail of CC2241. Packed inside its cargo space were twelve nuclear missiles, each with a lump of plastique explosive attached to their individual warheads, a blasting cap inserted inside each lump, and wires leading from the caps to the fuel cell power plant used to start up the auxiliary power plants that in turn powered up the fusion engines. The *Davis*'s primary puter was programmed to send a signal to the fuel cell power plant, which in turn would send an electrical current to each of the blasting caps, which would then detonate the plastique, which would then send a shock wave through each individual warhead that would detonate the TNT-derived torpex inside, which would then implode the uranium core, producing an atomic blast. It was all ad hoc, all Crater Trueblood jerry-rigged, and would have been considered crude by any exacting engineer. It also had a high probability of working.

Behind the *Jan Davis* and CC2241 was a crowhopper-crewed warpod with but one engine. On board the warpod were Crater, Petro, and Maria.

"I wonder what they're talking about," Maria said of her grandfather and father.

"No use worrying about it," Crater said. "You'll find out after we pick them up."

Maria pondered Crater. "You don't really think we'll pick them up, do you?"

Crater thought about telling her a comforting fib but knew she needed to hear the truth. "I'm not sure. They'll have to position that fuser just right, then tell the puter to give them enough time to detach the taxi and get a good distance away. It will take some skill, and the Colonel's the only one who can fly the fuser and probably the taxi too."

"My father can also pilot a fuser." When Crater didn't respond, she said, "You don't expect him to help, do you?"

Crater didn't meet her eyes. "I don't know him, just his reputation."

Maria shook her head. "When he's around the Colonel, he's a different man. He'll do his duty."

Crater wasn't certain what her father's duty was except to be punished for his crimes. He looked over at the bridge where Petro sat with Captain Valence. In another minute, they'd have to shut the lone engine down to conserve fuel, but the fuser had no such constraint. The Colonel could go full throttle until he had to flip the fuser over and decelerate to catch up and match the asteroid's velocity. As he'd told Maria, it would require perfect timing, which was another reason he wished he was sitting in the *Jan Davis*'s pilot seat. Tiger had programmed the *Davis*'s puter to accomplish the flight profile, but tweaking would be required. Crater felt agonizingly helpless. He needed to be aboard that fuser, and so did Petro!

"Come have a look," Petro called. "The pulsdar's got a good signal."

Crater and Maria flew over to the bridge to take a look. The gigantic blob that marked CC2241 in the center was shrunk down as Petro took the pulsdar scope to a wider range. "There's the *Davis*," Petro said, pointing at a pinprick of luminescence. "Acceleration complete. It's in the drift phase before flipping over."

"Anything showing up around Earth?" Crater asked.

"Nothing. Looks like they didn't have time to get their act together down there."

"Then it's up to the Colonel to save the world," Crater said.

"And the fuser's puter," Petro said. "Which is worrisome. We didn't have much time to program it."

Crater agreed, his worry and concern growing. "There's always something you forget when you're in a hurry."

"Well, if we did, I guess the Colonel will find out pretty soon," Petro said.

"And so will the world," Captain Valence added.

"You can do it, Grandfather," Maria whispered. "I know you can."

::: FIFTY-SIX

All right, Junior," the Colonel said. "We only have a few hours before this operation begins. I'm going to need your help."

His son looked up from the bunk where he'd been strapped in. "I don't want to talk to you."

The Colonel sighed. "Why not?"

"Because I'll be dead in a few minutes and I'd prefer to go into oblivion listening to my own thoughts, not yours."

"You're not going to be dead. We can do this."

Junior smiled. "Yes, I am. I took something. I'll go to sleep and not wake up."

The Colonel reached across the bunk and grabbed his son by his shoulders. "What's the antidote?"

"There isn't one, at least not anything on board this ship. Too bad, Father dear. You're not going to get the chance to interrogate me like a stern schoolteacher to an errant child, nor lecture me like a wise man to a fool. All you get to do is watch me die with hate for you spewing from my lips. Of course, what I feel is more than hate. I despise and detest you. Get away from me so I don't have your smell in my nostrils as I go on to the next place." He swatted at the Colonel's grip on him.

The Colonel desperately clutched his son to him. "I wasn't going to interrogate or lecture you, Junior. This isn't your fault. It's mine. I love you, son. That's all I wanted to say." Tears dribbled from the Colonel's eyes, tiny translucent spheres that fell slowly to the deck in the light artificial gravity caused by the accelerating fuser.

Junior was not impressed. "I hope I've made it perfectly clear that I don't love you."

The Colonel released his son, then bowed his head. "I should have been a better father."

"You should not have been a father at all," John High Eagle Medaris Jr. said, then closed his eyes and breathed his last.

The Colonel slowly pulled himself back to the cockpit where the sheriff sat staring at the controls set on automatic. "I've lost my boy, Sheriff," the Colonel said, settling into the pilot's seat.

"You lost him a long time ago, Colonel. Don't beat yourself up about it."

"I thought we would have time to talk." The Colonel felt stunned.

"How'd he do it?"

"A drug the Trainer woman gave him." The Colonel was lost in gloomy thoughts for a while, then said, "I wish he'd slit his wrists or stabbed himself or even shot himself. Taking a pill seems a cowardly way out."

"Well, Colonel, he couldn't meet your expectations, no matter what."

The Colonel paused. There was truth to what the sheriff said. "No, he couldn't. At least he gave me Maria."

"Did you tell him that?"

It hadn't occurred to the Colonel to tell his son about the one good thing he'd done with his life. "Surely he knew my opinion about that," he rationalized, then called up the fuser's puter. "How much longer until we catch CC2241?"

Two hours, seven minutes.

The sheriff shook his head. "I never thought I'd help save the world."

"We haven't saved it yet, Sheriff."

"But we will. This is in the bag, Colonel."

The Colonel was quiet, then said, "I've enjoyed your company over the years, Sheriff, and your loyalty."

The sheriff chuckled. "Nobody else would have me. In fact, most of the people on that world ahead would love to put me back in prison or hang me. You gave me a chance to start over. I appreciate that, Colonel."

"What I did was use you. I took your penchant for violence and put it to work for me."

"Well, it wasn't like I didn't know that."

The Colonel and the sheriff sat companionably until the puter announced, *Deceleration in thirty seconds. Please strap yourself in and brace until stabilization occurs.*

The sheriff gave an extra tug on his seat belt, then felt embarrassed. No seat belt was going to save him from being aboard a fuser rushing through space that was loaded with nuclear missiles.

The Earth in the viewport seemed to be moving, although it was actually the *Jan Davis* flipping over so that its engine could be restarted to decelerate the fuser as it caught up with the asteroid. When it was within five miles of it, the fuser would turn again, this time catching up with CC2241 and matching its speed.

Of course, that all depended on whether Crater and Petro had properly programmed the fuser's puter. Reflecting on the trust he had for Crater's abilities, the Colonel said, "I've always treated Crater unfairly. I regret that."

"I don't see why," the sheriff replied. "He was always a lot of trouble. How are you going to like him as a grandson-in-law? That's what I gathered from Maria and him, all that lovey-dovey talk."

The Colonel was fairly certain he'd never be around to find out the answer. Although the sheriff didn't seem to know it, the Colonel thought the odds of them surviving this mission were slim. He shrugged and said, "I think Maria and Crater will be fine. After a lot of trouble, of course. It's in her nature and his."

The fuser completed its flip and its three engines thundered. The artificial gravity produced by the deceleration was severe at first, then subsided to one Earth gravity. When the puter announced it was safe to move around, the sheriff released his seat belt and made a run for the waste collection system, there to rid himself of the fluid buildup that had occurred during the short period of weightlessness. The Colonel was next in line. Afterward, with gravity running along the z-axis of the fuser, they had to climb up a steep ladder to the cockpit. "I'm getting too old for this," the sheriff joked, and then thought how stupid he must sound to the Colonel, forty years his senior.

During the deceleration, the nose of the fuser was aimed toward space. The Colonel moved the camera in the tail until it was focused on the asteroid. He zoomed in on it and, just as expected, saw it was massive and gray but it also had an unusual consistency.

The sheriff peered at the viewscreen. "It's spongy looking," he said.

"Because it's a collection of boulders," the Colonel growled, "not a slab of basalt like we thought. The only thing holding its mass together is gravity."

"What happens if we blast it with nukes?"

"It won't get shoved the way Crater thought," the Colonel said. "It'll just get blown apart."

"Isn't that good?"

The Colonel studied the asteroid, but it was the study of ignorance. He didn't know what would happen. Would scattering the rocks do the job or would they simply come back together and keep on going? The Colonel thought about going to the taxi and using its communications to call Crater but then decided against it. Everything was set, and all the Colonel could do was carry on and hope and pray for the best.

The Colonel was not a praying man, but he now silently began to toss prayers up to heaven, and as he did he began to feel something warm inside him. Everything was going to be all right. He was sure of it. The Colonel sat with the sheriff in the cockpit and watched the asteroid get closer and closer.

"I wonder what they're doing on Earth," the sheriff said.

The Colonel gave it some thought, then said, "Maria called the company in Armstrong City who was supposed to call the Medaris family on Earth. The ranking member of the family on Earth is Rudy, my second son. Rudy's a levelheaded sort and will most likely contact the governments friendly to our business, leaving it up to them on how they'll tell their citizens or other governments if they tell them at all."

The Colonel's expression turned grim. "They're in the worst possible situation right now for a disaster. The countries of the old UCW are fighting civil wars, the other countries are trying to get on their feet economically after their war with the UCW. Their space assets are depleted, their fleets of warpods mostly grounded. If they know we're trying to stop this thing, all they can do is crawl into their holes and hope we do it."

The sheriff rubbed his face. "How did we ever get in this mess?"

"I am culpable," the Colonel said. "I financed the labs that made the crowhoppers, although, quite honestly, that wasn't my intention. I was just trying to see if we could make a better human. We got better humans all right, better killers at any rate. Then I came up with the idea of asteroid bombardment out of L5. It's astonishing to me now how clearly both ideas were crazy." He shook his head. "At the time they seemed perfectly correct avenues of thought and no one dared correct me. They knew I wouldn't listen anyway."

"You're still a great man, Colonel," the sheriff said.

"I did some good things," the Colonel agreed. "I'm willing to give myself credit for that, but I also recognize now how conceited and pompous I became, how unwilling I was to listen to anyone else but whatever random thoughts might be stirring through my mind at the time. I became corrupt, Sheriff, not the money-grubbing kind of corrupt, but the kind that's worse, the kind that gets into a man's head and makes him think that if he does anything, it's automatically the right thing."

"You know where I grew up, Colonel?" the sheriff asked. "I bet you don't, because I never put the same thing twice on any of my background documents. I grew up in a little town in Honduras. My father was a fisherman, a lobster diver, actually. He died pretty young and my mother ran off with a *Norte'*

Americano, leaving me, two brothers, and three sisters on the streets of La Ceiba. I took care of them as best I could. I learned to steal, and then when I was caught, I learned how to kill the policeman that caught me. Some rough men recruited me after that, and since I'd already killed, they made me into their killer for hire. I was only thirteen. Who would expect a teenaged hit man? I kind of thought of it as being a soldier, only not for a country but for my *patron*. When his enemies came for him, they not only killed him but nearly everyone in his family and employ. By then my brothers and sisters were working for him and they were gunned down. I was the only one to escape. After that I wandered the Earth, selling myself and my special skills to anyone who'd pay for them. I ended up in prison many times, but I was always able to bust out. I became a man who thought killing was so much a part of life that when I had a wife and wanted to be rid of her, I simply strangled her with my bare hands. When I ran away to the moon, I figured only to lie low for a while, then get back into the killing trade. Then when I came to Moontown, you made me your sheriff. It was most unexpected."

"I saw a man who'd spent a lot of time in prison and on the other side of the law," the Colonel said. "I figured I could teach you my law, whatever I thought it was each day, and you'd enforce it."

"And I did, as best I could. You were my *patron*. But then I found Carla, as sweet a wife as any lout like me ever had. And then we had Maria. Isn't it funny that we have a daughter with the same name as your granddaughter, Colonel? It was Carla's mother's name—that's how we picked it. Anyway, after a while, I started to see everything differently. I wanted to put my sins in a box and drop them into the deepest crater on the moon and turn myself into a good man. I never did it. I guess I was too far gone, but I wanted to. Do you think that counts for something, Colonel?"

"You are the only one who can answer that," the Colonel said. "You and your god."

"Yeah, I had a lot of talks to the preacher about that. I tried praying, but I don't know if I got through or not."

The Colonel met his eyes and put one hand on his shoulder. "Well, you just got through to me, so maybe you did."

The fuser engine stopped and the gravity slid back to zero. There were puffs from the directional jets, and the nose swung over. The asteroid filled the viewscreen.

"There were a lot of vibrations during the flight," the Colonel said. "Probably best if you went to the engine room and made certain all the connections to the warheads are secure."

"OK, Colonel," the sheriff said, "just don't be pushing any buttons up here that might make that mess go off."

"Don't worry. The puter will handle the detonations. Just check the connections and get back up here double quick. After we're positioned, we can get in the taxi and get away."

"Will do."

When the sheriff left, the Colonel remained in the cockpit with one hand on the cold reaction system in case the puter slid them in too close to the asteroid and he needed to correct their course. The puter, however, tweaked the *Jan Davis* in perfectly and then matched the asteroid's velocity. When the reaction control system continued to send out bursts of nitrogen, the Colonel studied the graphic of the fuser and the asteroid as the astronavigational system imagined it. Everything seemed perfect, so why were the cold jets still firing? The amount of nitrogen in the tanks was dwindling too.

"Puter," the Colonel said, "why is the reaction control system firing?"

To compensate for the drift to port, the puter answered.

"What is causing this drift?"

A nearby gravitational field.

The Colonel realized the error in the puter's programming. "Crater forgot the asteroid's gravitational force," he muttered. "How could he forget that?"

The force exerted by the asteroid wasn't much, but it was enough to require the fuser to keep working to maintain the correct distance between it and the CC2241. "Puter, switch to hot control jets," the Colonel ordered because the hot jets still had plenty of fuel.

Switching to hot jets, the puter said.

The Colonel felt a series of hard thumps. The hot jets were igniting, then cutting off, only to ignite again. The fuser rattled and jerked as the system blasted on and off. "Puter, why are the hot jets turning on and off?" the Colonel asked.

The hot control system is not designed to maintain position. The cold system is for that purpose.

"Can they maintain our position?"

Negative. Two hot-fire jets have already failed due to cracks.

"Switch back to cold."

Switching. Cold jet fuel down to three percent.

"Switch main puter control to taxi."

Switching.

"Sheriff, meet me in the taxi," the Colonel called and then left the cockpit and pulled himself along to the taxi airlock.

Before long, the sheriff arrived, wriggling through the

access hatch of the taxi and goggling at the size and proximity of the asteroid. "All the connections are secure, Colonel. Time for us to make a run for it?"

"We have a little problem, Sheriff," the Colonel said. "That big collection of rocks wants us to join it. We're down to only a few pounds of nitrogen left to steer away from it."

"How about the hot jets?"

"I suppose you felt that shaking a minute ago. That was them. They're not designed for fine-tuning and are now out of commission."

"Then we'd better get out of here before we get any closer."

"We can't go," the Colonel said, looking levelly at the sheriff. "We're going to have to use the taxi's guidance jets to maintain this position."

"But how will we—now, hold on, Colonel!"

"We had a good run, Sheriff."

Cold jet system down to zero point five percent, the puter warned.

"Puter, switch to the control jets on the taxi and maintain distance from the target," the Colonel said. Out of the corner of his eye, he saw the sheriff had drawn his pistol and aimed it at the Colonel's head. "Put that away, Sheriff," he said.

The sheriff sighed, then lowered his pistol and tucked it back in its holster. "I guess I always wanted to go out in a blaze of glory anyway."

"Your family will be well cared for," the Colonel said. "Since I knew there might be some, er, repercussions toward you if I died first, I put you and your family in my will."

"Thank you," the sheriff said. "Shall we tell the warpod they won't need to pick us up?"

"They'll figure it out. No use making them go on about

how heroic we are. We know the truth. Just a couple of old reprobates putting at least somewhat noble exclamation marks to our lives. Puter, start the timer for the special package. One-minute count should do."

Timer for special package started. One minute and counting.

"No audible countdown required," the Colonel said.

No audible countdown confirmed.

The sheriff raised his eyebrows and said, "I have a bottle of rum hidden away. Shall I get it?"

"If you think we have time."

"I'll do my best."

The sheriff disappeared down the hatch. For just a moment, the Colonel wondered if perhaps the sheriff was headed for the engine bay, there to pull all the wires from the warheads. Within fifteen seconds, however, he had returned with a bottle of rum. "It ain't easy to drink in zero-g," the sheriff said, "but if you put it to your lips and kind of move your head, you'll get a swig. Here, I'll show you."

The sheriff demonstrated, then handed the bottle to the Colonel. The Colonel followed the sheriff's example and managed to get a mouthful of the flavorful liquid imported from the Earth's Caribbean islands. "Good stuff," he said. He was about to hand the bottle back to the sheriff when the warheads detonated.

::: **FIFTY-SEVEN**

here it goes," Crater said. He didn't have to see it on the pulsdar. Even though thousands of miles away, the explosion was great enough that it lit up the asteroid, which, though his eyes were probably deceiving him, seemed to shudder and then expand.

Petro was on the pulsdar console. "We're getting an odd signal," he said. "The asteroid seems to have come apart."

Crater took a look. "It wasn't solid," he concluded. "It was a rubble pile. We calculated the explosion for a solid monolith."

Captain Valence said, "Puter, has the course of the target changed?"

Affirmative.

"Will it still intersect with the Earth?"

Target is unstable. Presently unable to predict final course.

Captain Valence frowned. "What does it mean by that?"

"The asteroid was pushed apart by the explosion but is now trying to reform. Until it does, we won't know its course."

"What about the taxi?" Maria asked.

Petro studied the pulsdar screen. "I don't see it."

Captain Valence nodded to his communications officer. "Call the taxi," he said.

The communications officer made the call. "Crater warpod to *Davis* taxi. Come in." He made the call eight more times with no response.

Maria said, "If he thought he was in trouble, Grandfather would have called us."

"Or he might have decided not to worry you," Crater said gently.

Maria shook her head. "He's not dead."

"We'll keep looking," Crater said, "but it was always going to be a close-run thing."

"You think they're dead, don't you?"

Crater unflinchingly looked into her eyes. "I think they are, yes. When they got close, they could see what the asteroid really was. Also, I realize now I forgot to figure the asteroid's gravitational force into my calculations. To maintain their position, they would have had to stay with it, using the fuser's reaction control system. I think the Colonel stuck it out to the end. That's what I think."

"Have you ever considered softening your truth, Crater Trueblood?" Maria demanded. "I didn't think so. I'm exactly the same, saying exactly what I mean all the time. If we get married, we're going to have to learn to tell a little white lie now and again."

"Are we getting married?"

"Of course we are."

Maria found herself in Crater's arms, but it didn't feel romantic, just sad. Still, she clung to him as if he was the only thing floating on an impossibly deep sea and she would drown if she didn't keep hanging on. She gave into her grief, her body racked with sobs.

"The asteroid's reforming into two chunks," Petro said. "I'm making them into two targets: 2241A and 2241B."

"Puter, predict course of 2241 A and B," Captain Valence said. "Inform as to intersection with Earth or near-intersection."

Both targets have wobble. Prediction seventy percent certainty.

"Acceptable."

Target 2241A will not intersect with Earth by a margin of eight thousand three hundred and eighty-two miles. Target 2241B will not intersect with Earth with a margin of ninety-three miles.

Cheers erupted from the warpod crew. "The Earth just dodged two bullets," Petro said, then looked over at Crater. He was still holding Maria, but his face was drawn. "What's wrong, brother?"

"Puter," Crater said, "factor in the Earth's atmosphere for target 2241B and check intersection with Earth."

Atmospheric drag will cause it to intersect the Earth.

"Where?"

The South Atlantic three hundred miles off Africa.

"They're going to take a pounding down there," Captain Valence said. "Shall we keep following?"

Crater nodded. "We need to get as close as we can to record what happens but keep track of our fuel. We'll want to get back to the moon."

Maria said sadly, "Poor Earth. Poor, poor Earth."

"That chunk will break up when it hits the atmosphere," Crater said. "It's going to cause a lot of damage, but at least it isn't going to destroy the planet."

Many hours later, after a thorough search of the area where the fuser taxi might be, and finding nothing, the warpod moved closer to Earth, its warpod cameras recording, while the people aboard watched silently from the bridge.

The Earth facing the warpod was dark. Fiery flashes of light streaked across it, then more flashes as the surface was struck with hundreds of impacts. It seemed as through the bombardment would never stop.

The warpod moved until it could see the Earth in sunlight. The atmosphere seemed washed out, the continents fuzzy. "Dust, ash, and water vapor are filling the air," Crater mused. He zoomed a camera in to look closer. "There are volcanoes in Central America that are smoking. Likely there are earthquakes causing the plates to shift, putting pressure on them."

Everyone on the warpod gasped when they saw another flash of light, this one above North America. "What's that?" Captain Valence gasped.

Crater studied the rising smoke. "I think it was a nuclear weapon. There's another one!"

"Oh, please, God, no," Maria prayed.

More flashes occurred. Captain Valence appraised the situation. "A general nuclear exchange," he said.

They continued to watch until Crater said, "I think we'd better be getting home, Captain."

"Yes," he said. "To your home, anyway. Will there be a place there for me and my crew?"

"If I have anything to say about it, Captain," Petro said, "you'll be welcome."

"I think we will all get behind that," Maria said. "We're all in this together now."

"Call the L5 station," Crater said. "Tell Crescent to evacuate aboard Captain Philippe's warpod and land at Armstrong City. We'll meet them there."

Captain Valence made the necessary adjustments, and the warpod made a long turn, lit its jets, and set a course for the moon to discover what the future might hold for a remnant of humanity that now called the little gray planetoid their only home.

::: FIFTY-EIGHT

The great bell in the tower of the new Cleomedes cathedral tolled slowly and mournfully to mark the third anniversary of the end of the world, at least as it had been known. Engraved on the bell, made of an alloy of tin, copper, and iron mined from the lunar wayback, was this inscription:

Nevertheless we, according to his promise, look for new heavens and a new earth, wherein dwelleth righteousness.

2 Peter 3:13 KJV

The Earth was still there, hanging in the lunar sky, a magnificent jewel pressed against the vast darkness of space, but lovely as it was, its colors were faded as if a veil had been drawn across the planet. In fact it had, the veil made of fine dust and ash from still-spewing volcanoes and the rubble thrown up by nuclear blasts. The Earth also seemed far whiter, vast areas in both the northern and southern hemispheres covered with fresh ice and snow.

There was still no commerce with the Earth. Before the asteroid strike, scramjet/rocket hybrids were used to reach orbit and then rendezvous with the Cyclers. Now dust and ash in the atmosphere made scramjet engines unsafe to operate, so they were all grounded. Only fully rocket-propelled craft could make it to space from the Earth, but there were only a few of them, none of them designed to carry people and not enough of them to carry significant cargo. The factories that had built them were all shut down, the economies of the nations in shambles where they were located. Starvation was also a worry for every nation, the crop yields shrunk by the reduced sunlight reaching the surface through the dust haze.

The people of the moon could communicate with the home planet through individuals on Earth transmitting on old-style radios. These radio operators told them that Earthian scientists were predicting that the air would be washed clean by the great storms that had erupted planet-wide, producing torrential rains and vast floods. It was as if the planet knew it had been damaged and was doing all that it could to cleanse itself. The air, these scientists said, should be clean enough for scramjet operations within twenty years.

The nuclear exchange had been caused by automatic systems that thought the incoming asteroid fragments were an attack. The effectiveness of the city-busting strikes had been limited because the dust and the ash had caused the missile targeting systems to go awry. Cities were missed with the nuclear detonations going off over the seas or deserts or mountainous regions. The people, animals, and plants in those areas suffered, but wholesale human slaughter was at least avoided.

After the initial exchange, the countries who'd launched them quickly shut the systems down and then went out of business, their leaders hiding from their angry citizenry.

The Earth was rebuilding, the amateur radiomen reported, but how that reconstruction would turn out, no one knew for certain. The hope was that the people on the moon would hold the seeds of civilization and be prepared to help their poor cousins on Earth when they were able. The radiomen also reported that churches were packed, the cataclysmic events paradoxically bringing out a new sense of wonder and even gratitude toward the Maker of the universe. In some ways, it was said, the people on Earth had never been happier. The challenge to survive had knitted them together like nothing had for centuries.

The people of the moon were also going through a period of adjustment. Still steadfastly against a central government, the Lunarians operated from city states. In Endless Dust, General Nero and Perpetually Hopeful had laid a test oxygen pipeline from Adolphus Crater into a vast dome that had transformed the small mining town into a pressurized farmland. Lakes and streams of water flowed through the acres, brought up by pumps from a deep well. Instead of biovat food, fresh produce was revolutionizing lunar cuisine. In Moontown and the other mining towns, the scrapes were still being worked. Some Helium-3 was carried up to the Cyclers and then sent down to Earth aboard spacecraft with ablative heat shields designed to land near fusion reactors that were still operable. This was charity from the moon, no payment expected. More of the precious isotope, however, was being stockpiled in anticipation of the atmosphere clearing on Earth and new fusion energy plants clamoring for replenishment.

All this history was running through Crater Trueblood's

mind as he listened to the tolling of the bell. Crater was the president of the Cleomedes-based Interstellar Transportation Company and was presiding over a memorial ceremony, his employees assembled around the ship the ITC was building to fly into deep space. After the bell finished its final toll, he asked for a prayer from the company reverend, who was the widow of the late sheriff of Moontown:

"Dear Lord, within our bounty on Luna, please do not let us forget the suffering of our fellow humans on the Earth, nor the suffering of her animals, the destruction of her vegetation, and the pain of her radiated surface and befouled atmosphere. We trust that You will allow Your Earth to heal and Your people of Luna to help when and where we can. Let us recall Paul's admonition in his letter to the Colossians: 'For by him were all things created, that are in heaven, and that are in earth, visible and invisible, whether thrones, or dominions, or principalities, or powers: all things were created by him, and for him: and he is before all things, and by him all things consist.' Let us therefore move ahead with confidence that all is unfolding as it should while recalling those who sacrificed themselves in an attempt to shield the Earth from its woes and to all those who are now seeking a new path and a new prosperity, this time even to the stars themselves."

The employees of the Interstellar Transportation Company amened the reverend's prayer and got back to work on the deep-space ship. Crater turned to his wife and the company's chief financial officer, Maria Medaris Trueblood, who was holding their baby boy, two months old. "He needs his diaper changed," Maria said and handed the baby to her husband. When Crater looked clueless, she added, "Ask the gillie. It knows how."

The gillie stayed in Crater's shirt pocket, although it said,

The baby stinks. After a few beats, it added, *But I love the little creature. I will not change its diaper, but I will teach it to read and write. It will be a great author.*

I will teach it its numbers, Maria's gillie said from her pocket. *It will be a theoretical physicist.*

It will need its own gillie, Crater's gillie said. *You should divide.*

I divided last time to give Crescent a new gillie after I went back to Maria. It's your turn.

Maria said, "Hush, you two. This is about changing Jack's diaper, not gillie mitosis, which no one wants to hear about."

The baby was named John High Eagle Medaris Trueblood, although he was mostly called "Little Jack."

"I'll show you how to change his diaper," Absalom the crowhopper volunteered. He held out his thick arms, and Crater gratefully gave up the baby, then followed them both into a bathroom to accomplish the deed.

Crescent smiled after the trio—man, crowhopper, and baby. She and Maria looked at one another, then over to the little girl who was playing with toys on the rug. Her name was Minerva and she was wearing the elastic suit that all children on the moon wore, which was designed to stress their muscles and bones and assure Earth-like development. "She's beautiful," Maria said, filling the awkward silence.

Crescent admired her own child. "Smart as paint too."

Maria smiled. "That's what the Colonel used to say about Crater."

"I know. Crater told me. The seedling doesn't fall far from the tree. And you're right. She's perfect. I was a little afraid..."

She left her fear unsaid, but Maria understood. "At least what Truvia said about that was true. Your eggs were the same as if they hadn't..."

Crescent finished Maria's sentence. "...manipulated mine in the petri dish to make me this way. Yes, I'm ugly but I'm the mother of a beautiful child."

Although Maria and Crescent were capable of admiring their children, the two women were not friends. Although she kept it buried in her heart, Maria resented what Crescent had done when she'd taken from Crater what she needed to fashion the child they now watched playing. Yes, Minerva was a perfect child—that could not be denied—but the child was a constant reminder to her of Crescent's breathtaking deceit.

Crescent sensed Maria's thoughts and agreed with them to an extent. It had been desperation that had led her to steal Crater's DNA, but it hadn't been right. Both women knew there was a long-delayed and probably painful conversation they needed to have. Since she found herself alone with Maria, a rare event, Crescent thought maybe now was the day to have it.

Before Crescent could speak up, Petro swung by. He was the ITC's chief of design and was forever busy on the puter drawing boards. There were as yet no markets for interstellar ships, but when the Earth got up and running, the ITC intended to be ready to provide one. The hope was that the people back on the world would be so tired of being cooped up on their planet that they would burst forth and carry themselves to the far reaches of the solar system and maybe even the galaxy. The ship that was being constructed was the first design, one that Crater and Petro intended to take on a test drive to Titan, an interesting moon that orbited Saturn.

"What are you ladies up to?" Petro asked.

"We're planning your wedding," Maria replied without hesitation.

"But first we need to find you a wife," Crescent added.

Petro laughed. "Don't waste your time. The two best gals on the moon are already taken."

"Riley's still around," Maria pointed out. "You ever think about her?"

"Aw, she and Tiger are an item. Wouldn't surprise me if they got hitched too. All this stuff about needing to have a baby boom on the moon to keep humanity going. Well, I don't intend to join in. I'll be around to teach the kids how to play cards and that other important uncle kind of stuff."

"You can teach Minerva to play poker, Petro," Crescent said, "but if I catch you showing her how to cheat, I'll demonstrate some crowhopper martial arts, starting with the Siberian stranglehold."

Petro's near-perpetual grin faded as he realized Crescent was serious. "I'll keep that in mind," he said and walked over to Minerva. The little golden-haired girl squealed at the sight of him and raced to throw herself into his arms.

"She loves Petro," Crescent said.

Maria laughed. "Well, maybe she'll marry somebody like him when she grows up!"

"Heaven forbid! Absalom would not be pleased at that prospect!" Crescent paused, then said, "My husband is a most excellent husband."

"As is mine," Maria replied, then lowered her voice so only Crescent could hear. "We need to have a conversation, one long put off, about Minerva."

Crescent lifted her chin. "Yes, I was just thinking the same thing."

Maria began tentatively. "She's so beautiful, but I think . . . I know you owe me an explanation."

"No, Maria," Crescent replied, "I don't. You were out of the picture at the time. I only owed an explanation to Crater, and I've done my best to explain to him what I did. He has forgiven me for my great sin. Your forgiveness I don't need."

Maria felt her face getting warm. Long-repressed anger was bubbling up. "Listen, Crescent—"

"No, you listen," Crescent interrupted. "I said I don't owe you an explanation, but I'm going to give you one anyway. Will you hear it?"

When Maria didn't answer, Crescent looked off into the distance as if looking back in time. "I love Crater. I have always loved him, even when I was so angry with him I could scarcely stand it. But it wasn't only because I wanted a part of him that I decided to have his child. It was because of you."

"Me?"

"Yes, because he loved *you* the way I loved *him*, and I knew how much that hurt. Every day I was with him, I saw how much not having you was tearing him up inside. He was always angry; his joy in life was nearly lost. At that time it was my judgment that you and Crater would never be together, and since I thought I was going to die as per the genetic specifications of the Phoenix Legion, I decided to have his child. I was too frightened to ask his permission. No, that's wrong. I didn't ask him because I knew he wouldn't agree, but I didn't care. I confess there was another reason I did what I did, and there was nothing altruistic about it. I decided to give *myself* a gift, a gift like none other. Hear me, Maria. I was deliberately born ugly and trained to be evil. Nothing about my life was ever supposed to be soft and good. Yet when I asked the doctor who'd treated his broken leg and had his tissue in her office what were the possibilities, her answer nearly made my decision for me. I would have Crater's child and grab a small scrap of joy from my miserable life. Of course, I also hoped Crater would transfer the love he had for you to our child and thus save himself."

Maria considered Crescent's words, and her confession. "It might have worked," she concluded. "Both Minerva and Little Jack are his special joy. I've never known him to be so happy. He's the old Crater, almost the way he was when I first met him so many years ago at that stupid fastbug race. But how did you do it, how did you convince the doctor to let you have his child?"

"Perpetually Hopeful arranged everything in Cleomedes, to take his cells and the artificial insemination."

"General Nero's wife helped you?"

"She's inordinately fond of Crater too. She and I had many talks about him. In fact, I think she's the one who first proposed that I have his child. She also thought it might make him happy. It's amazing what gold will do even for physicians, especially ones who owe their livelihood to the Neros."

Maria tried to digest everything Crescent had said. "But what you did . . . it's still unforgivable." She paused. "Isn't it?"

"Yes, but for some strange reason, it worked out in the end. I don't understand it, but oftentimes when you look back, even bad things seem to be for a reason, to make things fit the way they should."

"I can't really forgive you *yet*," Maria said as her anger subsided. "But I think I can accept what you've done."

"Just as I won't forgive you for what you did to Crater over the years," Crescent replied defiantly. "But I accept that you make him happy now."

Maria looked Crescent in the eye. "Fair enough," she said.

"Fair enough, indeed," Crescent replied.

Absalom came out of the bathroom first, followed by Crater holding Little Jack, now freshly diapered. Petro picked up Minerva and carried her, laughing, over to her mom. "She says she wants to go for a ride."

Crescent took the little girl. "Where do you want to go, Minerva?"

Minerva pointed straight up. "There!" she said.

"Well, I understood that!" Absalom said.

Crater swung Little Jack in his arms. The baby was giggling. "I think I've got a future fuser captain here."

"Maybe he'll go out to the stars," Maria said. "Maybe they both will, there to make a new world."

"Maybe that's why we're here on the moon," Crater said. "We're the cradle of a new civilization that looks forever outward. We've carved out a life on this frontier, and now we'll keep on going."

Petro looked doubtful. "Boy, Crater, don't turn into a philosopher. You're but an engineer. If there's philosophizin' that needs to be done, I'll do it."

"And what philosophy would that be, Petro?" Maria asked, her voice suddenly merry. She felt strangely relieved now that she and Crescent had managed to have the talk they'd both put off for so long. Now that it was done, although the air wasn't completely clear between them, there seemed to be a path forward.

Petro gave her question some thought, then said, "Make life fun. And if it isn't fun, you're doing something wrong." He chucked Minerva under the chin. When she giggled, he added, "And look after the kids. If you do, they're gonna take us to the stars!"

::: Reading Group Guide

1. At the end of *Crescent*, it wasn't clear whether Crater and Maria were going to end up together. Were you satisfied with their relationship at the end of *Lunar Rescue Company*? Do you think they made the right decision?

2. Although they are estranged, Crater can't seem to get Maria out of his mind and Maria can't seem to let go of Crater. Do you know relationships like that? Do they usually work out?

3. What did you think of Petro in this novel? What motivates him? Do you think he helps or hinders Crater? Would you like to be more like Petro or Crater?

4. Even though they are illegal and know it, would you like to have a gillie? What would you do with it?

5. Maria is tempted by the offer from Truvia to be the queen of the new civilization on the moon. What would you do in that situation?

6. Crescent's decision to have a baby tremendously affects Crater. Do you think she should have told him her plan? Do you sympathize with her? If you were Crater, what would you have done when you found out?

7. The crowhoppers we meet in this novel seem a little more human than the ones we met in the first two. Assuming the author wrote about them accurately, why do you think that is?

8. The Colonel's plan to place asteroids at L5 was to ensure the moon wouldn't be attacked. Does what happened help you to better understand the phrase, "unintended consequences"?

9. Although Truvia the Trainer was obviously a villain, are you able to sympathize with her situation? Why or why not?

10. If these novels were about real people, would you want to live as they do on the moon?

11. Crater, Maria, Crescent, and Petro form a company to build a ship capable of going to a nearby star, even though the trip would take decades. Do you think anyone will want to go? Why or why not?

12. At the end of the novel, Maria and Crescent talk about what Crescent did to have Crater's child. Crescent says she owes Maria no explanation although she gives her one, anyway. Maria believes Crescent owes her an apology. Who is right, in this case?

::: About the Author

Photo by Gary Cosby Jr., the
Decatur Daily

Homer Hickam is the author of the #1 *New York Times* bestseller *Rocket Boys*, which was made into the acclaimed movie *October Sky*. He is also the author of the bestseller *Torpedo Junction*, the award-winning memoir *Sky of Stone*, and the bestseller *Back to the Moon*. He is married to Linda Terry Hickam, and they live in Huntsville, Alabama.

Visit homerhickam.com for more information.

To learn more visit www.helium3novels.com